PARIS SOULS

To Otto-Jan, Blanche, Andreas, Lola and Oscar

DIRK VELGHE

PARIS SOULS

Unexpected Stories from the City of Light

HANNIBAL

FROM THE REVOLUTION TO THE PRESENT DAY

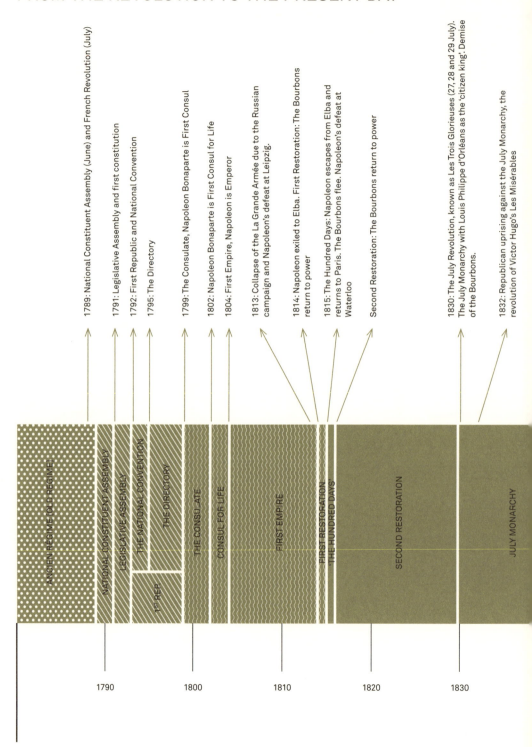

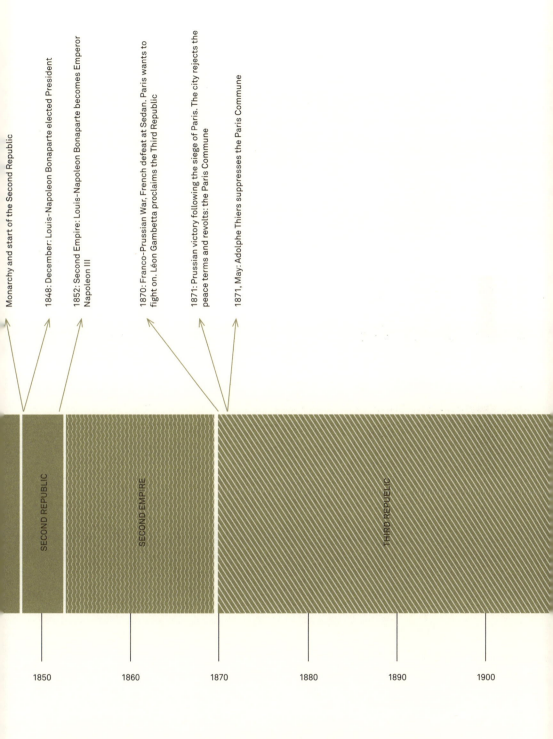

This simplified overview does not include all interim forms of government, transitional regimes or provisional governments. Certain historical events that were important for Paris have been added, however, such as the Siege of Paris during the Franco-Prussian War, the Paris Commune, the First and Second World Wars, the Occupation and Liberation, plus the post-war presidents.

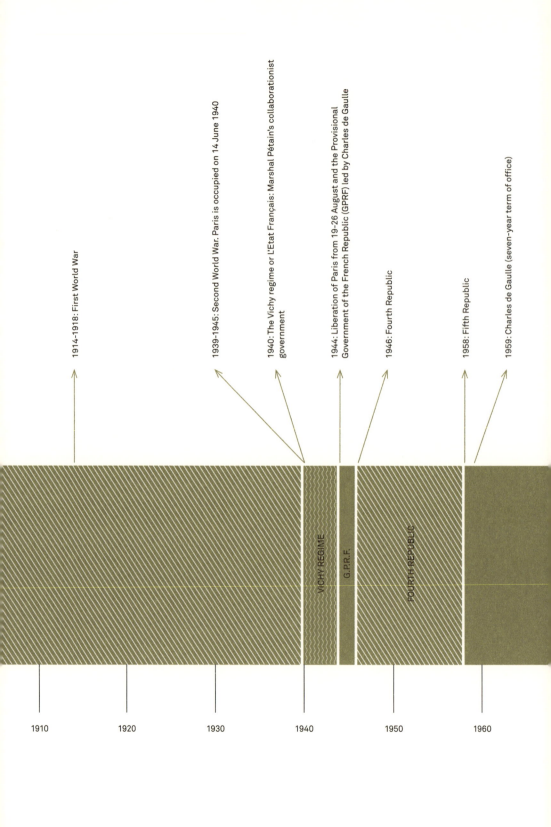

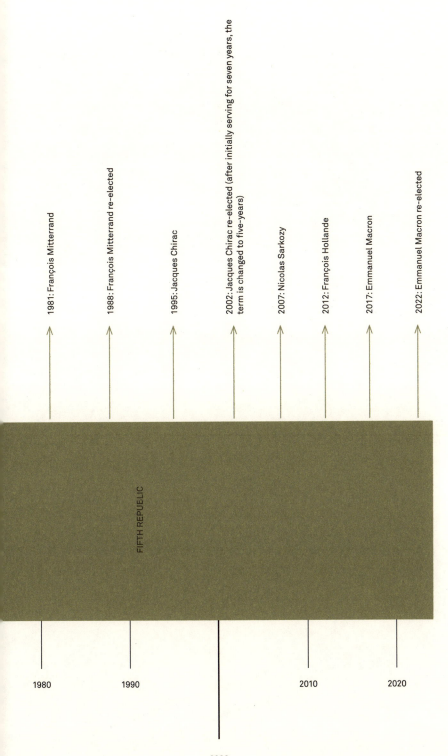

FOREWORD

p. 12

PART 1

RIGHT BANK, WEST

p. 15

PART 2

RIGHT BANK, EAST

p. 83

PART 3

LEFT BANK, WEST

p. 129

PART 4

LEFT BANK, EAST

p. 179

PART 5

MONCEAU & BATIGNOLLES

p. 261

ENDNOTES

p. 330

BIBLIOGRAPHY

p. 350

INDEX OF PEOPLE

p. 356

ACKNOWLEDGEMENTS

p. 366

FOREWORD

"An idea that is clear and precise even though false, will always have greater power in the world than an idea that is true but complex."

ALEXIS DE TOCQUEVILLE (1805-1859)

This book is about the extraordinary people who have coloured the City of Light and its rich history. A select group – historians and writers – could afford to do this with ink, others with oil paint or a camera, but the vast majority of Parisians were restricted to the only means at their disposal, which largely amounted to blood, sweat and tears. While the privileged few seem to be permanent fixtures in the literature on Paris, it is the lives of the latter group, the unusual suspects, that fascinate me the most. Men and women who nonetheless experienced incredible adventures: a gambler who became France's first central banker, a forgotten emperor, a nurse at the American Hospital who joined the *Résistance*, a world-famous artist's model who everyone has seen but no one knows, an assistant curator at the Musée du Jeu de Paume who risked her life for art, the anarchists who set Paris ablaze, the female publisher of *Ulysses* – at the time considered pornographic – or the descendants of Paris' great executioner dynasties. It is they, and their extraordinary fellow citizens, who populate this book. Even when you do encounter well-known figures such as Ho Chi Minh, Chanel, Arletty, Lenin or Picasso, they will probably surprise you by presenting a different, less polished side.

The quest for the soul of these characters is also a quest for their true selves. This was not always self-evident. On several occasions, I started a story with a fixed idea in my mind, only to dig deeper and find it totally turned on its head when an entirely different truth emerged: for example, in this book, the woman who was vilified in post-war France as *la hyène de la Gestapo* [the hyena of the Gestapo] undergoes a minor rehabilitation, and a president, a *Grand Homme de la Gauche* [Great man of the Left] falls from his pedestal. This brings us to the myths. The City of Light is rich in these and they are persistent. The French writer and dramaturge Raymond Queneau was forced to contend with them when editing his successful column in the newspaper *L'Intransigeant*. In 'Connaissez-vous Paris?' he asked the readers three questions every day. The answers appeared amongst the classified ads, which were even more eagerly devoured as a result. In order to substantiate his answers thoroughly, Queneau took a deep dive into the Bibliothèque Nationale, at that time still in the Rue de Richelieu. This is what he discovered: "a few visits sufficed to teach me that many books about Paris were copied from one another. That the same untruths, often corrected years before, still cropped up afresh, and that a small amount of *méthode historique* would nevertheless suffice to eliminate them for good". Did Georges-Eugène Haussmann, Prefect of Seine, who is presented in many a book about Paris as a destructive Attila, murder the city's soul? Was the Belle Époque a time of glitter and glamour, light-hearted operettas and uninhibited pleasure? Or did the flip side also reveal exploitation and budding anarchism, nationalist hysteria and anti-semitism, crime and violence? Leading French financiers and industrialists were surprised by the brutality of the occupying forces in 1940, leaving them with no option but to collaborate. Really? All myths. They are often so widespread and stubborn that the facts are not always sufficiently powerful to eliminate them.

Nevertheless, the facts often outstrip the fabrications; and the truth is more fascinating, more brutal or more shocking than the myth. So *une idée certaine* is a completely different kettle of fish to *une certaine idée*. For its inherent doubt and hesitation alone, the latter is still the most apt leitmotif for a quest of this kind.

"The enemy of history is morality", said the great historian of the French Revolution and the Empire, Patrice Gueniffey. In every era people view the facts in a different light. The fashion of the day. The bicentenary of Napoleon Bonaparte's death polarised national opinion in early 2021. At one extreme, the woke movement balked at the idea of commemorating a white, male misogynist who had re-imported slavery. At the other extreme was Eric Zemmour, then a columnist at *Le Figaro* who also hosted a wildly popular talk show on CNews, the French equivalent of Fox News in the United States. Zemmour, who went on to become a presidential candidate in 2022, believed that "Napoleon is the most influential personality in the country's history. So yes, *vive l'Empereur!*" After his day trip to Paris on 23 June 1940, Hitler ordered the destruction of Charles

Mangin's statue, a French general during the First World War. It irritated him. Just as the historical billboards on the Place de la Contrescarpe, such as '*Au Nègre Joyeux*', irritate the contemporary city authorities. These have since been transferred to the Musée Carnavalet. Different times, different morals.

Myth and morality are not the only reasons why seemingly alike citizens are bracketed together as saints or sinners. For the last surviving royalist romantics who believe in the battle-cry and motto of the Kingdom of France – *Montjoie! Saint Denis!* – the two world wars were not the worst things to happen to their country. No, these would be Robespierre and the French Revolution. For the radical republicans, the combatants on the barricades of the Commune are heroes; and the law-abiding, monarchist *Versaillais* that shot them down from on high, cowards. And vice versa.

It is through these will-o'-the-wisps that I have tried to bare the soul of my Parisians, in all their controversies and nuances, both in their trivial day-to-day concerns and in their grand *acte du siècle*, their 'deed of the century', be it an act of goodness or a crime. At the start of the book, a brief overview of France's political history makes it easier for the reader to situate the characters in their time. In these extraordinary histories, however, they do not appear in historical sequence, but are situated in the areas in which they lived and worked, were born and died, and where, for those who wish to get to know them better, their souls still roam. Thanks to the maps, Paris afficionados can meet them face-to-face through the still-visible reminders of their lives.

Dirk Velghe

PART 1

RIGHT BANK, WEST

———

1. Rose Valland's war   p. 18
Musée du Jeu de Paume,
1 place de la Concorde 75008

2. Chanel versus Wertheimer   p. 30
31 rue Cambon 75001

**3. Napoleon III,
the forgotten emperor**   p. 40
Place de l'Opéra 75009

4. Arletty's heart   p. 54
Théatre des Bouffes-Parisiens,
4 rue Monsigny 75002

5. Lenin's yellow jersey   p. 62
Bibliothèque de l'Institut national d'histoire
de l'art [INHA], Salle Labrouste,
58 rue de Richelieu 75002

6. John Law's 'shitty shares'   p. 72
Église Saint-Roch, 296 rue Saint-Honoré 75001

ROSE VALLAND'S WAR

1

On All Saints Day 1940, Rose Valland, assistant curator at the Musée du Jeu de Paume, is not bringing chrysanthemums for her deceased relatives. No, the sadness she feels is of a completely different order. 'Her' museum, of all places, has been commandeered by the Nazis as a triage centre from which to despatch their looted art across the Third Reich. For Rose, art is her vocation, and she decides to conduct an important task: to compile an inventory of the stolen works so that – who knows – one day they can be returned to their rightful owners. She soon realises the immense risks involved. The slightest error could be life-threatening.

‹ Rose Valland with artworks that she helped recover.

Rose Valland's war

THICK-SKINNED MAN WITH FELT HAT

The Jeu de Paume is a hive of activity: important visitors are due. Hundreds of artworks belonging to Jewish families or art dealers are hastily hung or propped against the walls. With her knowledge of art history and fluent German, Rose Valland must instruct the Nazis how to organise their improvised exhibition. As negotiated by her superior, *Monsieur* Jaujard, director of the Musées Nationaux, Rose is to keep an inventory of the works. But a man in uniform, clearly displeased, darts over and slams the notebook shut. No inventory! Meanwhile, heavily armed Luftwaffe soldiers stride into the building, where the museum's 'new personnel' are feverishly sorting the works, swastikas on their red armbands. They unload 400 crates in one day.[1] *Schnell!* Barking orders at one another, they pass the works from hand to hand. Some perish under their boots. Rose stifles a scream. Right before her eyes, and in the space of two short days – 1 and 2 November 1940 – the small but exquisite Musée du Jeu de Paume has been transformed into the headquarters of the sinister organisation that will systematically plunder France for the duration of the war: the Einsatzstab Reichsleiter Rosenberg (ERR) [Reichsleiter Rosenberg Taskforce]. It is named after its leader, Alfred Rosenberg, the Nazi ideologist responsible for the Party's racial theory and its concrete application, such as the persecution of Jews and the eradication of 'degenerate' art.

His representative in Paris, Baron Kurt von Behr, is in charge of the ERR antenna. Colonel von Behr is "tall and affable. His uniform cap conceals his face, which has the advantage for this ageing man of hiding his glass eye. He is not lacking in charm and speaks fluent French."[2] Rose endeavours to win his trust. She is successful, the war is still young, and the victors are flush with success. With Rose in his wake, the colonel makes a final inspection tour ahead of the crucial visit. In the evening, when the heavy doors of the Jeu de Paume swing shut, Rose, plus a handful of nightwatchmen who maintain the central heating, is the only French citizen to possess an *Ausweis* [pass] from Colonel von Behr. No one else is allowed near the heavily guarded treasure.

Sunday 3 November. Today is the day. The private exhibition opens its doors to a special guest, the Third Reich's second-in-command, Reichsmarschall Hermann Göring, mastermind of the German war economy and head of the Luftwaffe. Rose gazes anxiously at the entrance where soldiers form a guard of honour. She has heard a great deal about this hero of the skies, the eagle who had blasted his opponents from the air by the dozen during the First World War. Rose expects to see a soldier in full regalia when, all of a sudden, a lumbering, broad silhouette in the doorway blocks the low November light. "He's in plain clothes. A thick-skinned man wearing a felt hat, wrapped in an overcoat that almost touches the ground."[3] His art advisor and the keeper of his private collection shuffles in at his side. With a fat cigar in one hand and a cane in the other, with which he points out various details, Göring the connoisseur pontificates about the works.

So enchanted is that Nazi leader that he returns two days later with his private list. Cézanne's *Les Baigneuses*, and Renoir's *La Seine*, *La femme à la rose* and a *Nu couché* are immediately permitted to accompany him to Germany, along with twenty-seven additional masterpieces, including – appalling to every other Nazi, but not this art afficionado – *Place du Carrousel* by Pissarro, a Jew. Rose catches on straight away: this collector can get away with flouting the Führer's aesthetic guidelines. When Göring's private train pulls out of the Gare du Nord on 5 November, two carriages of stolen art are hitched to the back. He has also left behind an instruction for Paris: a decree stipulating that the ERR will henceforth decide which confiscated works will go to the Führer's collection – Hitler has the first choice – and which to his own. It will be difficult dealing with someone like that, Rose thinks.

SHOCKED ARYAN SOUL

Life has been hard for a long time. Two years previously, the marvellous bustle that still reigned supreme when the deputy curator organised international exhibitions in the shadow of the plane trees of the Tuileries suddenly gave way to another, altogether oppressive kind of commotion. It was triggered by the constant stream of news about the bitter fate of the art world in neighbouring Germany, from where numerous artists, collectors and dealers had fled to France. Every day brought bad news: seizures, appropriation, theft or destruction.

Hitler and his acolytes had decried modern art as the product of 'Jewish degeneration' long before the Nazis came to power in 1933. In their eyes, art was not just an aesthetic counterpart to their ideology or an arbitrary propaganda tool, but a battleground on which the very soul of the *Herrenvolk* would be fought. It was therefore enshrined into the Party's and the regime's *Weltanschauung*[4] [world view]. The Aryan soul was shocked, above all else, by Expressionism, Fauvism and Cubism, with their angular lines, distorted figures, fragmented forms, jarring colours and unnatural themes. The artists themselves, plus their collectors and dealers, were all Jews and Bolsheviks. The antidote was Germanic art, as practised by the Führer himself: his brand of figurative realism was harmonious, slightly romantic and conveyed a nostalgic yearning for the German Empire. Rose follows events on the opposite side of

Rose Valland's war

the Vosges mountains with suspicion. In Paris, as she puts pen to paper in the museum's inventory book for the very first time, on 20 January 1933, she has a strange feeling. Adolf Hitler had been appointed Chancellor of Germany just ten days earlier. The work that the Jeu de Paume has acquired is *Paysage* by Else Berg – a German-born Dutch painter of Jewish descent who would be murdered in Auschwitz on 19 November 1942.[5] Her angular, interpolating landscape painting contains none of the beautiful green undulations seen in the Führer's oeuvre. How unlucky.

At the National Socialist German Workers' Party (NSDAP) conference in Nuremberg in 1935, Hitler fulminated against *Entartete Kunst* [degenerate art]. Between 16,000 and 20,000 'wrong' artworks are removed from German museums, exchanged for 'Aryan works' or sold to feed the war industry. Furthermore, Göring and Hitler appropriate seminal historical works from Jewish collectors. With growing unease, Rose reads about the immense *Entartete Kunst* exhibition that is touring Germany in 1937. In twelve major cities, 3.2 million visitors[6] go to see 700 works by Jewish or 'exterminated' artists who had committed their 'mental illness' to canvas, marble or bronze. Children are forbidden. Each work is labelled with the price at which the museum acquired it, with the poisonous annotation "paid for with German tax money". In large, Gothic letters, visitors can read on the walls: "*Sie sehen es selbst!*" [See for yourself].[7] If exchange or sale does not work, the left-over "uglies" are burnt. Witness the 1,004 paintings and the 3,825 drawings and woodcuts that were thrown on the bonfire in Berlin's fire station on 20 March 1938.

In June 1939, 300 interested representatives of Belgian, American, Swedish, British and Swiss museums wait in the Grand Hôtel National in Lucerne for the opening of a large Nazi auction of art by degenerates such as Van Gogh, Ensor, Gauguin, Braque, Chagall, Derain, Matisse, Modigliani, Picasso, de Vlaminck, Kokoschka, Klee and many others. German Impressionists and Expressionists[8] are the main victims of the deadly campaign. A decree from June 1938 stipulates that they will not receive any compensation for confiscated works. Worse still, the German Ministry of Propaganda's 'valuation committee' decides to offload them all at rock-bottom prices to use the proceeds to buy Aryan art, such as the *Ghent Altarpiece* by the Van Eyck brothers – or war materials, as the case may be, "although the gross profit of the Lucerne auction, 300,000 Deutschmarks, is not even enough to buy a Tiger tank…"[9] There are no representatives of French museums at the Lucerne auction. They are preoccupied with an entirely different matter.

'LA JOCONDE A LE SOURIRE'

In March 1938, the world learns of the *Anschluss*: the annexation of Austria by the Third Reich. Exactly one year later, it is Czechoslovakia's turn. The alarm bells ring throughout Europe. Is France next in line? Jacques Jaujard, then still the deputy director of the Musées Nationaux,[10] refuses to wait for an answer and starts a major evacuation of French museums. The first of a whole series of convoys that will bring the collections to safety leaves on 27 September of that same year for the sixteenth-century Château de Chambord on the Loire. What was once Francis I's royal hunting lodge, boasting 440 rooms, has been designated by the museum management as a logistics centre from where the artworks will be despatched to safer places, mostly castles or monasteries deep in the heart of France.

Speed is of the essence. On 1 September 1939, Germany invades Poland. Two days later, Britain and France declare war. Yet nobody knew when hostilities would begin. Mr Jaujard accelerates the pace of removals: between 28 August and 28 December 1939, forty convoys, each with five to eight lorries, reach the banks of the Loire. Large-scale works travel in the Comédie Française's stage-set vehicles, so that by January 1940 only a few monumental sculptures, impossible to remove, remain in the Louvre. It is all accomplished in the nick of time. In May, Germany invades France. Rose Valland is requested by her superiors to accompany a number of unique masterpieces, such as the *Venus de Milo*, the *Nike of Samothrace*, Michelangelo's *Slaves* and the French crown jewels, to the Château de Valençay. It is there, in the middle of France, between Chambord and Châteauroux, that she learns of the French defeat. In three weeks, her country has been overrun. A thin tear runs down to the corner of her mouth – Paris is occupied.

The German *blitzkrieg* that erupted across France from May triggered, in turn, a second wave of art removals. As the storage facilities in the north are threatened, new convoys leave for the south. As all French men have been called up, women sit behind the steering wheels.[11] Driving seven-tonne lorries, they manoeuvre their country's patrimony through narrow village streets and along rugged mountain roads. Depots in close proximity to traffic junctions – meaning they could be bombed by the Royal Air Force – are relocated. Through the Resistance, London is informed where the art is stashed and, when the *Mona Lisa* arrives unscathed in the remote Château de Montal, on the edge of the Causses Regional Park, the BBC informs its French listeners in a crackling voice: "*La Joconde a le sourire - Je répète - La Joconde a le sourire.*" [The *Mona Lisa* is smiling – I repeat – the *Mona Lisa* is smiling].

Rose Valland's war

On 22 June 1940, the Franco-German Armistice is signed in Compiègne, and Rose Valland is back in Paris. For the first time, the deputy curator is confronted with Nazi hyper-efficiency: the largest art robbery in history was neither spontaneous nor improvised but based on meticulous reports of more than 1,000 pages each, compiled by Dr Kümmel, director general of the Berlin State Museums. By order of Propaganda minister Joseph Goebbels,[13] every important artwork and museum was listed. The Third Reich relied on Reichsmarschall Göring – an art expert with an extensive collection of looted works from Jewish collectors and museums in Germany, Austria, Czechoslovakia and Poland – to execute the orchestrated plundering. Now that France has surrendered, fresh horizons open up for the Nazis. He keeps daily track of his new conquests via photographs and notes. They will be published by Gallimard in 2015 under the title *Le catalogue Goering* [The Göring Catalogue]. [14]

SECRET INVENTORY

The Nazis demand works from French museums, from Dürer to Cranach and from Rubens to Van Dyck. The rest are to be stored in French depositories, the locations of which they now know. The Nazis are particularly interested in a work that Belgium has entrusted to France, and which is in the shelter of the Château de Pau at the foot of the Pyrenees: the *Ghent Altarpiece*, the masterpiece by the Van Eyck brothers. A month after the occupation of Paris, a diktat stipulates that the owners of artworks – French museums first and foremost – must register everything in their possession. Nor must they be moved without the permission of the occupying forces. France's cultural heritage is under threat and will be used, in due course, to enrich Hitler's or Göring's private collections – or to realise the Führer's dream: the largest and most important museum in the world, the Führermuseum in Linz, near his birthplace in Austria.

Yet the thousands of artworks in French museums are not nearly enough to satisfy the Nazi craving for art. No sooner is Paris occupied than they set their sights on a new prey. Troops confiscate the private collections of all the enemies of Nazism: Jews, Bolsheviks and Freemasons, as well as their depraved art dealers. Foreign minister Ribbentrop, a huge admirer of tapestries, and Otto Abetz, the Third Reich's new ambassador to Paris, also want their share. Their soldiers 'knock on the doors' of the great Jewish collectors, some of whom had fled abroad to save their lives. On 21 June – the Nazis had been in Paris for barely a fortnight – they break down the door of the Rothschild family mansion in the Rue Saint-Florentin. Their château in Ferrières, east of Paris, is also looted. The Germans complete their list while also dragging other Jewish family collections[15] and artworks from the galleries of major Jewish dealers, such as Georges Wildenstein and Paul Rosenberg, to the German Embassy. Daniel-Henry Kahnweiler, the Jewish art dealer for Picasso, Braque, Léger and other Cubists, sold his gallery at the last minute to his sister-in-law, the 'Aryan' Louise Leiris. The Nazis steal two hundred works[16] from Rosenberg alone who, in the meantime, had fled to America with his family. His gallery at 21, Rue La Boétie is renamed the 'Institut d'Etude des Questions Juives' (IEQJ). Ironically, it organises exhibitions from this address, such as *Le Juif et la France*, financed by the Gestapo and the German ambassador, Otto Abetz. The latter leans back in good spirits. He delights in the stolen works that grace the walls of his sumptuous city palace, the Hôtel de Beauharnais at 78, Rue de Lille.[17]

His collecting spree does not last long for there are new directives from Reichsleiter Alfred Rosenberg and his ERR, which will oversee all French art – whether public or private – on behalf of the Führer, and 'protect' it from vultures such as Abetz and Ribbentrop who are cutting corners. Ribbentrop has already hung some Parisian Gobelin tapestries in the Foreign Office building in Berlin. After a short but intense struggle between the Ministry and the Embassy on the one hand, and Rosenberg's ERR on the other, the ERR triumphs thanks to the decisive support of Reichsmarschall Göring. He too is champing at the bit to haul some of his ill-gotten gains to his estate.

To impose order on the chaos of looting, a new directive states that from November 1940, all confiscated works must be brought to the Jeu de Paume. This is where Rose Valland meets Göring for the first time. Over the next few years, the 'thick-skinned man with the felt hat' will return to the museum no fewer than twenty times to help himself to top works from French collections. By 1942, Göring has personally purloined ten Renoirs, an equal number of works by Degas, two Monets, three Sisleys, four Cézannes and five Van Goghs. The ERR sends the remainder to Germany and Austria or sells them to dealers, who in turn, resell the works on the international market, until every trace of them is lost, and all hopes of restitution are dashed. Or are they? Someone knows the exact number of works and all their particulars for they are listed in black and white in Rose Valland's secret notebooks, such as *"3 décembre 1941 – Le Ml Goering emportera demain, dans son train particulier [4 décembre au soir], les statues de l'hôtel Edouard de Rothschild... et une cinquantaine de tableaux – beaucoup sont des tableaux impressionnistes appartenant à la collection Rosenberg."* [3 December 1941 – Reichsmarschall Göring will remove tomorrow, in his private train (4 December in the evening), the statues from the hôtel Edouard de Rothschild... and about fifty paintings – many of them Impressionist paintings belonging to the Rosenberg collection]."[18]

Rose Valland's war

With the meticulous accuracy that she honed during her studies, the graduate from the École nationale supérieure des Beaux-Arts de Paris, the École du Louvre and the Institut d'Art et d'Archéologie notes the names of artists and artworks, owners, dealers and transporters, dates of arrival and departure of works, marks on crates, numbers and dates of convoys, along with their presumed destination over there, on the other side of the Rhine.

Hundreds of trains will leave Paris. Just as the convoys of Jews, communists, homosexuals, freemasons, gypsies and resistance fighters cross the points of the large marshalling yard of Drancy, north of Paris, on their way to Auschwitz and other final destinations, so too do thousands of artworks travel from the Jeu de Paume to their allotted destinations: masterpieces are sent to the romantic castle of Neuschwanstein, or that of Herrenchiemsee with its Versailles allure, or to the clifftop eyrie of Hohenschwangau. The rest are stacked in the Führerbau in Munich, in the Buxheim Charterhouse, Mikulov Castle in occupied Czechoslovakia and at other sites around Germany and Austria. In the Jeu de Paume, 'the Drancy of paintings',[19] Rose maintains the inventory to the best of her ability.

Rose completes her nocturnal notes with information gleaned from snippets of conversation, a discarded note or the contents of letters that she hastily copies. The Nazis suspect her of sabotage, stealing paperwork or sending signals to the enemy on no less than four occasions: such as when the building suddenly lit up in the middle of the night, in a Paris darkened for the Allied bombers. The Feldpolizei get involved. But each time, Rose manages to return to work and continue her monastic task.

THE ROOM OF MARTYRS

At the back of the first floor of the museum is *La chambre des martyrs*. An apt name for the room in which the Nazis stockpile the works stamped 'EK', *Entartete Kunst*. So as not to contaminate the other art, the room is screened with a heavy curtain. On 27 July 1943, Rose is powerless. Pen and paper are of no avail. The Jeu de Paume is surrounded by barbed wire and defensive obstacles known as *chevaux de frise* [Frisian horses]. A sentry armed with a machine gun keeps watch on a wooden tower near the entrance. Soldiers haul the EK works downstairs and hurl them into the flames. By Rose's reckoning, there are between 500 and 620 objects. A fine, high plume of smoke rises from the Jeu de Paume. On this summer evening that Rose will never forget, the ashes of the brushstrokes laid down by Miró, Valadon, Picasso, Léger, Klee, Ernst and others float above the treetops of the Tuileries, over the Seine, down the streets and across the city's squares.

When the Nazis appear to be facing defeat, roles are reversed in the Third Reich. Now it is their turn to conceal their loot and historical legacy. In a salt mine in Merkers, Germany, north-east of Frankfurt, they conceal all their gold, along with important artworks from Berlin and other German museums. But another precious hoard is concealed elsewhere: the portrait of Betty de Rothschild, wife of James, founder of the French branch of the Rothschild family, immortalised on canvas by Ingres; the *Ghent Altarpiece* from St Bavo's Cathedral in Ghent; Michelangelo's *Madonna* from the Church of Our Lady in Bruges; *The Astronomer* by Johannes Vermeer; and *The Last Supper* from the famous altarpiece by Dirk Bouts in Leuven. All masterpieces of European art, and every one of them concealed in the Altaussee salt mine in Austria.[21]

Paris, too, is nervous. On 6 June 1944, the Allies land in Normandy and begin their advance. Nevertheless, the cultural theft continues apace, as if the Nazis want to extract every last painting from the country. The Allied landings precipitate a fresh wave of confiscations. Not just paintings and sculptures but also valuable furniture is hauled off to the Jeu de Paume, including the unique collection belonging to the Jewish banker Moïse de Camondo, a passionate collector of seventeenth-century art. Rose Valland swallows hard. It is beyond comprehension. The de Camondo family are more French than the French. Everyone knew that Nissim, the banker's son and a decorated fighter pilot, had sacrificed his life for France in the First World War; and that his father had donated his entire collection, and the magnificent city palace in which it was housed, to the French state as a tribute to him, to be converted into a museum.[22] But the collaborationist French Vichy government spurned this bequest and allowed the Nazis to sack the Hôtel de Camondo on the Rue de Monceau. It elicited a bitter comment from Anne Sinclair, granddaughter of art dealer Paul Rosenberg, who was immortalised on canvas by Picasso as a child: "In the First World War, the Jews were good enough to serve as cannon fodder; twenty years later, they were considered traitors because they were born Jews."

Thousands of crates filled with artworks have already left the country – on 1 August 1944, the first day of the month in which Paris is liberated, 148 additional crates of masterpieces are added to the exodus. Like silent passengers, the artworks are crammed together like sardines, ready for a trip to Germany: Paul Cézanne, Claude Monet, Raoul Dufy, Paul Gauguin, Amedeo Modigliani, Auguste Renoir, Georges Braque, Edgar Degas, Henri de Toulouse-Lautrec, Maurice de Vlaminck, Maurice Utrillo, Pablo Picasso, Marie Laurencin, Pierre Bonnard and André Dunoyer de Segonzac. With sixty-four canvases, Picasso is the undisputed guest-of-honour in his carriage. Rose has carefully noted the

Rose Valland's war

contents of the cases – as she did the number of the train: 40044 – and the destination: Mikulov in Czechoslovakia.

The loot-filled train must leave Paris before it is too late. It is sealed and placed under armed guard. But as the Germans also want to get forty-seven other carriages with stolen furniture out of the city, the convoy's departure is delayed. Once underway, however, the train almost immediately grinds to a halt at the station of Aubervilliers, between Paris and Drancy. Technical problems. "*Trop long et trop chargé*", shout the French railway workers, who, with German submachine guns aimed at them, repair the defect. The convoy barely advances a kilometre before another breakdown forces it into a 48-hour stopover at the next village. This time, it's even more serious: the entire locomotive must be replaced. A setback for von Behr, but a success for Rose. The minute she discovers the fate of this priceless consignment she informs her director, Mr Jaujard. He, in turn, calls upon the Résistance-Fer [the Resistance arm of the French railways].[24] They have been sabotaging the Germans for days.

27 August: Paris has been liberated for two days and General von Choltitz has signed the German surrender. A little further on, everything starts to move: the locomotive has just pulled away when a miracle happens in the next village, Aulnay-sous-Bois. On learning of the ultimate kidnapping, a detachment of six volunteers from General Leclerc's second armoured division, which is leading the liberation of Paris, decides to halt the train. After a short but intense fire-fight, the German guards are overpowered and Picasso and company are freed. When Rose hears the news, she removes her trademark round glasses and rubs the nightmare from her eyes.[25] Her heart must have skipped a beat upon hearing that the intrepid lieutenant who liberated train no. 40044 is a young Frenchman called Alexandre Rosenberg. Opening the crates in Aulnay, he holds in his hands – to his complete surprise and intense emotion – the artworks stolen from his father's gallery.[26]

Rose Valland's war

2
CHANEL VERSUS WERTHEIMER

Rose and jasmine are the dominant notes of the iconic perfume Chanel Nº5. But the most successful bottle in the world also contains some not-so-floral accents, such as envy and greed, plus a hint of collaboration. It is a page that is often erased from the biography of the great couturier's fragrance. From her headquarters at 31, Rue Cambon, the 'Iron Lady of Perfume' fights a long-running and malodorous battle against the Jewish entrepreneurial family, the Wertheimers.[1] The majority stakeholders in Les Parfums Chanel since its inception are now the sole owners of the global Chanel empire. However, the Wertheimers came very close to losing their business to Mademoiselle Coco during the Second World War. Courtesy of the Nazis.

< Pierre Wertheimer with his
  inevitable bowler hat.

Chanel versus Wertheimer

THAT DAY AT THE RACES

The Grand Prix de Deauville is always thronged with beautiful people. Crowned heads of state, such as King Alfonso XIII of Spain and the Maharajah of Kapurthala, exotic princes and princesses, the Greek shipowner Zografos, and industrialists such as André Citroën and the brothers Pierre and Paul Wertheimer, all cross paths in the stands or on the new Promenade des Planches, which has been laid to prevent beachgoers from sinking up to their ankles in the sand. Gabrielle Chanel – *Coco* to her friends, *Mademoiselle* to her employees and the public – is also in attendance at this dazzling event in 1923. To her delight, numerous women are wearing her *pièces uniques*. Not to mention her hats, chicer versions of simple straw sun hats that are adorned with flowers or feathers. They are all the rage.

Coco's boutique, which had opened in the fashionable seaside resort in 1914,[2] cannot keep up with demand in the run-up to *la saison* on the '*Riviera Normande*'. Her *marinière* collection, in particular, is *en vogue* on both *L'Atlantique* and the Côte d'Azur: Chanel's designs – casual white shirts with sailor stripes, wide white trousers and thick blue jumpers – are inspired by the simple cuts and comfortable fabrics more typically associated with lingerie. She also offers knitted scarves against the mild sea breezes, and swimming costumes with plunging backs: daring at a time when corsets still constrict many women's physiques. Coco herself, however, has long since abandoned these suffocating straitjackets and even ran an advertisement in *Les Modes* in 1908 encouraging others to follow suit.[3] With great success. Her boutiques in Cannes, Biarritz and Paris – financed by an ex-lover who had died in an accident, Boy Capel – are also thriving. Given the prices, she caters to a particularly well-heeled clientele.

Théophile Bader is one such figure. He is a good friend of Coco's and the owner of the Galeries Lafayette on the Boulevard Haussmann in Paris. Under the cool awning of the champagne tent at the Grand Prix de Deauville, he introduces Coco to Pierre and Paul Wertheimer. The Wertheimers are successful Jewish entrepreneurs and thus ideally placed to help Coco realise her ambitious dreams. In the summer of 1920, with the help of talented 'nose' Ernest Beaux, once a perfumer to the tsar, she creates her own exclusive and exquisite perfume. She simply names it after the number on the bottle that she picks from the two series of samples that Beaux has prepared: bottle number five becomes 'Chanel N°5'.[4] Although her fragrance is a modest success in her boutiques, her dreams are far, far grander... and that demands capital.

Théophile Bader has prepared the meeting well. The Wertheimers are active in the aviation industry and already own the large French perfume and cosmetics company, Bourjois. With fire and passion, Chanel explains her ambitions: global success for her baby, N°5. The Wertheimers adore the races: their spirited stallion Epinard had won the Prix Yacowlef with a five-length-lead the previous year.[5] But they quickly forget the racetrack and are transfixed by the glittering black orbs under the equally dark eyelashes of the petite and gesticulating lady. The words that fall from her lips are as intoxicating as the clip of Sao Paulo's hooves, the winning thoroughbred. The spark has leapt.

FULL GALLOP

The Wertheimers and Coco establish 'Les Parfums Chanel' in 1924. The two brothers finance everything – production, distribution, marketing and sales – and shoulder all the risks. In view of this, they receive 70% of the company shares. Théophile Bader, who brokered the introduction and is providing distribution of the precious bottle through the Galeries Lafayette, receives 20%. Chanel, who has brought both the idea and the formula to the table but nothing in the way of money, receives the remaining 10%.[6] Chanel N°5 is surrounded by an air of exclusivity and luxury from the outset, underscored by an equally exclusive price. Chanel personally oversees the public relations and does a magnificent job.

She even makes it to Hollywood, where Sam Goldwyn, head of the Metro Goldwyn Mayer studio, invites her to design clothes for his stable of stars, including Gloria Swanson, Greta Garbo and Marlene Dietrich. The American studios roll out the red carpet for *Mademoiselle*, who is paid $1 million for her services, a fortune at the time, and equivalent to $75 million in today's terms.[7] The American media whip themselves into a frenzy over the innovative French couturier and her designs for the Hollywood stars. For her part, Coco has a knack for turning all media attention to one specific name, that of *Mademoiselle* Chanel.

Chanel is simultaneously conquering the Parisian stage. *Le Train Bleu* is causing a furore in the French capital. Jean Cocteau, an artistic jack-of-all-trades, has created the ballet opera for Serge Diaghilev's controversial Ballets Russes, with choreography by Bronislava Nijinska and music by Darius Milhaud. Picasso paints a giant version of his *Deux femmes courant sur la plage* for the set. From the moment it premieres in the Théâtre des Champs-Élysées in 1924, *Le Train Bleu* is an unbridled success. How could it be otherwise when so many great names have joined forces? Furthermore, the theme appeals to everyone's imagination. *Le Train Bleu* is the name of the exclusive night train that whisks the wealthy and carefree Parisians from the Gare de Lyon to their villas on the Riviera. It is a dazzling spectacle that transports audiences to a world of sun, sea and fashionable sports. The swimmers, tennis players and sunbathers are all dressed by Chanel.[8] *Le Train Bleu* receives an equally rapturous reception when it opens at the Coliseum in London. The principal dancer, Serge Lifar, reprises his performance in a signature Chanel costume at the Bal Racine in 1939.[9]

Chanel's opera and ballet designs only add to her artistic prestige and have a magical effect on brand awareness. Her name is on everyone's lips and in all the newspapers. The exposure not only boosts clothing sales, but also fuels demand for N°5. The perfume's phenomenal success in America and France soon filters through to other continents. By the mid-1930s, Chanel N°5 is a truly international brand. If Théophile Bader is delighted, then Pierre and Paul Wertheimer are ecstatic: the business is a runaway train, or to use an apt analogy, a racehorse on a winning streak.

AT WAR

Coco is less than pleased. She is downright angry about the situation. Her paltry 10% stake in this unforeseen success is now a source of conflict. *Mademoiselle* wants more. In 1935, she hires one of the best commercial lawyers in the country and takes legal action against the Wertheimers. *Maître* René de Chambrun is a descendant of the Marquis de Lafayette, who had assisted America in the fight for independence against the British in 1777. Long domiciled in the United States, his family has only recently returned to France. De Chambrun takes the 'see-you-in-court' style of advocacy that he has learnt in America and successfully imports it to his much more reserved homeland of France. In the meantime, the Wertheimers are ploughing a stack of fresh capital into the business with the aim of further extending the international brand's reach. In so doing, they remain loyal to Chanel and ensure that she retains her full 10% of shares with each fresh injection of cash.[10] Despite the legal attacks from Paris, the Wertheimers remain steadfast. Yet a dramatic turn of events soon forces them to yield.

As the rise of Nazi Germany plunges the world into the depths of despair, Coco is thrilled at the wealth of opportunities open to her in Paris. France capitulates on 22 June 1940, although the first German troops took up positions in Paris as early as 14 June. From July onwards, the commanding officers of the German Luftwaffe ensconce themselves in Coco's second home, the exclusive Ritz Hotel on the Place Vendôme. Göring maintains a suite in the establishment throughout the war. Another officer unpacking his cases in one of the rooms is a certain Hans von Dincklage. The Nazis' arrival forces Chanel to swap her prestigious high-ceilinged suite, with its double doors and view of the Colonne Vendôme, for a room at the back, which overlooks her offices and studios at

31, Rue Cambon, opposite the rear entrance to the Ritz. Although initially rancorous and aloof, Coco soon falls for the captivating charms of the strapping, blond, blue-eyed Hans. Recruited into the Weimar Republic's military intelligence services in 1919, he is identified as an *Abwehr* spy in France by the country's counterintelligence agency in 1935.[11] Chanel's relationship with her Nazi will continue for some fourteen years after the war ends.

Having a German spy as a lover naturally assists her case against the Wertheimers. Of even greater help, however, is a Nazi decree of 19 October 1940. It orders the 'Aryanisation of the French economy': companies run by Jewish businessmen are immediately placed under the control of provisional administrators who are tasked with selling them to Aryan industrialists,[12] such as Coco Chanel. Her choice of lawyer also proves to be auspicious. *Maître* de Chambrun has since married Josée Laval, the daughter of the French politician, Pierre Laval, who is the prime minister of the collaborationist Vichy regime. With his father-in-law installed as the head of the collaborationist government, de Chambrun's sense of grandeur grows. At the Ritz, he organises '*Les Banquets de la Table Ronde*' every three weeks: dinners with twenty-five Germans and an equal number of French guests – politicians, entrepreneurs and financiers – with the aim of 'facilitating a *rapprochement Franco-Allemand*',[13] and at which he, of course, is the greatest star of them all.[14]

More a businessman than a lawyer, de Chambrun is also one of the driving forces behind the idea of a huge *Banque Franco-Allemande*, with both countries in equal partnership and a starting capital of 1 billion francs.[15] The project collapses. De Chambrun enjoys far greater success, however, as a consultant for the perfume house Guerlain, which pays him 200,000 francs per month (the salary is merely a supplement to his many other lucrative activities).[16] Like so many other companies who rely upon the services of de Chambrun, Guerlain considers him to be their 'man for America' after the war. *Maître* de Chambrun has become an immensely powerful figure. Roses and moonlight finally seem within Coco's grasp, while the Wertheimers appeared to be hovering on the brink of disaster. With three trump cards in her hand – a Nazi lover, a Nazi decree and an all-powerful, Nazi lawyer – Coco plays her endgame.

Intuitive industrialists that they are, the Wertheimers had sensed the storm clouds gathering as early as 1940. Moreover, they know all about the fate of their brethren in Germany. That May, they quietly sell their 70% stake in Les Parfums Chanel, their cosmetics company Bourjois, and all their aviation interests to their French business partner, Félix Amiot. They escape to the United States via Brazil. The entrepreneurial family does not stay idle for long. The Wertheimers hire a secret agent who, in a life-or-death mission, smuggles gold into France to buy the

Chanel versus Wertheimer

ingredients needed to produce Chanel N°5 – which he first has to smuggle out of Grasse, and then France, before finally shipping them to the United States.[17] The James Bond of the day is one H. Gregory Thomas, who becomes the chairman of Chanel Inc. after the war, in recognition of these deeds. As the war rages on in Europe, the Wertheimers restart the production of N°5 in Hoboken, opposite Manhattan. With their in-depth knowledge of the entire production chain, the launch of the perfume on American soil is an instant success.

CHURCHILL TO THE RESCUE

Meanwhile, back in Paris, Coco has caught wind of the fact that Pierre Wertheimer's prestigious residence at 55, Avenue Foch, stands empty.[18] She believes that the Wertheimers have simply fled like the countless other Jewish families. *Mademoiselle* is already envisaging the revenue from their 70% stake flowing into her coffers. Until she discovers that Félix Amiot has silently replaced them as the primary shareholder. Legally speaking, the Wertheimers are under no obligation to inform Coco, as a minority shareholder, of the sale. In her anger, Chanel instructs her Nazi friend, Dr Kurt Blanke, of the Aryanisation Committee – headquartered in the Hotel Majestic on the Avenue Kléber – to turn the life of the majority shareholder upside down, with the aid of the French *Abwehr* spy Baron Louis de Vaufreland.[19] Félix Amiot is not only able to prove that he is 100% Aryan, but also that he has paid the correct price for the shares. Furthermore, the aircraft manufacturer has gone into partnership with the German company Junkers Flugzeug- und Motorenwerke to produce 370 planes – an order worth 1.2 billion francs.[20] The Aryanisation Committee is powerless to act against the new owner of Chanel N°5.

As the war progresses, it gradually dawns on Coco: she has played a high stakes game and lost. She realises that both her reputation and liberty are now at risk. The Allies have landed in Normandy and the Germans are becoming increasingly active. On 24 August 1944, five days after Chanel's sixty-first birthday, General Leclerc's second armoured division rolls into Paris while several factions of the Resistance are fighting pitched battles in the streets and across the city's rooftops. In the days and weeks that follow, collaborators are captured and executed. Thousands of women are publicly humiliated or worse for 'horizontal collaboration'. That Coco escapes is a near miracle. She is arrested and interrogated at the police prefecture before being collected by a chauffeur-driven car and driven straight to Lausanne, across the Swiss border.

The exact circumstances of her departure are still shrouded in mystery. The most plausible explanation for her 'salvation' is her long-standing friendship with Winston Churchill. As early as 1928, the British statesman and the couturier had hunted wild boar together on the French estate of Hugh Grosvenor, the Duke of Westminster, who was the designer's *chéri* at the time. A photograph taken at Mimizan in the Landes, the wooded coastal region just below Bordeaux, shows Churchill and a smiling Chanel, the latter in a riding hat, posing side-by-side with nervous-looking dogs at their feet. Grosvenor was so enamoured of Coco that he also gave her the land for her villa, 'La Pausa', in Roquebrune on the French Riviera,[21] making her the neighbour of the prime minister who leads Britain to victory in the Second World War. Chanel remains in exile in Switzerland, where she lives quietly with Von Dincklage until 1953. It is from here that she continues her battle with the Wertheimers.

AN OFFER SHE CAN'T REFUSE

The world is a different place after the war. The Wertheimers have not only purchased their perfume business back from Félix Amiot, but also regularised their aviation interests. In 1947, Pierre Wertheimer, who sees enormous opportunities for expansion and is tired of the legal wrangling, takes a conciliatory step. Coco is ready to listen. The 1924 contract is voided and instead of holding 10% of the shares, she will now receive 2% of the global turnover. It makes a huge difference: in today's terms, she receives the equivalent of an extra $25 million per year in profits. Furthermore, Pierre also gives her a $9 million share of the profits made on the wartime sales in America. At the age of sixty-five, Coco has suddenly become one of the richest women in the world.[22] Upon Paul Wertheimer's death in 1948, Pierre purchases the remaining 20% of shares from the heirs of Théophile Bader. In so doing, he becomes the sole owner of Les Parfums Chanel.

As relations with Coco continue to improve and the business returns to normal, Pierre devises an even 'better' arrangement. He will back the relaunch of Coco's couture business and guarantee her a fabulous monthly income. Wertheimer will also pay for her suite and expenses at the Ritz, which has been restored to its pre-war glory. Coco finally feels respected. Even though it means surrendering the rights to her couture business, she is pleased with the deal. Pierre becomes the owner of all current and future products bearing the Chanel name. For the rest of her life, *Mademoiselle* retains her grip on the creative reins as the designer and artistic director of the house – the job that later goes to Karl Lagerfeld. Throughout their lives, Pierre and Coco navigate a complex love-hate relationship, driven by 'the entrepreneur's passion for the woman he is exploiting'[23] and by the intriguing power play between a Jew and a Nazi sympathiser.

Chanel versus Wertheimer

Pierre Wertheimer dies in April 1965. Coco 'follows' him – although she would have balked at this turn of phrase – on Sunday 10 January 1971, in her luxurious suite at the Ritz. Rich beyond belief, but also lonely.

The perfume company continued to grow under the leadership of the Wertheimer grandchildren, Alain and Gérard, who assumed control in 1974. It is now a luxury empire with billions of dollars in turnover and, likewise, profits. In addition to the Chanel brand, the Wertheimers also own Holland & Holland, Erès, Orlebar Brown and Bell & Ross. They helped finance the renovation of the Palais Galliera fashion museum in Paris' Avenue Pierre 1er de Serbie, which reopened its doors in 2020. The family also owns Château Rauzan-Ségla, Château Canon, Château Berliquet, Domaine de l'Ile and Napa Valley's St Supéry Vineyards & Winery. All of these enterprises contribute to the fortunes of the family[24] whose clever and swift actions at the start of the Second World War not only saved their skins, but also their business interests.

On 6 February 2023, the Wertheimers took their friends and foes in the financial world by surprise once more. Together with the wealthy Peugeot and Dassault families – the former dynasty founded the eponymous car brand, while the latter are the aviation industrialists who changed their Jewish name Bloch to Dassault after the Second World War – they help finance the Rothschild family's attempt to delist its prestigious Franco-British merchant bank Rothschild & Co. But Alain and Gérard do not like to advertise their activities. On the contrary, they shun the media. In the few photos that do exist, however, mostly taken at the races, they are wearing somewhat anachronistic-looking bowler hats. This might well be racing etiquette but, at the same time, it can also be seen as a tribute to their grandfather, Pierre, the founder of the Chanel empire.

Chanel versus Wertheimer

NAPOLEON III, THE FORGOTTEN EMPEROR

3

"Industry is a machine that runs without a regulator. It does not care what driving force it uses. Like a true Saturn of labour, industry devours its own children and lives only by their deaths." Such words could easily be attributed to Karl Marx or Friedrich Engels, but surprisingly enough they were written by a rich, thirty-six-year-old prince – Louis-Napoleon Bonaparte, nephew of Napoleon – in an essay entitled Extinction du paupérisme *[The Extinction of Pauperism]. He wrote the treatise from his prison cell in 1844 while serving a life sentence. At the time, no one viewed this dreamer-adventurer as the comet who, in just six years, would ascend from prisoner to people's representative, president of the Republic and emperor of the French. But before all this could happen, the man who inspired the Second Empire must escape the heavily guarded Château de Ham.*

‹ Napoleon III, nephew of
Napoleon Bonaparte.

A NEW BONAPARTE

"Allez montez, mon cher ami!" Napoleon tenderly lifts his nephew and straightens the boy's uniform. Seven-year-old Louis-Napoleon Bonaparte is the son of Louis, the Emperor's younger brother, and his wife Hortense. She, in turn, is the daughter of Joséphine de Beauharnais, the Emperor's first great love and his first wife. The year is 1815. After escaping from Elba and reuniting with his army, Napoleon is back in the Palais des Tuileries in Paris. From whence the Bourbon king, Louis XVIII, has fled in disarray upon hearing the shocking news that 'the Eagle', as Napoleon is called, is at large. The Emperor is delighted to be reunited with his nephew. Little Louis-Napoleon gazes out of the window. A unit of the Imperial Guard marches past. It is a mere shadow of the Grande Armée but in the Emperor's mind, victory over the enemy nations, the ancient kingdoms of Europe, is still within reach.

As he embraces the young boy, the Emperor's heart bleeds. He pines for his own four-year-old son. His second wife, Marie-Louise of Austria, did not follow him into exile on Elba after his defeat in Leipzig but returned, with their child, to her imperial family in Vienna. Napoleon suffered disaster after disaster in 1813 and 1814. His Grande Armée was decimated during the Russian campaign, another 38,000 soldiers were lost at Leipzig, while 20,000 more were taken as prisoners of war. His first great love, the Empress Joséphine, had died, and Marie-Louise and his son are now living under enemy rule. Napoleon might have escaped Elba and returned to Paris, but emperors and monarchs throughout Europe are sharpening their swords in readiness for a final showdown with the Corsican. On 18 June 1815, Napoleon is defeated at Waterloo and exiled to Saint Helena, where he will die six years later. As Louis XVIII is reinstalling himself in the Tuileries upon his return from Ghent, where he had established a government-in-exile, the young Louis-Napoleon Bonaparte is en route to Switzerland with his mother. He will never see his uncle again. Yet the Imperial Guard's parade is etched upon his memory. Politics runs in the family, and it isn't long before it whets the appetite of the illustrious Emperor's young nephew.

At the age of twenty-two, Louis-Napoleon supports a conspiracy by the Carbonari, the secret society planning to install a liberal monarchy in Italy. He also joins the fight against the Papal States in Rome. But as soon as Austria despatches 20,000 soldiers to drive out the victorious revolutionaries, Louis-Napoleon turns tail and beats a hasty retreat to Paris – the city from which the new bourgeois king, Louis-Philippe d'Orléans, has been calling the shots since the July Revolution of 1830 (which is why his reign is referred to as the July Monarchy). Orléans tolerates Louis-Napoleon's presence in the city on two conditions: that he is there only briefly, and that he stays incognito. Nevertheless, the Parisians soon get wind of 'a new Bonaparte'. The young powerhouse is promptly exiled.

Louis-Napoleon is intent on causing a stir in the French capital; through a 'march on Paris', for example, just like his eminent uncle. He finds a friend and ally in the Duc de Persigny, his faithful right-hand man during his meteoric rise to the top.[1] But their clumsy plan is derailed in Strasbourg when they, and other assorted adventurers, call for revolution at the barrack gates. "*Soldats! Marchons contre les traîtres du pays!*" [Soldiers! Let us march against the country's traitors!]. The garrison springs into action: but only to arrest the bolshy prince. Persigny escapes. Thanks to the intercessions of Louis-Napoleon's mother, Orléans releases the captive on condition that he heads straight for America and stays away from Paris. The prince pays dutiful visits to Rio de Janeiro and New York. But when he publishes a book from Switzerland a few years later, detailing his 'political action' in Strasbourg, the French government cannot contain its exasperation. Orléans even threatens to attack Switzerland if it does not immediately expel the firebrand. Louis-Napoleon won't let it get that far. Despite accepting voluntary exile in London, he appears to have achieved his goal. In France, and Paris especially, there is renewed talk of 'that new Bonaparte'. Practice makes perfect.

He resumes his plotting the moment he sets foot in the British capital. This time, he will incite a garrison in Boulogne-sur-Mer to attack Orléans. A local general with a sentimental attachment to the Emperor offers his support. Louis-Napoleon sets sail for France on 5 August 1840 – full steam ahead – with an army of sympathetic Bonapartists under his belt, plus the ever-loyal Persigny. The 'Edinburgh Castle', supposedly hired for a cruise, is also carrying 100,000 gold francs. At the barrack gates in Boulogne, Louis-Napoleon reprises his theatrical stunt from Strasbourg. Astonished spectators are handed gold coins as they chant: "*A bas Orléans! Vive l'empereur!*" [Down with Orléans! Long live the Emperor!] But the rabble are chased onto the beach under a hail of gunfire from the Garde Nationale. Shot in the arm, Prince Bonaparte fails to reach his 'war fleet'. Sentenced to life imprisonment, he is hurled into the *cachot* [dungeon]. From *Le Journal des Débats* in Paris to *The Times* in London, the press has a field day. And the French? Louis-Napoleon is yesterday's news. They yearn for the return of their Napoleon's remains from Saint Helena. By the end of that same year, he is solemnly interred in the Cathédrale Saint-Louis-des-Invalides by King Louis-Philippe d'Orléans and his prime minister, Adolphe Thiers.

Napoleon III, the forgotten emperor

THE WAITING ROOM OF POWER

Unlike the illustrious Eagle, who once circled over Europe, his nephew has spent five years in a cage. In the heavily guarded Château de Ham, Louis-Napoleon managed to wangle a well-appointed room, a parlour with an extensive library, and a small laboratory in which to indulge his passion for chemical experiments. Provided he refrains from fomenting revolutions, he is generally left to his own devices. He reads the works of the early socialist thinkers, including Robert Owen and Louis Blanc, and formulates his own treatise on the eradication of poverty. Between chemistry and politics, he also finds time for his chambermaid, the captivating Eléonore Vergeot. That he fathers two sons with her is seen by the guards as a sign that he is gradually accepting his fate.

No one thinks anything of it, therefore, when a clog-wearing carpenter drags a few planks across the castle courtyard one fine spring day in May 1846. He pauses for a moment, glances disinterestedly around him, pulls his cap deeper over his eyes and sucks noisily on his pipe. The fellow hoists the planks onto his shoulder and saunters out of the gate. Two days later, Louis-Napoleon is back in London, where he snares the beautiful and wealthy actress Harriet Howard as a companion for further adventures. His own fortune, meanwhile, has been eaten up by his 'revolutions'. The twenty-three-year-old beauty saves him from bankruptcy. Moreover, she invests her own capital into her hero's propaganda campaign for the 1848 French elections. Things are getting serious, it's time to get down to business.

Tensions may have been running high in France in 1848, but the situation in Paris is downright explosive. Unemployment and poverty are soaring in tandem and, as in all the other European states, a year of revolt is brewing. The embattled populace takes to the streets on 22 February. The first deaths are recorded the next day, on the barricades across the Boulevard des Capucines. On 24 February, the insurgents storm the Palais des Tuileries. Louis-Philippe d'Orléans abdicates and flees to England. The idea of a French king is dead and buried in France, together with the July Monarchy. Alphonse de Lamartine, leader of the liberal Republicans, proclaims the Second Republic on 24 February 1848. Universal suffrage – read, for men only – is reinstated, the freedom of the press is restored and, in a true first for the era, slavery is abolished in the French colonies.

Somewhere at sea, the hunted Orléans and zealous Louis-Napoleon unwittingly cross paths. The former is heading for safety and peace in London, the latter for a political career in Paris. He offers his services in the capital but is sent packing. Indeed, the frail provisional government fears a return to authoritarianism with a Bonaparte in its ranks. For the very first time in his turbulent life, the hot-blooded Louis-Napoleon makes a wise decision. He keeps his head, returns to London, and waits.

There is nothing more he can do. The new government in Paris will not reverse the disaster. Persigny, for his part, cannot sit still. He establishes a *Comité napoléonien* in Paris, builds a network of supporters, and adds Louis-Napoleon to the list of candidates for the elections of 23 and 24 April.[2] Lo and behold, all good things come to he who waits. Thanks to his resounding name, political interventions and publications, Louis-Napoleon is elected *député* in Paris and of three additional *départements*. Lamartine, now genuinely alarmed by Louis-Napoleon's soaring popularity, immediately invokes the law on the 'exile of the Bonaparte family'. On Louis-Napoleon's game-board this means 'back to square one' for the umpteenth time. But the late emperor's nephew manages to keep himself in check once again.

That spring, the leaders of the Second Republic follow one another faster than the dishes in a bustling Parisian brasserie. A new government experiment to generate mass employment, the *Ateliers nationaux*, pushes France towards bankruptcy. The scheme is disbanded but the country descends into famine and violence, with Paris the worst hit. Yet this time round, neither writers nor enlightened nobles take to the barricades. The workers, the unemployed and the destitute are left to fend for themselves. Lamartine, newly elected by the Republicans with over 5 million votes, and his fellow politician, Victor Hugo, elected by the conservatives with almost 2 million votes, call for the guns to be turned on the people. As the tension mounts in Paris, someone in the British capital is devouring the French newspapers. For Louis-Napoleon, nothing is harder than keeping a low profile in his *salle d'attente* [waiting room], as he describes London.

Meanwhile, the bourgeoisie are sick and tired of the permanent insurgency in Paris. In the interests of commerce, it prefers 'a terrible end, rather than unending horror', which is exactly how the wealthy middle classes perceive the rising 'red tide'. The riot acquires its name from the red flags on the barricades, which are waving for the first time in history. The *Tricolore* has all but disappeared; the barricades are manned by a rabble calling themselves 'communists'. This is a new and deeply unsettling phenomenon. A *union sacrée* of Orléanists, legitimists, republicans and socialists decide to stop the riots.[3] The provisional government readies itself for battle. Gardes Mobiles, mainly comprising thugs, are co-opted into the Garde Nationale. Troops are recalled from the provinces, bayonets sharpened, cannon aligned. The city is teetering on the brink of war.

By late June, the barricades have become impossible to count. General Eugène Cavaignac, ex-governor of Algeria and head of the conservative

Napoleon III, the forgotten emperor

Republicans, supresses the riot with a rabid fanaticism. More than 5,000 people are killed. Cavaignac pursues the survivors down the narrowest alleyways to execute them, even as they surrender. With the red flags shot down in flames, the General asserts his authority over the government. The revolution of 1848 is dead. As the blood dries on the streets of Paris, a certain someone exits their 'London waiting room' with bulging travelling trunks. On this occasion, he has packed for a longer stay.

ETERNAL BUT FLEETING LOYALTY

Unsullied by the bloody repression of the citizens, Louis-Napoleon Bonaparte stands in the first direct presidential election on 10 December 1848. The Republicans field the conservative candidates Lamartine and Cavaignac, while the Socialists back the progressive Alexandre Ledru-Rollin. François-Vincent Raspail throws in his lot with the Socialists. In opposition is a brand-new movement, the Parti de l'Ordre [Party of Order]. It has succeeded in uniting monarchists, clerics, the haute bourgeoisie, and large swathes of Bonapartists under the dictates of innate politician Adolphe Thiers and newcomer Louis-Napoleon Bonaparte. The latter's exercises in political agitation will now serve him well.

Louis-Napoleon focuses his campaign on Paris, while his *comités de soutien* [election committees] set their sights on the rest of the country. From their headquarters on the Place Vendôme, militants, poster pasters, letter writers and pamphlet distributors conquer the hearts of Parisians. After all the bloodshed, they long for order and peace. Louis-Napoleon shakes hands in the barracks, debates with writer-politicians such as Hugo and Pierre-Joseph Proudhon, and above all else, succeeds in winning over the press – previously unwaveringly hostile – to his cause. What the journalists and public do not realise, however, is that the campaign is funded by a cash injection from his wealthy admirer in London.

The elections turn to triumph: Louis-Napoleon Bonaparte is declared president of the Second Republic. With 5.5 million votes to his name, he wins a huge margin over the next candidate, Cavaignac (1.5 million votes). The new president promptly transplants his London paramour to Paris and installs her in the Rue du Cirque, literally within walking distance of the Elysée Palace.[4] Just before Christmas in that turbulent year of 1848, the President takes the oath of office before the Assemblée. As Louis-Napoleon solemnly swears "eternal allegiance to the one and indivisible democratic Republic", the *députés* catch their breath. Another Bonaparte: it is an emotional moment. It has started to snow. No one sees the fleeting transience of the snowflakes swirling above the

Assemblée as an omen. But Louis-Napoleon's pledge of "eternal loyalty" and the "democratic Republic" will only survive another three years.

One constitutional point vexes Louis-Napoleon from the outset: "The president is elected for four years, renewal is impossible." He cannot accomplish his immense plans in such a short space of time. Therefore, a year before the end of his term, at daybreak on Tuesday 2 December 1851, hundreds of white posters hang in Paris. In the drizzling rain, people are dumbfounded by the message: parliament has been dissolved. New elections will follow. Meanwhile, President Louis-Napoleon Bonaparte exhorts the army, "the nation's elite", to "defend national sovereignty" in the name of the French people. A coup d'état.

Seasoned conspirator that he is, Louis-Napoleon and the Duc de Morny, his half-brother, plus the indefatigable Persigny, have prepared the coup well. The army, administration and the prefect of police, including all forty-eight commissioners, are in on the plot. Morny, the mastermind of the coup, is appointed minister of the interior, although he is quickly replaced by Persigny. Louis-Napoleon's bosom friend, Émile de Maupas, formerly prefect of the Garonne, takes over the Parisian force. His man in the army, General Saint-Arnaud, becomes minister of war, while his confidant, minister Achille Fould, a Jewish banker converted to Protestantism, is tasked with stabilising the markets during the transition period. Just before dawn, a hundred or so troublemakers from the Assemblée, mostly Republicans and 'reds', have already been lifted from their beds. His former supporter, Adolphe Thiers, and other members of his own Parti de l'Ordre are also detained. The Assemblée is seized by the army. Paris is occupied by 54,000 soldiers. At 11am, the President parades down the Champs-Élysées to the applause of his troops.

Elsewhere in the city, some 300 assorted parliamentarians beg the army to defend the Republic, with utterly unforeseen consequences – the army places them under lock and key. La Montagne, the left-wing Republican party, is outlawed. Its leaders, Alexandre Ledru-Rollin and Louis Blanc, flee the country. Even General Cavaignac, the 'butcher' of the 1848 'red revolution', is forced to watch his cell in the Mazas prison in the Faubourg Saint-Antoine draw closer and closer from the tiny window of a police vehicle. Random shots are fired and a hundred or so malcontents are killed, but the tumult is quickly contained. But unlike before, the people do not take to the streets en masse in defence of the Republic and its representatives. They remember how they were abandoned in the summer of 1848, three years previously, when thousands of people died on the barricades. "*Le peuple est aux fenêtres, le bourgeois seul est dans la rue*," [The people are at the windows, the bourgeois alone are in the street] is how Hippolyte Babou, writer and friend of Charles Baudelaire, sketched the working-class indifference to the coup d'état. Persigny, not entirely unsympathetic, has an inspired idea: three weeks later, on 20 and 21 December 1851, a huge referendum is held. The French are asked to declare their confidence (or not) in the president. The response is overwhelming: 7,439,216 affirmative votes versus 640,737 negative. Encouraged by the outpouring of adoration and with the help of the ever-zealous Persigny, the President ventures to take another step.

THE EMPIRE OF PEACE

On 2 December 1852, a year to the day after his coup, Louis-Napoleon proclaims himself 'Napoleon III, Emperor of the French'. France becomes the 'Second Empire', an initially authoritarian dictatorship that, from 1860, becomes increasingly 'enlightened'. The imperial motto is already promising: *L'Empire, c'est la paix* [The Empire is peace]. This instantly reassures the neighbouring princes who haven't forgotten Uncle Napoleon. Napoleon III, however, does not wish to seek glory on the battlefield but via social and economic innovation. Under his leadership, Paris must surpass London, and France all other nations.

To Georges-Eugène Haussmann, the new prefect for Paris who was nominated by none other than Persigny, he entrusts a magisterial plan for *l'embellissement* of Paris. Haussmann turns it into a total project that encompasses the overlapping spheres of sanitation, transport and beautification. Paris becomes 'the' construction site of the century in the blink of an eye. Visible reminders of the era include the Opéra Garnier, the Théatre du Châtelet, the Théatre de la Ville, numerous boulevards, parks and squares, and bridges and stations such as the Pont Saint-Michel, the Gare du Nord and the Gare de Lyon. Invisible to the naked eye are the kilometres of aqueducts that siphon healthy drinking water to the city for the first time, and the sewers that channel wastewater to underground collectors. The impetus for the works can be traced back to the Emperor's famous uncle. For a city that suffered cholera epidemics in 1832, 1849 and 1853, the infrastructure is essential.

Two remarkable world exhibitions, the first in 1855 and the second in 1867, perfectly illustrate the fruits of these imperial policies. Millions of international visitors gather beneath the grandiose metal arches of halls and palaces built especially for the occasion – some of which are designed by Gustave Eiffel, a young engineer who has yet to make his mark. In these veritable temples of modernity, people marvel at new inventions and their scientific, commercial, agricultural and industrial applications. In the category *nouveautés militaires*, France proudly showcases its modern ambulances and mobile field cookers. Prussia steals the show with its state-of-the-art Krupp cannon, weighing 50 tonnes, with which it will shell Paris only a few years later.

Queen Victoria also attends and there is talk of building a tunnel under the English Channel. Another world-famous canal opens in 1869, at Suez. The French railway network expands exponentially, transporting raw materials and people to the farthest reaches of the empire. New stations are opened in Paris, allowing visitors to travel right into the heart of the city. On the Left Bank, they shop at Le Bon Marché which opened its doors in 1852, and on the Right Bank, they frequent the Grands Magasins du Printemps, or Monsieur Louis Vuitton, the *emballeur-malletier* who opened his chic *maroquinerie* at 4, Rue des Capucines in 1854. New colonial sorties into North Africa, Senegal, Gabon, Djibouti, Madagascar, New Caledonia, Polynesia and Indochina boost trade. The French overseas territories, which spanned 300,000 square kilometres in 1850, stretch to 1,000,000 square kilometres by 1870. The financial world responds to the dynamism, and the major banks that we know today, such as Crédit Lyonnais and Société Générale, open their doors.

At the same time, the new emperor tries to temper the excesses of growth. Basic living standards, such as housing, health and hygiene, come on in leaps and bounds thanks to Haussmann's work. Sunday labour is outlawed, the first *mutuelles* and pension funds see the light of day, the right to strike is ratified, and the article in the *Code civil* that automatically favours the employer in workplace disputes is abolished. Primary education is not only compulsory but also free. Girls are finally admitted to secondary school. Socially and economically, the age of Napoleon III is difficult to categorise under a single heading. At times an extreme liberal, at others a utopian socialist, he strove to keep economic and social expansion in line. He even joked about his political support base: "*L'impératrice est légitimiste, Morny est orléaniste, le Prince Napoleon est républicain et je suis moi-même socialiste. Il n'y a qu'un seul bonapartiste, c'est Persigny, et il est fou.*" [The Empress is Legitimist, Morny is Orléanist, Prince Napoleon is Republican and I am a Socialist; the only Bonapartist is Persigny, and he is mad].[5] Ordinary workers were generally much better off at the end of his reign in 1870 than they were during the July Monarchy or Second Republic. In terms of social legislature, France was the most progressive country in Europe at the time.[6]

Peace did not fare as well under Napoleon III. Some thirty sites in Paris are named after Second Empire victories or military campaigns. Boulevard Sébastopol, Avenue Malakoff, Pont de l'Alma and the Rue de la Crimée all refer to the Crimean War (1853-1856); Boulevard Magenta, Rue de Solférino, Rue de Turbigo, Rue Palestro and Quai Montebello hark back to victories over the Austrians, in support of Italian unification (1859); Place Abd-El-Kader alludes

Napoleon III, the forgotten emperor

to the 'humanitarian intervention' aimed at preventing the wholesale slaughter of Christians in Syria and Lebanon (1860); while Rue de Pali-Kao, Rue de Saïgon and Rue d'Annam all refer to the military actions in China and Indochina (1858-1863).

Napoleon III and Queen Victoria launch a joint military expedition in China following the massacre of missionaries and seizure of trade ships in the country. After capturing Canton in 1859, the troops set fire to the Imperial Summer Palace in Peking in 1860. The looted Chinese artworks are carefully shipped to Napoleon III's own imperial summer palace at Fontainebleau as well as to the British Museum, which had just celebrated its centenary. France's military campaigns in China and Indochina will haunt the country for years to come, eventually culminating in the Vietnam War. Ironically, Paris also boasts a Place de Mexico, named after the country in which Napoleon III suffered a bitter defeat following a long and torturous campaign (1861-1867), although the square was named at a later date. The forgotten emperor's only Mexican victory was at Cerro del Borrego in 1862, hence the Rue du Borrégo, a narrow street on the outskirts of the city.

Napoleon III's meddling in international politics – and his interference in neighbouring Italy in particular – riles his enemies. Just a few weeks prior to the gala opening of the World's Fair, an Italian refugee, Giovanni Pianori, fires two shots at the Emperor in the Bois de Boulogne. The ruler escapes unhurt but Pianori loses his head. The next attack is bloodier still. Felice Orsini hurls three bombs at the imperial carriage near the former opera on the Rue Le Peletier. The result: 12 dead and 30 wounded, the guillotine for Orsini, and an opulent new opera house for Paris – shaken by these public attacks, Napoleon III commissions a new opera house from the young architect Charles Garnier, with a separate entrance for his carriage. Once safe inside, he will be able to walk straight to his imperial box. Although the works begin in 1861 during the Second Empire, everything comes to a standstill during the Franco-Prussian War and the ensuing Commune uprising. Napoleon III did not live to see the inauguration of the Opéra Garnier in 1875, but the five N medallions above the entrance nod to their patron to this very day.

LA FÊTE IMPÉRIALE

Meanwhile, Paris is in a celebratory mood, especially at the imperial residences, the Palais des Tuileries and Versailles, the latter of which Napoleon III has restored to its former glory to impress visiting overseas monarchs. At the 'autumn castle' of Compiègne, north of Paris, the Emperor and Empress organise their coveted *Séries*. In four sets of six days each, in October and November, the imperial couple invite hundreds of artists, scientists, industrialists, bankers, writers, heads of state and politicians to call on them. Empress Eugénie leads the protocol according to the theme of the *Série*: *'élégante'*, *'sérieuse'*, *'militaire'* or *'scientifique'*. Strict rules are followed. On Wednesdays, a train of invitees departs from the Gare du Nord for Compiègne at 2.33pm sharp, where the guests are welcomed in full regalia. According to the Emperor's political agenda, the attendees 'mingle' at receptions and dinners. Business is discussed, plans forged, problems solved.

Impérial diplomacy is running at full pelt. Napoleon III does not seem perturbed by Otto von Bismarck and Wilhelm I of Prussia at this time. French engineer and diplomat Ferdinand de Lesseps, the Empress's cousin, whips bankers into a frenzy with his Suez project, while chemist Louis Pasteur obtains funding for his laboratory at the Sorbonne. The Emperor dreams of a large international hotel next to the new opera house. "Isn't that a godsend for you, *mes chers messieurs Pereire*?" Isaac and Emile Pereire, the enterprising financiers at Crédit Mobilier – in which Morny also participates – are always on the lookout for opportunities. *Et voilà!* In 1862, the Empress Eugénie opens the era's most palatial hotel, now known as the Grand Hotel Intercontinental, opposite the Opéra Garnier. From its restaurant – the Café de la Paix, still trading today – the Empress enthusiastically imparts to the assembled journalists that she feels 'as much at home here as at the Tuileries or at Fontainebleau".

La Fête impériale is a well-oiled machine that solidly drives the Second Empire onwards. But every so often, a grain of sand gets stuck in the works. Victor Hugo is one of Napoleon III's most prominent opponents. Angry and disillusioned, this great writer – a member of the Académie Française, mayor of the 8th *arrondissement* and Republican *député* – left France directly after the coup. Initially from Brussels, but later from Jersey and Guernsey, he assails Napoleon III's regime with books such as *Napoléon le Petit* [Napoleon the Little], *Les Châtiments* [Castigations] and *Histoire d'un crime* [The History of a Crime], as well as in pamphlets and essays. His abuse is unstinting. By way of just a few examples: "A nullity"; "that little one is a bastard, he has stolen his name, his birth is a disgrace"; "a man of middle height, cold, pale, slow in his movements, having the air of a person not quite awake"; "He has a heavy moustache... and a lifeless eye... he is a vulgar, commonplace personage, puerile, theatrical, and vain.... He loves finery, display, feathers, embroidery, tinsel and spangles, big words, and grand titles – everything that makes a noise and glitter, all the glassware of power. In his capacity of cousin to the battle of Austerlitz, he dresses as a general"; "This man lies as other men breathe" and so on. Hugo keeps it up for

Napoleon III, the forgotten emperor

twenty years. It earns him a fortune in copyrights and the Emperor a growing wave of enemies. In the end, his antagonists get the upper hand. Napoleon III messes up.

SOLITARY GRAVE

Where did it all go wrong? Did his adventurous spirit or his 'short fuse' finally get the better of him? By the summer of 1870, a diplomatic dispute between France and Prussia is spiralling out of control. On 19 July, an enraged Napoleon III declares war on Prussia. In less than a month, the French army is overrun and, on 2 September, Napoleon III is trounced at the Battle of Sedan. His Empire of Peace is felled by a war, of all things. In March 1871, Bismarck exiles the imprisoned Louis-Napoleon to Chislehurst, to the south of London. There, the defeated Emperor writes several more books and dreams of a triumphant return, just like his uncle from Elba. It is not to be. A fall from his horse leads to complications and Napoleon III dies, aged 65, on 9 January 1873.

Napoleon III has long been shrouded by a *légende noire* that portrays him as a villain. The social progress achieved during the Second Empire has only recently been recognised. Workers, for example, were better off at the end of Napoleon III's reign, in 1870, than they were in 1850.[7] Indeed, to dismiss him with the nickname 'Boustrapa' – after the initials of offensives in Boulogne, Strasbourg and Paris – or *un pantin insignifiant* [an insignificant puppet], is to do the man a grave historical injustice. But the French never took Napoleon III to their hearts. Unlike his uncle, Napoleon, he never captured the world's attention or inspired hundreds of authors. The difference in status between Napoleon and Napoleon III is perfectly summarised in this one sentence: "In history, the imperial uncle is a name, his nephew a number."[8]

Napoleon's mortal remains are interred in a magnificent red quartz tomb in the gilded Cathédrale Saint-Louis-des-Invalides in central Paris, beneath the exquisite dome by Jules Hardouin-Mansart. Napoleon III's body, on the other hand, lies in St Michael's Abbey, a church in Farnborough in southern England. In 2007, the French authorities rejected an application to exhume his body and reunite it with that of his illustrious uncle. The only place in Paris named after Napoleon III is the *parvis* [forecourt] in front of the Gare du Nord. Everyone walks across it, yet no one ever thinks of the Emperor. Perhaps because all eyes are now on artist Richard Texier's 7-metre-high, winged red sculpture, *Angel Bear*. Worse still: voices are rising to deprive him of even this vague honour. *"Pourquoi ne pas débaptiser des voies dont le nom est comme un déshonneur urbain: la place Napoléon III devant la gare du Nord, ...?"* ["Why not rename roads whose names are an urban disgrace: the Place Napoléon III in front of the Gare du Nord, ...?][9]

Tourists, schoolchildren, and Napoleon acolytes throng the Dôme des Invalides every day. The most popular souvenir in the Musée de l'Armée's gift shop is a sheet of cardboard. You can fold it into the great Emperor-General's iconic bicorne in three quick steps. Every visitor wears one. People brandish them aloft, just like Napoleon at Waterloo, who waves his hat for the very last time from his rearing Arabian thoroughbred, Marengo. His horse is also the subject of a Parisian scandal. When Les Invalides reopened in late April 2021, after a long lockdown, people were greeted with a sacrilegious sight. The horse's skeleton was hovering above Napoleon's tomb. It turned out to be a plastic replica of the bones that have been on display at the National Army Museum in London since the British captured Napoleon's steed at Waterloo in 1815. An everlasting humiliation to the French. *Memento Marengo* was a temporary installation by French artist Pascal Convert, who saw it as utterly harmless. But the public were outraged: "*C'est de la folie, ils sont fous, suspendre un Bucéphale en plastique dans une nécropole nationale confiée à la garde de l'armée française*." [It's madness, they're crazy, hanging a plastic Bucephalus in a national necropolis entrusted to the protection of the French army]. 10.4 million tweets, and counting, demand the immediate removal of 'the thing'. Following widespread and fractious debates, everyone waited with bated breath for President Macron to visit the tomb on 5 May: the bicentenary of the death of one of the greatest heroes in French history. Lo and behold, that day – momentarily perhaps – the bones of the late Marengo were nowhere to be seen. With only a year until the presidential elections, Emmanuel Macron made the best of a bad job.

In Farnborough's little church, on the other hand, time stands still. Silence reigns. A stillness punctured only by the chanting of a handful of Benedictine monks, who dutifully maintain a daily prayer vigil for Napoleon III, the forgotten emperor of the French.

Napoleon III, the forgotten emperor

The actress Arletty: *"My heart is French but... "*.

4

ARLETTY'S HEART

After the Liberation of Paris in late August 1944, accounts had to be settled. France's most popular actress, Arletty, must also pay – for a love affair with a German officer. The star of Hôtel du Nord *and dozens of other films, plays, revues and musicals is hauled in for questioning. But* l'amour *is not a crime in Arletty's eyes. With her imperious theatrical voice and piquant retorts, she gives as good as she gets.*

"You slept with a German?"
"Ah! If you hadn't let them in, I wouldn't be sleeping with them!"
"It's our fault then?"
"Well, in any case, the French surrender wasn't my idea!"

The verbal sledgehammer pounds away, delivering blow after blow. It enrages the Milices Patriotiques [patriotic militia] on the other side of the table. Arletty delivers another punch – one too many as it turns out. An officer jumps to his feet and aims his machine gun. All forty-six years of her tumultuous life flash before her eyes. It was so good in the beginning...

Arletty's heart

FORBIDDEN LOVE

Léonie Bathiat, nineteen years old and infatuated, has just moved into a young banker's house in Garches, to the west of Paris. Their chic Art-Nouveau villa, Modern'Castel, was designed by Hector Guimard, the architect who bequeathed Paris her magnificent metro canopies. Their next-door neighbour – who resides in the no-less prestigious Bel Respiro – is a certain Coco Chanel. They become firm friends and Léonie, on her banker's arm, acquaints herself with 'the better side of Paris': the theatres, restaurants and especially *le gratin*, the upper crust of Parisian society. Not bad for a young typist from Clermont-Ferrand, the daughter of a tram engineer and a *lingère*, a ready-to-wear seamstress.

Does it need to be said that Léonie is gorgeous? She finds work as a model at Paul Poiret's illustrious *maison*. She changes her name to 'Arlette', which is more palatable in her new environment, and soon swaps her banker for an art dealer, the latter of whom recommends her talent to the director of the Théâtre des Capucines on the eponymous boulevard. Thrilled by her potential, the impresario gives her name an American twist: 'Arletty' is born. The freshly-minted actress dazzles in the comedy *C.G.T Roi* – pronounced: *Si j'étais Roi* – as early as 19 October 1919. It is a satire on the omnipotence of the French Communist Party's powerful trade union, the Confédération Générale du Travail.[1] It marks the start of what will become a stellar career.

More than twenty years later, on 25 March 1941, Arletty attends a concert in occupied Paris. She is oblivious to the music. She is fixated on the row behind, where a tall, handsome, German officer with blonde hair and blue eyes is seated, imposing in his grey uniform. Arletty's friend, Josée Laval – the daughter of Pierre Laval, prime minister of the collaborationist Vichy regime – knows him: Hans-Jürgen Soehring. Josée handles the post-concert introductions. Arletty's heart is pounding. Hans-Jürgen speaks perfect French. Josée has confided that he belongs to the Luftwaffe's War Council. More impressive still – according to her friend – is that he was due to compete in the Berlin Olympics but had to withdraw on account of a stupid accident. An athlete to boot! He's thirty-three, and she's forty-three, but love is ageless.

Like all the other Luftwaffe officers, Soehring has installed himself at The Ritz on the Place Vendôme, along with Reichsmarschall Göring, head of the division. Coco Chanel, coincidentally, also lived there throughout the war with Hans von Dincklage, her own German officer. The girlfriends didn't just fall for the enemy but also for youth: Dincklage was more than a decade younger than Coco. Arletty and Soehring spend two blissful years together, dining on oysters and champagne at The Ritz and at Voisin, the restaurant just around the corner from the Place Vendôme. She is applauded everywhere, takes holidays on the French Riviera and goes horse riding with Hans-Jürgen in the woods of the Château de Condé. But above all, she is acting for top directors such as Sacha Guitry, Marcel Carné and Pierre Brasseur. By the spring of 1943, Arletty is netting 100,000 francs a week, an income some 160 times higher than that of the average Parisian family.[2] It is not money worries that keeps her awake at night, therefore, but something of an entirely different nature.

NO CHILD OF PARADISE

All 600 seats are sold out. Again. The poster reads: 'Arletty in the musical *Voulez-vous jouer avec moâ* [Do you want to play with me?] by Marcel Achard, directed by Pierre Brasseur.' Arletty plays Isabelle, a blonde ballerina who fends off the advances of Rascasse, Crockson and Auguste, the three clowns who are vying for her hand, with witty retorts and racy banter: "*Voulez-vous jouer avec moâ?*" she asks them with an accent straight from the *faubourgs* [suburbs]. Silence. As the piano and clarinets stir, Arletty's voice goes straight to the heart. "*Voulez-vous jouer avec moi / Le jeu d'amour, la tendre guerre?*" [Do you want to play with me / The game of love, the tender war]. At the close, as the music dies down, she stares into the auditorium and gives it her all, in that slow and raw parlando so unique to Arletty. "*Voulez-vous jouer avec moi / Un jour, un an, la vie entière? / ... Avec moi*" [Do you want to play with me / A day, a year, your whole life? / ... With me.]

A salvo of bravos erupts. The audience, French and German alike, go wild. Arletty beams and blows kisses with her hands. But beyond the flocked walls of the Bouffes-Parisiens, a plush 1827 *bonbonnière* on the Rue Monsigny, the mood is bleak. It's been three years since the Germans took Paris. Arletty's own heart is subdued, though you would never guess it from her stage performances. At forty-five, she is a genuine star, with roles in films, theatre, operettas, revues and musicals to her name. She is in the midst of filming her thirty-eighth feature film, *Les Enfants du paradis*, based on a screenplay by Jacques Prévert and directed by Marcel Carné. But its title leaves a bitter taste in her mouth, because what is also in the making is a child... and her baby will not be an *enfant du paradis*, of that she is certain.

The father-to-be, her officer, has been redeployed to Sicily to counter the Allied landing. Her doubts multiply. Forty-five, what age is that to have a child? Will Hans-Jürgen ever return? And even if he does, what then? Will the Germans still be in power? How can she juggle a child and her extreme work commitments? And also, with her impossible love life? She is not just besotted with

Arletty's heart

Hans-Jürgen, but also with Antoinette, a younger, wealthy aristocrat who has joined the Resistance. A German and a freedom fighter. Could it be more irreconcilable? Two loves, *le jeu d'amour*. She can't think straight. She feels as drab as Hans-Jürgen's uniform. Arletty decides to have an abortion. Marcel Carné, who has already directed her in the hugely successful film *Hôtel du Nord*, coaches her through this difficult time. The protagonist of *Les Enfants du paradis* is so pale and wan that he is forced to reshoot numerous scenes for his future masterpiece. But the show must go on.

Surprising news arrives in early June 1944. The Allies have landed in Normandy and are advancing towards Paris. Her friends, including the German ambassador Otto Abetz and his French wife Suzanne, pack their bags. They invite Arletty to flee, to accompany them to Germany. Coco Chanel, who is in the same situation, offers a little more reassurance – although she too will ultimately escape to Switzerland where she will live in exile until 1953. The screenwriter and director Sacha Guitry, her friend, says there is no need to worry, but by the time Hans-Jürgen implores her to head for his homeland, his regiment has already been redeployed to Poland to repel the Russian offensive. Other startling news stills her heart: Georges Mandel's bullet-ridden body is found in the forest of Fontainebleau. Mandel served as France's minister of the interior until the eve of the war. As a Jew and supporter of the Resistance, he had been transferred to Buchenwald. He was one of Arletty's dearest friends and admirers. The murder is a stark warning from the French 'Gestapo', the Milices, to the resistance fighters who have stepped up their activities to support the Allied advance. Arletty is distraught. She is caught between a rock and a hard place. Flee? *Non! Après tout*, what has she done wrong? Falling in love with a German, is that really such a crime?

'JUST SHOOT ME!'

As the battle for Paris rages through the streets and across the rooftops, the hunt for collaborators has already begun. The French Communist Party newspaper, *L'Humanité*, runs the following headline on 22 August 1944: *MORT AUX BOCHES ET AUX TRAITRES!* [DEATH TO THE KRAUTS AND TRAITORS!] Two days later, it adopts an even more uncompromising tone: *A CHAQUE PARISIEN SON BOCHE!* [EVERY PARISIAN GET A KRAUT!] In the heat of the conflict, no one differentiates between the German soldiers, nicknamed *Boches*, and those that fraternise with them. Arletty's apartment windows on the Quai de Conti are smashed by the Resistance. The actress goes into hiding. At this point, she hears her name announced on Radio Alger: she has been added to a list of famous

French citizens slated for execution. Despite her steadfast belief that love is not a crime, she is desperately afraid. Love or not, sleeping with the enemy is called 'horizontal collaboration'.

With the city purged of Germans, certain Resistance fighters – mostly delinquents and turncoat collaborators – trade their pistols and rifles for scissors and hair clippers. It is late August. 'People's courts' are springing up all over Paris: men with white ribbon armbands pull up chairs to kerb-side tables. They tend to be members of the Forces Françaises de l'Intérieur (FFI), the Franc-Tireurs et Partisans (FTP) or the Milices. Women are accosted, taunted and forced to sit. They are shorn bald. Some are daubed with swastikas and assaulted. Arletty has witnessed the *cortèges de tondues* [processions of shorn women] in the city: open lorries filled with bald women who cower behind chicken wire. They are booed. Whitewashed letters on the lorry bonnets proclaim: *les poules à boches* [Kraut floozies].

When Arletty ventures back into the capital on 4 September, Paris has been liberated for just under a week. She takes a room at the Hôtel Lancaster but the police, who have been scouring the registers for years, immediately pounce. She is removed and imprisoned in Drancy, a large camp in a converted goods yard to the north of Paris – the trains taking deportees to Auschwitz have literally only just stopped running from here. Arletty is interviewed several times over. As she continually impresses upon the inquisitors, she is 'still someone'. The prickly retorts get under their skin. "Are you about to tell us that you are a Gaullist?" To which Arletty replies: "Gaullist? *Non... Gauloise!*" She offers the questioner a Gauloise cigarette. It is the last straw. *Assez!* One of interviewers jumps to his feet and aims his submachine gun. Arletty will later testify that she didn't mince words, not even then: *"J'ai suivi mon instinct.... J'ai dit: dépêchez-vous de me faire sauter, que je ne vois plus vos sales gueules! Et ça a été fini, la mitraillette enlevée et tout!"* [I followed my instinct.... I said: 'hurry up and shoot me, so that I can't see your dirty faces anymore!' And that was it, the machine gun was put down and everything!][3] Thanks to her 'instinct', Arletty survives the arbitrary interrogations but is brought before the Commission de l'Épuration du Cinéma Français [Commission for the Purification of French Cinema]. It is they who will pass the final verdict.

INTERNATIONAL ARSE

The commission is lenient. Of the 4,200 French actors and actresses to stand trial, fewer than 100 are punished,[4] with Tino Rossi, the 'Corsican nightingale', amongst them. Only two are sentenced to death: Jean Mamy and Jean-Marquès

Arletty's heart

Rivière, a filmmaker and screenwriter respectively, who were responsible for *Forces occultes* [Occult Forces], a propaganda film alleging an anti-French conspiracy between Jews and Freemasons.[5] This was not, however, an isolated example. In *Le Paradis soviétique* [The Soviet Paradise], it is the communists who are conspiring, while the Jews take the lead again in *Le Péril juif* [The Jewish Peril] and *Les Corrupteurs* [The Corrupters]. The storylines are interchangeable: set to terrifying music, giant black spiders descend upon Paris and weave a web that suffocates the good Frenchmen.

Alongside the films made by the German Propaganda-Abteilung [Propaganda Department], the other main source of disinformation in France was the production house La Continentale. Founded by the German Embassy and the Vichy regime, it prided itself on making 100 per cent French films, thus reaching the true heart of the population. La Continentale was a relatively prolific operation: it made thirty of the 220 films made in France between 1940 and 1944. Arletty refused all their commissions. The post-war Commission de l'Épuration du Cinéma Français knew perfectly well that she lost out on millions of francs as a result. Pending her hearing, Arletty remains incarcerated but is able to leave prison to continue filming *Les Enfants du paradis*. Released on 9 March 1945, the film is a resounding success. Three weeks before its premiere, on 23 February, she is brought to trial. The atmosphere is more civilised compared to the brutal last days of the Liberation. "It is alleged that you had a love affair with a German officer. You were consequently arrested and interned at Drancy. Please explain yourself."

Arletty launches into her account. "I acknowledge the facts. During the Occupation, from 1941 to 1943, I was in a relationship with a German officer, answering to the name of Soehring. I was introduced to him by a friend, Madame de Chambrun [Josée Laval, married to René de Chambrun]. Major Soehring was handsome, with a marvellous physique. A friendship developed and I confess to becoming his mistress. I want to categorically state that I am not guilty of collaborating during the Occupation, despite having frequent opportunities to do so. I refused to act for German producers and, in particular, for La Continentale. I rejected any roles with collaborationist streaks. I was pressurised by the German propaganda department to tour Germany, to be presented as a big star in the country. And I always rebuffed their advances with a myriad excuses. At one point, Otto Abetz wanted me to leave Paris and flee to Baden-Baden. I resolutely refused, stating that I was a Parisienne through and through, and that nothing could top Paris-Paris. Other than my lover, I did not associate with the Germans, and I never asked them for anything, except for permission to drive my car during the Occupation."[6]

Her argument was certainly compelling, but Arletty wouldn't be Arletty if she didn't have the last, coruscating word: "*Messieurs: mon cœur est français, mais je l'avoue... mon cul est international!*" [My heart is French but, I must confess, my arse is international!]. At least, this is how it has gone down in history, although the line is missing from the official transcript. Perhaps she flung it at her interrogators during a preliminary interview because it is Arletty through and through. Another scenario is that the immortal one-liner was penned by none-other than Henri Jeanson, the inimitable scriptwriter behind *Hôtel du Nord*.[7] Whatever the case, the Commission de l'Épuration du Cinéma Français did not indict Arletty. She was, however, issued with a three-year professional ban as penance for her German love affair. She later starred in numerous films and plays, and would also contribute to documentaries on Georges Braque, Jacques Prévert, Marcel Carné, Bernard Blier and all the other friends she outlived, for Arletty – whom the French also knew as Raymonde from *Hôtel du Nord*, Garance from *Les Enfants du paradis,* Loulou from *Fric-Frac*, Dominique from *Les Visiteurs du soir*, Inès from *Huis Clos* or Blanche from *L'Air de Paris* – lived to a ripe old age. The curtain finally fell for the 94-year-old actress on 23 July 1992. She died in her flat in the Rue de Rémusat in the 16th *arrondissement* of Paris, the city she refused to trade for love.

Arletty's heart

The Salle Labrouste in the Rue de Richelieu library,
where Lenin found warmth and inspiration.

5

LENIN'S YELLOW JERSEY

Cycling lost a talented rider to the October Revolution. For Lenin, as it emerged during his exile in Paris, had a particular fondness for the sport. With his muscular legs, heart of steel and incredible stamina, the future President of the Council of People's Commissars of the Soviet Union had all the makings of a Tour de France winner. But it was not to be. Instead of slipping into the yellow jersey, he threw himself into the proletariat.

Lenin's yellow jersey

THE ALPS AND THE COL DU GALIBIER

Following the failure of the Russian Revolution in 1905, Vladimir Ilyich Ulyanov – better known as Lenin – is on the run in Europe. After many peregrinations and with the tsar's secret police in hot pursuit, the Bolshevik lays down his *valises* in Paris. It is not his first visit: Lenin had previously attended a conference[1] in the city and also passed through on his way to a congress organised by the Russian Social Democratic Workers' Party in which he represents the Bolshevik faction. Lenin, his wife Nadezhda Krupskaya, and his mother-in-law Elizaveta Vasilievna Tistrova, will live in Paris from 1908 to 1912.[2]

The journey from Geneva – "a petty bourgeois lake with stagnant water"[3] – to Paris is exhausting. In those days, émigrés left nothing behind. Which is why, in December 1908, crates of simple furniture, boxes of books, Cyrillic printing stencils and files relating to *Proletari*, Lenin's Bolshevik newspaper, pulled into the Gare de Lyon. Once they have secured their accommodation in the 14th *arrondissement* at 24, Rue Beaunier, Lenin and Nadezhda return to the baggage office to collect their belongings.

Attention! Lenin chastises the heavy-handed workmen as they unload their most precious possessions: two rock-solid bicycles of German manufacture. A gift from his mother. They will be invaluable in Paris while they prepare for the next coup against the tsar. This time, the right time, swears the author of *What is to Be Done?* a.k.a. a practical guide to a successful revolution. And he is right. Lenin and his Bolsheviks will storm the Winter Palace in Petrograd in 1917, thereby ending almost four centuries of Tsarist rule. The rest is history. But what the books don't tell you, however, is that the first leader of the Soviet Union was as much a talented cyclist as a gifted orator. We often see him in his pulpit made of planks, from where – in the famous photo with cap in hand and Trotsky to his right – he whips the proletarian masses into a frenzy. With a red flag instead of *le maillot jaune*.

Like many of the people in his sights – the international proletariat – Lenin assiduously follows the Tour de France. In 1911, the cyclists cross the Alps for the first time in the Tour's history[4] and conquer the Col du Galibier. On 30 July, they ride the final stage from Le Havre to Paris: a flat 377-kilometre stretch along the Seine. The sun is blazing on the day of the *Arrivée*. But duty calls. Lenin has a revolution to teach. Just a few months previously he had established a clandestine school in an old workshop in Longjumeau, an unassuming village 20 kilometres south of Paris. The building has two doors. Non-negotiable. Lenin has to be able to escape his enemies, in this case the Okhrana, the tsar's secret police, who will invariably find their way to Paris. In Longjumeau, hidden from their prying eyes, Lenin is training the Party cadres that the 1905 revolution so desperately lacked. He skips the race.

SUSPICIOUS SUSTENANCE

Nevertheless, the elated crowds cheer on the winner of the stage, Marcel Godivier, and Gustave Garrigou, who is wearing the yellow jersey.[5] They have reached Boulogne-Billancourt, and the *Arrivée* is in sight! *Allez!* Caps fly into the air. Tapped barrels pour forth a steady stream of Irancy wine.[6] Chased by the peloton, the lead cyclists fly across the bridge over the Seine, straight across the white finishing line in the Parc des Princes. A mere 20 kilometres away, the nascent Russian Communist Party leader and his comrades are studying dialectical materialism. Just as Lenin closes the school gate after an exhausting session, Garrigou, punching the air with both fists, rides his victory lap into the frenzied stadium. Applauded by huge swathes of the working classes.

To the delight of its ever-increasing readership, the radical socialist newspaper *L'Humanité* devotes extensive coverage to the Tour de France. Lenin devours the reports. The riders covered 5,344 kilometres at an average speed of 27.3 kilometres per hour. Moreover, the German Kaiser Wilhem II has decided, as of 1910, to ban the race from his territory. Alsace and Lorraine have belonged to Germany since the Franco-Prussian War of 1870/1, but an exception had always been made for the Tour. Until now. The news fuels Lenin's pessimism about the prospect of a new war. But it is the Duboc affair that truly grabs the cycling afficionado's attention.

Lenin's affinity with the rider, the second overall, grows with every word he reads. Paul Duboc, nicknamed *La Pomme* due to his physique, has been chasing Garrigou from the start. At Stage 10, he suddenly falls ill. He has been drinking from a water bottle passed by a teammate, François Lafourcade. It seems to have been sabotaged. The suspicious liquid derails Duboc. The second-placed rider starts to deteriorate. Every finger points to Garrigou, who has the most to gain from Duboc's decline. The accusations are serious. Poisoning. Such is the uproar that the wearer of the yellow jersey receives a bodyguard. When the Tour passes through Rouen, Duboc's hometown, the race organisers force Garrigou to don an elaborate disguise.[7] They fear he will be dragged off his bike and lynched by Duboc's supporters. Reading all this, Lenin briefly touches his throat. Poison; a fall from a bridge; a cycling accident. With the Okhrana agents now in Paris, it could happen to him at any moment.

Lenin's yellow jersey

THE TSAR'S RETURN

The hated secret police, now fixated on running Lenin to ground, was founded in 1881, in response to the assassination of Tsar Alexander II. Originally intended to protect the imperial family, the Okhrana became a wide-ranging, anti-revolutionary octopus with tentacles stretching far beyond the Tsarist empire. The Zagranichnaya Okhrana, or overseas office, opened in Paris in 1883.[8] Its agents had been working in the city, home to the mother of all revolutions, for over a decade. Yet compared to Moscow or St Petersburg, Paris is a tolerant free state where, by the end of the nineteenth century, the Russian *émigré* community has swelled to more than 5,000 members. Disgraced aristocrats, revolutionaries, anarchists, terrorists and other assorted opponents of the Romanovs have all flocked to the City of Light. It is a fishpond for Bolsheviks and Mensheviks alike. Early in the second half of the nineteenth century, it is General Mezentsov, chief of the tsar's *cabinet noir*, who spies on them in Paris. In between his shadowy dealings, he invests part of his fortune in the theatrical career of the *grande horizontale* Blanche d'Antigny, on whom he lavishes precious jewels and Russian sables.

One of his successors, General Harting, opens the Okhrana's annexe in Paris. He is given two offices in the Imperial Consulate of Russia at 97, Rue de Grenelle, on the Left Bank. The ground-floor windows of this gloomy building are protected by the original wrought-iron bars to this very day. Lenin must remain vigilant and do everything in his power to avoid the so-called 'Harting'. But the general is not a general at all. He is none other than an *agent-provocateur* named Heckelmann, who was convicted fifteen years earlier at the Cour d'Assises de la Seine for bomb-throwing. The tsar's entourage had secured his release and everything was brushed under the carpet.

Meanwhile, the Okhrana is hand in glove with the French Sûreté Générale. The Russian agents are given permission to open letters in the post office on the Rue Gay-Lussac, in the district with the highest density of Russian migrants.[9] The French welcome the development: it saves them having to monitor the foreign insurgent scum and frees up their time to trace their own internal enemies – anarchist bombers and the invincible Jules Bonnot and his gang, who are terrorising the country with their robberies. The Okhrana's eyes and ears are everywhere. *L'oeil de Moscou voit et sait tout* [The eye of Moscow sees and knows everything]. It is safer outside the city.

READY FOR THE FINAL SPRINT

Lenin discovers Longjumeau while cycling past the southern city limits. From their little flat at 4, Rue Marie-Rose, also in the 14th *arrondissement*, to which they had moved in the summer of 1909, the Bolshevik leader and Nadezhda regularly explore the wooded area south of Paris. They ride their bicycles along the banks of the Yvette and climb the hills in the vast forests of the Haute Vallée de Chevreuse. After these excursions, they often take a bouquet of wildflowers to Elizaveta,[10] who is in charge of the revolutionary couple's day-to-day affairs. Lenin never shirks a 100-kilometre ride for a 'family visit'[11] to the socialist writer Paul Lafargue. The latter might well be the author of the unpalatable book *The Right to Be Lazy*, but he is married to Laura Marx,[12] the daughter of Lenin's great idol. That makes up for everything.

In *Memories of Lenin*, Nadezhda recounts that her "Volodya [the diminutive of Vladimir] is enjoying the summer in Paris. He has organised work outside the city, cycles a lot, bathes and is pleased with our stay here. This week we both cycled like crazy. We did three rides of 70-75 kilometres each and crossed three forests. It was very pleasant. Volodya is keen on tours where we leave at six to seven in the morning to return late in the evening."[13] This is beyond impressive, in the eyes of cycling historian Marco Lebreton,[14] because bikes in that day and age had steel frames and weighed as much as 15 kilos.

Lenin's love of cycling is wholly consistent with the Party line. Even more than the hammer or the sickle, the body is the worker's weapon. It must be kept in peak condition. Cycling, walking and gymnastics are strongly recommended. From Paris, Lenin sets a good example: "After waking up, he exercised his muscles through gymnastics. For, in his eyes, a good revolutionary should always possess the strength to endure trials, keep his head straight in captivity, and have the bravery to escape."[15] After the October Revolution, the statistics of gymnastics clubs in the Soviet Union surpassed those of grain and coal production. Sport will allow the new man that is born from the communist society to achieve his true potential: "Everyone will be able to choose for himself the physical activity by which he can pursue and achieve his total personal realisation," writes the father of the Russian Revolution in his *Collected Works*.[16] In 1921, 'the conquest of the masses' is the central theme at the third congress of the Comintern, the one and only Communist International. During the festivities, Lenin, with itchy legs, launches a new department: the Red Sport International.[17]

Lenin's yellow jersey

In the eyes of the Comintern founder, a second ideological reason exists for singing the praises of bicycles: their ability to draw women into the cult of the body – and by extension, the revolution. The uprising is an exercise "in equality", according to *What Is to Be Done?* Men and women side-by-side. Which explains why the Bolshevik leader not only cycles with Nadezhda but also with Ludmila Stal, Serafima Hopner and Inessa Armand. These women are no shrinking violets. They fought the Romanovs in 1905 and spent long periods locked in the tsar's dungeons. Whether they were set free or managed to escape, they found their way to Paris, where they supported their leader in his struggle.

One of them, Inessa Armand, is a model student in the classroom. As well as in bed. On the role of women in the class struggle, Nadezhda and Lenin are open-minded. They are fond of Inessa and maintain an almost perfect *ménage à trois*. Inessa is a full-blooded Bolshevik, battle- and prison-hardened, but she escaped via Finland in 1909, moving first to Brussels, and later to Paris. She eventually followed Lenin and Nadezhda to Russia and helped them overthrow the Tsar in 1917. After the October Revolution, she led the women's division of the Central Committee of the Bolshevik Party, amongst other things.[18] Following her premature death from cholera in 1920, Lenin and Nadezhda unofficially adopt her five children from her marriage to Alexander Armand. As a token of love and loyalty, Lenin arranges for Inessa to be interred in the Kremlin's wall – the Pantheon of Moscow, so to speak. A privilege reserved only for the bravest heroes of the class struggle.

A struggle that is already fomenting in Paris where Lenin cycles from place to place. From a party or faction meeting to a speaking engagement. Or from the Bolsheviks' socialist restaurant in the Rue de la Glacière to their employment office for newly arrived refugees in the Rue du Parc-de-Montsouris. To relax from time to time or to escape the 48-square-metre flat and his mother-in-law, Lenin does not just cycle in the woods and valleys; fascinated by everything aeronautical, he also enjoys attending the aviation meetings at Brétigny, Etampes and Athis-Mons, the origins of Orly airport. Blériot flew across the English Channel for the first time in 1909, while Roland Garros flew from Paris to London and Madrid and back in 1911.

Lenin is thrilled by it all. He makes feverish day trips to airports 40 kilometres from Paris. The Okhrana are not inclined to pursue their prey over such long distances. Yet in Juvisy, just beyond Athis-Mons, he is brutally run off his bike in 1909 while completely distracted by the spectacle in the sky. Lenin fears the worst. Harting! The Okhrana! But before he can flee from his fallen bicycle, a

French voice calls out. Of all people, it is the chauffeur of a stiff-necked vicomte who extends the apologies.[19] Only then does the people's tribune realise that he has not been hit by the tsar's secret agents. A *Vicomte*!? Lenin makes the class enemy pay for the repairs.

A bicycle was an expensive item in those days. A new model cost around 100 francs.[20] Like a true racer, Lenin lovingly cares for his steel steeds. He diligently greases the moving parts and sends the cycles into a short hibernation in the cellars of the Rue Marie-Rose. But with the first rays of spring, they soon reappear. He polishes them with devotion, checks the tyres and fills them with air. One day he returns home, carrying his broken bike. Out on the pavement it transpires that the Bolshevik is an accomplished repairman: "Lenin disassembles and straightens the fork with unusual alacrity and repairs the pedals."[21]

THE LAST MILE

As the summer draws to a close, so too does the Longjumeau school. As the newly qualified Leninists file back to Russia to preach the revolution, Lenin commits his theories to paper. But a cold draught soon starts to penetrate the chinks in the rickety windows of the Rue Marie-Rose. Searching for a more suitable place to study and write, Lenin miraculously discovers an earthly paradise: summer temperatures, light and space, plants and flowers, all in the middle of the ashen, frozen city. Paradise is the Salle Labrouste of the Bibliothèque Nationale at 28, Rue de Richelieu. With its ornate columns, arches, cupolas and paintings, it is a slice of Byzantium in Paris.

But the joy is short-lived: a *gardien* throws the stranger out. The Russian needs a French citizen's letter of recommendation to gain access to the country's illustrious patrimony. Lenin's landlord refuses. For the average French bourgeois capitalist, such as the latter, Russia is a godlike, beneficent nation that stretches all the way from just under the polar cap to distant Abkhazia. Holy Russia, led by the paternalistic Tsar, is brimming with magnificent churches and cathedrals, multicoloured onion domes, snow-covered wooden dachas, precious icons and troikas with tinkling sleighbells that glide across the frozen tundra. In Paris, people are warming to Diaghilev's *Ballets Russes* and its star dancers, Nijinsky and La Karsavina. The landlord is apoplectic. What proletariat? "All nihilists ... it will end in disaster!"[22] Louis-Henri Roblin, *député* to the *Socialistes unifiés* in the Chambre des Députés, finally writes Lenin's crucial letter.

Back at the Rue de Richelieu, Lenin stares open-mouthed at the thousands of books. His eye travels from the shelves to the high ceiling cupolas. Supported by elegant pillars, they scatter the winter light across the long reading tables.

Lenin's yellow jersey

From his desk, his gaze wanders to the walls. The rows of books are surmounted by painted friezes, filled with trees and plants. Colourful birds flit between their crowns. Following their lines of flight, he discovers the giant windows at the back of the room, through which low shafts of sunlight penetrate the hall. The nimble orator is speechless. Full of awe and admiration, he strides into the sanctuary. The frozen exile finds that the Henri Labrouste reading room, named after the architect who constructed the space in 1868,[23] is equipped with every modern comfort. The long reading tables are illuminated by gaslight. Over a hundred lampshades cast a warm, yellowish glow across the wooden surfaces. Warm air is blown into the room through ornate cast-iron elements around the perimeter.[24]

But the most important thing of all, as far as the perished Bolshevik is concerned, is below the desks: hot water pipes. Lenin warms his frozen feet on the scalding metal. A marvel of the era. "The reading room is a clever combination of architectural heritage and modern technology."[25] It is here that the hunted Bolshevik starts to thaw and find peace – and inspiration. His curiosity knows no bounds. He draws valuable political lessons from his study of the French Revolution, those of 1830 and 1832, the bloody workers' revolt of 1848 and the Paris Commune uprising. Such revolutions were well-intentioned, no doubt, but fuelled by directionless missiles and lacking in strategy, they were all doomed to failure. No. A successful revolution needs a clear political doctrine that can be implemented by the proletarian masses, whose momentum will be steered by well-trained Party cadres. Preferably the ones in Longjumeau.

Once the reading lights have been extinguished and the gates of heaven swing shut, Lenin finds himself back in the cold. But the caretaker to whom he entrusts his precious bicycle during his visits to the Bibliothèque Nationale comes rushing up, gesticulating wildly. The Okhrana! No. *Comment est-ce possible!* His bike is missing. Stolen. A tragedy. What to do? At the next meeting of the cell at the newly opened Café de la Rotonde[26] on the Boulevard du Montparnasse, Lenin insists that his comrades and future members of the Politburo – Kamenev and Zinoviev[27] – go halves on a replacement. Lenin's bicycle is common property. It is a tool, no more no less, at the service of the revolution. Which is beckoning. Just before the summer of 1912, Lenin, Nadezhda and the eternal Elizaveta move to Poland, closer to their target. The humble furniture, crates of books, files and Cyrillic printing stencils are neatly stacked in the baggage car. One last time, the wearer of the red jersey checks that his bikes are securely fastened.

A few weeks later, he writes to his mother from Kraków: "In Paris, it is very difficult to live with modest means. It is an exhausting city. But to spend some time there, make visits or take a tour, there is no better and more enjoyable metropolis. It completely changed my mindset."[28]

NO POSTHUMOUS VICTORY

Almost a century after the October Revolution, the final stage of the 2010 Tour de France departs from Longjumeau, of all places[29] – from the front gate of Lenin's former communist school. Deep in his mausoleum, the racing cyclist of the proletariat rubs his hands: his talent is finally being acknowledged. Certain details, however, spoil the posthumous fun: the building at 17, Grande-Rue, where Lenin and Nadezhda worked themselves to the bone during lessons, now accommodates a restaurant, the 'Lénine Kebab'. Worse still, the street has been renamed the Rue du Président François Mitterrand, a 'revisionist'. Sinful. But that is not all.

Joaquim Rodriguez – or 'Purito' to his fans – from the Russian team Katusha has won an earlier stage, the tough route from Bourg-de-Péage to Mende. The local Lenin Association is cock-a-hoop and wants to honour the 'Russians'. It declares 2010 to be *l'Année France-Russie* [France-Russia Year] and 2011 – how could it be otherwise? – *l'Année Lénine à Longjumeau* [Lenin in Longjumeau Year]. Red flags with hammer and sickle and banners with images of *Lénine* adorn the departure point. The locals want photos of Purito and the other Katusha riders, Daniel Moreno and Alberto Losada – with a red flag and in front of the studio where their idol assembled the very first members of the Central Committee. Their excitement is irrepressible.

But it is all too much for the reactionary mayor of Longjumeau, the deep-blue Nathalie Kosciusko-Morizet, or 'NKM' to the French. This prominent member of *Les Républicains* is better known as Nicolas Sarkozy's spokeswoman in the 2012 presidential election. The colour red works on her like the proverbial rag to a bull. *Balayez-moi ce bazar!* [Sweep up this mess!] The helmeted CRS (Compagnies Républicaines de Sécurité), brandishing batons, are in position. It beggars belief. One would expect better manners from the great-granddaughter of André Morizet, a founder of the French Communist Party, and a man who actually shook *Lénine's* hand.

Lenin's yellow jersey

Plate owned by a Dutch shareholder who was ruined by the 'Mississippi Bubble'.

6

JOHN LAW'S 'SHITTY SHARES'

In Venice, halfway between St Mark's Square and the Gallerie dell'Accademia, lies the San Moisè Church. Anyone entering the dark portal from the bright light of the lagoon runs the risk of unwittingly stepping on a grave. A small diamond-shaped stone at the entrance bears the inscription Honori et memorial Joannis Law Edinburgensis Regii Galliarum Aerarii Praefecti Clarissimi, *which loosely translates as: 'In memory of John Law of Edinburgh, the most distinguished financial controller to the French kings.'[1] How did France's first central banker, and also the entrepreneur of an international trading company, end up beneath a tile in an Italian church instead of a Parisian mausoleum?*

John Law's 'shitty shares'

SPECULATION

On 21 April in the year 1671, celebrations are afoot in the household of the Scottish goldsmith and Royal Mint employee, William Law of Lauriston. He and his wife Jane have just held their new-born son over the baptismal font in St Giles' Cathedral, Edinburgh. 'Their John' reveals himself to be a mathematical prodigy at an early age. He puts his talent to good use by gambling at cards. But playing games of chance in Edinburgh is not very lucrative. While his father continues to mint coins, John decides to try his luck in London, but with calamitous results. Embroiled in all kinds of financial dealings, he kills his opponent in a duel at the age of twenty-three. The circumstances are disputed but Law is sent to the gallows. With the help of his friends and his savings, he manages to escape from Newgate Prison, that vestibule of hell "where death is both a mercy and a salvation".[2]

Law, who seemed to have inherited a fondness for coins with his mother's milk, reaches the Netherlands and falls under the spell of securities. The bills of exchange issued by the Bank of Amsterdam are universally trusted because they are backed by the reserves of merchants and entrepreneurs. With ears alert, he listens to the forerunners of today's short sellers. They spread negative reports about the United East India Company to send its share price plummeting before going in for the kill. From these 'speculation' specialists, he learns how to buy and sell shares without owning them himself. He absorbs this new knowledge with alacrity. Law soon realises that the Amsterdam Stock Exchange is more exciting than any casino.[3] But his plan to organise a state lottery in the Netherlands comes to nothing. He then travels to Genoa and Venice, the great mercantile cities of the age. He is a trader by day and a gambler by night – although he finds commerce a game and gambling more like work. All his profits are ploughed into a flourishing portfolio of shares on the London Stock Exchange.

Law returns to Scotland in 1705. It is a culture shock. The feudal clans, whose sole interests are agriculture, cattle breeding and land, have plunged his country into even deeper poverty. The Scots do not engage in trade – the source of all wealth and prosperity in Law's eyes – and the Scottish kingdom is limping behind that of England, which is booming. He sees no other option but to change this state of affairs. Encouraged by his financial successes, he commits his ideas to paper. In his book, *Money and Trade Considered, with a Proposal for Supplying the Nation with Money*, Law advocates the creation of a Scottish mercantile bank. He draws on the model of the Bank of England, which issues paper money backed by the value of arable and agricultural land. His explanation of the paradox of values has lost none of its freshness: "Water is of great use, yet of little Value; Because the Quantity of Water is much greater than the Demand for it. Diamonds are of little use, yet of great Value, because the Demand for Diamonds is much greater, than the Quantity of them."[4] Taking grain and wine as alternative examples, Law demonstrates that the value of a commodity is determined primarily by supply and demand.

He submits his plans to the Scottish parliament, but it has bigger fish to fry: the vote on the Acts of Union (1707) that will unite the kingdoms of Scotland and England. Law doesn't wait around for the result. Although a free man in Scotland, and the scion of a reputable family no less, he is nothing but an escaped convict and murderer in England. Where to next? Where on the Continent might his insights stand a chance? Which country, like Scotland, is still saddled with mediaeval structures, traditional agriculture and a gold standard?

PHILOSOPHER'S STONE

France – a feudal country with an absolute monarchy – meets all Law's criteria. In Paris, given the parlous state of the French finances, Nicolas Desmarets, the *contrôleur général des finances* to Louis XIV, is all ears. Law all but convinces Desmarets that paper money can not only replace coins but also drive trade, the source of all wealth. Trade is based solely on trust. When there is trust, banknotes can play the same role as gold, but without the hassle of coinage and the risks involved in transporting the precious metal. "Is he a Catholic?" inquires the Sun King, who, with the revocation of the Edict of Nantes, has just driven the last Protestants from his land.[5] "Because pagans are not to be trusted. We will not do business with them."[6] Alas. The gates of Versailles remain firmly shut and France lurches further into debt. It is not until after Louis XIV's death that Law is finally granted an audience at court, on 2 September 1715, where the regent, Philippe d'Orléans, is temporarily overseeing the administration until Louis XV reaches maturity.

"I have discovered the secret of the philosopher's stone: how to make gold from paper,"[7] bluffs the champion gambler to Orléans. It is music to the regent's ears. The financial hole dug by the Sun King appears to be inversely proportional to his charisma. According to the calculations made by Desmarets' successor, the Duc de Noailles, public debt has reached 3.5 billion *livres* with a deficit of 80 million per annum due to war and excessive spending.[8] Orléans believes the Scot might well have the solution: a new state bank, overseen by the *Conseil Royal*, to finance trade via public securities, collect taxes and supervise the fiscal management of the Crown. For Noailles, it is too much all at once: "*Non.*" Law refuses to let Orléans off the hook, however. At the gaming table,

John Law's 'shitty shares'

he outlines the grand ideas behind his *système*. Admittedly, it is unlike anything the regent has ever heard. "*Imaginez-vous*: a French United East India Company *comme en Hollande*, but without competitors. *Une compagnie mondiale* with a monopoly! Not run by private shareholders, but by a public bank *toute comme la Banque d'Angleterre*, which also issues the company's shares. *Quel pétard*! And all governed by *sa majesté*."

Despite having been rejected by the *Conseil Financier*, Orléans authorises the plan on 20 May 1716. The Banque Générale Privée is established below Law's prestigious residence, the current 18, Place Vendôme.[9] The bank issues paper notes in fixed-value denominations with guarantees that rapidly win the public's trust: '*La Banque promet payer au Porteur à vüe Dix livres Tournois en especes d'Argent, valeur reçüe*'[10] [The Bank promises to pay the Bearer on demand Ten *livres Tournois* in Silver coins, value received] – 'in silver coins' is literally stated on the notes. Orléans, deputising for the king, personally entrusts a million *livres* to the new bank.[11] For the first time in history, the French people see banknotes. This had previously been the privilege only of the Swedes, the Genoese, the Venetians, the Dutch and the English: countries that were thriving economically and where more and more people were enjoying the fruits of prosperity. With these examples, Law continues to assail the regent. Orléans capitulates and orders that, from 1717, all taxes must be paid in notes issued by the Banque Générale Privée. Not there yet, Law thinks, but a step in the right direction.

NEW FORTUNE

In addition to his relentless lobbying for a government bank, Law toils away on the second aspect of his grand idea: a trading company. He acquired the monopoly on French trade with her American colony, 'the Sleeping Beauty' of Louisiana, as early as 1717. After all, the French cannot compete with the Spanish silver from Potosi or the Portuguese gold from Brazil. Although Quebec was founded as early as 1608 and a West India Company established fifty-six years later under Richelieu's impetus, it did not amount to much. While the English, Spanish and Portuguese are unashamedly focusing on commerce and wealth, the French seem fixated on territory and *découvertes*. Except for René Robert Cavelier de La Salle, who is making good money from the Canadian fur trade. He is the first Frenchman to sail down the Mississippi river to its mouth, and who, in 1682, on behalf of Louis XIV, commandeers all the regions he crosses on his expedition. In honour of the monarch, he christens the territory 'Louisiana'. The new French colony comprises a long strip of land, running from the Mississippi delta to the heights of the Midwest – about a quarter of the present-day United States.[12] Repeated wars with the Dutch Republic and Spain, however, and a long struggle with the League of Augsburg,[13] meant that only modest gains had hitherto been made in the newly conquered land. But now, via the resurrected Compagnie d'Occident led by John Law, its new main shareholder, the wheels will finally turn.

In 1718, the Compagnie founds a new city at the mouth of the Mississippi river and settles it with several thousand impoverished Germans from the Rhineland, Switzerland and Alsace. Law names the city *La Nouvelle-Orléans* [New Orleans] as a tribute to the obliging regent. The ambitious company receives starting capital of 100 million *livres*, an unprecedented sum for the time. Shares, which are available to everyone, are priced at 500 *livres* each. Even Philippe d'Orléans participates in the public offering. The shares sell smoothly and rise in value. A thrilled Orléans extends Law's privileges: the Compagnie is granted a monopoly on the tobacco trade and is also permitted to absorb the Compagnie du Sénégal, the Compagnie de la Chine, and the Compagnie des Indes Orientales. Law effects a lightning-fast turnaround, turning a modest enterprise on its last legs into a truly global concern in just two short years: the new operation is immediately called the Compagnie du Mississippi by the French. The trading company and the Banque Générale Privée are as prosperous as each other. But the best Christmas present that year is the renaming of Law's private bank to the Banque Royale. The royal seal of approval not only hastens the dissemination of paper money but also the sale of the Compagnie's shares. Things are going well for Law.

Just as Cardinals Richelieu and Mazarin before him had slowly but surely centralised all political power in the figures of Louis XIII and XIV, Law gradually shifts France's financial might into his own hands. In 1719, he acquires the rights to the royal mint and snatches the licence to collect all indirect taxes from a rival financier. By the summer of that year, the Scottish Protestant, banker and entrepreneur is on the brink of realising his *système*, but a single asset – and ultimately the most important one – is missing.

CALCULATED PRAYERS

In the Église Saint-Roch on the Rue Saint-Honoré, Law is lost in thought. Were he a Catholic, this would be his parish church, given his residence on the Place Vendôme. And so it *will* be, *enfin*. This is where France's first true central banker will finally be laid to rest, alongside Le Nôtre, the landscape architect of Versailles, and Pierre Corneille, the author of *Le Cid* that is on everyone's lips in France. There could be no more fitting place for him, the saviour of the

John Law's 'shitty shares'

bankrupt nation. His dreams of eternal rest are fleeting. Sunk not in prayers but in calculations, he has a flash of inspiration. When it rains, the makeshift roof of the church is a sorry sight for the parishioners, and the broken façade an embarrassment for the parish priest. These problems can be turned into opportunities. Ostensibly, it works like this: Abbé de Tencin, the cardinal and archbishop of Lyon whose tentacles stretch all the way to Paris, will give Law a religious makeover, while the latter, for his part, will fund a new roof and façade for the church. In reality, however, the stakes are much higher than a heap of tiles and bricks. Law's appointment as *contrôleur général des finances* has a single, non-negotiable precondition: he must be a Catholic. Given the financial power he has amassed, this is the final piece of his plan. It will give him control over the finances of the entire country.

Unsurprisingly, de Tencin offers to convert the powerful pagan. Law is introduced to him through Madame de Tencin, the archbishop's beautiful sister. Claudine, an ex-nun who has been released from her vows, is just one of the women with whom the banker maintains relations.[14] Everything Law touches turns to gold, Orléans is his political patron and de Tencin his spiritual one. However wealthy and ambitious the de Tencins already are, the cardinal and ex-nun want to convert their money chest into a veritable horn of plenty in exchange for rebranding Law. And what quicker way to do it than through a wad of shares from the financial success story of the century, the Compagnie du Mississippi? On 17 September 1719, in the Église Saint-Roch, Abbé de Tencin pours water three times over the mastermind who will make him untold riches: "*Jean Law, je te baptise au nom du Père et du Fils et du Saint-Esprit. Amen.*" The cleric rubs the ointment firmly, as if hoping it will make the share prices rise even faster.

On 5 January 1720, less than four months after his conversion, Law pockets his appointment as *contrôleur général des finances*. He thus follows in the footsteps of Colbert, Pontchartrain, Chamillart and Desmarets, the highest servants of the late Sun King. In addition to holding absolute power over the finances of France – Law is now de facto the country's first central banker – he also acquires some personal property: the Hôtel de Nevers, with all the allure of a palace, on the Rue de Richelieu (part of today's Bibliothèque Nationale); the adjacent Palais Mazarin, in the style of the Place des Vosges, on the Rue des Petits Champs, where the company's headquarters are located; a third of the properties on the Place Vendôme; more than a dozen estates; several plantations in Louisiana and, for 100 million *livres*, shares in the Compagnie du Mississippi.[15] After countless moves on the chessboard, the London duellist finally sees his dream come true. It will turn into a nightmare that very same year.

'FANTAISIE'

Whether Protestant or Catholic, Law prefers gambling to praying. If the *système* Law, as everyone calls it, is to continue to triumph, it needs *fantaisies*. Success stories. This prompts Law to praise Louisiana as a paradise from which gold, silver, silk, tobacco, furs and spices will start to flow. 'Savages' crowd the wharves to ship their supplies to Europe. The tobacco plantations rejoice in the good care of 700 French soldiers, 500 French settlers and 850 *nègres*.[16] It is a hugely lucrative business: tobacco is heavily taxed, the price does not suffer from competition and the cost of production is low thanks to slave labour. Moreover, the climate is extremely mild, yonder in the new Garden of Eden.

Besides *fantaisies*, the 'system' also needs financial tools. This is where Law excels. To acquire a share in one of the 'subsidiaries' (the various trading companies) the French must simultaneously buy four shares in the 'mother' (the Compagnie du Mississippi), thereby accelerating the price. Furthermore, the Banque Royale is happy to lend people money to buy shares in the company. The bank pays a 'pension on advance' to wealthy citizens who decide to invest. Those who cash in their shares get their deposit back immediately. At least in the beginning, when Law is still able to rob Peter to pay Paul. Everyone either buys or wants to buy, the fever rises proportionally to the price, and Law sets a good example by being the first major purchaser of each new issue. Shares purchased in early 1718 at 500 *livres* peak at 9,000 in the autumn of 1719 and exceed 10,000 *livres* a month later.[17]

The rush is unstoppable. People fight for shares at the door of the company's sales office in the narrow Rue Quincampoix. Merchants pawn their businesses and aristocrats sell their lands and family jewels in order to join this get-rich-quick scheme. The street is too small, and the exchangers, speculators and resellers of the company's shares sit behind their tables as far as the Rue des Lombards and the Église Saint-Merri. The tumult rubs off on other businesses: "Like an army on campaign, the cohort of *agioteurs* drags a heap of prostitutes and thieves in its wake."[18] The sales cause such a hullabaloo that a bell opens and closes the street's share trading, just as at the Marché des Innocents, Paris' largest food market. During the permitted trading hours, a twelve-man permanent guard is stationed in the street, while Law himself enjoys the protection of sixteen *gardes suisses*. Everyone wants to see and talk to him, because who can possibly resist them, those shares? 20,000 *livres*, invested in 1718, are worth 2 million by 1720. For the first time in history, the word *millionnaire* is used.[19]

John Law's 'shitty shares'

MESSAGES FROM HELL

Meanwhile, back in Louisiana, the fantasy of Law's colonial paradise is hard to reconcile with the reality. Along the twisting Mississippi, which floods its banks, there is precious little to cultivate. Settlers and slaves not bitten by insects and poisonous snakes end up between the jaws of alligators or under the tomahawks of American Indians.[20] It is even worse in the delta: 80 per cent of settlers and slaves die within the year from starvation or tropical diseases such as yellow fever.[21] The crack in Law's *système* becomes visible with the return of a ship from Louisiana after the winter of 1720. There is no silver or gold on board, just thirty seriously ill, exhausted sailors. The harbour police quarantine them at Le Havre. In a last show of strength, the unfortunate men hurl a mailbag onto the quay. "Letters from *Nouvelle Orléans*?" "Nay, messages from hell!"[22] When a second ship arrives with a similar cargo, the bad news spreads faster than rats abandoning a sinking ship. The Garden of Eden turns out to be an infectious inferno.

Another reality is that food prices in Paris have doubled in two years.[23] The spread of paper money, coupled with the stock boom, has created an illusion of wealth that sends inflation soaring. The Banque Royale finds itself in dire straits. To prop it up, it is taken over by the Compagnie du Mississippi, whose shares begin to plummet, from 9,000 *livres* on 16 May 1720 to 4,200 *livres* on 31 May. The first windows in the Rue Quincampoix are broken. Law is under house arrest after ruined people storm his carriage to lynch him. His *hôtel* on the Place Vendôme is boarded up. The Banque Royale closes its books. Orléans can no longer be reached. The harm is done. Trust – the basis of everything, *dixit* Law – has evaporated. In September, the price of Mississippi shares crashes to 2,000 and in December to 1,000 *livres*. After the winter, the bank and trading company appear to have melted with the snow and Law has fled across the Alps, to Venice. Deprived of his fortune, which has been seized by the French crown, he returns to gambling. An activity he pursues until his death in 1729.

After the Banque Royale and Compagnie du Mississippi debacle, the French crown abolishes paper money and stock exchange trading – a ban that lasts for generations. The French monarchy consequently stumbles from one financial crisis to another, until its bankruptcy eventually triggers the French Revolution. The Compagnie du Mississippi's 'castle in the air' leaves countless participants with an almighty hangover. To remind himself daily of the dangers of the stock market, a Dutch shareholder has embittered warnings painted on his porcelain. One plate shows a man displaying his empty pockets: "*Pardie [bij God], al myn*

Actien kwyt!" [My God, all my shares gone!] On another, a man raises his leg to relieve himself: "*SchijtActien en windhandel*" [Shitty shares and speculation].[24]

Bubbles are of all times.

John Law's 'shitty shares'

PART 2

RIGHT BANK, EAST

———

1. Les grandes horizontales p. 86
Folies Bergère, 32 rue Richer 75009

2. 'Why did they kill Jaurès?' p. 98
Rue de Montmartre & rue du Croissant 75002

3. Selling the Eiffel Tower p. 110
La Poste, 16 rue Etienne Marcel 75002

4. Attila p. 116
Place de l'Hôtel de Ville 75004

On 'actress' Liane de Pougy: *"She plays better lying down than standing"*.

RIGHT BANK, EAST

1

LES GRANDES HORIZONTALES

The French term grande horizontale *is not derived from geometry or architecture, but from prostitution. For the vast majority of prostitutes working in mid-nineteenth- and early twentieth-century Paris, selling sex is a means of survival. Destitution and exploitation are rife. Yet a rare handful of women manage to ascend the social ladder from their supine positions. On chaises longues and in opulent beds, these empresses of paid love work their way into the ranks of the so-called* grandes horizontales. *Beauty, singing ability or acting talent all help, but unbridled ambition and dogged determination are the true keys to reaching the top and earning a fortune as a* grisette, lorette, cocotte *or* demi-mondaine.

S'OFFRIR UNE DANSEUSE [TREAT YOURSELF TO A DANCER]

A concise guide to making it as a *grande horizontale* might read as follows. Forget the common customers and consort with a wealthy, preferably older client: a rich merchant, senior civil servant or his military equivalent. Fan the flames of desire until he is completely hooked. If marriage is on the cards, so much the better! Don't hesitate, get wed, it's the first step to climbing out of the gutter. Meanwhile, discreetly service your other customers. If your husband passes away: great! Don't immediately squander his legacy: this is a trap into which many have fallen. Invest the money in your career instead. Perfect your language skills, learn to act, sing, play the piano, or better still, take up ballet. For is it not to the glorious opera ballets (as immortalised in Edgar Degas' fragile depictions of girls in tutus leaping across the stage) that wealthy gentlemen flock in order to *s'offrir une danseuse*?[1] 'Treating oneself to a dancer' is such a popular pastime that the expression soon becomes a euphemism for business takeovers motivated by pleasure rather than profit.[2]

If your rich husband shows no sign of giving up the ghost, get divorced or drive him to despair. As soon as you have bagged your inheritance, reclaim your freedom. Repeat this scenario over and over again, until you fall into the arms of a prince, king, emperor or tsar – or a wealthy industrialist. But always in your bed and on your terms. Avoid children.[3] Enhance your prestige by giving your name aristocratic connotations: one only has to think of Valtesse de la Bigne, Liane de Pougy, Blanche d'Antigny, Emilienne d'Alençon or the Marquise de La Païva. Choose wisely, however: Nini Patte-en-l'Air [Nini 'Legs-in-the-Air'] may sound cheerful but it will not be universally admired. In better society, the name will ruin you before you can get your legs into the air. The exceptionally beautiful, however, do not always need to ennoble their names. For the Spanish-born Agustina Otero, it suffices to be called 'La Belle Otero', while Rosine Bernhardt, the illegitimate child of a Dutch mother and a father of unknown nationality, simply changes her first name to Sarah. As Sarah Bernhardt, she brings the house down at an early age, earning as much for her stage performances as for her work behind the scenes.

A report from 1871, in the age of the Third Republic, reveals how much a night with a *grande horizontale* can cost.[4] The newly installed government wants to eradicate the Second Empire spearheaded by Emperor Napoleon III, the man who had led France to an ignoble defeat in the Franco-Prussian war. It instructs the Parisian vice squad, the so-called *Brigade mondaine*, to clean up the racy files on Napoleon III's lackeys. Subject to a moral investigation: the Duc de Morny, half-brother to the Emperor and architect of the regime;

the Duc de Persigny, minister of the interior and loyal confidant of Napoleon III; not to mention the Princes Murat and Poniatowski, Baron Oudinot and other Bonapartists – *grandes horizontales* such as Fanny Lear and Sarah Bernhardt, can charge these wealthy gentlemen up to 1,000 francs per *'passe'*, the unitary measure of prostitution. Since a franc in the age of Napoleon III is now worth €15.97 (in 2020), it means they are earning the equivalent of almost €16,000 per *'passe'*. This can feed and clothe a *Brigade* member's family for years. Added to which are the expensive gifts; for example, the imperial police chief under the tsar gives his favourite courtesan, Blanche d'Antigny, some 50,000 francs worth of jewellery. Her gems would be worth €800,000 today.

The investigation targets these gentlemen of state but turns a blind eye to the *grandes horizontales*. After all, they will soon have the new rulers under the sheets. Even so, they are still listed by name in the *Registre des courtisanes de la préfecture de police de Paris* by 1875.[5] Some of the more successful ladies of dubious morals come from well-to-do milieus, such as the aristocratic Countess de Castiglione – *'la perle d'Italie'* – or Cléo de Mérode, who later takes great pains to distance herself from her past. Sarah Bernhardt is fortunate in that her aunt is the mistress of the powerful Duc de Morny. In her autobiography, *Ma double vie*, she recalls that he paid for her education. Most *grandes horizontales,* however, are born into poverty. Some, such as Valtesse de la Bigne and La Belle Otero, are weaned on prostitution. The fact that they manage to drag themselves out of the gutter and acquire both fame and wealth is testimony to their exceptional entrepreneurial skills.

EGO, VALTESSE DE LA BIGNE

Émilie-Louise Delabigne is a seamstress and *grisette*[6] (a name derived from the grey cloth jackets worn by female garment workers) who, like many of her ilk, supplements her wages by moonlighting as a prostitute. Her mother, herself a whore in the former Rue de Paradis-Poissonnière, recommends her thirteen-year-old daughter to her clients: 'You'll see, the little one is going to be a marvel! She's going to be amazing!'[7] The men in her mother's room stink of 'urine and burnt lard'. Émilie-Louise wants to do better: rather a rich prostitute than a poor worker. As soon as she is old enough, she branches out on her own as a *lorette*, the name given to girls who received their clients in rented rooms around l'Église Notre-Dame-de-Lorette in the 9th *arrondissement*. Every Sunday, she dances in the Bal Mabille, a busy open-air dance venue. She also earns extra money as a *verseuse* [hostess] in a brasserie for soldiers on the Champ de Mars and as an extra in the Folies Bergère revues.

Les grandes horizontales

In 1871, following the Franco-Prussian War and the Paris Commune, the new owner of the Folies Bergère, Léon Sari, instigates several radical changes. He adds a catwalk and a winter garden to the venue and the boring musical performances make way for operettas, pantomimes, circus songs and dance routines. From November 1886, Georges Grison, a talented journalist at *Le Figaro*, organises performances that fuse all these ingredients into a new kind of spectacle, the 'revue-ballet'. The dazzling shows sweep people off their feet. 'The success of *Place au Jeûne*, the revue-ballet by Messrs Buguet and Grison in the Folies Bergère, is confirmed by the overcrowded halls each night', *Le Figaro* enthusiastically reports on 13 December 1886. In early 1900, Victor de Cottens adds feathers and sequins to the increasingly exciting revue. Everything is swaying, waving, shimmering and glittering. It marks the beginning of '*la folle histoire des Folies Bergère*'.[8]

As all the *grandes horizontales* once flaunted themselves at the venue, the Folies Bergère is the launch pad of choice for girls with stars in their eyes. Such as Émilie-Louise Delabigne. With her unbridled ambition, she becomes the mistress of Jacques Offenbach, a successful composer and owner of the theatre Les Bouffes Parisiens, situated on the Rue Monsigny, the prosperous axis between the Opéra and the Bourse. It is also where numerous bankers, lesser nobles and industrialists reside. Delabigne pays the requisite attention to her name: after careful consideration, she conflates the regal form of address '*votre altesse*' into the grandiose-sounding 'Valtesse' and decides to write her surname with a lower case 'd'. Valtesse de la Bigne: it works. Bed-hopping will soon be a thing of the past, however. So too, old Offenbach and his devoted affection. Valtesse is on the lookout for yet bigger prey.

Her first victim is the scion of an aristocratic Polish family, Prince Lubomirski. He installs Émilie-Louise in a luxurious flat on the Rue Saint-Georges. It is a pleasing enough step, but Valtesse has read the manual from cover to cover. She ruins and abandons her prince before moving on to an even grander figure. Emperor Napoleon III – lover or admirer? – elevates her to the nobility. 'Valtesse' becomes 'Comtesse' de la Bigne. The painter Edouard Detaille is given the delicate task of portraying the wholly fictitious aristocratic members of the 'glorious La Bigne family'. As a motto, the new countess simply picks 'Ego', meaning 'I'. She has the three stylised letters applied to her stationery, her porcelain tableware and the ceilings of her sumptuous villa in the residential surroundings of Ville-d'Avray, between Paris and Versailles.[9] Here, she counts Léon Gambetta, prime minister of France and minister of foreign affairs, as her neighbour. In her *lit de parade*, a sumptuous, gilded bed with a mint-coloured canopy, she enchants her admirers and financiers but also teaches young courtesans all the tricks of highly paid love.[10]

Passionately fond of the mild sea breeze along the Côte d'Azur, the Countess builds a house – Villa des Aigles – in the hills near Monte Carlo. The scent of thyme, rosemary and lavender are worlds away from the stench of urine and burnt lard that emanated from the men in her mother's bedroom. 'Ego' dies at the age of fifty-two. Immortalised by Edouard Manet, she can still be admired in the Henry and Louisine Osborne Havemeyer room at the Metropolitan Museum of Art in New York.[11] These early collectors of Impressionist art, an American sugar magnate and his wife, fell in love with the genre when it was deeply unfashionable in France and barely worth a *sou*. Did the chic Havemeyers ever discover who was really hiding behind Manet's soft pastel hues?

EMILIENNE D'ALENÇON

Emilienne André is a caretaker's daughter from the Rue des Martyrs, the street that climbs from Notre-Dame-de-Lorette straight to Montmartre – the martyr's mountain. At the age of fifteen, she becomes Emilienne d'Alençon and wins standing ovations at the popular Casino de Paris.[12] In her fabulous act, *'Emilienne et ses ânes savants'* [Emilienne and her Performing Donkeys], she balances on a narrow plank with a pair of donkeys. Colourful posters entice Parisians to come and see the spectacle with their own eyes. Not everyone who buys a ticket is interested in the animals. Emilienne is soon to be found kicking her heels up at the Folies Bergère. Transcending the revues, she graduates to the exalted Théatre des Variétés on the Boulevard Montmartre, which is owned and directed many years later, from 1991 to 2005, by the French actor Jean-Paul Belmondo.

Emilienne also enjoys her fair share of liaisons. After some initial scrambling she marries and abandons first a jockey and then a nobleman, the Duc d'Uzès, whom she leaves 3 million francs poorer.[13] Her next quarry is the wealthy Étienne Balsan. The son of a textile industrialist who has built a fortune outfitting the French army,[14] he was Coco Chanel's first great love. With Balsan as her calling card, Emilienne d'Alençon rises rapidly through the social ranks. The voluptuous donkey-tamer of yesteryear now deigns to welcome men such as King Edward VII of Great Britain, Kaiser Wilhelm II of Germany and King Leopold II of Belgium to her bed.[15] The one thing she cannot avoid, however, is the First World War. Like Valtesse de la Bigne, *La d'Alençon* spends her last days in fashionable Monaco, far away from the rough and randy donkeys and their human counterparts, whom she had once charged a few *sous* for a brief *soulagement à la main* when first starting out.

Les grandes horizontales

BLANCHE D'ANTIGNY

Marie-Ernestine Antigny hails from a decidedly better milieu. Her father is a carpenter and parish sacristan. Yet she forsakes respectability for the love of a Romanian, with whom she elopes at the tender age of fifteen. Taught to ride horses by gypsies in Bucharest, she returns to Paris and finds work as an Amazon in the Cirque Napoléon, the precursor of the Winter Circus on the corner of the Rue Amelot and the Boulevard du Temple.[16] It is not here, however, but under the colourful lanterns of the Bal Mabille that she attracts the attention of Prince Alexander Gorchakov. The solemn Chancellor of the Russian Empire is sixty-five years old, balding, wears tiny spectacles and – a godsend – is in poor physical health. She is whisked away to St Petersburg by her admirer, whereupon he instantly fades into the background.

The young Frenchwoman launches herself into the world of the Russian aristocracy... and triumphs. At the age of twenty-two, she is the mistress of the powerful General Mezentsov, chief of the tsar's secret police. Head over heels in love, he showers her with kisses, roubles, jewels and furs. It is all too much. Unable to tolerate the competition, the Tsarina expels Blanche d'Antigny (as she has taken to calling herself). But Mezentsov cannot get her out of his head. The Russian decides to finance her theatrical comeback in Paris. He pays for her apartment, for the theatre, performers, publicity, the orchestra and everything else that is necessary for Blanche to shine. At the long-awaited premiere at the Théâtre du Palais-Royal on 3 July 1868, Mezentsov's investment is shown up for what it actually is: spectacularly ill-judged. The theatrical press conclude that Blanche is better off riding than acting.

Any other actress would have hanged herself at such a devastating review, but Blanche sees the premiere as an unqualified success: after all, perhaps there is someone in the audience whose wealth eclipses that of her Russian spy chief? Raphaël Bischoffsheim, an affluent banker, is happy to respond to her advances. He smothers Blanche in kisses and diamonds. Gustave Courbet immortalises her in his *La dame aux bijoux*. The painting shows the flame-haired *grande horizontale* struggling to select an item from her crammed jewellery box. But she succumbs to boredom. Perhaps she can climb just one step higher after all? It is her undoing. The manual is unequivocal on this point: do not get ahead of yourself. She is dropped by her banker. A theatrical tour in Egypt is a failure – the curtain has to be lowered at the Alexandria performance due to the incessant jeering.

Blanche d'Antigny dies of typhoid fever in Paris at the age of thirty-four, tended by her devoted and still chief of the secret police, Mezentsov, who continues to visit. Her neat corner apartment at 93, Boulevard Haussmann might not be a villa in Monaco but it is far more sophisticated than her birthplace: Martizay, a godforsaken village on the edge of the Brenne forests and lakes, a midpoint in the no man's land between Châteauroux and Poitiers. Moreover, her portrait by Gustave Courbet continues to adorn the walls of the Musée des Beaux-Arts in Caen. A rare honour.

LIANE DE POUGY DE LA PÉNITENCE

At the age of sixteen, Anne-Marie Chassaigne abandons her husband and child for the lure of Paris, where she learns her trade in several *maisons closes*. Instructed in the art of social climbing by her friend Valtesse de la Bigne, she develops her talent as a *magicienne* and acrobat in the Folies Bergère. She is adored by the public. Anne-Marie Chassaigne, a soldier's daughter from the village of La Flèche in the Sarthe, quickly metamorphosises into the seductive Liane de Pougy, a denizen of Paris. She is made for the stage, according to reviews. On 14 January 1902, *Le Figaro* hails her performance in the Folies Bergère 'a brilliant success…. She receives rapturous applause and makes several curtain calls.'

Liane de Pougy enjoys a meteoric rise after the revues: she goes from being a mime artist at the Olympia to treading the boards in serious theatres. Yet she is soon brought back down to Earth: 'She plays better lying down than standing'.[17] La Pougy subsequently marries a Romanian prince who is fifteen years her junior, Georges Ghika. Another transgression of the manual: it is an ill-fated union. After a lavish life filled with brothels, dancing and lovers, Liane de Pougy repents and, after a 'good conversation with the *mère supérieure* of Saint Agnes' refuge',[18] puts the hustle and bustle of Paris behind her for good. Under her new, now profoundly hagiographical name, Anne-Marie-Madeleine de la Pénitence, she enters the convent of the Third Order of Saint Dominic near Lausanne. Here, she seeks atonement for her sins. There must have been many: after her death, her confessor declares that she had devoted herself to convent life with such fervour that 'she was almost a saint'.[19]

LA BELLE OTERO

'Almost saintly' is not a description one can apply to Spanish-born Agustina (Caroline) Otero. Born into a miserable family, and with a prostitute mother, Caroline Otero learns flamenco dancing at the age of thirteen from her first lover. That might sound very modern and appealing were it not for the fact that he also pushes her into prostitution. Following several detours around Marseille

Les grandes horizontales

and Monte Carlo, the 'Spanish Beauty' arrives in Paris. At the Folies Bergère she monopolises the role of the '*belle étrangère*'. Multiple conquests later – including a Spanish banker, an American impresario, a French minister, the leader of the French Socialist Party (Aristide Briand), a Russian grand duke, British and Belgian kings (Edward VII and Leopold II, respectively) and a tsar (Nicholas II) – and La Belle Otero's star glitters brightly in the firmament of the City of Light.

She is not interested in a noble-sounding appellation because men are already entranced by her beauty. Quite literally. La Belle Otero incites several of her lovers to fight duels and she is the direct cause of six suicides. As a result of which she is also nicknamed '*la sirène des suicides*'.[20] In 1915, after several charity performances for the excited French soldiers behind the Front, the country's most beautiful woman demonstrates her wealth by purchasing the sumptuous Villa Caroline in Nice for 15 million dollars. Yet La Belle Otero ends up as poor as she started out: living in a tiny room of a shabby *hotel garni*, having gambled away her entire fortune.

THE MARQUISE DE PAÏVA

The richest and boldest of all the *grandes horizontales* dies in opulence. Born in a freezing alley in the Moscow ghetto, Esther Lachmann, daughter of a Jewish-Polish weaver, initially marries a tailor. After bearing a child, Esther embarks on a solo journey to Paris. Upon her arrival, she ensnares Henri Herz, a virtuoso pianist and professor at the Conservatoire. Henri's piano compositions may delight the ears, but they do not yield nearly as much as the wealth of the Portuguese Marquis Araùjo de Païva. The marquis gives Esther the *hôtel particulier* at 28, Place Saint Georges, which is as beautiful today as it ever was (but should not be confused with the *hôtel* that she commissioned later in life). By dint of her marriage to her Portuguese marquis, Esther trades her Jewish name for a Catholic one: Thérèse.

The girl from the ghetto, now the Marquise de Païva, is a true devotee of the *grande horizontale* manual. The day after the wedding, with the contract in her pocket (in which the Marquis not only grants her a furnished house but also £40,000), she ends their relationship by letter. The grandee slinks away with a broken heart and a bleeding bank account. He subsequently commits suicide. Since the aristocratic name of her ill-fated husband is so illustrious, La Païva retains it as a means of ensnaring her third victim. The German nobleman, steel and mining magnate, Guido Henckel von Donnersmarck, turns out to be the long-awaited bullseye. His fortune is limitless. Thérèse converts to Protestantism and becomes – in the German style – Theresia. Head over heels in love, Guido gives his mistress an annual income of £80,000 and, furthermore, the Château de Pontchartrain, a beautiful U-shaped castle with extensive gardens and farmlands, flanked by the royal residences of Versailles and Rambouillet.

But the Marquise's love of metropolitan life, salons and the opera wins out. With Guido's money, she treats herself to another new, dazzling *hôtel* at 25, Avenue des Champs-Élysées. Here, she hosts glittering parties at which the Goncourt brothers, Théophile Gautier, Léon Gambetta, Ernest Renan and many other Second Empire luminaries toast the success of Napoleon III. When La Païva finally marries her magnate in 1871, after the defeat of the French by the Prussians, she suddenly finds herself the wife of a hated enemy. The newly unified Germany imposes reparations of 5 billion francs upon France, to be paid in three years, and annexes Alsace and Lorraine. Grand receptions at the Hôtel La Païva are now a thing of the past. After accusations of spying for Otto von Bismarck, the new German chancellor, she and Von Donnersmarck depart for Germany, never to return to the country in which she rose from being an immigrant to a marquise and ultimately an empress of love.

Her luxurious urban palace is now a public monument. Slightly set back from the Avenue, its extravagant façade immediately catches the eye. The sumptuous interior is even more baroque than that of La Païva's first home on the Place Saint-Georges. In the soaring entrance hall, a shimmering and unique staircase in yellow onyx, which is the reason the building was listed as an historical monument, leads to a wealth of grand spaces, including ballrooms. The bathrooms resemble Moorish hammams. The largest, used by La Païva herself, is graced with a bath and three taps. Legend has it that milk flowed from the first tap, lemonade from the second, and champagne from the third. In a setting such as this, it is wholly plausible.

CLÉO DE MÉRODE

In her best-selling memoir *The Second Sex*, published by Gallimard in 1949, philosopher Simone de Beauvoir discusses, amongst other things, Cléo de Mérode. She calls her a courtesan and places her on a par with the *grandes horizontales*. At the time of publication, the seventy-four-year-old de Mérode has been absent from the stage for fifteen years and is living a quiet and affluent life in her spacious flat on the Rue de Téhéran in the 9th *arrondissement*. De Beauvoir is unaware that she is still alive. De Mérode, however, is not enamoured of the fresh publicity. *Moi, une pute?* In no time at all, a registered letter drops through Gallimard's letterbox, in which one *Maître* Boiteau, on behalf of the *grande danseuse*, demands 5 million francs in compensation.

Les grandes horizontales

Gallimard's lawyer, *Maître* Garçon, mounts the defence that de Beauvoir is simply alluding to the vague twilight zone between 'the art of the dancer and the *volupté*'. He argues that such practitioners are occasionally compelled to 'please'. Moreover, in the past, when such publicity was good for her career, she never – *jamais!* – distanced herself from such associations. Her sudden indignation, therefore, is wholly motivated by financial gain. *Maître* Boiteau refutes the accusation – *au contraire!* – and proves that Cléo de Mérode is of independent means thanks to the generous salary she had commanded at the Opéra Garnier between 1895 and 1925. The judge sentences Gallimard to damages of 1 symbolic franc, instead of the requested 5 million, and Simone de Beauvoir is forced to redact her book and remove all references to de Mérode.[21]

How could it have come to this, asks the elderly Cléo, all these false associations with the *grandes horizontales*? A reputation against which the former *danseuse* has been fighting for years. As the illegitimate daughter of a Belgian baroness and an Austrian nobleman, who retains her financial independence and enjoys a solid education, Cléo de Mérode dances her way from the Folies Bergère to the Opéra Garnier and performs for the crowned heads of Europe. In terms of beauty, she is in no way inferior to La Belle Otero. In 1896, aged just twenty-one, she wins a beauty contest organised by the authoritative weekly magazine *L'Illustration*, in the presence of the soprano Sybil Anderson and the famous actresses Cécile Sorel and Sarah Bernhardt. She is photographed by the greatest photographers of the day, including Nadar and Léopold-Émile Reutlinger, and appears in all the media. With her innocent looks, she enjoys posing for posters, portraits and postcards that proclaim her beauty to all four corners of the world. Is it any surprise that she attracts the attention of several prominent and reputable gentlemen? Tsar Nicholas II, in particular, regularly visits Paris in order to behold the beauty that graces his much-cherished postcard.

In the same year as the beauty contest, 1896, the sculptor Alexandre Falguière exhibits a new work at the summer Salon in Paris: the naked, voluptuous *La Danseuse*. The woman's face is undeniably that of La Mérode. Moreover, the sculpture elicits intense press speculation: the body is so like the dancer's that people assume it was cast from her naked body. Scandal! Cléo de Mérode issues denials in every conceivable language. She finally admits to posing for the sculpture but says that 'Falguière, the traitor, has broken his promise to clothe my body'.[22] The furore dissipates over the summer, only for a hurricane to unleash itself in September. The Belgian king, Leopold II, is said to have swooned at the sight of de Mérode during her 'sublime performance' in *Aïda* at the Opéra Garnier.[23] The monarch pays incognito visits to her home and showers her with flowers and kisses. A few days later, the Belgian king effectively makes a public appearance with 'his' Cléo in the foyer of the Opéra. In one fell swoop, Leopold – then sixty-one years old – confirms the rumours about his new mistress, who is forty years his junior.

De Mérode cannot stay young and wild forever. Concerned about her reputation, she publishes the autobiographical *Le ballet de ma vie*[24] in 1955, at the age of eighty. In the book, she issues indulgent rebuttals of the numerous alleged affairs. Right up until her death in 1966, the *danseuse* does all she can to erase the image of her being a *grande horizontale*. Her final resting place, in the 90th division of Père-Lachaise cemetery, is perhaps a little unfortunate from this perspective. She is interred near Oscar Wilde, the English poet-dandy who was notorious for his sexual excesses and scandals. As if to protect her from Wilde's immoral influence, a grieving woman in flowing robes leans piously over de Mérode's red granite tomb. But it is not her infamous neighbour who has her turning in her grave on 22 September 2015. On that day, a new exhibition opens at the Musée d'Orsay, '*Splendeurs et misères. Images de la prostitution, 1850–1910*'. At the heart of the installation stands an alluring nude. A dancer. Signed by Alexandre Falguière.

Les grandes horizontales

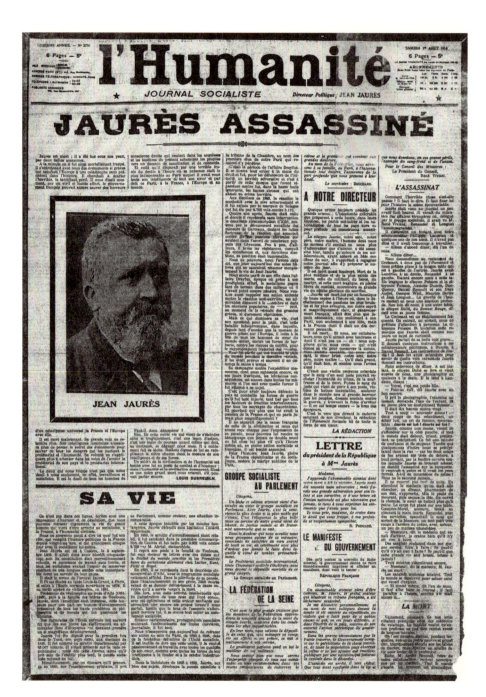

L'Humanité, 1 August 1914.

2

'WHY DID THEY KILL JAURÈS?'

Friday, 31 July 1914: "How did this terrible disaster happen? We must document. We must record this dreadful event for history!" Journalist Marcel Cachin, utterly distraught, files his copy on the murder of his employer, Jean Jaurès. The socialist MP, co-founder of the Section Française de l'Internationale Ouvrière *[French Section of the Workers' International] (SFIO), founder and political director of the socialist newspaper* l'Humanité, *had been assassinated a couple of hours previously at the Café du Croissant in the Rue Montmartre, just two buildings down from the editorial offices. It is midnight; Cachin's copy must hit the presses. Paris is about to be plunged into turmoil.*

LOVERS... STALKED BY DEATH

Saturday, 1 August 1914. *Jaurès assassiné!* This is not the only bad news to reach Paris on that turbulent day, the first day of the First World War: "Germany declares war on Russia!" It is reported in all the evening papers. The conflict has become a reality, and Jean Jaurès is one of its first casualties. A month earlier, Archduke Franz Ferdinand of Austria-Hungary had been assassinated by a Serbian student in Sarajevo. This previously local Balkan flare-up between Serbia and Austria-Hungary has since spilled over into Europe, dragging Russia and Germany into the fray. Russia takes Serbia's side; Germany aligns itself with Austria-Hungary. Retaliative threats and reprisals have spiralled out of control. Austria has just bombed the Serbian capital Belgrade. The flames are licking at the doors of Europe. Yet Jean Jaurès is determined to extinguish the blaze.

Jaurès is fresh from an emergency meeting of the International Socialist Bureau in Brussels. Convened on Wednesday, 29 July 1914, delegates included Emile Vandervelde from Belgium, Hugo Haase and Rosa Luxemburg from Germany, Friedrich Adler from Austria and representatives from the Netherlands, Italy, Switzerland, Bohemia and Hungary. Luxemburg and Jaurès had proposed a coordinated and immediate general strike in France, Belgium and Germany. The march to war could be slowed by crippling industrial output and transport links. In the time gained, Germany could bring Austria to its senses, and France could ask its ally Russia to rein in Serbia. It all sounds so logical and clear. But once again, the Bureau is divided. Pacifists Luxemburg and Jaurès are defeated; a general strike is a step too far. While the International is opposed to militarism, imperialism and aggression, it balks at pacifism. Self-defence in the face of aggression is permissible.[1]

The socialist leaders issue a woolly statement and promise to exert pressure on the government to halt the warmongering. Jaurès messages his editorial office in Paris as soon as the meeting ends. The next day, his newspaper proclaims the *"volonté pacifique du prolétariat mondial"* [peaceful will of the world proletariat].[2] Jaurès and Rosa Luxemburg are disappointed in the Bureau's weakness; the general strike would have packed a persuasive punch. Both are due to address a major peace rally in Brussels that same evening. Rosa Luxemburg refuses to speak,[3] but Jaurès holds his nerve. At the Cirque Royal, which is packed to the gills, he rouses the audience. When he broaches the subject of the approaching conflict, silence reigns: "When I see lovers strolling through the city," – Jaurès chooses his words carefully as he scans the room – "I feel that death is already stalking them." After his speech, the workers march through Brussels, brandishing white placards emblazoned with '*Guerre à la guerre!*' [War on war!] and chanting the *Internationale*, over and over again.[4]

With his image of lovers heading towards death, Jaurès is the first to translate the anonymous cannon fodder – which military leaders and monarchs have historically disregarded – into real people made of flesh and blood. Rulers such as the tsar and the kaiser will yet again be sacrificing hundreds of thousands of people, with neither rank nor station, on the altar of a senseless war. For the European establishment, it is an unprecedented message from a brand-new voice. But a highly undesirable discourse. By this point in time, however, the socialists are afraid of their own shadows. They receive nothing but public opprobrium in France and Germany. In Paris and Berlin, they are accused of being unpatriotic, or worse – of collaborating with the enemy. Jaurès is heedless. But applause is thin on the ground. He is almost a lone pacifist within his own International. A few days later, the Belgian Labour Party cancels a peace march at the Cirque Royal, and when the Kaiser declares, "I know no parties anymore, I know only Germans!", the country's socialists close ranks and take up arms against their 'comrades' from Russia and Europe. But in France, a solitary man refuses to abandon the cause.

Thursday, 30 July 1914. Jaurès reaches Paris after an exhausting train journey from Brussels. Dramatic news has landed on the editorial desk: general mobilisation in Russia! Although expected, it is nevertheless a shock. The news, in bold black-and-white, makes the headlines everywhere. If Russia does not rescind the order immediately, Germany will have no option but to follow suit. At which point, the die is cast. In Jaurès' opinion, Russia is the only country that can pull Europe back from the brink.

Friday, 31 July 1914. As promised in Brussels, Jaurès contacts the French prime minister, his friend and party colleague, René Viviani. Together, they stood at the cradle of *l'Humanité*. But he is drowning in endless crisis meetings with his cabinet. Jaurès then pleads with his right-hand man, Abel Ferry, to insist that the president of France, Raymond Poincaré, acts as the ultimate intermediary with Tsar Nicholas II. Poincaré and Viviani had met with the tsar in St Petersburg just the week beforehand. They immediately despatch a telegram: "mobilisation equals war, Russia must turn back immediately!" The prime minister thanks Jaurès *très cordialement* for his *vision remarquable* and wishes him *une bonne soirée*. In the light of subsequent events, it is a cynical salutation.

When Jaurès leaves the corridors of the Assemblée Nationale at the Palais Bourbon later that afternoon, the weather is oppressively hot. He finds some shade in the narrow, high-walled Rue de l'Université. The respite is brief because once he reaches the open ground before the Pont de la Concorde, the leaden

'Why did they kill Jaurès?'

heat hits him for six. Jaurès has no time to spare, not even for a refreshing glass of beer. He wants to launch a final appeal in next day's *l'Humanité* and, in so doing, to reinforce his political intervention. A taxi stops. Jaurès alights near the Bourse, the epicentre of the Parisian press. It is pointless trying to drive to the offices of *l'Humanité* in the Rue Montmartre. All the newspapers have their own printing presses and the street is blocked from dawn to dusk with paper delivery lorries. His office is but a five-minute walk from the Bourse. Jaurès uses the time to summarise the whirlwind of recent events for his editorial. But those familiar with his brisk gait and rotund figure would immediately have noticed that something was wrong. For the imposing socialist leader walks slowly along, hunched over, his gaze trained on the ground. He is tired. Tired of fighting for peace.

DREAMS OF A BEAUTIFUL WAR

While Jaurès is still hoping for peace, the military leaders in Britain, France, Russia and Germany have long been dreaming of a beautiful war. After all the preparations in all the camps, there must and will be fighting. The military top brass in France, led by Field Marshal Joffre, is brandishing 'Plan XVII'. So-called because it has been updated seventeen times since the Franco-Prussian War of 1870/1, which will finally be avenged.[5] The French and Russian military commanders have dutifully been making annual revisions to the Franco-Russian convention. But under the influence of their belligerent ambitions, it has evolved from a defensive treaty to an attack plan. It would be a shame not to use it, they think. Across the Channel, the British and French military leaders have been colluding against Germany since 1905, even attending each other's manoeuvres. "In consultation, they selected French landing bases and made provisions for a front from Charleroi to Namur and on into the Ardennes, in anticipation of a German invasion."[6] Finally, in Germany, General von Moltke, alongside his senior military advisors, is polishing the 1906 Schlieffen Plan into a strategic gem.

Germany had approved a war budget, generous enough to guarantee a well-equipped army, as early as 1913.[7] A militaristic microbe has spread unchecked throughout Europe: the battle plans are firmly in place (with or without the knowledge of the politicians and monarchs). The closer the conflict creeps, the more impotent the ruling class – as Tsar Nicholas II and Kaiser Wilhelm II soon discover. Their generals square up to each other like playground bullies. The two monarchs are cousins. They are well acquainted thanks to weddings, funerals and coronations, and enjoy shared holidays on their imperial yachts in the Baltic Sea. As if to prove further their fidelity to the world, they wear each other's military uniforms on ceremonial occasions. They address one another as Nicky and Willy and call their uncle, King Edward VII of Great Britain, Bertie. At the latter's funeral in 1910, the Kaiser wore the "scarlet uniform of British field marshals".[8] Conversely, at the wedding banquet for Kaiser Wilhelm's only daughter in 1913 in Berlin, Bertie's successor, King George V – call me Georgie – posed in his Prussian uniform and sported a genuine *Pickelhaube* on his head.[9]

Until the very last hours, before their armies will smash the world to smithereens, they maintain a lively correspondence – invariably signing off with the familiar Nicky, Willy or Georgie – as a sign that they are doing their utmost to stave off disaster. It is a veritable compendium of hypocrisy and deceit. "The war was already decided upon and the whole flood of telegrams between the governments of Russia and Germany was only the staging [*mise en scène*] of an historical drama....", wrote Sergei Dobrorolski, a former lieutenant general in the Tsarist army, some years later.[10] In one of his 'ultimate' messages, the German Kaiser wrote to his cousin, the Tsar: "In my endeavours to maintain the peace of the world I have gone to the utmost limit possible. The responsibility for the disaster which is now threatening the whole civilised world will not be laid at my door. In this moment it still lies in your power to avert it. Nobody is threatening the honour or power of Russia who can well afford to await the result of my mediation. My friendship for you and your empire, transmitted to me by my grandfather on his deathbed has always been sacred to me and I have honestly often backed up Russia when she was in serious trouble especially in her last war. The peace of Europe may still be maintained by you, if Russia will agree to stop the military measures which must threaten Germany and Austro-Hungary."[11]

Even if they had been sincere, they had long since lost the power to turn the situation around. The French and German chiefs of staff are firmly in control. In Russia, General Dobrorolski and his staff have relieved the Tsar of his mobilisation duties, while in Germany, the Kaiser is backed into a corner. Blood will be spilled. France fares no better. The prime minister, Viviani, an inexperienced socialist and pacifist, is under the thumb of the assertive and experienced president, Poincaré. Poincaré is a liberal Republican who correctly gauges the ambitions of the Ecole Supérieure de Guerre and its director, General Ferdinand Foch: "*La victoire, c'est la volonté!*" [Victory is willpower!]. Grit, guts and zest, or enthusiasm in other words, are the cries rising from the military academy. The moment has arrived when the great plan – *l'offensive d'outrance* [attack to excess] – will lead France to a glorious victory.

'Why did they kill Jaurès?'

What some regard as the ultimate patriotic and military duty, Jaurès views as a leap into the abyss. As he steps into the Rue Montmartre, lost in thought, he bumps into several colleagues from the evening paper *La Liberté*. They are utterly shaken. That afternoon, the Netherlands had called for general mobilisation and Germany had declared a *drohende Kriegsgefahr* [imminent threat of war]. They scurry off; they have to get the news into the late edition of the paper. A ghastly escalation, thinks Jaurès. Under the blazing evening sun he removes his coat, folds it over his arm and rolls up his shirt sleeves. On the threshold of the newspaper building, he glances up at the sky. "*Quelle affaire*. And on such a beautiful, warm summer day." It is the final day of July, and his last one on Earth.

TRAGIC HOURS

Jaurès enters the editorial office just before 8pm. Landrieu, the general manager, requests an instant update: how did the meeting with the prime minister go? Jaurès shuts the door. They gesticulate and pace around the small office. Behind the glass wall, the journalists put down their pens. They follow the gestures with the utmost concentration. Landrieu looks as depressed as Jaurès. He throws his arms in the air, a sign of pure despondence – not because they will be working late again tonight, but because they all know that the disaster is inevitable.

A colleague makes a welcome suggestion: "*Allons d'abord dîner!*" [First, let's go and eat!] Why not? Jaurès and his colleagues cross the Rue du Croissant to the café of the same name (today's Bistrot du Croissant), which stands at the junction with the Rue Montmartre. The place is thronged with journalists from newspapers of all creeds, as always. They are often at each other's throats, both on paper and, occasionally, in duels. But here, the editors fraternise with *un petit coup de rouge* [a little glass of red]. The café does a roaring trade because the offices of *L'Aurore*, *La Liberté*, *La Presse*, *La France*, *L'Univers*, *Le Radical*, *l'Humanité*, *La Patrie*, *Le Siècle*, *La République*, *L'Intransigeant* and *Le Soleil*, not to mention the weeklies *Le Jockey* and *Le Journal des Voyages*, are all located on the Rue Montmartre or the Rue du Croissant. Contributors to *Le Figaro* on the Rue Drouot or *Le Temps* on the Rue du Faubourg-Montmartre also occasionally stop by to glean news and ideas.

Like true habitués, the journalists from *l'Humanité* install themselves at their long table to the left of the entrance. Everyone needs a break. Jaurès sits in his usual seat, his back to the window. It is open. A cooling evening breeze gently lifts the curtains. At another table, Dolié, a journalist from *Le Bonnet rouge*, stands up. He comes over to show Jaurès a photograph of his young daughter. Jaurès smiles affectionately and congratulates the man warmly. A regular greets

Jaurès from afar; he shakes hands with two other diners. For a brief moment his worries dissipate. Suddenly, the curtain is yanked apart from outside. An arm swings into the room and presses a pistol to the back of the statesman's head. Two shots later, Jaurès is dead.

The next day, Saturday, 1 August 1914, Germany declares war on Russia, and upon France a mere two days later. Britain enters the war in the next twenty-four hours. The ticking timebomb of the First World War has finally exploded in all its ferocity; Jaurès has narrowly missed its detonation.

"Jaurès! Jaurès! On a tué Jaurès!" [Jaurès! Jaurès! Jaurès has been assassinated!] The lights go on along the Rue Montmartre as the street descends into chaos. Men and women in nightclothes, some with children in their arms, lean out of windows to catch a glimpse of the unfolding drama. A crowd gathers outside the café. An ambulance waits with its doors wide open. Inside, where Jaurès' body has been carefully laid out on a table, the panic-stricken party leaders crowd into the room. There are no words.

From the newspaper district around the Bourse, news quickly spreads across the city. In the eastern districts of Belleville, Ménilmontant and Charonne – the traditional working-class neighbourhoods – the people pour onto the streets and emotions run high. *"La place Gambetta était noire de monde."* [The Place Gambetta was full of people].[12] The demonstrations last well into the night on the Faubourg Saint-Antoine. But the better neighbourhoods to the west of Paris are eerily calm. From Neuilly to Auteuil, and in the residential 7th and 8th *arrondissements*, the streets are deserted. Under the soft light of the golden lanterns illuminating the private mansions and chic apartments around the École Militaire, an occasional sigh is uttered, *"Enfin!"* [Finally!] Or even approving whispers: *"Bien fait!"* [Well done!] By no means every French citizen opposes the war.

French ultra-nationalists and the military top brass had long been seeking revenge for what the Prussians did to France in 1870/1: starving Paris, annexing Alsace and Lorraine, and extorting five billion francs in war reparations. The publicly humiliating Dreyfus affair still stings. Just when Germany is about to be taught a lesson by glorious France and its allies, a reprehensible pacifist throws a spanner in the works. He – Jean Jaurès – the "bearded socialist", the "national traitor" is *"vendu à l'Allemagne"* [in hock to Germany] and *"l'homme du Kaiser"* [the Kaiser's man]. The general populace also harbours strong anti-German sentiments. The soldiers leaving the Gare du Nord for the Front are waved off to rapturous applause. On the Rue Montorgueil, with its perennially busy market, proponents of the war smash German-sounding signboards. Soup-maker Kub's shop on the nearby Rue Tiquetonne is hit. He will poison the French with his

'Why did they kill Jaurès?'

'German' fare. Further down the street, tailor Yarf quickly scrambles his name to 'Fray' and posts a notice declaring his intention to enlist in the army as soon as possible.[13] His shop windows remain intact.

'LE PEUPLE EN ARMES'

The morning after Jaurès' assassination, Parisian newspapers reflect upon the polarisation around the impending war. At one extreme, *l'Humanité, journal socialiste*, publishes an extensive tribute to its leader. The newspaper runs the headline "*Jaurès assassiné*" and surrounds his photo with a black mourning frame. Not a word here about the military developments. At the other extreme, *L'Action Française, organe du nationalisme intégral*, bellows: "*La France sous les armes*" [France takes up arms]. Not a word about the assassination of Jaurès. Only 'everyone's friend', *Le Petit Parisien, le plus fort tirage des journaux du monde entier*, reports both news items. Under the imposing headline "*Heures tragiques*" [Tragic hours], people could read in smaller type: "*La situation internationale s'aggrave*" [The international situation is worsening] and "*On a assassiné Jaurès*" [Jaurès is assassinated].

After the killing, the perpetrator is instantly overpowered in the environs of the Café du Croissant. A twenty-nine-year-old man called Raoul Villain. The motive is recorded, with a rare degree of elegance, in the transcript of his initial interrogation at the commissariat: "I have been contemplating the attack on Jaurès for a long time. He is very harmful to his home country. With his attitude towards *la loi des trois ans*, he has betrayed France. That has made me frenzied with rage. It is at that moment that I decided to get rid of him."[14]

La loi des trois ans [the three-year law] is a simple matter. In France, the general staff had been anticipating a war with Germany since 1913. Back then, however, Germany boasted 850,000 serving soldiers (out of a population of 67 million). France, on the other hand, only had recourse to 480,000 (out of a population of 39 million). An unacceptable discrepancy. The French military therefore called for the conscription period to be extended from two to three years. With immediate effect. Jaurès jumped on the barricades. He delivered a blistering attack on the law in the Chambre des Députés on 17 and 18 June 1913.[15] To no avail. He marshalled as many as 204 *députés* against the extension, but 324 voted in favour. In the Senate, 244 members voted for and only thirty-seven against.[16] The law was passed on 7 August. The upshot being that the recruits of 1911, who were about to be demobilised, were landed with an extra year's service.

The introduction of the *Loi des trois ans* not only led to rebellion in the barracks, it also caused deep rifts in French political life and society. Nationalists and militarists were pro. Radical socialists and pacifists were contra. Jaurès was the figurehead of the latter group. He believed that France should not stoke the threat of war but, moreover, saw the army in a radically different light. It is worth noting that the troops did not just maintain order in 1913; they were also deployed against striking workers, many of whom were shot. In his 700-page book *L'Armée nouvelle* (1910) [Democracy and Military Service, 1916], Jaurès argued that armies are defensive rather than offensive forces. Moreover, that defence is a civic duty. But popular conscription and armed civilians, organised into militias; that is anarchy, *quelle horreur!* The conservative *Dieu, Patrie, Famille* [God, Country and Family] camp, and the entire military establishment, are as enraged as they are perplexed. For everyone under that banner, Jean Jaurès is a dangerous man. Yet for many other compatriots, his relentless crusade for peace makes him an especially beloved figure. Others despise him. Like Raoul Villain.

A GOOD PATRIOT

While studying archaeology at the École du Louvre, the young Raoul Villain crossed paths with the ultra-nationalist Ligue des jeunes amis de l'Alsace-Lorraine [League of Young Friends of Alsace-Lorraine]. The two regions that the Prussians took from France after France's defeat in 1871. The Ligue wanted them back, and a new war cannot come soon enough. Amidst this bellicose milieu, Villain is radicalised. Furthermore, his family circumstances are not conducive to a balanced lifestyle. His mother suffered from early dementia and had been institutionalised twenty years previously. Raoul was nine at the time. With his father, a lawyer in Reims, he has "a poor to no relationship".

Villain stands trial in 1919. The war has just ended and France is in full victory mode. Senior military officers and nationalists have a firm grip on the case. They find Villain rather formidable – after all, didn't the *Loi des trois ans* allow France to increase its deployable troops to 750,000 men in record time? Didn't France win the war as a result? Won! *Hélas!* Had the law been defeated by traitors like Jaurès, France would surely have lost! These bitter reproaches ricochet around the walls of the courtroom like bullets. In the pleadings, Villain's defence lawyers assert that he was only "performing his duties as a good patriot". The jury is won over. Thanks to the post-war tumult of victory and his unhappy childhood, Villain is immediately released. Worse still, the court orders Jaurès' widow to pay the court costs.[17]

'Why did they kill Jaurès?'

Jaurès was unable to prevent the mass slaughter of millions of people during the First World War, but he was one of the first to make it a subject of debate. He fought for peace with all his might and paid the ultimate price. In his poignant, raw *chanson*, Jacques Brel reminds us of Jaurès' place in history. A time when young people were exploited by rampant industrialisation and consumed by war. Yet Jaurès nevertheless saw those young people as his country's future.

...

Si par malheur ils survivaient
C'était pour partir à la guerre
C'était pour finir à la guerre
Aux ordres de quelques sabreurs
Qui exigeaient du bout des lèvres
Qu'ils aillent ouvrir au champ d'horreur
Leurs vingt ans qui n'avaient pu naître
Et ils mouraient à pleine peur
Tout miséreux oui notre bon Maître
Couvert de prêtres oui notre Monsieur

Demandez-vous belle jeunesse
Le temps de l'ombre d'un souvenir
Le temps du souffle d'un soupir
Pourquoi ont-ils tué Jaurès?[18]

Jacques Brel, 'Jaures' from the album Les Marquises (1977)

'Why did they kill Jaurès?'

Victor Lustig caught in America, but still smiling for the press.

RIGHT BANK, EAST

3

SELLING THE EIFFEL TOWER

It is April 1925. Picture, if you will, the chic Hôtel de Crillon on the Place de la Concorde, where six gentlemen are gathering to discuss a business deal of the utmost secrecy and sensitivity: the sale of the Eiffel Tower. The vantage point of their prestigious third-floor suite affords them a magnificent view of the pride and glory of the 1889 Exposition Universelle: a gigantic celebration in steel of the French Revolution's centenary. Seated around the table we see five entrepreneurs representing prominent French scrap merchants. The sixth gentleman is a senior official from the Ministry of Postes, Télégraphes et Téléphones (PTT), the body that manages the Eiffel Tower. It is he who has brought this ensemble together. The sales pitch can now commence.

READY FOR THE SCRAPHEAP

Although this steel structure is world famous for its impressive height, the cost of its maintenance is also rocketing skywards. To evade financial loss, Paris now wishes to sell off the tower's 18,038 wrought-iron sections and its 2.5 million bolts.[1] Startling news as this may be, it is nevertheless a fact that another of the Exposition's architectural marvels, the Gallerie des Machines, has already been demolished. Conditions of sale are laid out neatly in the professionally drafted specifications. The entire operation is a state secret; only the new president of the republic, *Monsieur* Gaston Doumergue, has been kept abreast of the situation, as well as a few *personnes très haut placées* in his immediate circle. In view of the sensitivity of the matter – the Eiffel Tower now being the overarching symbol of the city both at home and abroad – this sale is to be made public only once the deal has been sealed. The contract will be awarded to the highest bidder and tenders must be submitted within three days. That concludes the briefing thus far by one of the PTT's directors general: *Monsieur* Victor Lustig, in attendance, present and correct.

As stated in the agenda, on the meeting's conclusion the party is to proceed to the tower on a joint working visit, thus allowing the scrap specialists to ascertain the parlous state of the monument for themselves. With confident gait, the director general strides past the long queue of people and, with his retinue in tow, heads straight for the entrance. The mere presentation of his PTT pass permits the company to ascend at once to the third level at a height of three hundred metres. It is at this juncture that the situation becomes all too plain: either the Eiffel Tower must be demolished, or else it must undergo wholesale restoration, an investment out of the question for a country scrambling to right itself after the devastating blows suffered in the Great War. Mr Lustig's guests are convinced: opportunity is staring them in the face.

Essentially, the scrap merchants are just as their name implies: entrepreneurs dealing in scrap iron. However, the senior official is anything but the man he purports to be. His visiting card and his PTT access pass have been skilfully counterfeited thanks to one Robert Tourbillon, a former circus artist and Lustig's stooge at Les Postes. Notorious master-swindler that Lustig is, this is far from his first venture. Leaving aside the scrap merchants now hanging on his every word, by this time Lustig has already amassed a good many victims, especially among the wealthier passengers aboard transatlantic shipping lines. He has relieved them of their financial tonnage by way of 'palming', 'slipping' and other poker-related sleights of hand. Long before they ever see through him, the ship has docked and he has hit the road. That aside, he has a particular gift for

RIGHT BANK, EAST

horse racing cons and property market fiddles. Back in Paris, it is while reading the paper that he spies an article on the increasingly burdensome cost of the Eiffel Tower. How terribly inspiring! Without paying for his coffee, he vanishes at once from his sunlit pavement table, armed with the newspaper that the Café Le Nemours always provides its customers.

BRIBERY OR GENUINE OFFICIALDOM?

Victor Lustig is not only a cunning fox but also an excellent psychologist. He sells the Eiffel Tower *not* to the highest bidder – each of the five scrap merchants submits an offer – but to the man exhibiting the greatest eagerness and the weakest personality: André Poisson. Some time later, it is with bated breath and trembling hands that Poisson opens the envelope containing the official letter from the PTT. "It's ours!" he cheers. In his mind's eye he is already entering the upper echelons of the Parisian business world, a champagne flute in hand. But his wife is hesitant; it really is a lot of money to be playing with. And why were the negotiations not held at the headquarters of Les Postes in the Rue Étienne Marcel? She requires a further interview. Lustig knows that this will be a delicate exercise. Fortunately, he can rely on a self-composed list comprising ten codes of conduct that meet with success in situations such as these. The first commandment: listen patiently and don't speak in haste.

At the second interview, Lustig changes his tone. The formerly reserved director general is now all ears to *madame*'s concerns. He nods, listens attentively and gives reassuring answers to all her questions. "*Oui, madame*, the contract is being awarded to the highest bidder and that is your husband. But for us it's also a matter of trust. We have to be certain that the contract will be executed precisely on schedule and in line with prescribed procedure. That is why our decision has been to choose a sound and solid business such as that built by your husband." *Madame* Poisson straightens in her chair, proud as a peacock. André really *has* gone places with his scrap iron after all.

When, at her insistence, the scrap merchant asks Lustig one last time whether he really is an official from *Les Postes*, the swindler plays his final card. "But, yes, of course!" Lustig assures them and then adds conspiratorially: "But as you'll know, Monsieur Poisson, we civil servants, no matter how high in rank, are in receipt of only a modest stipend. You'll understand that, in order to assign the commission to you definitively, this compels me to request a small bonus for myself, a trifle. I trust that something of that order might indeed be possible in view of the healthy profit you'll be making from the project." In other words, money under the table. What Lustig does next is a lesson in top salesmanship:

Selling the Eiffel Tower

leave the 'clients' alone for a moment to get them to convince each other. "Would you excuse me?" he asks politely and goes off to wash his hands. Mme and Mr Poisson are now entirely alone in the suite. "You see! Under the table! That's proof enough this man's a real government official!" whispers a now wholly convinced *madame* to her husband.

One day later Poisson hands over the bribe, along with the advance payment of 250,000 French francs.[2] Immediately afterwards, Victor Lustig boards the train to Austria. From majestic coffee houses in Vienna he pores over foreign newspapers with acute interest. Nothing. Even the French press has not a single word to say about the affair in Paris. Meanwhile, poor old Poisson is not feeling up to filing a complaint. He is keeping a low profile out of pure shame. What could he say if it came out that he had paid a bribe? His entire reputation would be flushed into the sewer. As it is, for several days now *madame* has not been on speaking terms with him.

A EUROPEAN COUNT

On the back of this great success, Lustig tries out his Eiffel scam a second time. On this occasion, however, he is unmasked, although he succeeds in slipping away to the United States just in time. There, he claims at first to be a certain Count Lustig with centuries of aristocratic lineage behind him, as well as numerous castles peppered throughout Europe. Given that Lustig speaks five languages and appears to know Europe from Budapest to Paris like the back of his hand, it all sounds highly plausible. The count keeps in step with the times: "He was not the hand-kissing type of count – too keen for that. Instead of theatrical, he was always the reserved, dignified nobleman", writes *The New York Times* later in an analysis of his criminal profile.[3]

Besides his incarnation as a count, Lustig has many other identities and lugs around their accompanying disguises in his travelling trunks and suitcases. Today he is a rabbi, tomorrow a priest, the day after a banker. One morning, in the guise of a diligent bellboy at a swish hotel, he hauls out onto the street the expensive luggage of an important guest. Around the block he throws off his cap and his jacket with the gold epaulettes, thrusts the suitcases into a waiting taxi and vanishes. This is Lustig *par excellence*: forever surprising and with nerves of steel. Rumour has it that, via an investment scam, he has even managed to con the notorious Al 'Scarface' Capone.

Ultimately, seeking an easier way to earn money, Lustig the chameleon morphs into a gangster. The fastest road to riches is to print your own money. Transforming himself yet again, this time into one Robert V. Miller, Lustig embarks on counterfeiting. He is soon flying too close to the sun. On 10 May

1935 he is arrested and placed under lock and key at the reputedly 'inescapable' Federal House of Detention in Manhattan. When – regardless – the bird has flown the nest, the guards discover an intriguing note left in his cell: "Law was not made by God, and Men can be wrong".[4] In other words, Lustig is justifying his escape with a nod to *Les Misérables*: a European count really ought to know his classics, after all.

His bid for freedom does not last very long. On 28 September of the very same year Lustig is re-arrested, this time in Pittsburgh. He is sentenced to fifteen years' incarceration, and on this occasion the authorities do not take any chances. Lustig is sent to Alcatraz, the notorious prison stuck on a lonely rock in San Francisco Bay. Legend will have it that he also died there behind iron bars that served as a daily reminder of the Eiffel Tower. But those are not the facts. In early March 1947 he develops a lung infection and is transferred to the Medical Center for Federal Prisoners in Springfield, Missouri. It is there that he dies on 11 March. His death certificate states his true profession in blunt terms: 'Usual occupation: Apprentice Salesman & Counterfeiter',[5] albeit a world-class one. For anyone feeling sufficiently inspired to try following in his footsteps, here are Lustig's 'ten commandments', as retrieved from among his personal effects:

Listen patiently and don't speak in haste.
Never look bored.
Wait for someone else to bring up politics and then follow their lead.
Wait for someone else to bring up religion and then follow their lead.
Don't talk about sex until someone else brings up the subject;
be discreet in that regard.
Never bring up someone's illness or affliction unless it's extremely visible.
Never delve into someone's personal life; be patient, they will tell you by and by.
Never brag about yourself; let the circumstances reveal your importance.
Never be untidy.
Never get drunk.

Caricature from *La Ménagerie Impériale* [The Imperial Zoo]: Haussmann, the 'ever-renovating' beaver.

RIGHT BANK, EAST

4

ATTILA

One evening in 1854, a dim glow illuminates one of the smaller windows in the roof of the Hôtel de Ville [town hall]. It is late, but Georges-Eugène Haussmann is still immersed in paperwork for an important meeting the next day. He is not in his large office but in a modest private study a few corridors down in the Hôtel de Ville. He rereads a paragraph: "Paris is an immense workshop of decay, where misery, plague and disease reinforce each other, where neither sunlight nor air penetrates the narrow alleys, where plants wither, and four out of seven children die within the year."[1]

SHRIVELLED BREASTS

Four out of seven. Haussmann closes his eyes and thinks of Henriette and Valentine, his daughters aged ten and thirteen. The author of the book in his hands, a certain Victor Considerant, is a socialist and philosopher, everything that Haussmann is not. Yet the newly appointed *préfet de la Seine* knows that every word this graduate of the École Polytechnique has written is the truth. He himself was twice evacuated from Paris to the countryside as a child. He overcame his asthma but it was a close shave. He casts the book aside and skims Dr Bayard's report on the state of Paris's countless rented rooms. Ruthless owners hire them by the night. "In a 5-metre-square room, I discovered twenty-three individuals, men and children combined, on five beds. The stench was so bad that I was overcome by disgust. It even extinguished my candle. A sour, unbearable miasma emanated from their shoes and clothes, overpowering all other smells."[2] Even more striking is the account by Dr Alexandre Baudet-Dulary, a *député*: "Women are dying on straw mattresses without blankets, surrounded by starving children. Yes, I have seen children hopelessly sucking on the empty and shrivelled breasts of languishing mothers, deprived of any help, either for them or for their children."[3]

Haussmann was twenty-four when a cholera epidemic hit Paris in 1832. It killed more than 20,000 residents in less than six months, including the former prime minister and ex-central banker, Casimir-Pierre Perier. He was not poor. Nor was General Jean Lamarque. The beloved military leader's funeral brought 100,000 Parisians onto the streets, creating the perfect conditions for that year's revolution. Lamarque's sudden death was exploited by the Republicans in an attempt to overthrow the July Monarchy. The crowd was already in thrall to them, Haussmann recalls, and the procession had not even departed. It did not develop into a major revolution, however, just a few hundred dead.

While the harrowing misery behind the 1832 revolution inspired Victor Hugo to write *Les Misérables*, Haussmann sees it as illustrative of how disease and misery could make a city 'explode'. He leans back, loosens his collar a little, and ponders the proximity of death to his own room that catastrophic year. A record number of people had died of cholera in the street behind his building, the former Rue de la Mortellerie that runs parallel to the Seine. The residents believed the street was cursed due to the inclusion of the word *mort* [death] and demanded it be changed. To keep the peace, the city made a special exception. It is now called the Rue de l'Hôtel-de-Ville.

16,000 Parisians died of cholera in 1849. This time, it was the death of Thomas-Robert Bugeaud, Marshal of France, the country's highest-ranking officer, that disturbed everyone. He seemed invincible behind the walls of his fine *hôtel* on the Quai Voltaire; until people realised that the marshy banks of the Seine were so disease-ridden that infections spread much faster in his neighbourhood than anywhere else in the city.

RATS AND FLYING URINE

The toxic river water was not the only risk. Overcrowding was getting worse by the day. The population of Paris stood at 714,000 in 1817. Forty years later, in 1857, Haussmann's colleagues counted 1.2 million, not including the 330,000 *zonards*.[4] These were the inhabitants of *La Zone*, a neglected no man's land between the ancient Mur des Fermiers Généraux, Louis XVI's old toll gate, and the new ramparts built by Adolphe Thiers in 1844. Over 1.5 million Parisians used the Seine for drinking water. Yet, in addition to all the human waste, it also contained the effluence from textile dyers, tanneries and other industries. All things considered, very little had changed since Haussmann's school days when, as a young child, he had picked his way through dirty narrow alleys on the way to the Lycée Henry IV, whilst simultaneously dodging rats and flying urine from night buckets. His predecessors, at least those worth mentioning, including the Comte de Rambuteau, had made the odd improvement here and there, but all progress was quickly undone by neglect and exponential population growth.

When Haussmann assumed office in June 1853, Paris was the most populous and filthiest city in Europe and riddled with crime and prostitution. He realises, high up in his little study in the Hôtel de Ville, that his task far exceeds the mere *embellissement de Paris*. He will tackle all the issues in one fell swoop – or none of them. He rises, extinguishes the light and opens the door to his bedroom. Knowing that he will have to work day and night, the new *préfet* had already moved into the Hôtel de Ville. He will resume the discussion with his employer, Napoleon III, emperor of the Second Empire, tomorrow.

Napoleon III was initially elected president of the Second Republic in 1848, following the first popular uprising that is worthy of the name. Three years later, he buried it with a cold-hearted coup. Louis-Napoleon Bonaparte, Napoleon's nephew, proclaimed France an empire and christened himself Emperor Napoleon III.[5] His Second Empire is a tribute to the vanquished regime of his illustrious uncle, Napoleon Bonaparte. As the supreme power – the Assemblée has been dissolved and the press muzzled – Napoleon III is keen to make his mark on history. Louis-Napoleon had fled to England after his uncle's defeat at Waterloo, where he was impressed by the British Empire's 'new' capital. Rebuilt after the Great Fire of 1666, it now exudes an air of grandeur. Napoleon III hates

Attila

the idea of his own city being inferior: Paris will outshine London, the city of Wellington, his uncle's gravedigger. Victoria might be Queen, but he, Napoleon III, is an Emperor! And he will prove it.

After wrangling over the budget for his ambitious beautification dreams, the emperor sacks Jean-Jacques Berger, the incumbent *préfet de la Seine*. On the recommendation of the Duc de Persigny, his minister of the interior, he appoints Georges-Eugène Haussmann as his successor on 22 June 1853. Haussmann, forty-four at the time, is a law graduate from the Sorbonne, who also happens to have a music degree from the Conservatoire under his belt. A highly versatile man. He has a track record as a *sous-préfet* and *préfet* of other *départements*, such as the Var, the Yonne and the Gironde, where he resolutely defused an Orléanist insurrection. Of all the *préfectures*, that of the Seine is by far the most prestigious. His appointment is the culmination of his seriousness and dedication to the cause of state order.

On his first day, the emperor hands him a multi-coloured map detailing His Majesty's vision for *l'embellissement de la ville*. But with his tall stature of 1.92 metres,[6] confident gaze and, above all, his in-depth knowledge of the city and its issues, Haussmann makes it clear he is not just going to execute a colour-coded plan. Health, prosperity and political stability are indivisible in Haussmann's mind. People who are healthy can work. Those who work have an income. Those who have an income have food. Those who have food want to be left alone. No more revolutions, no more chaos. If Haussmann hates anything, it is revolution and chaos.

His real challenge is to transform Paris – simultaneously a source of epidemics, a place of poverty and a hotbed of revolutions – into a healthy, prosperous city. Modest he is not. Haussmann manages to interweave Napoleon III's aesthetic dreams into his own holy trinity: *assainissement, circulation, embellissement.*[7] Sanitation, mobility, and then – only then – embellishment. The new cholera epidemic of 1854, which claims 143,000 victims across France, lends weight to his plea. The emperor capitulates. The new *préfet* incorporates the emperor's scheme into his own, thereby creating a Haussmann plan. In so doing, he convinces him that Paris must change as much below ground as above, that the entire city infrastructure must be overhauled and that – now for the delicate part – it will cost money. Much more than currently envisaged. Don't worry, the emperor reassures, all 50,000 bonds of our state loan flew out the door within a fortnight last year.[8] The money is rolling in. *Allez-y!*

THE BIG CLEAN

Thus far, Haussmann has fought hard. Coming from a Protestant family with roots in Alsace, his ascent in the now Royalist-Catholic, then Orléanist hierarchy has not been plain sailing. Haussmann learnt to be wary from an early age. An instinct that prompts him to surround himself with specialists with whom he is personally acquainted. To name them individually: Baltard, Alphand, Davioud, Belgrand, Deschamps and Marville. They will become his mainstays in the turbulent adventure that will plunge Parisians into a giant, noisy construction pit for many years to come. One that will also drag him into a political quagmire and a financial vortex – of which Haussmann, at this point, has no inkling.

He initially appoints Victor Baltard as the city architect. He has a team of thirty-six designers at his disposal, most of them graduates of the École des Beaux Arts. The 'Regulations of June 1859' are a major milestone for the team as they enable the unique, mile-long façades in creamy beige stone to be built. "All houses will have cut stone façades with balconies, cornices and mouldings. The horizontal lines of the façades will be stopped and supported at their ends by pilasters or consoles established outside the party wall, so as to make an architectural whole."[9] They all have a similar vertical arrangement. At the base, a ground floor for commercial activities or stables – tens of thousands of horses still 'live' in central Paris at that time. Then a *petit étage* for the storage of goods or as domestic staff quarters. Up above, several *étages nobles* with tall windows, moulded ceilings and grand balconies. Finally, one or more low-ceilinged floors, often without balconies, and a roof in grey slate, later in zinc. Haussmann extends the uniformity from north to south and east to west. Baltard also designs Les Halles as part of the commission, ten monumental covered market buildings in brick, cast iron and glass. Despite their glorious appearances in numerous books and films, Les Halles are closed in 1969 and later demolished under the administration of President Georges Pompidou.

Adolphe Alphand is Haussmann's gardener. He is a civil engineer rather than an architect. Alphand builds the Bois de Boulogne and the Bois de Vincennes, levels the Trocadéro, and designs the Champ-de-Mars, the Parc Monceau and the Parc Montsouris. From the historic limestone quarry of the Buttes-Chaumont, he conjures an idyllic park with waterfalls, ponds and footbridges. Alphand also creates the Avenue de l'Observatoire, the Square de Batignolles and dozens of similar counterparts. Landscape architect Jean-Pierre Barillet-Deschamps is a trusted assistant. The Jardin du Luxembourg fares less well. 'La Pépinière de Paris', the city's nursery, loses 12 hectares of greenery. "From what was once the most beautiful tree nursery in Europe and

Attila

the world, 14,000 fruit trees came every year and were sold immediately, as well as more than 700 different *cépages*, the finest collection of vines in France."[10] Haussmann made no mention of this in his *Mémoires*. The architect of the École des Beaux Arts, Gabriel Davioud, oversees its layout. He sketches the fountains, lampposts, benches, kiosks, advertising columns and – in a touch of inspired elegance – the *chalets de nécessité* [public lavatories]. It is Davioud who bestows a casual unity upon the Parisian streetscape, and who is also to be thanked for the majestic Fontaine Saint-Michel opposite the bridge of the same name.

Haussmann's hydrogeologist is Eugène Belgrand. An civil engineer with an additional degree from the École Polytechnique, he maps the entire natural water system below Paris and the Seine basin. Belgrand gives every street its own sewer. This is a true first. He reroutes wells, builds aqueducts to carry water from the rivers Dhuys and Vanne to Paris over distances of more than 100 kilometres, constructs large water reservoirs, and designs yet another world first: the giant *collecteur* at Asnières, in the bend of the Seine between Clichy and Argenteuil. For the first time in its history, Paris has healthy drinking water.

Haussmann turns to his right-hand man, Eugène Deschamps, for administrative matters. He oversees all the city services that must seamlessly work together in the new Paris. Deschamps does an outstanding job, which prompts Haussmann to make him director of the *Plan de Paris*. Healthcare is another vital consideration. Henceforth, central hospitals will only treat emergencies. The long-term sick will be nursed in the outskirts or at home. Haussmann recruits 160 doctors and an equal number of midwives for this purpose. Dr Léon Le Fort described the new healthcare system in his *Paris Guide*, published on the occasion of the 1867 World's Fair: "This service must be for France, and especially for Paris, a moment of glory, because neither England nor Germany have, in this respect, anything comparable."[11]

Last but not least, Charles Marville is Haussmann's photographer. Marville had previously worked for the Louvre where he compiled a photographic inventory of the collection for posterity. He repeats the task for Haussmann. Marville documents all the buildings and neighbourhoods that are demolished, as a record of their original condition. His photographs often depict scenes of great suffering. It is hard to believe, when studying them, that Paris is just a few years away from becoming the 'the City of Light' for the entire world, and a true beacon of modernity.

Haussmann himself oversees the major, sight-defining interventions, the above-ground breakthroughs and connections, as well as the major multibranched intersections, such as the Place de l'Etoile. On the right bank, he connects the Rue de Rivoli and the Rue Saint-Antoine to the Bastille, and then onwards to the Avenue Daumesnil and up to the Bois de Vincennes. On the left bank, he connects the Palais Bourbon via the Boulevard Saint-Germain, the Pont de Sully over the Seine and the Boulevard Henri IV to the Bastille. He thus creates an east-west axis on each bank. From north to south, he connects the Gare de l'Est to the Observatoire de Paris via the Boulevard Sébastopol and the Boulevard Saint-Michel. This diagonally connects the Place de la Nation, in the south-west of the city, to the Place de la République via the Boulevard Voltaire, and further via the Boulevard de Magenta to the Gare du Nord in the north-east of the city. To show that he is not sentimental, his birthplace in the Faubourg-du-Roule does not escape unscathed. It makes way for the Boulevard Haussmann.

THE END OF THE PARTY

Other than his confidants, Haussmann has no friends in Paris. The tens of thousands of dispossessed hate him, the politicians fear him and the bankers pray that his gigantic enterprise will succeed. Not all prayers help. Alongside a number of smaller banks, the famous Crédit Mobilier, established by brothers Émile and Isaac Pereire, is declared bankrupt in 1867 due to speculation. Money from two additional government loans, one for 250 million francs in 1865 and another for 260 million francs in 1869, is released without difficulty. Haussmann's opponents are getting nervous, so too his chief accounting officer. Three colleagues have died from exhaustion since his appointment.[12]

The eleven mayors who lost power when their districts were annexed to Paris in 1860 are also out to get the *artiste démolisseur*. But the capital now comprises twenty *arrondissements*, and everything can be executed on a much grander scale. As the Socialists, Republicans and Orléanists are unable to undermine the emperor politically, they set their sights on his *préfet* instead. The latter utilised every opportunity afforded him as an autocrat and, admittedly, the wholesale transformation of Paris might not have been possible under a parliamentary democracy. *Députés* Jules Favre and Ernest Picard attack Haussmann in parliament, describing him as the 'Attila of Expropriations'.[13] Jules Ferry, the republican journalist and politician, writes scathing articles on Haussmann's financial strategy for *Le Temps*. They cause a huge outcry and are collated into a book. With a nod to Offenbach's *Les Contes d'Hoffmann*, Ferry entitles his book *Les Comptes fantastiques d'Haussmann,* or, Haussmann's fairytale accounts.

But the *préfet* is not just a set-builder, he is also a *dramatis personae*. The impeccably dressed Haussmann, like all men of standing, is found in the city's best establishments. Occasionally on the arm of Mademoiselle Marie Rôze, a singer from the Opéra Comique, at other times on that of Mademoiselle

Attila

Cellier, a dancer from the Opéra, with whom he fathers a daughter, Eugénie. Coincidentally the name of the empress. Or was this a gesture to flatter the emperor? The extent of Haussmann's personal largesse is unknown. Later, during the Belle Époque, rumours circulated that Napoleon III and Valentine, the *préfet*'s youngest daughter, were lovers. They allegedly had a son, Jules-Hadrien Hadot. But the whispers were dismissed as *"des subterfuges de feuilletoniste"*,[14] the fabrications of serial fiction writers. Haussmann may not have been the strict reformed Protestant he claimed to be, for although he had been married to Octavie de Laharpe since 1838, the *préfet* participated in *la fête impériale*, as the numerous parties and receptions – frivolous customs and fleeting affairs included – were called. They were held at the imperial court in Paris and, during the autumn, at the Château de Compiègne. But the party cannot go on forever.

The crack in Napoleon III's omnipotence slowly but surely widens. As early as 1860, he softens his grip on the political sphere and allows parliament and the press to re-establish a profile, albeit a low one. Not only Republicans, but also Orléanists, such as Adolphe Thiers, want him gone. When Napoleon III, sick and tired, entrusts the government leadership to Émile Ollivier in early 1870, the game is truly up for Haussmann. Ollivier is an "enemy of youth" and demands the *préfet*'s head. Napoleon III offers it up to save his own skin. Only to apparently lose his own head some six months later when he declares war on Prussia over a mere trifle, thereby plunging the new city and its inhabitants into the debacle of the century – the Franco-Prussian War – and the inexorable civil war that followed.

Haussmann dies three times. The first time at his deposition in 1870. What a humiliation! The second time on witnessing his city, rebuilt and remodelled with such extraordinary effort, destroyed and set ablaze during the Paris Commune; and a third time in 1891, when Haussmann himself, a kind of human monument, gives up the ghost, at the age of eight-two.

STREET FIGHTS

Haussmann also received a posthumous kicking from the left-wing socialists. In a remarkable essay of 1938, Marxist cultural philosopher Walter Benjamin interprets the *préfet*'s schemes in a militaristic light: "Haussmann's activity is incorporated into Napoleonic imperialism which favours investment capitalism... The real aim of Haussmann's works was to secure the city against the possibility of civil war. He wanted to make it impossible ever to construct barricades in the streets of Paris... The broader streets made construction of barricades impossible and the streets were made in straight lines to connect the workers' districts to the barracks."[15] By allowing rapid troop deployment and hindering the erection of barricades, the interventions spared the bourgeoisie the misery of popular uprisings, thereby nipping the Parisian propensity for revolutions in the bud. Haussmann's wide, straight boulevards, writes a Republican *député* and opponent of the works, were so designed "because cannonballs can't take the first right."[16]

Yet Nicolas Chaudun, who conducted meticulous research for his remarkable book *Haussmann au crible* (2000) [Haussmann Under the Microscope], did not find any evidence to suggest army interference in the *préfet's* plans.[17] Nor any interest in Haussmann's part in military affairs. In a note dated 8 July 1857, however, Haussmann draws the emperor's attention to the direct link between social unrest and the urbanisation scheme: "If we are not one day to be overrun by the revolutionary cannons from our *faubourgs*, we must march on them today with spade and pickaxe in hand."[18] Haussmann also confesses in his *Mémoires* that his covering of the Canal Saint-Martin facilitated military control of the Faubourg Saint-Antoine, pretty much the cradle of every rebellion. But this may have a logical inference from the theories underpinning his urbanisation scheme. Haussmann's *Mémoires* contain more episodes of such *Hineininterpretierungen,* or wishful thinking, such as the fact that he was baptised in the Protestant Église de l'Oratoire, the oldest chapel of the Louvre, on the Rue Saint-Honoré. A mark of sophistication. In reality, Haussmann was christened in his parents' house at 55, Faubourg-du-Roule.

Whatever the case, if helping the army was his real intention, then he failed spectacularly. During the Paris Commune of 1871, a year after he resigned, barricades appeared all over his boulevards and squares. An unparalleled number. The biggest and tallest yet erected. And they were fought over with unprecedented ferocity. To such an extent that the rebellious *communards* chased the ordinary troops, *Les Versaillais*, who strove to restore order, from the city – only for them to return. On 26 May 1871, on the antepenultimate day of the *Semaine sanglante* [Bloody Week], in which the streets of the Paris Commune were drenched in blood, ex-*préfet* Haussmann witnessed his familiar Hôtel de Ville go up in flames. His office, his designs, his private quarters, the city archives, the population register and Delacroix's magnificent ceiling painting in the Salon de la Paix, where he gave numerous receptions under blue skies with mythological heroes, were reduced to ashes. Along with many other buildings and monuments across smouldering Paris.

In the city burning before his eyes, Haussmann, in a tenure of just sixteen years and six months had: built more than 64 kilometres of new roads; constructed over 100,000 new homes; tripled the number of gas lanterns; planted

Attila

80,000 trees along boulevards and avenues; and laid 585 kilometres of sewers and underground water pipes.[19] Yet it was only a third-class conveyance that transported his body to Père-Lachaise.[20] The eponymous Boulevard Haussmann would not be completed until 1926, and he did not gain a statue on the avenue until 1989, under the auspices of Jacques Chirac, then Mayor of Paris. With head held high, cloak draped around his shoulders and his perennial portfolio under his arm, the *préfet* gazes out, as though surveying his works.

To some, Georges-Eugène Haussmann will always be an Attila, a barbarian who destroyed the soul of Paris, a beaver who escaped from the imperial zoo and excavated the city for his personal gain. To others, he is a visionary who catapulted the semi-mediaeval Paris into the future. Whatever the case, his former arch-enemy, the republican Jules Simon, professor and politician, wrote in *Le Gaulois*: "Haussmann achieved more in ten years than we had managed in half a century."[21] Judge for yourself.

Attila

PART 3

LEFT BANK, WEST

———

1. Odéonia p. 132
7 and 12 rue de l'Odéon 75006

2. Bonny and Lafont p. 146
68 rue Bonaparte 75006

3. The hyena of the Gestapo? p. 154
61 rue des Saints-Pères 75006

4. Boillot, the Torpedo p. 168
Esplanade des Invalides 75007

James Joyce, Sylvia Beach and Adrienne Monnier at Shakespeare & Company.

LEFT BANK, WEST

ODÉONIA

1

They are not saints, but patron saints. Nobody does more than Adrienne Monnier and Sylvia Beach to encourage, feed, house, finance, publish or hide the new generation of post-WW1 writers from persecution. The book-sellers from the Rue de l'Odéon love their authors, books and readers. And one another. In what could be called The Improbable Adventures of Adrienne and Sylvia, *happy passages alternate with dark chapters. But time and time again, the bosom friends courageously turn the page.*

LOVE OF BOOKS

"I love America." Adrienne, the Frenchwoman, breaks the ice. The American is still clutching the letter bearing the address of La Maison des Amis des Livres and glancing nervously around. Here, the books are propping up the ceiling. "And I love France", she replies.[1]

Adrienne Monnier keeps her shop ticking over. Not that it's easy, selling books in the middle of a war. But rents are low in Paris in 1915. Moreover, she is helped by a blessing in disguise: after an accident at work, her father, who sorts letters on the train for Les Postes, receives an invalidity allowance of 10,000 francs. He gives the money to his daughter, who dreams of starting her own bookshop. Adrienne's mother, Philiberte, has always championed her child's education – Latin, history, philosophy and, wholly unexpectedly for a woman from the Massif des Bauges, one of the most isolated parts of the Savoie: theosophy.

This leaves Adrienne with a fondness for Buddhism, a sharp mind and conversational adroitness. She understands the impact of words, of silences in a debate, and refuses to be intimidated by verbal aggression. Having just turned eighteen, she wants to study English in London. Naturally this is allowed; it is the language of the British Empire, after all. The future. For Adrienne, however, it is less about the language and more about the company of Suzanne Bonnière, her best friend from secondary school. After a love-infused year on the other side of the Channel, Adrienne returns to France. She starts work at the Université des Annales. It organises conferences for the weekly magazine *Les Annales politiques et littéraires*[2] whose editorial team are based in the Rue Hérold, close to the Place des Victoires on the Right Bank. Adrienne finds *Les Annales* a stuffy concern with conventional values. This is not what she wants. The Left Bank is the cradle of innovation, home to the interesting publishers that modern poets and writers frequent – the other side of the Seine exerts a magnetic pull on the young woman.

On 15 November 1915, the wooden façade has been painted and the name of the business emblazoned across the entire width of the building in large, white capitals: LA MAISON DES AMIS DES LIVRES. In an ideal location, close to multiple publishers, Adrienne Monnier opens her bookshop at 7, Rue de l'Odéon. It soon develops into more than just a business. There are tables and chairs where people can sit with a book or discuss a work. Framed photos of authors and artworks adorn the walls – where they are not crammed with books. Deploying her organisational talent from her time at *Les Annales*, right from the outset Adrienne snares Paul Valéry and Guillaume Apollinaire, who recite their poetry in La Maison. The writers André Gide and Jules Romains read from their works. For André Breton, writer, poet and essayist, La Maison is "the most interesting hotbed of ideas of the era".[3] Everyone who's anyone in the expanding field of modern literature bumps into one another in the shop. When Sylvia and Adrienne first clap eyes on one another, La Maison is already a vibrant literary address. Jacques Prévert compares Adrienne's shop to a *"hall de gare"*[4] [station concourse], where everyone's paths cross.

SCHOOLGIRL

Sylvia Beach is the middle of three daughters born to the Protestant pastor, Sylvester Beach, and Eleanor Orbison from Baltimore, a coastal city in Maryland. In 1901, her father receives an international promotion. The entire family moves to Paris, where he is appointed assistant minister at the American Church on the Quai d'Orsay. As a teenager, Sylvia has a taste of a different world. In Paris, everything is lighter and more relaxed. Less puritanical. The family returns to the United States in 1906, where her father becomes a minister in Princeton, New Jersey. Her mother Eleanor is extremely unhappy with her overbearing pastor. She encourages Sylvia to explore the world, and to continue her studies. The tense atmosphere at home leaves the young woman with two marked traits: an aversion to both religion and men. Inspired by her carefree teenage years in Paris, Sylvia returns to Europe. She studies Spanish in Madrid and Italian in Florence. When the First World War erupts, she returns to France. There is no appetite for female ambulance drivers at the Front, and Sylvia is not a nurse. So she studies French literature at the Sorbonne instead. Although the guns are thundering at just a day's journey from Paris, the university remains open. A poetry magazine that Sylvia is struggling to find is said to be for sale at a specialist shop on the Left Bank.

Thus, on a windy day in March 1917, she pushes open the door of La Maison des Amis des Livres. There is a gust of wind. Pages flutter. Sylvia's hat is blown across the pavement. The bookseller hurries after it. That's when the spark is ignited. Adrienne hands Sylvia more than just a hat. The Frenchwoman also places her heart and soul in the American's hands. For more than fifteen years their love will be entirely mutual, albeit not without its trials. Adrienne is twenty-five and Sylvia thirty. Outwardly, the two could not be more differ-ent. Adrienne "looks like a former nun, devoted to the service of literature. She has scraped-back hair, a round, unblushing face that disapproves of any semblance of coquetry, and a pair of bright, twinkling eyes."[5] In her long skirts – from which she is inseparable – she resembles "a French milkmaid from the

Odéonia

135

eighteenth century".[6] This may seem a harsh judgement but it is not: anyone who sees a photo of Adrienne, with her dark high-waisted skirts that fall to the floor, is immediately reminded of the alpine meadows of the Massif des Bauges. Adrienne could not care less about her appearance and disdains new fashions. Sylvia, on the other hand, is tall and slim, and generally wears a jacket and a skirt that falls to below the knee, "with a white schoolgirl's collar and hairdo, in the style of Colette's *Claudine à l'Ecole*".[7] Be that as it may, the same fire burns in both.

THE BARD FROM STRATFORD-UPON-AVON

The recognition that Adrienne wants for contemporary French writers, Sylvia wants for their anglophone counterparts. With the $3,000 that her mother has saved, augmented by Adrienne's verve and drive, Sylvia Beach opens her own bookshop on 17 November 1919 at 8, Rue Dupuytren. Shakespeare and Company is tiny and situated around the corner from the Rue de l'Odéon. If Sylvia and Adrienne's offering is innovative, then so is their business model. Customers can borrow books to see if they like them before making a purchase. It seems naïve but it works effectively. Customers choose their books after an in-depth discussion with Adrienne or Sylvia and gladly return for their next book.

Riding the wave of her initial success, after two years Sylvia permits herself new, more spacious premises, this time at 12, Rue de l'Odéon, opposite Adrienne's shop. Looking for all the world like an English pub, a signboard hangs outside bearing the likeness of the bard from Stratford-upon-Avon. He looks on with satisfaction as his anglophone descendants flock to the Rue de l'Odéon.

THE TASTE OF FREEDOM

Not all the American soldiers make it home after the First World War. 117,000 of them rest in peace in the war cemeteries of Europe. Others have stayed voluntarily. Some even return after a short sojourn in their homeland. Paris has always been a popular destination for Americans. They come to expand their cultural horizons or to fraternise with the descendants of Rochambeau and Lafayette, who helped fight for American independence. After the First World War, the exchange rates are favourable and life is cheap. Ernest Hemingway tells the readers of the *Toronto Star* that a Canadian can live comfortably on $1,000 a year in Paris.[8] For some overseas visitors, the city has an altogether different advantage. Many young journalists, writers, musicians and visual artists find American provincialism limiting. The war brings F. Scott Fitzgerald, John Dos Passos, Ezra Pound, Dashiell Hammett and T.S. Eliot, to name but a few of the most famous, into contact with Paris. No matter how brief their stay, the experience is an unforgettable one. "They loved the freedom to write without censorship and to drink alcohol without being arrested."[9] Paris is not only associated with freedom of thought but also of skin colour, which is the antithesis of the situation in America. For many people, the land of the free is anything but.

380,000 black American soldiers, always strictly segregated in all-black units, have risked their lives at the Front just like their white fellow citizens. But they were not appreciated in the same way in their homeland. The black heroes of the 369th Infantry Regiment, to whom France awards the Croix de Guerre[10] for their exceptional courage, were excluded from the 1917 farewell parade in the United States. Put in uniform and empowered with self-confidence at the Front, they are seen as a threat to the strict racial segregation upon which the American social order is built. In 1917, Senator James K. Vardaman from Mississippi criticises the participation of black soldiers in the war: "Impress the negro with the fact that he is defending the flag, inflate his untutored soul with military airs, teach him that it is his duty to keep the emblem of the Nation flying triumphantly in the air... it is but a short step to the conclusion that his political rights must be respected."[11] This is akin to death for the majority of white Americans.

After enduring the trenches, freezing conditions, barrages, hunger and gas, the black soldiers are no longer prepared to take orders willy-nilly from white people. Their return sparks serious race riots, which go down in history as the 'Red Summer' of 1919. Hundreds of black veterans are imprisoned, dozens more are lynched and murdered. While white Americans hang the black soldier L.B. Reed, suspected of having a relationship with a white woman, from the bridge over the Sunflower River in Clarksdale, Mississippi,[12] in Paris the black fighter pilot Eugene Bullard marries Marcelle Eugénie Straumann. Bullard has been decorated by France with the Légion d'Honneur, the Croix de Guerre and the Croix du Combattant Volontaire.

Also in Paris, the French are pricking up their ears to the first sounds of jazz. It goes down a storm. The 'black devils' of the 369th Infantry Regiment, the 'Harlem Hellfighters', are responsible for transplanting their music to Europe.[13] Although forbidden by the US authorities from participating in the Victory Parade through Paris, the French invite their marching band to give a concert. The American band sets the Théâtre des Champs-Élysées alight. A single evening is such an overwhelming success that it is extended by six weeks. Immediately after the war, the black Mitchell's Jazz Kings, led by drummer Louis Mitchell, receive equally rapturous applause at the Casino de Paris in the Rue de Clichy. These are the first of a whole string of black musicians who will continue to enrapture

Odéonia

Paris for a long time to come. The Revue Nègre creates a furore at the Théâtre des Champs-Élysées in 1925. This time it is Josephine Baker, the black dancer in the famous banana dress, who turns heads. Then, in 1930, the song that Vincent Scotto composes for Josephine resounds in the revue *Paris qui me remue*: "*J'ai deux amours / Mon pays et Paris / Par eux toujours / Mon cœur est ravi. Manhattan est belle / Mais à quoi bon le nier / Ce qui m'ensorcelle / C'est Paris, c'est Paris tout entier.*" ["I have two loves / My country and Paris / For them always / My heart is thrilled. Manhattan is beautiful / But what's the use of denying / That what bewitches me / Is Paris, it's the whole of Paris."] The City of Light conquers the hearts of the whole world. White or black, it makes no difference in Paris.

The same is true of homosexuals and lesbians. One of the earliest Shakespeare and Company supporters is the American writer Gertrude Stein from Allegheny, Pennsylvania. Along with her partner Alice Babette Toklas from San Francisco, she swapped America for Paris as early as 1903. They live in the Rue de Fleurus, where they host a well-attended salon. In addition to writers, visual artists such as Picasso and Matisse also call around. When Sylvia Beach arrives in Paris, Gertrude Stein is already a cult figure. Other couples follow in the footsteps of Stein and Toklas, such as Janet Flanner, who has been writing for *The New Yorker* from Paris for fifty years, and her partner Solita Solano. Djuna Barnes, the great love of the writer Natalie Clifford Barney, describes "the leading figures of All Parisian Lesbians"[14] in her eccentric *Ladies Almanack* from 1928. Anything goes in Paris. The reverberations of sexual freedom also reach the sculptor Thelma Wood, the painter Romaine Brooks and the photographer Berenice Abbott, who also trade the United States for Paris. Gertrude Stein writes to a friend in New York: "It is there that we all were, and it was very natural for us to be there".[15] 'There' is not only Paris, but also and above all 'Odéonia', as Adrienne and Sylvia call their neighbourhood. From the Théâtre de l'Odéon, with its book stalls beneath the arcades, to the Carrefour de l'Odéon on the Boulevard Saint-Germain, antique shops, carpet dealers, a printer, a publishing house and two bookshops attract the cream of international literary talent.

PORNOGRAPHY!

In the meantime, Adrienne introduces her French authors to their anglophone counterparts, and Sylvia vice versa: "Sylvia carried the pollen like a bee. She fertilised the writers".[16] This cross-pollination between French and anglophone literature works brilliantly. In its series *Cabinet Cosmopolite*, the French publisher Stock issues translations of Katherine Mansfield, D.H. Lawrence and Virginia Woolf. Gallimard introduces John Dos Passos, William Faulkner and Erskine

Caldwell to the French, and Plon publishes E.M. Forster and Joyce's 1914 short story collection *Dubliners*.[17]

Jane Heap and Margaret Anderson, two friends from New York, gain first-hand experience of the contrast between Paris and the puritanical America of the early 1920s. In April 1920, they publish a sample of *Ulysses* – the great 'work in progress' on which James Joyce is labouring in Paris – in their literary magazine *The Little Review*. Pornography! The court issues Jane and Margaret with a $50 fine for 'obscenities'. Despite Judge John Woolsey of the US District Court in New York admitting that beyond the sexual context, *Ulysses* appears to be a "sincere and honest"[18] book, the publisher Ben Huebsch reneges on his decision to print the work. British publishers are also reluctant to get their fingers burnt. It is a catastrophe for the Irish writer, just as he has moved to the French capital from Trieste with his wife Nora Barnacle and his two children. Ever since their first meeting, James Joyce has been using Sylvia Beach's tiny kitchen behind her bookshop as an office. Joyce writes, whilst Sylvia helps him with his correspondence. This is not unusual. For the anglophone writers that turn up, Sylvia acts as a bank, post office, cook, psychologist and hotelier. Now she also becomes an investor. So fierce is Sylvia's belief in Joyce's masterpiece that she decides to publish it at her own risk. Her first outlay is on a prospectus with an order form that she sends to potential customers: "*Ulysses* by James Joyce will be published in the Autumn of 1921 by Shakespeare and Company – Sylvia Beach – 8, Rue Dupuytren, Paris, VIe."[19] Sylvia proofreads all the texts and borrows money to finance the printing: 700 pages sewn in hardback and with a plain blue cover: *Ulysses* by James Joyce.[20] It costs her a fortune. And her health.

On 2 February 1922, on the very day of James Joyce's fortieth birthday, his magnum opus sees the light of day. The publication ban from the American court works to the book's advantage. All the newspapers have written about it. For or against. Within three months, 35,000 copies of *Ulysses* are sold. The costs mount with every reprinting but the profits are slow to materialise. Joyce convinces Sylvia – on the verge of a nervous breakdown – to relinquish the rights to a large publishing house. Random House in America offers him $45,000 dollars.[21] In Britain, The Bodley Head from London reels in the prize much later. This is a bitter pill for Sylvia. Joyce has totally forgotten her; she does not regain a single franc of her investment. What she does receive is reflected glory. But despite that prestige, she can barely save Shakespeare and Company from bankruptcy.

Odéonia

INJURIES

The Great Depression knocks on Shakespeare and Company's door in the early 1930s. American customers stay away and writers return home. When André Gide hears that Shakespeare and Company is to shut up shop, he founds 'The Friends of Shakespeare and Company' in a frenzy of French solidarity. Jean Schlumberger, Jean Paulhan, André Maurois, Georges Duhamel, Valéry Larbaud and Jules Romains head a list of 200 authors who pay the minimum amount of 200 francs per year to attend Shakespeare and Company's lectures and debates. From the United States, authors and family send gifts, and on the sign above the door, Shakespeare clamps his lips firmly shut to prevent all this goodwill dribbling away.

If the Great Depression hounded them from Paris, the Spanish Civil War (1936-1939) brings a considerable number of anglophone journalists and writers back to the continent. Some join the fight on the side of the Republicans. But the sheer volume of German fighter planes that come to Francisco Franco's aid is overwhelming. More than half a million Spanish refugees are imprisoned in camps in France. The writers return to Paris. Their books describe the cruelties of the war. In his studio on the Rue des Grands Augustins, a stone's throw from Odéonia, Picasso paints the dismembered people and animals of Guernica.

In the meantime, things are looking up at Shakespeare and Company. But not for the love between Adrienne and Sylvia. During a visit to her father and sister in the United States – her mother Eleanor had moved back to Paris years before and had died there – Sylvia suffers from heavy bleeding. She undergoes a hysterectomy in a hospital in Connecticut. While she recovers from her operation, Adrienne rearranges her own affairs in Paris. In both her heart and her apartment, she replaces Sylvia with Gisèle Freund, a young German-Jewish photographer who has been making a name for herself in Paris since 1929. This is a bitter blow for Sylvia. Upon her return from America, she moves into the studio above Shakespeare and Company.

But the three remain friends. Every day, Sylvia buys vegetables at the Marché de Buci,[22] Adrienne cooks for all three of them, and as of old, smothers her nutritious dishes with her Savoyarde sauce, while Gisèle takes beautiful photos of the writers who visit. The wounds heal, and everything settles down somewhat in Odéonia. Whereupon the Germans once again appear on the horizon.

KULTURKAMPF

Adrienne and Sylvia are prepared. Warning signs have been emanating from Nazi Germany since 1933. The pair shelter writers, poets and other artists who, like Gisèle, have fled the country. Adrienne hides the Hungarian-Jewish writer Arthur Koestler in her apartment and she helps the German-Jewish Marxist cultural philosopher Walter Benjamin escape from Paris to Lourdes.[23] The American writer Henry Miller and the American-Jewish photographer Man Ray also flee to the South of France. James Joyce, for whom Sylvia cherishes a warm friendship despite his 'forgetfulness', tries to reach Switzerland with his family. Gisèle Freund waits until the Germans are firing upon the Parisian suburbs before finally fleeing.[24]

In 1926, the Préfecture de Police registers 26,000 Americans in Paris.[25] In September 1939 their number has swelled to 30,000.[26] Even though America is not yet involved in the war and Germany will not attack France until May 1940, 25,000 Americans head back home. Sylvia Beach stays. Paris has been declared an 'open city' by the French government, which has fled, and the Nazis occupy the capital on 14 June 1940. "*Achtung!*" The order from the loudspeakers reverberates against the façades. A Wehrmacht vehicle drives through the Rue de l'Odéon and announces the curfew. This marks the start of years of struggle. On the market in the Rue de Buci, groaning stalls are reduced to skeletons of empty planks and trestles within a week. The swastika flies above all official buildings. Censorship strikes Adrienne and Sylvia. Their English and American magazines are banned, their writers persecuted because of their work or for having joined the Resistance. The Nazis replace André Gide with the antisemitic author Pierre Drieu la Rochelle as head of the prestigious *Nouvelle Revue Française*. Along with a clique of French writers and journalists,[27] Drieu la Rochelle aligns himself with their *Kulturkampf* [culture war].

The year ends badly for Sylvia. A letter from America announces the death of her father. There is more bad news to come. After months of waiting, Joyce manages to cross the Swiss border with his wife and son. Their daughter remains behind in France. Her absence, coupled with the hostile reactions to his new book *Finnegans Wake*[28] and a lack of money, undermines his already poor health. The author of *Ulysses* dies on 13 January after an emergency operation in the Red Cross Hospital in Zurich. In Paris, Odéonia goes into mourning. The borders of the small but international kingdom are narrowed to the walls of La Maison des Amis des Livres and those of Shakespeare and Company. Inside, Adrienne, Sylvia and Françoise Bernheim, a young Jewish volunteer, persevere. Before long she becomes Françoise-with-the-yellow-star.

Odéonia

By the spring of 1941, the American community in Paris has shrunk to 2,000 residents. Women, men and children. No longer protected by their embassy,[29] all they can still depend upon is the safety net of the American Hospital in Neuilly, The American Library in the Rue de Téhéran, the American Church on the Quai d'Orsay and the American Cathedral of the Holy Trinity on the Avenue Georges V. As the American faithful pray to the Lord for deliverance from the Nazis and the end of the war, Germany's ally Japan bombs the US naval base in Pearl Harbor on Sunday 7 December. Four days later, Germany declares war on America. At a stroke, the Americans in Paris become enemies of the Third Reich.

Still before Christmas, the Nazis arrest 340 American men and imprison them in Frontstalag 122, also known as 'Camp de Royallieu', to the north of Paris. At Shakespeare and Company, Wehrmacht soldiers and the Gestapo come and leaf through Sylvia Beach's 'hostile' books. One day, one of them asks for the copy of *Finnegans Wake* from the shop window. Sylvia refuses. "That is my own copy. It's not for sale." Aggrieved, the man warns her that they could seize her shop. The door closes with a bang. Sylvia does not hesitate. Valuable manuscripts[30] and letters, as well as her collection of books, are all housed on the premises. Adrienne, Françoise-with-the-yellow-star and a few hastily assembled friends ferry books and documents to the fourth floor of Adrienne's private home at number 18. They dismantle the racks and pack up the photographs. Painter friends from the Rue de l'Odéon obliterate every possible reference to the shop, both indoors and outside. When the Nazis return that evening, Shakespeare and Company already seems to have been swept away by the Seine. On the carefully packed-away signboard, Shakespeare closes his eyes. Forever.

ZOO

On 24 September 1942, Sylvia, bike in hand, is returning home. She had heard that there was honey for sale in a shop near the Église de la Madeleine, on the Right Bank. Madame Allier, the faithful concierge, is in floods of tears. Sylvia comforts her. "But no, Miss Sylvia." This is not about Madame Allier: the Germans are actually searching for Sylvia. A truck approaches. Residents, shopkeepers and passers-by surround her in a protective ring. The truck is loaded with other American women, and Sylvia must join them. In the absence of a better alternative – the prisons are full of enemies of the Third Reich – the Nazis hold them in the Jardin d'Acclimatation, as the Parisians call the zoo in the Bois de Boulogne. From there, they are taken by train to Vittel. A number of dilapidated hotels in the fashionable spa town are fenced in with barbed wire. More than 1,000 women are imprisoned in Frontstalag 194. Above their heads, the swastikas flutter in the breeze from the Vosges.

In March of the following year, Sylvia's name crackles from the loudspeakers. Adrienne has finally secured her release – albeit with the help of Jacques Benoist-Méchin, an early friend of Shakespeare and Company,[31] now minister of police in the collaborationist Vichy government. Free once more, Sylvia goes into hiding in Paris.[32] But every night she steals to La Maison in the Rue de l'Odéon. There, together with Adrienne, she proofreads copy for the publications of the clandestine *Éditions de Minuit*.[33] Their writer friends sign their work under assumed names: 'Vercors', the region in which the Nazis are unable to break the spirit of the Resistance, is the author of *Le Silence de la Mer*, a.k.a. Jean Bruller; 'François la Colère' is Louis Aragon; 'Forez' is François Mauriac; 'Mortagne', publisher of the underground newspaper *Libération*, is Claude Morgan; while 'Jean Noir' is the poet Jean Cassou. Jean Paulhan, mainstay of La Maison des Amis des Livres, is discovered and imprisoned. Françoise-with-the-yellow-star-Bernheim of Shakespeare and Company is arrested in a round-up and transported to Auschwitz. She never returns.

Despite his literary embassy being closed, it is Shakespeare who makes Odéonia spring back onto its feet. In March 1944, a revival of his play *The Life and Death of King John* is staged to great acclaim at the Théâtre de l'Odéon. Besides Adrienne, several German officers are sitting in the audience. They glance around, slightly more nervous than the previous year. The opening words of a passage, which in the first year had slipped past unnoticed, now have the French on the edges of their seats: "Never such a power / For any foreign preparation / Was levied in the body of a land. / The copy of your speed is learn'd by them; / For when you should be told they do prepare, / The tidings come that they are all arrived." At the latter words applause breaks out, and the audience delivers a standing ovation.

For months, years, the French have been hoping for overseas help to expel the occupier. The theatrical company holds its breath. Quiet quickly returns. Clutching their caps and white with fury, the Wehrmacht officers leave the hall. But in people's minds, the Liberation has already begun. In the air too: on the edge of Paris the Allies bomb the Renault factory in Neuilly[34] and other industrial sites that the Nazis have used for their war economy.

SYLVIA!

From their window, Adrienne and Sylvia see it all happen. "At the foot of the Rue de l'Odéon from behind a barricade of furniture, stoves, rubbish bins and other

Odéonia

items, young men sporting the armband of the Forces Françaises de l'Intérieur (FFI) and a strange arsenal of weapons take aim at the Germans on the steps of the theatre further up the street. On 24 August, the Second Armoured Division under General Leclerc – finally – rolls into Paris.

"Sylvia! Sylvia!" It is Maurice Saillet, Adrienne Monnier's young employee, who comes running into the street. "Sylvia, Hemingway is here!" Adrienne encapsulates the indescribable happiness they all feel: "Sylvia stormed down the stairs four at a time. My sister and I saw her jump and be lifted up by two Michelangelo-shaped arms, her legs swinging in the air."[36] Hemingway and his self-assembled 'Hem Division', a chaotic bunch of French and Americans, first chase a few German snipers from the rooftops of Odéonia before liberating the wine cellar of Hemingway's beloved Ritz Hotel. After the war, Sylvia moves in with her cache of books and Maurice Saillet takes over the Maison des Amis des Livres from Adrienne. Sylvia and Adrienne remain close friends. In 1951, the painful disorder Adrienne has had for a long time receives a name: Ménière's disease. Adrienne halts the decline herself. On 19 June 1955, Sylvia visits her friend in the Hôpital Cochin near the Observatory. Adrienne is no longer responding. She lies in a coma after taking an overdose of medication and dies the next day.

Sylvia leaves her collection of 5,000 books to the American Library which, thanks to its own patron saint – Clara Longworth de Chambrun – has survived the war. In June 1962, forty years after the publication of *Ulysses*, the 75-year-old Sylvia Beach travels to Dublin for the opening of the James Joyce Tower and Museum. Did the journey tax her strength too greatly, or did she live at triple the intensity of other people? On 5 October of the same year, the book of Sylvia's life closes, in her studio above her life's work in the Rue de l'Odéon. A tear wells up in the eye of the English bard who once guarded the entrance.

With twinkling eyes beneath blonde curls, Sylvia Beach Whitman, daughter of Sylvia Beach fan George Whitman, continues the work of her namesake. No longer at 12, Rue de l'Odéon, but in the Rue de la Bûcherie,[37] still on the Left Bank of the Seine. Especially for her, Shakespeare has extended the border of Odéonia to encompass the address.

Odéonia

Henri Lafont and a sombre-looking Pierre Bonny in court.

2

BONNY AND LAFONT

Henri Lafont, biting his nails, and Pierre Bonny, gloom-ridden, are on trial. "From 24 December onwards, bitterly cold weather has swept through the northern and eastern regions – a situation not seen since the end of November 1942." Again, on Boxing Day 1944, it froze all day. In the dreary courtyard of the Montrouge barracks, the snow is already as hard as the underlying cobblestones. As the small procession files out, a murder of crows takes flight. Someone is coughing, a man with a cigarette. Others carry rifles. A scuffle breaks out in the rear with much pushing and pulling. One of the men is dragging his feet: not because of the biting cold, but because of the assembled firing squad. The man with the cigarette allows himself to be tied to the first post, the guns pointed at his heart. Even now, Henri Lafont has no regrets. Just before the order "take aim", he jeers at the chaplain: "Les cons, faudrait moderniser tout cela. Envoyez une belle Nana à la place d'un curé!"[1] *[The idiots, you should modernise all this. Send a beautiful girl instead of a priest!] The signal is given, the shots reverberate against the barrack walls. Lafont falls. His comrade Pierre Bonny has been struggling all morning, whining and begging for mercy. He slumps at the post, making it harder to aim. The second signal rapidly follows. The guns discharge. Bonny, too, is dead.*

PIOUS RESISTANCE

Which is worse, collaborating criminals or criminal collaborators? Bonny and Lafont are both. As run-of-the-mill Parisian gangsters, *recyclés du grand banditisme* [recruited from the criminal underworld],[2] they place their expertise at the disposal of the Gestapo during the early days of the Occupation. Their sinister organisation, known as the Carlingue, metes out death and destruction to all who stand in its way. Bonny and Lafont grow rich. They haul their victims to their robber's den in the Rue Lauriston, many of whom do not survive their 'interrogations'. On 20 July 1943, at the Au Voeu de Louis XIII bookshop at 68, Rue Bonaparte, they set a trap for *La Défense de la France*, a Resistance network. Geneviève de Gaulle, niece of the illustrious general, happens to visit the shop on the day in question.

Au Voeu de Louis XIII is a religious bookshop with a Catholic tenor. The name alludes to the collection of prayers and devotional acts that the childless Louis XIII addressed to the Blessed Virgin between 1632 and 1638 in the hope of conceiving an heir – and with success: his son, the future Louis XIV, was born on 5 September 1638. This literary shrine, operated by one Madame Wagner, is stuffed to the gills with hagiographies, Lourdes travel guides and Bibles in every conceivable language. No one suspects that the *La Défense de la France* is operating from the back rooms. To all intents and purposes, the shop is the covert editorial office of the organisation's banned newspaper. Its staff, which ranges from students to experienced Resistance members, hold clandestine meetings during which they deliver their copy or discuss plans. But they are not quite cautious enough! In early June 1943, Philippe Viannay, the network's founder, smells a rat. He wants to relocate the cell. But it takes time, too much time. Bonny and Lafont pay a visit to the shop on the evening of 19 July, and not to purchase a guide to Lourdes. Madame Wagner happens to be out of town. Her stand-in is captured, the trap is set.

The very next morning, the game is up. Unsuspecting journalists arrive with bag loads of incriminating literature. They are immediately overpowered by Bonny and Lafont's accomplices and restrained in the back of the shop. As many as eighty people are 'captured' that day. Bonny and Lafont are jubilant. Until Resistance fighter Pierre Marx – for one brief moment – threatens to derail everything. As the men from the Carlingue try to apprehend him, he draws a gun and shoots. But misses. Bonny, who is well trained, immediately fires back. Accurately. Badly wounded, Pierre flees and collapses in the metro. The Germans take over and carry him to the La Pitié-Salpêtrière hospital, now exclusively staffed by German doctors. Instead of receiving treatment, he is subjected to a brutal interrogation. Marx eventually slips into a coma and dies.[3]

LEFT BANK, WEST

'PAPERS!'

Meanwhile, back at the bookshop, a tall lady enters the room. At that precise moment, Bonny and Lafont have no idea of the prize before them. For her part, and thanks to Resistance publications, Geneviève de Gaulle immediately recognises the faces of the criminals who address her listlessly.

"*Bonjour madame*," Bonny nods sheepishly. "*Puis-je vous aider?*"

Geneviève quickly puts on a false front. "Certainly, monsieur, I have come to collect the Bible I ordered a while ago."

"*Et à quel nom, madame?*" continues Bonny.

"*Madame Lecomte, Germaine Lecomte*," Geneviève dissembles.

"Ah, I don't know anything about it," Bonny replies, for once truthfully. "But wait a moment, please. Madame Wagner will be here shortly. She will certainly help you."

In full knowledge that Madame Wagner is out of town, Geneviève maintains her composure.

"*Très bien*, then I'll run an errand first and come back," she takes a step towards the door.

"*Madame Lecomte!*" Lafont aggressively intervenes. "*Papiers s'il vous plaît!*" Bonny snatches the bag from her hands. In addition to a telling list of fellow Resistance fighters, they discover her true identity.

"*Pas vrai!*" they triumphantly exclaim. To have captured General de Gaulle's niece is almost beyond their comprehension. The family of that damned officer who, from the safety of London, is inciting France against the Reich. Drunk with glory, they drive to their 'offices' in the Rue Lauriston with their loot. There, they set to work on Geneviève for the first time. But they realise that this catch is too big for them, too important. They hand Geneviève over to the Gestapo, who in February 1944, transport her to Ravensbrück, a concentration camp for women north of Berlin. Heinrich Himmler immediately realises her value. She is imprisoned in the camp bunker upon her arrival. The guards are allowed to rough her up but, at the same time, must keep her alive. After all, Himmler wants to use her as his passport in the event of a German defeat. The Red Army beats him to it, however, in April 1945. The Russians liberate the camp and Geneviève, scarred and battered, is released. Charles de Gaulle is devastated by his niece's ordeal: "*Cela m'a laminé l'âme*" [it has crushed my soul], he later wrote.[4]

Bonny and Lafont

YOU WILL CALL ME 'BOSS'!

Bonny and Lafont unleash their own Reign of Terror during the Occupation of Paris,[5] a dark mixture of crime and collaboration. Bonny hails from the milieu of the Sûreté, the French intelligence services. After a career peppered with as many failures as successes, he is finally imprisoned for corruption, blackmail and assault in 1935. Upon his release, he becomes a self-employed private detective. No one knows the art of espionage quite like Bonny. He is an expert in handling firearms. He also boasts an extensive network of contacts, ranging from criminals to far-right political agitators. Bonny's 'expertise' takes Parisian collaboration in the Second World War to the next level: "He took a professional approach to the services offered at the Rue Lauriston", is how historian Jean-Paul Cointet summarised his questionable role.[6]

His partner in crime, Henri Chamberlin, a.k.a. Lafont, is no layabout either. He is head of the Carlingue. Lafont is a dyed-in-the-wool villain with an extensive criminal record. Which is why, at the start of the conflict, in 1939, he is locked up in the prison in Fresnes, south of Paris. Since the declaration of war, the French government has been using it as a detention centre for German citizens, to prevent them forming a 'fifth column' and attacking France from within. Lafont gets on with them like a house on fire. On 14 June 1940, German troops roll into Paris, *ville ouverte* [open city]. Those who can, flee the capital. Henri Lafont prefers to stay. He returns to the city, against the flow of refugees, in the company of two Germans he has befriended in Fresnes. In Paris, he finds his way to the occupier. The criminal turns collaborator.

Now that the Germans rule the roost in Paris, Lafont receives his reward: he is hired by the Abwehr, the German intelligence services. To help the occupiers infiltrate the Resistance networks via a French organisation, the Carlingue was created and headed by Lafont. Lafont decides to recruit his shock troops amongst the criminals in Fresnes. He arrives at the prison with a Gestapo-issued permit and enrols some thirty former inmates. Burglars, forgers, extortionists, rapists, traffickers and murderers. "*Tu es libre*," he tells them one by one. "*Mais tu m'appelleras patron!*" [You are free, but you will call me boss!] These flunkies will do the nastiest jobs for their master, of the kind that even the Gestapo refuse to sully their hands with at the start of the Occupation. These are the men who plant the bombs that destroy several synagogues in Paris on the nights of 2 and 3 October 1941. "You see, even the French don't really like the Jews," Helmut Knochen, deputy commander of the Sicherheitspolizei (SiPo), the security police, crows triumphantly. Later investigations showed that Knochen personally issued the order.

ABOVE THE LAW

In the meantime, business is booming for Bonny and Lafont. In between torturing Resistance fighters, they help themselves to Jewish property and steal the belongings of other deportees. A profitable trade in forged papers swells their coffers yet further, as do the bribes their victims pay to prevent the thugs from turning them over to the Gestapo. Bonny and Lafont turn a blind eye to those who can pay. After their appointment as head of purchases at the Wehrmacht, a sham post *par excellence*, their income reaches astronomical proportions. And they enjoy the fruits of their labour: they live the high life, throw decadent parties and drive a Bentley and Jaguar – all of which is conspicuous enough in Occupied Paris, where hunger and misery are gradually spreading. But the Carlingue bodyguards protect them from any potential Resistance attacks. Bonny and Lafont are now above the law.

To reward them for the unique dedication and sterling results, Helmut Knochen puts Bonny and Lafont in charge of the newly established Devisenschutzkommando [Foreign Exchange Protection Commando]. The aim is to track the flow of capital out of German control, mostly towards Switzerland. Bonny and Lafont are given a 20 per cent commission on the funds they uncover. They become less personally involved in the torture and executions as a result, preferring instead to focus their attention on their more lucrative Occupation-related activities. In gratitude, they give Knochen a Bentley as a wedding present. Meanwhile, the Abwehr, SS and Gestapo commanders spoil them rotten with celebratory entertainment at Le One-Two-Two, the luxury brothel at 122, Rue de Provence. To his pride, Lafont even acquires German citizenship. To help the Germans combat the seemingly indefatigable efforts of the Resistance, known as the Maquis, Lafont reaches out to his superiors with a bright idea: a new division of thugs from North Africa that he will recruit through his contacts. His notorious Brigade Nord-Africaine terrorises entire regions and is responsible for several mass executions of civilians, including those at Mussidan (52 victims), Saint-Germain du Salembre (34 victims) and Brantôme (25 victims). For these special 'achievements', Lafont is promoted to the rank of captain.[7]

Times are changing. With the Allies closing in as of June 1944, the Parisian Resistance redoubles its efforts in mid-August. Bonny and Lafont don't just see one fly in the ointment but a whole swarm. They destroy as much evidence as they can from the Rue Lauriston and flee. An anonymous farmhouse outside Paris becomes their hideout. It only takes a few days before Bonny and Lafont are located, along with the latter's mistress. The farmstead is surrounded. Upon their arrest, the companions are found to be in possession of 2.5 million French

Bonny and Lafont

francs in cash. The opportunistic Bonny confesses everything during his interrogation. To save his skin, he betrays numerous Carlingue lieutenants and fake Resistance fighters. Things hot up in Paris as a result.

His grovelling attitude is only moderately appreciated. The judge calls him *"une carpette"*, a doormat, especially when compared to his comrade Lafont, who is intractable. Kidnapping, torture, murder, theft, swindling, extortion, criminal appropriation of fixed and movable property, treason: the list of charges is long. The delinquent duo is sentenced to death. Lafont knows the offences are unforgivable. He makes peace with the situation. A few days before his execution, he reflects upon his wartime activities with *Maître* Drieu, his lawyer, without chagrin: "I have no regrets, Madame. It was worth it for four years amongst orchids, dahlias and Bentleys. I lived ten times faster, that's all."[8]

Bonny and Lafont

Violette Morris in male attire at the lesbian club *Le Monocle*.

LEFT BANK, WEST

THE HYENA OF THE GESTAPO?

3

Wednesday, 26 April 1944: it's another wartime day of sunshine, the rays warming the hinterland of Deauville and Honfleur. Normandy has enjoyed particularly dry weather for some time now and, as a result, clouds of dust betray the approach of any car from a distance. It has just gone six in the evening. On département road D27, between the sleepy hamlets of Épaignes and Lieurey, the men see the black Citroën traction avant ploughing ahead through a landscape of fields. La voilà! 'La' referring not to 'la voiture' but to 'elle': that is to say 'she', the woman behind the wheel. Violette Morris is on her way back to Paris when suddenly, after a bend in the road, a large farmer's cart rolls out on to the cobblestones, blocking her path. Rounds of submachine gunfire riddle the car, its driver and its passengers. Among the latter are Claude and Henri Bailleul, fourteen and twelve years old. Six weeks before the Normandy landings, the Resistance is eliminating the 'hyena of the Gestapo'. Fair enough, you might say, but what about those children…?

'JUST WHO ARE THESE CRAZED FURIES?'

In 1893, Violette is the third child to be born to the Morris family. They live on the Left Bank of the Seine at 61, Rue des Saints-Pères, the narrow section between the Boulevard Saint-Germain and the Rue de Grenelle. Coincidentally, this is the same house in which the film director and writer couple Marceline Loridan [née Rozenberg] and Joris Ivens[1] will later live. However, although they may have shared the same house, the lives of Marceline and Violette could not be further apart: being Jewish, the sixteen-year-old Marceline is deported from Paris to Auschwitz, but ultimately survives the war; at that same time in Paris, the word is that the fifty-year-old Violette is hunting down Jews and Resistance fighters, but she does *not* survive the war. There is also one other difference; in all likelihood, the biography of Marceline Loridan-Ivens[2] squares with the truth, whereas that relating to Violette Morris[3] does not.

Violette's mother, Élisabeth Sakakini, hails from a wealthy Jewish family in the Levant. Her maternal grandfather lives off his investments. Her paternal grandfather is a general, and her father, Jacques Morris, is a captain. Each of these officers has been awarded the Ordre National de la Légion d'Honneur. Consequently, her parents are delighted when their firstborn is a boy – Paul – because he can continue the family name and its military tradition. Alas, little Paul dies after only a few months. The next child is a girl: Louise Marie. Much to the regret of these gentlemen officers, so too is the next: Violette – even if she does display boyish traits pretty much from the outset.

To ensure that his girls receive a decent education, Captain Morris sends them to the Couvent de L'Assomption de Huy, a convent between Namur and Liège. Unlike other convents of the time, the sisters of Huy are not adherents to the negation of the body, otherwise viewed as the instrument of sin, potential feelings for which should be nipped in the bud. No, these sisters know how to make talent blossom in the girls entrusted to their care. Violette is in her element and excels at basketball, hockey and running. Sister Ellis, a British nun, becomes her first trainer and encourages the girl to participate in school swimming and athletics competitions in England. Later, between the wars as a young woman, Violette will return to England to improve on the then world record for discus throwing.

At the age of fifteen, Violette is 1.66 metres tall, weighs 74 kilos and has a shoulder circumference of 1.2 metres. "*Un garçon manqué*", writes *Le Miroir des Sports*.[4] At seventeen, she is boxing against male opponents, and in 1913, aged twenty, she finishes fifth as the only female participant in the French championships for long distance swimming. In 1914 – when France had already been mobilised against Germany for the past 20 days – she is married at the town hall in the 8th *arrondissement*'s Rue de Lisbonne beneath a swirling ceiling fresco[5] depicting a female figure with angel's wings as she starts her ascent to the heavens. Flying is a sport in its own right, thinks Violette. Her bridegroom, Cyprien, goes off to fight at the Front a few days later and Violette, true to form as the granddaughter of General Morris, joins the war effort, initially as a motorcycle dispatch rider and then as an ambulance driver for the Red Cross. They have been looking for someone who will take on dangerous assignments. In 1916, Violette slaloms between the craters and command posts at Verdun. She gets pleurisy for her trouble. She recovers quickly and, a year later, takes part in the first French women's athletics championships, away from the Front. It is around this time that Violette ceases to hide her sexual preference for women.[6] Violette and Cyprien are childless and divorce after the war. This suits Violette perfectly and, with relish, she goes on to represent the French tricolour at the many subsequent international competitions aimed at helping Europe forget the anguish of the First World War.

Although the rest of the country may still be in trauma, in Paris the first ripples of the Roaring Twenties are being felt. The *zeitgeist* is one of pushing the boundaries, upsetting age-old traditions and challenging conventional standards of morality and decency. However, when it comes to any given field of sport, women still have to fight for their rightful place. "A woman is built not to fight, but to procreate."[7] So says Pierre de Coubertin in 1900 at the second modern Olympic Games, in Paris, where he sets the 'right example' by prohibiting the participation of women. Only golf and tennis are permissible. History fondly recalls such names as the tennis star Suzanne Lenglen, the French sportswoman who was also an elegant ambassador for Parisian chic and good taste. Rather more poorly remembered by posterity is Violette Morris who, owing to subsequent events, few now associate as a sports champion, breaking barriers in all disciplines and at numerous championships. At the time, however, she is bagging medals and trophies in decidedly male fields such as javelin throwing, football, cycling, and motorcycle and car racing. If Lenglen is entrancing the aristocracy, Violette is beguiling the masses. Men and women throughout France look up to her. The former because she challenges and intrigues them, the latter because Violette is giving the men tit-for-tat. Violette smokes in public, dresses like a man, has a man's haircut and a man's way of talking. In the France of the early 1920s, she is a controversial figure, often making the front page of the newspapers.

On its front page in the 21 August 1922 edition, *Le Figaro* bursts with admiration for Violette, but there is a sting in the editorial tail: "Not a single

The hyena of the Gestapo?

feminist victory carries the force of Miss Morris's triumphs in weight throwing." But next there's the wagging finger: "Yet do we not see that, through those weights, she is simultaneously throwing off the subservience of her sex, centuries of repression? Just who are these crazed furies? What a sorrowful spectacle of physical degradation lies in those feral eyes, distorted bodies and contorted mouths, simply to reach their end goal. We wish upon women challenges other than braving wind and dust. The fact is that violent exercise was probably not made for women."[8]

Violette puts the critics behind her, just as she does her male competitors at the popular Bol d'Or of 1927, a gruelling motor racing event in which drivers must cover as many kilometres as possible in 24 hours on a tricky route through woodland along the Seine between Saint-Germain-en-Laye and Poissy. As the winner, Violette Morris comes in at just under 1,700 kilometres in her indefatigable Benjamin. Her successes in motor racing make Violette more famous and loved than ever: "*La plus intrépide des sportives de notre pays*" [the most intrepid sportswoman in our country], writes *Le Miroir des Sports*. However, while Violette may be adored by some, she is increasingly becoming a hate figure for others: conservative sports bodies, journalists and politicians cannot stomach her attitude and loathe her unashamed openness about her sexual orientation. The Fédération Féminine Sportive de France (FFSF) is anything but amused either. Its most popular 'show pony' ultimately threatens to break-up the Fédération in acrimony.

A RETURN TO ORDER

At the peak of Violette's glory, reactions to her hit home. A row about her masculine attire leads to the withdrawal of her sports licence, which means she is unable to compete in the 1928 Olympic Games in Amsterdam or in other competitions. Her clothing is merely the pretext, an excuse. The real reason is more deeply seated; after a decade, the invigorating force of the Roaring Twenties has run its course and, from 1930 on, right of centre and far right political parties enter the scene along with their paramilitary organisations. They seek a return to order. Their new values are '*travail, famille, patrie*' [work, family homeland].

This divorcée, lesbian sports champion who 'wears the trousers' does not fit that image. In 1929, she makes a drastic decision that only makes matters worse. Perhaps it is because of discomfort with her self-image and a desire to be even more of a man, but whatever the case, she decides to have her breasts removed, making her an early transgender icon. Her explanation is that she needs "to get closer to the steering wheel in her racing car".[9] Her voluntary double mastectomy is seen as unacceptable behaviour in a France that needs mothers to 'repopulate' the nation after the demographic cull inflicted by the First World War. It is not only patriotic France that is shocked, but also the sports world which gives her a firm thumbs down. The Joan of Arc of sport is downgraded to a corrupter of youth.[10] Although Violette does not take this lying down and sues the Fédération, she still loses the 'trousers case'. Her sporting life is over.

In the early 1930s, Violette seeks out a new *raison d'être*. As a motoring enthusiast, she opens a car accessories business on the Rue Roger-Bacon in the Ternes quarter of the 17th *arrondissement*. This goes under all too soon. In a photograph by Brassaï from 1932, taken in Le Monocle, a lesbian club on the Boulevard Edgar Quinet, a corpulent man in suit, tie and pocket handkerchief is holding his arm around an elegant woman. The woman is unmistakably a woman. The man, however, is no man but Violette Morris.[11] On 11 January 1933, Violent moves into the houseboat *La Mouette* moored on the Seine in Neuilly and earns a living by performing as an *artiste lyrique*, a cultural discipline that she had already been pursuing whilst engaged in competitive sports. But life is not to be lyrical for Violette. Every so often there is drinking and partying aboard *La Mouette*. Sometimes rather too much, such as on Boxing Day 1937, when her life takes a dramatic turn and a drunken man attempts to attack her... and Violette shoots him in self-defence. This is borne out by the subsequent investigation. Violette goes free, but her already sullied coat of arms has been still further tarnished: she's killed someone!

A woman who openly expresses her sexual orientation, prefers being a man rather than a woman, who behaves wholly as if she were a man, who makes a mockery of the sports bodies, who defeats men on their own turf, who has had her breasts removed and, lastly, who has shot a man dead: these are the fatal puzzle pieces laid out for all to see when explanations come in the wake of the Liberation in 1944.

HIMMLER'S CLOSE ACQUAINTANCES

It is an incontrovertible fact that Violette chooses the wrong side in the war. Just before the outbreak of hostilities she is still regularly chauffeuring her friend Jean Cocteau – the creative jack-of-all-trades – to his lover, the actor Jean Marais, mobilised to the Front. After the Occupation of Paris,[12] however, it is Christian Sarton du Jonchay whom she drives around, a pilot she has known since before the war – after all, flying has also been a dream of hers alongside motor racing. Only, the thing is... du Jonchay is a wrong 'un. He is principal private secretary to

The hyena of the Gestapo?

Pierre Laval, the prime minister of the collaborationist government under the Vichy regime of Marshal Pétain. It is du Jonchay who opens the gates of Vichy to Violette. They lead to collaboration and black marketeering. It is this that places the former sports champion on the radar of an agency established by General de Gaulle: the Bureau Central de Renseignements et d'Action (BCRA) [Central Bureau of Intelligence and Operations][13] of the Free French government in London. With economic collaboration rife in France – at every level – the BCRA feels it has other fish to fry. But when the Liberation comes, and in contrast to previous reports obtained, the Bureau suddenly receives certain highly incriminating information about said V. Morris.

It appears from new reports and statements taken from the Resistance after the Liberation that, in 1936, having been ousted by the Fédération Féminine Sportive de France, Violette had accepted an invitation to the Olympic Games in Berlin from none other than Hitler. The Nazis are said to have received the former top athlete with great ceremony. Inspired by German power and charmed by the Third Reich's adoration of physical athleticism, it is then that she began to spy for Nazi Germany. She is said to have secured top-secret plans about the Maginot Line,[14] passing them on to the enemy. According to yet another strand of information, Violette – who at that time is a fifty-year-old, overweight, mannish lesbian without breasts – has been mistress to Himmler, the 'most powerful man in Europe' after Hitler. What is more, the senior officers of the SS and its intelligence arm the Sicherheitsdienst in Paris, Helmut Knochen and Karl Oberg, are also said to have been lured into her love nest. Together with Pierre Bonny and Henri Lafont (lowlife criminals, black marketeers and founders of the Carlingue, the French equivalent of the Gestapo), she has been hunting down the Resistance, Jews and anyone standing in the way of the Third Reich. Blind with rage for what the French have done to her, she is said to have personally tortured her quarry to the point of death. Sometimes this is in the Carlingue's cellars at 93, Rue Lauriston, other times in the Gestapo version at 11, Rue des Saussaies or in the basement at 180, Rue de la Pompe. These addresses alone are enough to have any Parisian break into a cold sweat. Meanwhile, her black-market empire has flourished, making her a fortune.

Consequently, the order from the Haut commandement de la Résistance in London comes not a moment too soon so as to prevent anything worse happening. The telegram is unequivocal: "Kill spy Violette Morris immediately by any means possible – Stop – Detect and eliminate agents in contact with her – Stop – Priority order – End."[16] The rain of bullets that one week later steeps the Normandy coast's dry hinterland in blood puts paid to the crimes of this diabolical hyena. This task is performed by the Maquis Surcouf, the

Resistance network led by charismatic Resistance fighter and local grocer, Robert Leblanc. Leblanc's men find on Violette's body a Gestapo membership card and a list of Resistance workers' names and hideouts. There is no doubt they would have been dealt with by Violette Morris in her notorious style. Shot dead alongside her in the car are a couple of *charcutiers*, their two children and their son-in-law. After their execution, Robert Leblanc reports to his superiors as follows: "The infamous French Gestapo agent Violette Morris and her friends, the Bailleul family of Beuzeville, 'close acquaintances of Himmler', head of the Gestapo and to whose organisation they contributed, were apprehended and executed on the road between Épaignes and Lieurey, while they were travelling *en route* to Paris".[17]

One year after the war's end, he makes this submission once again to the French police. Hearings of this kind were initiated after 8 May 1945, with the Resistance having to account for particular executions. These hearings give a good deal of leeway to the Resistance in those few weeks before the Normandy landings, but this does not include the shooting of children. And so it is that Leblanc is incarcerated in Bernay Prison, a stone's throw from the D27 where the events unfolded. He wants to be released as soon as he can. But how?

MONSTROUS LIES

"The problem with the story of Violette Morris's death is that two children were killed by the Resistance and, consequently, it was necessary afterwards to justify this execution, and that is how the storytelling got started. She was accused of being a Gestapo agent, but the dossiers are a blank on that subject, there is nothing."[18] By stating in new research from 2011 that the dossiers are a blank, French historian Marie-Josèphe Bonnet touches a painful nerve. The problem is the death of the children; there needs to be an explanation that excuses their execution vis-à-vis the post-war authorities, one which keeps intact French sympathy for the heroes of the Resistance. That explanation goes by the name of Violette Morris. Her historically unconventional lifestyle and the prejudices attached to it are fertile soil in which to sow hate.

Consequently, numerous testimonies, articles and books looking back on the Second World War and the Resistance peel away the image of the fêted sports champion to reveal a spy and fearsome accomplice to the Occupier. Above all, it is the author Raymond Ruffin, "considered one of the most serious diarists of the period 1939-1945",[19] who pulls out all the stops to highlight her crimes. In two biographies, this diarist deftly pieces together the parts of the puzzle as supplied to him by Violette's controversial life. Whereas his first publication in 1989,

The hyena of the Gestapo?

La Diablesse – La véritable histoire de Violette Morris,[20] maintains a description of the lesbian former athlete as a she-devil, spy and mistress to the Occupier in the possession of a Gestapo membership card [sic], his follow-up to this work fifteen years later mutates her into a bloodthirsty beast of prey: *Violette Morris – La hyène de la Gestap.*[21]

"That list of resistance members that the Maquis Surcouf finds on Violette's body does not exist and never existed; it is not to be found in any archive anywhere. Likewise, the order from London to execute Violette Morris is false. The telegram in question was fabricated afterwards. Her membership of the Gestapo? By the time of his second biography, Ruffin had tumbled to the fact that the Gestapo did not issue membership cards; instead, the author simply replaces this with the expression *ses papiers d'identité.*" Bonnet reveals not only this but much more besides in her research publication *Violette Morris – Histoire d'une scandaleuse* (2011). Step by step, and with unquestionable precision, the historian wades through archives, correspondence and even bank accounts. In so doing she unravels the myth created after the Liberation of France by the Resistance for the purpose of placing blame for the death of the Bailleul children and the son-in-law Henri Hémery squarely on the shoulders of the former sports champion.

Violette Morris's sin was one of economic collaboration, a sin she had in common with so many other French citizens, none of whom was ever executed on that charge.[22] Yet Violette's bank account was hardly burgeoning as a result of that complicity, which implies that her assignments were of little importance. In other words, and contrary to the allegations, she did not earn a fortune at all. Nor was Violette a spy; she did not secure the Maginot Line plans, never mind pass them on to the enemy. She was no more Himmler's mistress than the Beuzeville *charcutiers* were the Nazi leader's 'close acquaintances'. Nor was this fifty-year-old, overweight, mannishly close-cropped woman without breasts the mistress to Knochen and Oberg in Paris. She never hunted down Resistance fighters or Jews – her mother, Élisabeth Sakakini was Jewish. Violette never tortured anybody either, any more than the Bailleul children betrayed their teacher to the Germans, a deed levelled at them by the Resistance. Finally, the son-in-law was neither a Gestapo informer nor an officer as he was characterised in varying versions of the story. Yet, thanks to all the accusations directed at the occupants of that bullet-riddled Citroën, the damage had been done and, to a greater or lesser extent, they all 'deserved' a bullet in the head.

In the weeks prior to the Normandy landings, the local Resistance groups become anxious and proceed to execute collaborators. So it is that at the beginning of June they also shoot dead the Bailleul's neighbour, the café owner Beaudouin, along with his family at their home on the market square in Beuzeville. Are the Resistance leaders jockeying for the position of their own underground group? Are they settling scores before the Allies arrive? Are they eyeing up potential medals of honour? Looking for promotion? Given all the weighty baggage from her past, Violette Morris is the perfect target for an 'act of heroism'. The deaths of the 'treacherous teenagers' is an *accident de parcours*. Collateral damage. Four days after the raid, Robert Leblanc is promoted to the rank of *arrondissement* military commander.[23]

The ten-man command unit, their names cited by Bonnet, probably never thought they would be called to account for their actions. They succeed in getting away with it only by creating a monster accountable for deeds more heinous by far than the death of two children, a monster that must be stopped in its tracks to prevent worse from happening. That monster is the hyena, Violette Morris.

SMALL FRY AND BIG FISH

What are we to make of the execution of Violette, the *charcutier* and the café owner and their families – small-scale entrepreneurs in Beuzeville – when set against the impunity given to the biggest French economic collaborators, bankers and industrialists? They emerge from the war wealthy, pursue their business interests, hold political office and, at a ripe old age, slip away peacefully in their beds. In her in-depth study *Industriels et banquiers français sous l'Occupation* (2013), the French historian Annie Lacroix-Riz demonstrates that, contrary to popular belief, the worlds of high finance and big industry did not start collaborating economically *after* the Occupation of France but *before* it. Well before the war, and notably after 1933 when Hitler comes to power, French bankers and industrialists are eyeing the social and political model of Nazi Germany.[24] A parliament rendered powerless, a censored press, muzzled trade unions, reduced wages and extended working hours, lock-outs at will, unregulated price fixing: French bosses can only dream of such things. However, the most appealing aspect of all is the elimination of their Jewish business partners or competitors.

In addition to this, Hitler is offering higher prices for their raw materials and products than they get from the Conseil National de Défense, which results in them bending over backwards to feed the German war machine. In 1939, an engineer from steel and weapons manufacturer Krupp attests to the fact that "two thirds of the steel that we use comes from French businesses, particularly those in North Africa."[25] The Compagnie Française des Mines de Bor, the jewel in the crown of the French group Champin-Mirabaud which had run into financial

The hyena of the Gestapo?

trouble, is wholly resuscitated thanks to German rearmament. In fact, French industry exerts itself so much on behalf of Germany that its own national armaments programme suffers in the face of it. "As a result of this," argues Lacroix-Riz, "the great majority of contemporary French bankers and industrialists contributed towards the defeat [of France]."[26]

Many show no reticence in voicing their opinion. "I don't give a damn about the Conseil National de Défense!"[27] cries a furious Louis Renault, founder of the eponymous car factory when, in 1939, France asks him to produce more military vehicles for his own country. Renault boasts so much about his visits to Hitler that those in his circle nickname him *Hitler m'a dit* [Hitler-told-me].[28] His nephew-in-law, François Lehideux, general director of the Société Anonyme des Usines Renault, and Jacques Barnaud, general director of the merchant bank Banque Worms, jointly encourages other French senior executives to found Franco-German cartels and *sociétés mixtes* [mixed companies] with German businesses, such as those between Rhône-Poulenc and IG Farben, or between La Société d'Électrochimie et d'Électrométallurgie des Aciéries Électriques d'Ugine (SECEM) and Deutsche Gold- und Silber-Scheideanstalt (Degussa). Later, in its factory in Villers-Saint-Sépulcre in the Oise region, SECEM will go on to manufacture lethal Zyklon B pellets for the extermination camps.

At the same time, the high finance and big industry sectors are funding far-right political parties and paramilitary organisations. Pierre Taittinger, the great champagne and hospitality trade industrialist and a Nazi sympathiser, is sponsoring the youth league Jeunesses Patriotes and the group La Cagoule, to which the founder of L'Oréal, Eugène Schueller, also belongs. Since before the war, the paramilitary organisation La Cagoule has been committing armed attacks to disrupt the French Third Republic, so hated by entrepreneurial France with its strikes and its Popular Front government. "Fortunately, Hitler is going to put this house back in order",[29] asserts Georges Lang, chairman of the large printing group Curial-Archereau.

Once the Reich has occupied France, the bankers and industrialists intensify their collaboration. They fill important posts in the Vichy government and enrich themselves at the expense of the French people who pay the bill for German occupation by way of personal income tax: from 25 June 1940, the Banque de France deposits 400 million francs a day in occupation costs into the account of the Reichskreditkasse of Paris (RKK). After November 1942, this rises to 500 million – the Allied invasion of North Africa having increased the occupier's outgoings. "Simultaneously, the capital held by the big French banks doubles or triples, the profits of the *société mixte* Théraplix quadruple, the stock price increases sevenfold for 35 major stock exchange-listed companies, including 4 banks, 6 insurers, 7 coal mines, 5 railway companies, 13 gas and electricity companies... and so it goes on. The assets held by François Lehideux, the aforementioned nephew-in-law of Louis Renault, are estimated at 104,492,000 francs even by the end of 1943."[30] A fortune at that time. No, those engaged in high finance and big industry are *not* "brutally confronted" by an occupying force that "leaves them with no option open other than enforced cooperation". On the contrary, they welcome their 'preferred partners' with open arms so that, together, they can create the continental, economic superpower of their dreams.

Jean Bichelonne, a politician in the Vichy government who, before the war, was chief of staff to the French armaments minister, advocates radical integration with Germany. To that end, he organises the Service du Travail Obligatoire [STO], which sends hundreds of thousands of French citizens into the German armaments industry. Just before fleeing to Germany at the end of the war, he states: "Gentlemen, Germany's armies have been defeated, all our work has been for nothing, we've put our money on the wrong horse. You can now throw dice or play cards to bet on where I'm going to be hanged or shot."[31] But neither outcome comes to pass. Bichelonne dies prematurely from a pulmonary embolism. Barnaud the banker lives to be 69, cosmetics boss Schueller reaches 76, champagne king Taittinger 78, and car maker Lehideux 94. All expand their business ventures after the war. As leader of the provisional government that France operates after the Liberation, Charles de Gaulle does not want investigation and punishment; instead, his goal is to look to the future and to rebuild the nation with every player involved. Consequently, far from the dusty lane where once upon a time Violette Morris, the Bailleuls, their children and their son-in-law were riddled with bullets, the collaborationist men at the top (scarcely any women were among their number, with rare exceptions such as Coco Chanel[32]) gave up the ghost peacefully in their beds in Paris. There, they were surrounded by their heirs, some of whom do their utmost to eradicate these dark pages from their corporate history with the help of communications agencies and law firms.

THE TRUTH WINS OUT IN THE END (OR DOES IT?)

Violette has neither children nor heirs; she has neither communications gurus nor lawyers. That is why the Parisian-of-so-many-faults has remained for decades the perfect pretext for the deadly raid on *département* road D27, as well as a highly commercial but defenceless subject for magazines and books. Who would ever be bothered to seek the truth? Nevertheless, the truth has come to light. However, the truth is not enough. The stubbornness of the lies becomes

The hyena of the Gestapo?

apparent in 2017. After the death of the French writer and journalist Roger Grenier, Gallimard publishes his correspondence with his close friend Brassaï, the photographer who took the aforementioned photograph of Violette Morris at the lesbian club Le Monocle. Without batting an eyelid or adding a footnote, and six years *after* the research conducted by Marie-Josèphe Bonnet, a reputable publisher and likewise author once again has this to say about Violette: "In 1936, Hitler's government invited her to the Olympic Games in Berlin as a guest of honour and recruited her as a spy. She furnished information about the Maginot Line and, under the Occupation, belonged to the French Gestapo, became to all intents and purposes a torturer and ended up being killed by the Resistance in 1944."[33]

When asked by a journalist for *France Culture* about the tenacity with which – even to this day – Violette Morris is branded as 'the hyena of the Gestapo', Marie-Josèphe Bonnet replies with the dilemma familiar to many historians: "When you've built up such a legend, you can't dislodge it with facts."[34]

The hyena of the Gestapo?

Georges Boillot at the wheel of his Torpedo.

4

BOILLOT,
THE TORPEDO

On 30 May 1914, the French motor racing driver Georges Boillot, the king of the steering wheel, is racing towards victory in the Indianapolis 500-Mile Race. But tyre trouble means that his fellow countryman René Thomas wins the prestigious American prize. Two months later, Boillot shoots out of the starting blocks at the Lyon Grand Prix. Revenge for Indianapolis! His Peugeot L76 – la torpille [the torpedo] – has no pity for the Mercedes of Christian Lautenschlager, the German who challenges him in vain. The French are confident of victory: Boillot already has two Grands Prix trophies to his name and his lead is now significant... until the final circuit, when black smoke plumes up from beneath his bonnet. Lautenschlager wins, on French soil. Less than a month later, the Germans are back, for a much bigger battle. Race circuits make way for trenches and the symbolic torpilles *become real torpedoes. Miraculously, Paris is let off the hook: the German advance stops at the Marne, and that is partly thanks to Boillot.*

A LION AT THE WHEEL

Germany's declaration of war on France[1] falls on the very day of Georges Boillot's 30th birthday – 3 August 1914. In the photos from Indianapolis, he stares proudly into the lens, posing in his new magic box on wheels. With jet-black, slicked-back hair, spirited dark eyes and a black moustache above his self-confident smile, he resembles an Italian. His *joie de vivre* is unmistakable: Boillot feels in the prime of his life. The industrious young mechanic has made his own luck. In 1908, at the age of 24, he joins the Lion-Peugeot team, the competition arm of the illustrious brand. He immediately wins the Grand Prix for *voiturettes* [lightweight cars], in Dieppe. A year later, he triumphs in the same category in a packed Vélodrome d'Hiver[2] on the Rue Nélaton in Paris. The young Boillot sweeps from victory to victory.

But he dreams of more – the trophy of the international Grand Prix de l'Automobile Club de France. The racing mechanic makes his dream a reality. Two years in a row, in 1912 in Dieppe and in 1913 in Amiens, he triumphs over the British, Germans, Italians and single Belgian, Josef Christiaens, who competes in an Excelsior. With his new machine, the Peugeot L76, Georges Boillot beats them all. On the Place de la Concorde, the champagne flows freely in the discreet halls of the sumptuous palace of the Automobile Club de France, the oldest in the world.[3] The French are once again a force to be reckoned with.

The *L Soixante-Seize* is a devil. The L stands for Lion, derived from the name Lion-Peugeot, and the *soixante-seize* [seventy-six] for the cylinder capacity. For some time now, the competition arm of the brand has been running on empty. The Italians at Fiat and the Germans at Mercedes are performing considerably better. It is Georges Boillot who convinces Peugeot to give its racing programme a fresh boost. Together with the co-drivers Jules Goux and Paolo Zuccarelli and the engineer Ernest Henry, Boillot forms a small cell, and with the financial blessing of the big car manufacturer they build a technological wonder in a warehouse near Paris: a compact, four-cylinder monobloc engine with a capacity of 7,600 cc and with – for the first time in history – four valves per cylinder and a dual overhead camshaft (DOHC).

This compact engine with a dry sump system allows the driver to sit lower down in the chassis, which delivers a reduced centre of gravity, and therefore greatly improved roadholding. In addition, they equip their engine with a hemispherical combustion chamber and a central spark plug, also completely new for this era. Finally, to ensure that the competition is left trailing far behind them, they equip the engine with a fixed drive shaft whereas the competitor engines are still propelled by a chain. What's more, the design of the L76 is perfectly streamlined, from nose to tail. With its engine that now produces 148hp, *la torpille* – the torpedo, as it is immediately dubbed – achieves a speed of over 190 kilometres per hour.

Because of the technical hocus pocus, Peugeot's official engineers call Georges Boillot and his friends *les charlatans*. But as soon as their monster puts its rubber feet on the tarmac, the charlatans smash all existing records. In addition to numerous other victories, Boillot is the only person to win the Grand Prix de l'Automobile Club de France and the Course de Côte du Mont Ventoux twice in a row. His friend Jules Goux wins the Indianapolis trophy in 1913 with the same car. On 4 July 1914, before the infamous duel with Lautenschlager – which he loses due to an overheated engine – he once again banishes his demons. This is his final race. On a circuit, that is.

GENERAL WITHOUT AN ARMY

Halfway through the summer of 1914, the First World War is raging in all its ferocity. After their murderous and incendiary passage through Belgium, the German First, Second and Third Armies led by the generals von Kluck, von Bülow and von Hausen are advancing towards France like a flying scythe. Four further German armies stand ready in Alsace, Lorraine and in the Vosges. The French do not sit idly by. On 7 August they invade their former province of Alsace. The advance is short-lived. By the end of August, they have been brought to a standstill. The supremacy of the Germans means that the French are obliged to retreat towards Paris.

There, President Poincaré has just appointed the socialist René Viviani as his new prime minister, but he is not given much time to govern. On 3 September, German Uhlans[4] are already bivouacking just a few dozen kilometres to the north of Paris on a reconnaissance mission. That same day, Poincaré and his government turn their backs on the French capital and flee to Bordeaux. A third of Parisians leave the city,[5] but those who stay take a dim view of these *tournedos à la bordelaise*.[6] By fleeing, the French government wants to avoid a repeat of their painful confinement during the Franco-Prussian War of 1870/1, when the Prussians surrounded and hermetically sealed off the city.[7]

From 4 September, the Parisians come under the control of the military governor of Paris, General Joseph Gallieni. Gallieni is ordered by Alexandre Millerand, minister of war, to defend Paris *à outrance* [to the utmost]. "Do you fully understand, minister, what *à outrance* means in military terms?", Gallieni asks Millerand, who sits in a waiting car with his head in his hands, ready to disappear to Bordeaux. "It means: destruction, ruins, blown-up bridges, burning

Boillot, the Torpedo

cupolas." *"A outrance!"* Millerand confirms with a gravedigger stare. To Gallieni it feels like a death sentence, he is convinced that he is staying behind to be killed.[8]

Gallieni is a general with extensive experience but no army. All the troops are stationed at the Front in the north and the east of the country. In Vitry-le-François, halfway between Paris and Nancy, the brand-new French commander-in-chief General Joffre[9] is establishing his Grand Quartier général. From there he directs the movements of his generals Lanrezac, Ruffey, de Langle de Cary, de Castelnau and Dubail. Together their armies form a line of defence that stretches from Maubeuge in the *département* of Nord right through to Belfort in the Vosges. Unlike von Moltke, Chef des Grossen Generalstabes [Chief of the Great German General Staff], who dictates the manoeuvres from his office in Berlin, Joffre is in direct contact with his generals. For this he must spend long hours braving the French fields and roads behind the Front. The blond, moustachioed general finds a brilliant solution for this, which combines business with pleasure: he has Grand Prix winner Georges Boillot[10] drive him around at a speed of some 115 kilometres per hour.

So Boillot becomes General Joffre's chauffeur. At least, that's what the great American historian Barbara Tuchman claims in *The Guns of August* (1962), her unsurpassed account of the first month of the First World War. According to a friend of Boillot's, who was a freelance staffer on the trendy sports magazine *La Vie au grand air*,[11] this is nevertheless a myth.[12] In 1914, Joffre's official chauffeur is a descendent of the noble d'Albufera family.[13] In 1915, however, he leaves this position to enrol in the artillery school at Fontainebleau where he becomes a specialist in heavy artillery tractors. So, it is perfectly possible that Boillot occasionally drove General Joffre. This is not disputed. Historical sources, however, such as the yellowing editions of *La Vie au grand air,* have only recently become digitally available, and they show how Boillot is deployed for dangerous missions – for drives that demand precision, courage and daring. The chicanes of the Grand Prix are nothing in comparison to the constant slaloming between rifle bullets and bomb craters during the war.

'SEE YOU IN SIX WEEKS' TIME'

On the German side, everything is going like clockwork in early August. More specifically, it is in accordance with the infamous Schlieffen Plan: a cunning military strategy to eliminate the French army as quickly as possible during a war with France. That plan has been sitting in the German Ministry of War yearning to be put into action since 1905. Crucial to this attack scenario is the advance of the German First Army. This must advance in a wide arc along the

English Channel. Once to the south of Paris, it must swing inland to attack the French defence from the rear and drive the French armies towards the German Sixth and Seventh Armies. The job must be completed within six weeks. Kaiser Wilhelm II will then deploy his troops against the Russians on the Eastern Front. The Kaiser is enthusiastic. "You will be home before the leaves fall from the trees",[14] are his words as he addresses his departing soldiers.

Six weeks. A rapid annihilation of the French army. This is, however, without 'the mistake' by the German veteran von Kluck. Or Gallieni's bravado. Von Kluck succeeded in skilfully surrounding Paris during the Franco-Prussian War and is hand-picked by von Moltke to execute the plan to perfection: go past Paris and take it under your arm in a turn to the east. But his troops are tired. They grumble. For a whole month now, von Kluck has been driving them at breakneck speed through Belgium and northern France. The Belgian army has blown up railway lines and bridges and hindered their supply of munitions, food and medication. Yet the German general presses his troops to go even faster, towards Paris. So, they stumble on, "their faces coated with dust and their uniforms in tatters. They look like living scarecrows".[15] The general knows this. He deliberates.

What contributed to his 'fatal' decision? Fear of exhaustion and mutiny in his own ranks? The urge to attack the retreating Frenchmen – on 24 August Joffre has given the order to implement a general retreat – from behind? The message from von Bülow to merge von Kluck's First Army with his Second Army and deal the decisive blow to the French together? Whatever his reasons, on 30 August, von Kluck decides to abandon the Schlieffen Plan. To the north of Paris, still above Chantilly, he swings left with his kilometres-long column. Straight to the east. Officers pretend to the endlessly plodding soldiers that they are still marching on Paris.[16] This is the only way to keep them moving. Paris, there they will find refreshment. The following day, a French scout uncovers the new direction of the march.

In his residence in the Hôtel des Invalides, in the Rue de Grenelle, Gallieni sits for a moment. Sixty-five years old and recently recalled out of retirement, he needs to catch his breath upon hearing the news. The city no longer appears to be von Kluck's first target. It is only on 2 September, after great difficulty and some threats, that the French Sixth Army has been put at the Paris military governor's disposal for the defence of the city. But this fantastic news changes everything. This vital alumnus of the military academy of Saint-Cyr recovers his youthful, offensive dynamism: "They are swinging back! They are offering us their flank!"[17] Gallieni cheers. Now that the Germans are no longer directly threatening Paris, the French general decides to send his troops to the Front. To the Marne. The good

Boillot, the Torpedo

news from Paris and the arrival of the British Expeditionary Force under Sir John French, which in the meantime has joined the French, also restores General Joffre's confidence. He decides upon a counter-attack. It is 6 September 1914, and the decisive Battle of the Marne begins.

TAXI TO THE FRONT

Sending troops from Paris is easier said than done. The presence of the Germans in such large numbers means that the train traffic in Nord is totally disrupted. The French trains are unable to cope with the sudden transportation of thousands of men to the Marne. Gallieni makes an historic decision. He convokes the taxis of Paris. Up until the war there had been about 12,000 of them driving around,[18] but thousands of them have been stabled since the start of hostilities. Their drivers are fighting in the army. Gallieni finds just enough vehicles to transport the last 6,000 soldiers, who are unable to travel north on the ailing trains, to the Front. On the same day as the French offensive, hundreds of hooting taxis appear on the parade ground in front of Les Invalides. Red-coloured Renaults, but also the Dion Boutons, Brasiers and Unics. It is an impressive spectacle that fills the entire esplanade, up to the Pont Alexandre III. Spectators applaud the drivers. Then it begins – for three days and two nights, the taxis of Paris transport the foot soldiers to the Front. On the morning of 8 September, the exhausted troops at the Marne receive unexpected reinforcement from Paris. The news spreads like wildfire. It warms hearts in the French trenches.

Regardless of how heroically the infantrymen spring from the taxis, they are the proverbial drop in the ocean. At the Marne, a million German soldiers face a million French and British soldiers. On one side, von Moltke carries out his gambits, whilst on the other Joffre makes his countermoves. It is a deadly game of chess in which huge effort is being expended. A few thousand pawns do not make a difference. To everyone's astonishment, the Battle of the Marne ends in a defeat for the Germans. On 9 September they beat a retreat. Unlike Waterloo in 1815, the Franco-Prussian War in 1870/1, and the Second World War, the Germans do not reach the French capital during the First World War. However, this is far from being a sensational victory for the French, Belgians and British: "Every opportunity for a short war – an absolute precondition for a rapid German victory – was now lost for good."[19] From Ypres to beyond Verdun, both camps dig in for a long, bloody battle.

Yet the Marne taxis become four-wheeled war heroes of a kind. A myth, held up in school textbooks and national historiography as a decisive factor that helped halt the Germans' advance. Above all, Gallieni's action has a psychological impact on the hard-pressed French at the Front: it shows that the French army is prepared to do anything to prevent the Germans from overrunning them.[20] The owners of the Parisian taxi firm, the Compagnie Française des Automobiles de Place, are in the money as a result – for the journeys to the Marne, Comte André Walewski, Baron Rognat and the Banque Mirabaud & Cie receive the erstwhile princely sum of 70,012 francs: the exact figure on the taxis' meters.[21]

THE FALLING LEAF

In 1916, Georges Boillot is promoted to second lieutenant and driving instructor for the French troops. But giving lessons behind the front line bores him. He thrives on adrenaline. The Battle of Verdun is approaching and the French have an acute shortage of fighter pilots. Since the first dogfights in autumn 1914, General Joffre has been sending circulars calling for volunteers. By 1916 it is clear that whoever wins in the air wins the war. General Pétain, at that point a captain in the First Army fighting in Verdun, does not mince his words: "If we are chased from the sky, it's simple, Verdun will be lost!!"[22] The would-be pilots must have good eyesight, good health and a civilian aviation licence. That hits the mark! Boillot fulfils all three requirements. During his years as king of the steering wheel he obtained his aviator's diploma number 395. This comes in useful now. After a short training course, Boillot is literally on cloud nine.

Up there in the sky, Boillot fine-tunes his technique. Looping-the-loop, the falling leaf, upward and downward spins: Boillot plays with all the aerobatic manoeuvres. But he is more than simply skilled at performing tricks, he is also fearless. Just as he wanted to win on the racetrack, he now wants to win in the sky. On 31 March 1916, he shoots down the first Germans from the sky above Lachapelle-sous-Rougemont, between Belfort and Mulhouse, with his Nieuport 11. Encouraged by his successes, he wipes the skies clean of enemy planes from dawn to dusk. Aviatiks and Albatrosses fall to earth in pieces. He's had enough of tinkering on the sidelines. Boillot asks for a transfer. He wants to join the fight in the eye of the storm. Above Verdun.

His victories garner Boillot the distinction of the Légion d'honneur, Croix de guerre avec palme.[23] "His recent quarries have delivered him this star of the courageous. The municipality of Valentigney [Boillot's birthplace] can be proud of such a soldier",[24] a local newspaper writes on 19 May 1916. "We send him our heartfelt congratulations!" But what use is a medal to a man? In the morning of the same day on which the congratulations from his home village are printed in the newspaper, Boillot poses – again with a broad smile – in front of his plane.

Boillot, the Torpedo

There is a large white B painted on the side at the back.[25] Standing beside him is his friend, second lieutenant Jean Navarre, 'the scourge of the Boches'. After a successful day with Navarre, Boillot takes off for a flight in the evening sun. Come on, another Aviatik or an Albatros. Boillot invites Navarre to join him in the hunt. *La chasse aux Boches.* But the talented pilot who is incapable of submitting to military discipline – which his superiors overlook because he shoots down so many enemy planes – is not in the mood this time. He has just completed 31 flying hours. No, the 'scourge of the Boches' needs to rest for a while. Boillot takes off alone. The bullet from the Aviatik that kills him cuts straight through him and exits his body just above the heart. Boillot crashes in Vadelaincourt, inside the French lines.

No one is aware of a sweetheart. In case of accident, his father, Monsieur Louis Boillot of 37, Rue d'Antin in Paris, must be informed, as states the soldier's military index card.[26] On 1 September 1921, three years after the war, a short notice appears in the magazine *Omnia – Revue pratique de locomotion*, under the heading '*Echos et variétés*': Boillot's younger brother, André, also a racing driver and winner of the Targa Florio 1919,[27] is bringing the mortal remains of "the renowned champion of automobile races, who fell in the line of duty at Verdun"[28] from Vadelaincourt to Paris. In silence. No flowers or wreaths, but in the presence of many of Boillot's friends, fellow soldiers, members of the Automobile Club de France and supporters. In subdued silence they come to support their Grand Prix and war hero in his final race: "Come on Boillot, come on!"

Boillot, the Torpedo

PART 4

LEFT BANK, EAST

1. Castor and Pollux p. 182
Jardin des Plantes, 57 rue Cuvier 75005

2. The secret of the Grand Mosque p. 194
Grande Mosquée de Paris,
2bis place du Puits de l'Ermite, 75005

3. Doctor Jack and nurse Toquette p. 202
8 rue Tournefort 75005

4. The party in the Rue Toullier p. 210
9 rue Toullier 75005

5. Made in Paris: p. 218
the People's Republic of China
and the war in Vietnam
Sorbonne, 1 rue Victor Cousin 75005

6. Mytherrand p. 226
22 rue de Bièvre 75005

7. Picasso's 'red period' p. 244
7 rue des Grands-Augustins 75006

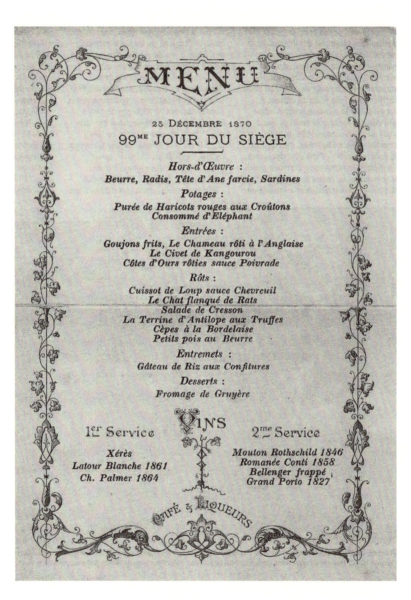

On the Christmas menu in 1870: elephant, camel, kangaroo, rat and cat.

1

CASTOR AND POLLUX

Despite Christmas falling on a Sunday in 1870, Paris is not celebrating. For 99 days now, the Prussians have been keeping the city hermetically sealed. The Parisians are numb and famished. First horses, then dogs, cats and rats appear on people's plates. In the better restaurants, such as Voisin on the corner of the Rue Saint-Honoré and the Rue Cambon, the most well-to-do are served up something rather more exotic this evening: elephant consommé and roast leg of camel.[1] The cynical thing about the Franco-Prussian War is that the Prussian statesman Otto von Bismarck is interested neither in Paris nor in France, but in his personal dream: the unification of Germany. Following wars with Denmark and with Austria, the Prussian prime minister now has his eye on France. An ordeal for the proud capital, Paris.

IRON AND BLOOD

Bismarck knows France and the French better than they know him. At the invitation of the French Emperor Napoleon III and Empress Eugénie, he visits the 1855 Exposition Universelle in Paris, where he is given a grand reception. A few years later, Bismarck is ambassador to Paris.[2] Not for long, but long enough to get an idea of the country's status. Napoleon III also invites Bismarck to the 1867 Exposition Universelle, this time with Wilhelm I, the new king of Prussia. During this visit, Wilhelm I and Bismarck attend the imperial *Séries*, the sensational diplomatic parties thrown by the imperial couple at their autumn residence, the Château de Compiègne.[3] Here, the Emperor of the French introduces them to other heads of state and to the cream of society: top politicians, scientists, artists, writers, industrialists and bankers. While his king immerses himself in the discussions, Bismarck keeps his eyes and ears wide open, with his plan at the back of his mind.

The moustachioed nationalist, anti-liberal and anti-democrat believes that "not through speeches and majority decisions will the great questions of the day be decided ... but by iron and blood".[4] To this end, as Prussian prime minister, he has equipped his country with a superior army. He firmly believes in an external enemy as a means of uniting the divided German states, and has already unleashed and won two bloody wars: one against Denmark in 1864 and one against Austria in 1866. These successes have had the desired effect, allowing him to unite a number of German principalities to create the North German Confederation. France must help him weld these to the states of the South German Confederation to create a new country: Germany.

Less pleasant than their encounters at the *Séries* in Compiègne, even downright painful, is their visit to the Théatre des Variétés. Bismarck and Wilhelm I do not laugh along with the audience. In his comic opera *La Grande-Duchesse de Gérolstein*, Jacques Offenbach, despite having himself been born in Cologne, openly makes fun of the Prussians' military voracity. Helmuth von Moltke,[5] Chief of Staff of the Prussian army, is disparagingly portrayed as *le Général Boum*, a blundering general of a small German principality. Hilarity all round. But in their red velvet seats, Wilhelm I and Bismarck jump to their feet as if they had sat on their spiked helmets. Days later, during the French military parade in Longchamp, Bismarck waits for his sovereign by France's pitifully inadequate cannon:[6] mere playthings. On their own stand, the Prussians exhibit their rapidly reloadable, steel cannon made by Krupp.

Back in Berlin, Bismarck takes stock. By comparison with the Prussian military machine, the French army is now a mere shadow of Napoleon

LEFT BANK, EAST

Bonaparte's *Grande Armée*. Internal political disputes undermine the authority of Napoleon III and his Second Empire. Over the course of its eighteen-year history, the empire has moved from being an authoritarian regime to a liberal dictatorship that is on its last legs. The Assemblée Nationale sessions are more akin to performances of the Opéra Comique on the Rue Favart. Republicans, Orléanists, Bonapartists, royalists and liberals taunt one another in the chamber. What Bismarck has also discovered is the French emperor's short fuse, a Corsican trait, unmistakably inherited from his uncle Napoleon Bonaparte. He contemplates his next move. It falls like a gift from Heaven. Neither in Prussia, nor in France, but – who'd have imagined it? – in Spain.

Queen Isabella II of Spain has fled her country after the 1868 revolution. The Spanish throne is vacant. Although Bismarck is well aware that Isabella has French roots from the Bourbon dynasty, the master chess player advances a member of the Prussian royal family: Leopold, Prince of Hohenzollern-Sigmaringen. This causes consternation among the French and their emperor. Napoleon III already regards the Prussians on his eastern border as a threat, but an even greater number on his southern border he sees as an encirclement. Napoleon III protests to Wilhelm I, who is sympathetic. To allay French fears, the Prussian king withdraws the candidature of Hohenzollern-Sigmaringen. For the king, who is immersed in an invigorating water cure at the fashionable Bad Ems on the banks of the Rhine, this is the end of the matter.

Napoleon III, however, is uncomfortable with the situation. The unexpected diplomatic step from the Spanish opens his eyes: an increasingly aggressive Prussia is unleashing war after war in Europe. When will it be his empire's turn? Through the French ambassador in Prussia, Napoleon III asks for guarantees that Wilhelm I will also waive a Prussian candidature for the Spanish throne in the future. A mildly irritated Wilhelm I has run out of patience. He repeats in friendly but precise terms to the French ambassador that he has nothing more to add to the withdrawal of the Prussian candidature and sends a telegram via his prime minister, Otto von Bismarck. Bismarck sees a great opportunity to give a decisive push to his unification plans. He edits the contents of the royal telegram and changes the tone from friendly but firm, to arrogant and condescending. The new version reads as follows: "His Majesty the King of Prussia has declined to receive the French ambassador again and has informed him via his serving *aide de camp* that His Majesty has nothing more to add to his decision."[7] A refusal to receive the French imperial ambassador? Conveying the message through whichever *aide de camp* happened to be on duty? How much more can a king belittle an emperor? The next day Bismarck ensures that his manipulated message is leaked to the press. *Boom!*

Castor and Pollux

KING WILHELM'S MUCK-SCRAPER

The empire of Napoleon III has been insulted. Deeply offended by the content and tone of the telegram, France declares war on Prussia on 19 July 1870. Crowds on the boulevards and avenues scream "Down with Prussia! To Berlin! To Berlin!"[8] The warning of the moderate revolutionary leader Mirabeau – "Prussia is not a country with an army, but an army with a country"[9] – is totally ignored. With French victories in Crimea and at Solferino in Italy[10] in the bag, the emperor will teach the king a lesson in humility. His *Proclamation de L'Empereur* burns with Baroque rhetoric: "There are solemn moments in the life of people, when the national sense of honour, violently excited, imposes itself with irresistible force, dominates all interests, and alone takes in hand the direction of the destinies of the country. One of those decisive hours has sounded for France. Prussia, towards whom both during and since the war of 1866 we have shown the most conciliatory disposition, has taken no account of our good wishes and our enduring forbearance. Launched on the path of invasion, she has provoked mistrust everywhere, necessitated exaggerated armaments, and has turned Europe into a camp, where reigned nothing but uncertainty and fear of the morrow. A last incident has come to show the instability of international relations, and to prove the gravity of the situation. In light of Prussia's new posturing, we made known our protests. They were evaded and were followed on the part of Prussia by contemptuous acts. Our country resented this treatment with profound irritation, and immediately a cry for war resounded from one end of France to the other... The glorious flag which we once more unfurl before those who have provoked us is the same which bore throughout Europe the civilising idea of our great revolution. It represents the same principles and will inspire the same devotion... May God bless our efforts! A great people which defends a just cause is invincible. Paris, 23 July 1870."[11]

On 2 September, a month and a half after the bombastic *Proclamation*, Bismarck defeats Napoleon III at Sedan. In Paris, the mood remains triumphant. "The confidence and enthusiasm are immense",[12] proclaims *Le Temps,* which backs the emperor. But on the same day, Empress Eugénie receives an urgent message from her husband: "The army is defeated, I have been taken prisoner."[13] The French losses are substantial. A broken Napoleon III hands over his sword to Bismarck. The falsified telegram from Bad Ems proves to have been a masterstroke: immediately after the French declaration of war, the South German Confederation and the North German Confederation closed ranks, and Bavaria, Baden, Hessen and Württemberg joined the battle against France. When the defeat is announced in Paris the next day, the city is in shock. Thousands of citizens – workers and bourgeois alike – converge in front of the Assemblée at

LEFT BANK, EAST

the Palais Bourbon. *La Marseillaise,* banned since the beginning of the Second Empire, sounds out from the throats of all present. The words "To Berlin!" are replaced with: "Down with the Empire! Long live the Republic!"

In Paris, Napoleon III, instigator of the war, becomes the scapegoat. In a caricature *Le décrotteur du roi Guillaume*, the muck-scraper of King Wilhelm, the defeated Emperor, with a tear in his eye, cleans the boots of the Prussian sovereign. The latter barks at him: "Come on Badinguet [one of the Emperor's nicknames], faster than that!"[14] On 4 September at the Hôtel de Ville – a street in Paris has been named after this date[15] – the radical republican *député* Léon Gambetta proclaims the Third Republic,[16] the first without revolution and bloodshed. Along with other moderate republicans, Gambetta forms the Government of National Defence in Paris that will negotiate with Bismarck. The talks are held in the requisitioned Château de Ferrières, the country estate of banker James de Rothschild, in the wooded areas outside the eastern city walls. They are inconclusive.

GAMBETTA'S BALLOON

On 20 September, the Prussians stand at the gates of Paris. But Bismarck does not intend to accept any kind of military loss. What he does want is to see the costs of his military campaign reimbursed, and to annex France's eastern provinces. With winter on its way, he resolves to besiege the city. To starve it into submission. Initially, Paris holds firm. With garrisons that have escaped from the hell of Sedan, marines and cannoneers from Brest, Lorient or Cherbourg, supplemented by reservists, customs officers, gendarmes, veterans and *gardiens de la paix* from across the country, they succeed in putting together a 'new army' of 207,000 men.[17] In addition, Paris has its own Garde Nationale, but due to their untrustworthiness in the revolutions of 1830 and 1848 – in both of which they defected to the side of the people – Napoleon III has reduced their number to 30,000. Now, however, Paris needs combatants. The town halls of all the *arrondissements* rapidly recruit new guardsmen: workers, craftsmen, day labourers and the unemployed. They arm them and offer a rate of 1.50 francs or 30 sous (*trente-sous*) per day, supplemented by 75 centimes for their spouse and 25 centimes per child.[18] From one day to the next, the siege puts paid to all trade and provisioning. Unemployment rises as a result. This leads to an unprecedented rush on uniforms and wages. Before long the Garde Nationale has more than 300,000 members. Paris can call upon a total of 523,000 men at the start of the siege, almost three times the number of the 182,000 Prussians. The number of cannon that are cast in Paris or have been dragged in from other regions is

Castor and Pollux

also superior to that of the enemy: 2,600 of them on the French side, compared to the Prussians' 1,138.[19] But those are not the numbers that count.

First and foremost, there is no unity of command. The generals of the regular army keep their troops at arm's length from the *trente-sous*. Those are the untrustworthy, undisciplined members of the Garde Nationale, of whom only a minority knows how to use their weapons and who are led by self-appointed 'leaders', often the man with the biggest mouth in the neighbourhood. "Everyone commands, no one obeys."[20] But what is left of *la troupe,* the army, is also a hotchpotch. A cannoneer from Brest does not understand what an officer from Grenoble is telling him to do. What's more, the French cannon are no match for the Prussian ones.

The regular army makes several courageous sallies to break the blockade: at Châtillon in the south, Clamart in the west and Champigny in the east. But each time the earth is stained red with French blood. The Parisians therefore try a different tack. On 7 October, the wind is blowing in the right direction. It is coming from the east, an excellent opportunity to float to the west. Hundreds of Parisians, including the writers Victor Hugo and Alphonse Daudet, converge on the Place Saint-Pierre in Montmartre. With bated breath they wait for the starting signal. Their fresh hope, the *Armand-Barbès* balloon, is already filled with the gas that in normal times is used to illuminate Paris. Suddenly the order sounds out: "*Lâchez tout!*" All the ropes are released. The balloon ascends into the sky. On board are Léon Gambetta, his friend, politician and writer Eugène Spuller, and the aeronaut Trichet. They are going to mobilise the rest of France to relieve Paris. In between the Prussian bullets and cannon balls, the courageous trio floats over the battle lines of the siege. Encouraged by this new weapon, the encircled Parisians launch a total of 66 balloons. Some contain soldiers, but the majority contain post. More than two million letters leave Paris by balloon.

But after just five flight hours, Gambetta's balloon lands on the banks of the Somme near Montdidier. Others land in the sea or in rural areas. A few float over Belgium, including *L'Egalité*, navigated by balloonist and scientist Wilfrid de Fonvielle, which is stranded near Leuven. In the Netherlands, Vibert lands his *Steenackers* near Harderwijk, and *La Poste de Paris*, navigated by Turbiaux, lands near Venray. But it is balloonist Paul Rolier who breaks the record for going astray. With his *La Ville d'Orléans* he travels 1,246 kilometres to Lifjell, Norway, to seek help for his besieged fellow townspeople. No one shows up.

ELEPHANT CUTLETS AND EAGLE FILLET

Flocks of sheep and goats wander down the Champs-Élysées, cattle graze on the squares, and the city parks are transformed into vegetable gardens. The Parisians fetch drinking water from a number of sources in the city and from the river that flows beneath the unfinished Opéra Garnier. With all the added troops from the provinces, Paris has 2.2 million mouths to feed.[21] When all food sources have been used up before winter, the Parisians start on the rats, dogs and cats. *Boucheries canines et félines* [dog and cat butchers] pop up everywhere. New signs appear of their wares: *Newfoundland, basset, poodle, terrier, bulldog.* The market leader is Carteret et Cie. Under the motto *résistance à outrance* [resistance to the last] it buys up the Parisians' animals for 'reasonable prices'. Their abattoir in the Rue Curial in La Villette processes the meat, which is then sold in the market hall of Saint-Germain in strips, as sausages, or prepared. In the famished Paris of winter 1870, horsemeat costs 20 francs per kilo, cat meat 15 francs, dog meat 8 francs and rat meat 1 franc.[22] By comparison, vegetables are ruinously expensive: carrots cost 75 francs and onions 80 francs. Towering above the rest is the price of the butter: 160 francs, equivalent to 106 days' salary of a member of the Garde Nationale, whilst the entire siege lasts 'just' 130 days. After a time, all the four-legged creatures have been devoured, as have all the vegetables. The hunger is starting to bite.

The only place where live animals can still be found is in the Ménagerie, Paris' zoo in the Jardin des Plantes.[23] The lions, tigers, camels and other exotic animals are real crowd-pullers, but the most popular are two Asian elephants. Their names – Castor and Pollux – come from the constellation Gemini. Countless children have already enjoyed a ride in the swinging basket on their broad backs. The gentle giants and other animals have been a source of joy, surprise and pleasure for Parisians for years. Now, with the threatening Krupp cannon on the hills around the city, the friends from the Ménagerie are suddenly saddled with a different destiny.

In order to avoid shocking the population too greatly, a slaughter list is drawn up in order of popularity. The least favourite specimens, such as the reptiles, are first for the chop. These are followed by the kangaroos, the antelopes, the zebras, the camels, the bears and the yaks. Their meat goes to butchers; their bones, where possible, to the Galerie de Paléontologie et d'Anatomie Comparée [Paleontology and Comparative Anatomy Gallery] in the Rue Buffon, on the edge of the Jardin des Plantes. There, their skeletons are expertly reconstructed in the service of science. Displayed as if they are stampeding ahead, they surprise every visitor who opens the doors of this wonderful place to this

Castor and Pollux

day. Right at the bottom of the slaughter list are the much-loved Castor and Pollux. The fact that they are brother and sister only serves to enhance the compassion the general public feels towards them. The children of Paris are in floods of tears. But to no avail. With a series of well-aimed dumdum bullets, the Garde Nationale fells the pair. Only the monkeys escape the slaughter. When the Garde Nationale arrives, a large group of demonstrators has collected in front of their cage chanting "No to the monkeys!" Monkeys closely resemble humans. It is a bridge too far.

Monsieur Deboos, owner of the Boucherie Anglaise on the Boulevard Haussmann, buys the bodies of Castor and Pollux. He flays the elephants and sells them in fillets to the city's better restaurants, such as the Jockey Club and Voisin. Only the well-to-do can afford a seat in such establishments. Chef Alexandre-Etienne Choron of the restaurant Voisin, inventor of the world-famous 'sauce Choron', puts the elephant meat alongside other exotic animal preparations on his Christmas menu. "Cat flanked with rats" is probably one of the most remarkable courses in the history of French gastronomy. Choron also serves excellent wines as an accompaniment: La Tour Blanche 1861, Château Palmer 1864, Mouton Rothschild 1846, Romanée Conti 1858 and 'Bellenger frappé'. On 24 January 1871, Le Figaro advertises elephant cutlets from the maison Douix, kidneys and zebra fillet from the maison Martin which, "by the time this article appears will also have eagle on sale".[24] How much the eagle meat will cost, we do not know. But we do know the price of raven: "In January, a raven costs 2.50 francs."[25]

For the vast majority of ordinary Parisians, it is a bleak and chilly Christmas, and the worst Christmas Eve since time immemorial. On 6 January of the new year 1871, the temperature in Paris falls to -15°C. The Seine freezes over for three weeks. As if to keep themselves warm, the Prussians treat the city to a merciless bombardment. They particularly focus on the hospitals Val-de-Grâce, la Salpêtrière, la Pitié and Lourcine and on the domes of the Panthéon and the church of the Sorbonne: "They are changing all the traditions of civilised countries."[26] Paris is numbed.

GERMAN CELEBRATIONS IN VERSAILLES

The Prussians are celebrating. Of the eastern French cities that put up opposition, Metz is the latest to fall, and Orléans, briefly recaptured by the Armée de la Loire, is again in Prussian hands. France is on its knees. Bismarck and Wilhelm I do not wait for the fall of Paris to celebrate their victory. Their war with France has paid off: the South German Confederation has joined its North German counterpart and is thus united to form a new country, Germany. On 18 January 1871, Bismarck has invited 600 officers to the Château de Versailles, all of them princes of the unified principalities. In the gilded Hall of Mirrors, King Wilhelm I appears on a green velvet podium – from beneath a canopy with the Prussian standard and dozens of battle pennants, his proud gaze sweeps across the spiked helmets. Bismarck is depicted in a white uniform and high jackboots in *The Proclamation of Wilhelm as Kaiser of the new German Reich in Versailles 1871* by Anton von Werner, painted in 1885. With his chest thrust forward, he gazes up at his sovereign. His head is bare as a sign of respect. His white-gloved hand clasps the spike of his gleaming helmet.

Then comes the signal. Bismarck strides to the front, as the officers look on in silence. In a solemn tone the Prussian prime minister proclaims the German Empire. Beneath the crystal chandeliers where the French absolutist kings once strode, and their queens and mistresses added an extra shine to the parquet with their long hooped skirts, King Wilhelm I becomes Kaiser Wilhelm I. He appoints his prime minister as chancellor on the spot. To deafening cries of "hurrah!" and "long live the Kaiser!" unsheathed sabres and spiked helmets fly up into the air. With a combative cadence, the military choir launches into the newly composed march *Prussia's Glory*. Champagne corks from French cellars are popped. Their triumphant explosions sound like lovely cannon shots to Bismarck's ears.

The day after the crowning of the kaiser at Versailles, the Garde Nationale, for its part, ventures to make two final sallies in Buzenval to the east and in Montretout to the west of the city. Although heroic, they lead nowhere, except to thousands more deaths. Irritated, the Prussians reduce the western suburb of Saint-Cloud, with its royal castle, to ashes. In Paris, General Trochu, leader of the Government of National Defence, judges the situation to be hopeless. He sends his minister of foreign affairs, Jules Favre, to Bismarck. The brand-new chancellor lays down his conditions: the relinquishing of Alsace and Lorraine, 5 billion francs in reparations spread over three years, with the occupation of France until the moment that the last franc has been paid, and a victory parade on the Champs-Élysées. The armistice is signed on 28 January 1871: the Franco-Prussian War is at an end.

When the battle-weary Parisians discover the conditions of the agreement, they muster all their courage and rise up defiantly. On 18 March 1871, the city announces itself to be self-governing: La Commune de Paris. In so doing, it is heading for one of the most dramatic moments in its history. From Versailles, Adolphe Thiers, a 74-year old dyed-in-the-wool conservative and member of the Académie Française, appointed by the newly elected Assemblée Nationale as

Castor and Pollux

'head of the executive power of the republic', restores order in Paris. This turns into a blood-soaked tragedy in which the French fight against the French, with the Prussians looking on from the hills surrounding the city. The battle of the 'reactionary' Versailles against the 'revolutionary' *communards* ends in an orgy of violence: *la Semaine sanglante* [the Bloody Week], from 21 to 28 May 1871, in which the *communards* fare the worse.

But just as with Napoleon Bonaparte, here it is not the winner but the loser who goes down in history with a legendary sympathy. More than 200 years after Waterloo, Napoleon exerts a vastly superior appeal to the global imagination than Wellington, Blücher and the Prince of Orange put together. The same is true of the *communards*. In the 150 years following their battle, more ink has flowed than blood during the fighting – numerous books, commemorations, Chinese postcards, postage stamps from all the former Eastern Bloc countries, paintings, posters and photos keep the memory of the Parisian fighters alive.

Just as in all hagiographies, the heroes in one account are the cowards in another. But what has been proven irrefutably is that the Paris Commune created more victims[27] and led to more buildings being destroyed[28] that the two subsequent world wars put together. These are deeply rooted in this French-Prussian appetiser in which Germany was united on the back of the French. And on those of Castor and Pollux.

Castor and Pollux

Rector Si Kaddour Benghabrit with German officers at the Grand Mosque.

2

THE SECRET OF THE GRAND MOSQUE

"Wonderful! It reminds me of Marrakesh!", SS-Standartenführer Helmut Knochen compliments the rector of the Grand Mosque in passable French. Behind the sculpted gate that is carefully opened for him, water splashes in an azure fountain, orange trees are in bloom and azaleas shimmer in the spring sunshine – a breath of fresh air in occupied Paris. "Welcome, Herr Colonel." Only someone with the status of rector Si Kaddour Benghabrit can afford to address the Nazi with the equivalent of his French rank. "We will start your tour in the library." In the meantime, one floor below, in the cellars of this metropolitan paradise, a certain Simon is being renamed Salim.

ALLIES OF THE THIRD REICH

As soon as Helmut Knochen has selected the stately, five-storey Second Empire villa at 72, Avenue Foch as headquarters of the Gestapo in France, he can get stuck into his duties.[1] One of these is the nationwide rollout of the SS-Reichsführer Heinrich Himmler's 'Muslim plan'. In Muslims, Himmler sees motivated allies in the battle against the Jews. Is it not true that according to the Islamic faith, anyone who takes up arms against the Jewish arch-enemy is rewarded with a place in paradise? For this reason, Himmler wants the Muslim world, particularly in the French and British colonies, to join forces with the Third Reich.[2] It is for the same reason that he does not incorporate Muslim soldiers into the regular German army, but directly into the SS. With the blessing of Hajji Amin al-Husseini, Grand Mufti of Jerusalem, several Islamic SS-divisions are established.[3] The ties with the Muslim community must be strengthened in the French capital too, and who better to help with this than their spiritual leader, the rector of the Grand Mosque of Paris?

Si Kaddour Benghabrit – 'Si' is short for Sidi and is as deferential as Sir – is an Islamic and legal scholar with a distinguished service record with the French administration in Algeria, and with successful diplomatic missions in North Africa under his belt. It is to him that the Grand Mosque owes its existence. The complex was built after Benghabrit had pressed the French government for a gesture in recognition of the thousands of Muslims who died for their country in the First World War. At Verdun alone, 70,000 Muslims perished between 21 February and the end of October 1916. In recognition of the past, the Grand Mosque opens its doors on 15 July 1926,[4] the day after the celebration of the French national holiday. Benghabrit is known to be a brilliant man: highly educated, cultivated and with a circle of friends and acquaintances that he has expanded over the years across religious, cultural, political and language divides.[5] The most Parisian of Muslims is also widely honoured and respected in the international community.

The Nazis must therefore treat him with great care. As a result, the first visits after the occupation of Paris on 14 June 1940 are extremely friendly. The SS officers and other representatives of the Third Reich, such as Prince Ratibor, allow themselves to be taken on convivial tours of the Grand Mosque. In the shadow of Benghabrit's charisma, Knochen's men sip mint tea and discuss with the rector how to deal with their common enemy, world Jewry. There is no need for them to wear their constricting caps emblazoned with the skull and crossbones beneath the swaying palms and orange trees. What's more, the honey-sweet cornes de gazelle, stuffed dates and baklava are a delicious treat.

LEFT BANK, EAST

The SS is not insensible to all this oriental enchantment, and during this first summer in Paris they visit the Grand Mosque more frequently than necessary – life cannot be all work and no play, after all.

MUSIC FROM THE CELLAR

In autumn 1940, it becomes clear that the oriental oasis of the Grand Mosque is a mirage. The SS has the irksome duty of drawing up the following message in the offices of General Weygand, minister of national defence in the collaborationist Vichy government: "The occupying authorities suspect the personnel of the Mosque of Paris of issuing fraudulent birth certificates to interested parties, whereby the latter are presented as members of the Islamic faith. The imam is urgently commanded to desist from such practices. Indeed, it appears that a number of Jews are taking advantage of forgeries of this kind to conceal their true identity."[6] From now on, Rector Benghabrit and his staff are closely monitored.

Halfway through the war, the mood has shifted completely. Thousands of Jews have already been deported from France. Also from Paris. With the large-scale round-ups of 1941 and the Vélodrome d'Hiver round-up of 16 and 17 July 1942,[7] the Nazis accelerate their plans. They cannot expect active cooperation from Rector Benghabrit. His principle is clear: religion yes, politics no. The Grand Mosque continues to devote itself strictly to its religious tasks: the provision of food and clothing to fellow-believers in need; the washing and burial in accordance with the rules of the some 1,500 Muslims who die at home, in Paris' hospitals or prisons during the war;[8] and the celebration of the established religious feasts. Benghabrit defies the request of his Grand Mufti to rally the Muslim community in the French colonies and Algeria to support Nazi Germany. He is arrested.[9] There is little with which the Nazis can charge him, however, and they soon have no choice but to release him.

After the losses in Stalingrad in early February 1943, the Third Reich suffers a fresh blow in May. In Tunisia, the German and Italian troops surrender to the Allies. The 223,000 Algerian, Moroccan and Tunisian Muslims who fight with the Allies in the regrouped Armée d'Afrique,[10] make everything clear for the Germans: Himmler's plan has failed, the Muslims have not turned out to be supporters. The relations between the Third Reich and the Islamic world definitively turn sour. In Paris, the pleasant visits to the Grand Mosque have morphed into round-ups. No longer do the Gestapo men remove their shoes when entering the prayer hall; instead they bring along their barking Alsatians. Rector Benghabrit maintains his dignity, despite his abhorrence for the pounding SS boots on the steps of his mosque and the incursions into the discreet hammam, illuminated

The secret of the Grand Mosque

only by the light filtering through vivid stained-glass windows, and where, to their frustration, the SS men find only a few terrified women.

Nevertheless, there really is something to discover in the mosque. In the cellars, assistants are executing a top-secret task for the rector's musical pride and joy, Simon Halali. Simon's father is of Turkish origin, but his mother is Jewish, which also makes him a Jew. At the age of fourteen he leaves Algeria, and at the age of seventeen he is already singing in the Arabic-Andalusian clubs of Paris. Simon is a virtuoso player of the *darbuka*, a type of Middle Eastern drum. His stirring music is so popular that he tours the whole of Europe and North Africa, until the outbreak of the war drives him back to Paris. In France, he can still earn money in the Grand Mosque's café-restaurant. But this is precisely where vigilance is now required.

Under the all-seeing eye of the SS and their acolytes, it is impossible for Simon to retain his Hebrew name and Jewish identity. Rector Benghabrit resolves to change Simon's name to Salim. The Jew becomes a Muslim, complete with an 'authentic' birth certificate. This contrivance allows Simon to escape arrest, deportation and death. Unfortunately the same is not true of his younger sister Berthe (Beïa) Halali. On 17 August 1943 the SS arrest her, and her seven-month-old baby Claude, in her home in the Rue François Miron in the Marais. Berthe Halali is gassed in Auschwitz on 7 September, and her baby dies three weeks later.[11] The musician and the rector survive the war. Si Kaddour Benghabrit dies in 1954 in Paris. Salim Halali dies in 2005, following a glittering musical career that would never have happened without the courage and support of the Grand Mosque's rector.

IMAGINARY FOREFATHER

After the war, peace returns to the mosque. Until 1983, when a certain Albert Assouline, doctor and former Jewish resistance fighter, comes out with the story that he, along with 1,732 other members of the Resistance, hid in the Grand Mosque between 1940 and 1944.[12] According to Assouline, the rector and his staff helped Jews, pilots and members of the Resistance to escape, through corridors and tunnels that led to the Seine. The Grand Mosque of Paris seems unexpectedly to have been an active hub of the Resistance. The historians and researchers who delve into the history of the Resistance and the Holocaust in France are flabbergasted: this is a totally new piece of information.

In 1991, the broadcaster previously known as FR3 airs a documentary by Derri Berkani, *La Mosquée de Paris: une résistance oubliée* [The Mosque of Paris: A Forgotten Resistance]. In the programme, a second witness, Doctor Ahmed

Somia, a Muslim who works at the Hôpital Franco-Musulman in Bobigny, confirms Assouline's story. Nevertheless, written traces or documents are nowhere to be found. Still other witnesses recount how the influential advocate and politician Simone Veil was also hiding out in the cellars of the Grand Mosque. Simone Veil denies this: as much as she would like to believe that Muslims and Jews helped one another, she was not there because she was staying in Nice at the time, in the 'free zone'. Serge and Beate Klarsfeld, founders of the French organisation that protected the interests of the children of Jewish victims in the Second World War, also raised their eyebrows. In their reputable documentation centre, which was able to determine the identity of thousands of Jews who were persecuted in and deported from France, no trace can be found of possible rescue operations via the Grand Mosque in Paris.[13]

Yet in books, documentaries, comics and films, a new myth is born: the Grand Mosque of Paris as a clandestine hub of the Resistance, and as the saviour of Jews and other persecuted people. One of the most popular films on the theme, *Les Hommes Libres* (2011) by Ismaël Ferroukhi, with Michael Lonsdale in the role of Rector Benghabrit and Mahmoud Shalaby playing Salim Halali, includes an unforgettable scene. When incriminating rumours about the successful musician of the Grand Mosque are circulating, the SS again interrogates Rector Benghabrit. "How long has he been a Muslim? But my dear Sirs, what a question, you see... Since forever, he was born a Muslim. Go and meet his ancestors." He dares the SS to verify the claims at the large Islamic cemetery in Bobigny, just outside Paris. Here, the Nazis do indeed find the grave of Salim's father, marked "Brahim Halali, 1885-1939" in Arabic script. For the stonemasons employed by the ingenious rector, carving this 'old' inscription into an anonymous tombstone was no mean feat. But it works: the SS falls for it and allows Halali to keep on singing... in the film.

RIGHTEOUS ARABS

Of course, Bobigny cemetery really does exist, although the tombstone does not. Indeed, it has never existed: Salim's father was called Fradj and was born in 1892, not in 1885. But it is irrelevant. The story of the falsification is a wonderful invention and, when it comes to fiction, the imagination reigns supreme. It is only when the film-makers ask for the scientific advice of Professor Benjamin Stora, an authority on the history of Algeria and Islam, that the debate is rekindled. As the number of Jews and members of the Resistance said to have been helped by the mosque keeps on rising – from 1,732 according to Albert Assouline to 15,000 according to the Israeli newspaper *Yedioth Ahronoth* of

The secret of the Grand Mosque

16 February 2013[14] – multiple experts take up their pens in order, finally, to differentiate fact from fiction.

But the facts are not easy to find, as is apparent from the debate that has been raging ever since.[15] At this point in time, the most accurate conclusion is that there was no organised Resistance network active in the Grand Mosque of Paris, and that falsified birth certificates were not systematically issued to Jews. However, Rector Benghabrit and his staff did save the life of Salim Halali and also those of several other, predominately Sephardic, Jews. Among them were Georgette Astorg, pianist in the Radio France orchestra, and Oro Tardieu-Boganim, a Jewish nurse of Moroccan origin who worked at the Hôpital Franco-Musulman in Bobigny where there was an active Resistance network.[16] By night she helped operate on wounded pilots and members of the Resistance there. Behind the always carefully locked door of the pharmacy at the Hôpital Franco-Musulman, there was more to be found than simply medication; and anyone requiring a longer recovery period was placed in the tuberculosis ward, where the Gestapo and Vichy police rarely ventured for fear of contagion – an ideal hiding place.[17]

How many people escaped death thanks to Rector Benghabrit and the Grand Mosque of Paris? Albert Assouline, who lit the imaginative fuse, can no longer be heard, and neither can Ahmed Somia, as both died in 1994. When the French Yad Vashem Commission[18] put the question to Salim Halali in 2004, he was already a resident of the care home at Vallauris, and "his comments [were] incoherent in light of his condition".[19] According to the director of the care home, he was suffering from a form of Alzheimer's disease.[20] Today, the debate seems to have stalled. All the pros and cons have been weighed up, all the arguments have been examined. It is striking that the most exciting contribution did not come from experts, but from Mohammed Aïssaoui, journalist at *Le Figaro littéraire*. He conducted the most comprehensive and credible search for witnesses into the role played by the Grand Mosque.[21]

His thorough work makes one thing clear: it is not fair that there is not a single Muslim among the more than 3,900 names that grace the 'Wall of the Righteous' in Paris' Marais quarter, the memorial with which Yad Vashem honours the French who risked their own lives to save Jews during the Second World War. Aïssaoui hopes that within a reasonable timespan, Arabs can also be recognised as 'Righteous' by Yad Vashem.[22] In the meantime, no one can say for certain exactly which lives were saved there in the cellars of the Grand Mosque of Paris. It is a secret that only Rector Benghabrit knows, and one that he has almost certainly taken with him, for eternity, to his simple grave in the garden of his mosque.

The secret of the Grand Mosque

Dr Sumner Jackson (at the back in white doctor's coat and tie) and his team at the American Hospital in Neuilly.

3

DOCTOR JACK AND NURSE TOQUETTE

Thursday 13 June 1940, 9.45pm. On the rooftop of the American Hospital in Neuilly, Doctor Sumner Jackson gazes into the distance. Through the haze of his cigarette he watches the smoke rising over Paris, punctuated with flashes of light. On the other side of the Seine, behind the vast forests of Saint-Germain-en-Laye, the Germans are approaching. He estimates that tomorrow, or the day after at the latest, they will reach Neuilly. The next day, the first Germans enter Paris. They will occupy the city for four years, two months and thirteen days. Dr Jackson manages to hold onto his post for the duration of the war. With the help of his wife, he not only employs an inventive ruse to keep the Germans out of his hospital, but he also saves the lives of hundreds of Allied pilots, parachutists and resistance fighters.

TRAPPED

Some 30,000 Americans are living in Paris just before the Second World War. But when Britain and France declare war on Germany following the invasion of Poland in September 1939, it triggers a mass exodus of 25,000 residents back to the US.[1] The remaining 5,000 American citizens in Paris are more or less tolerated by the occupying forces during the first year of the war. Their situation takes a dramatic and unexpected turn on 7 December 1941, however, with the Japanese bombardment of Pearl Harbor, the American naval base in the Hawaiian Archipelago, followed four days later by Germany's declaration of war on the US on 11 December. Now that their homeland is directly involved in the war, the Americans in Paris are trapped. Overnight, they become enemies of the Third Reich. Many are arrested and imprisoned in camps outside Paris.

Dr Jackson's boss, the renowned physician Thierry de Martel – one of the most celebrated neurosurgeons in France – prepares for the arrival of the Germans with the same meticulousness that he reserves for the operating theatre. On the morning of 14 June he shaves with the utmost care, as is his habit; he dresses and retires to his study in his elegant apartment at 18, Rue Weber, near the Champs-Élysées.[2] There, he sits on the sofa and injects himself with strychnine. To his friend, William Bullitt, the American Ambassador in Paris, he leaves a dry farewell note: "I promised you not to leave Paris, but I didn't say if I'd stay dead or alive. *Adieu*. Martel."[3] Dr Martel is not the only person to commit suicide at this time. Reeling from the shock, the hospital board hands over the clinical management of the facility to Dr Jackson, a surgeon and urologist. This will be the doctor's second war.

After studying medicine, Jackson joins the Massachusetts General Hospital in Boston, but leaves in 1916 to fight alongside the British Army on the Western Front. He is thirty-one years old. During the second Battle of the Somme he operates on thousands of wounded soldiers. Bullet wounds, scrapes, burns, gangrene, gas poisoning, the infamous *gueule cassée* (in which the victims lost a jaw or part of their face) – Dr Jackson sees it all. When America joins the Allies in April 1917, he transfers to the US army. That same year, at the American Red Cross Hospital No. 2 in Paris, he meets Charlotte Sylvie Barrelet de Ricout, a nurse after his own heart. They marry immediately. 'Jack' and 'Toquette' – Charlotte's nickname, an affectionate reference to her family's dog – return to the United States after the Armistice in November 1918.

But they do not remain on the other side of the ocean for long. After all, they are not only in love with each other but also with Paris. They return to the city in 1923. Jack spends two years in specialised training at the École de Médecine before

LEFT BANK, EAST

commencing a new career at the American Hospital in Paris in 1925. In 1928, Toquette gives birth to their son, Phillip. Under Jack's leadership, this renowned institution, which was founded in 1909 to provide American medical care to expatriate students, tourists, businessmen and diplomatic staff, grows and flourishes.

FULL

The situation alters in 1940. The Germans are heading back to the city. Although they had been held back on the Marne during the First World War, they are now marching towards Paris. Jack exhales one last cloud of smoke. He extinguishes his cigarette and quickly descends. It has been frantic since the fighting began last month. Some 60,000 French soldiers have been killed in less than two months, between 10 May and 22 June. Of the civilian population, 21,000 people have lost their lives. In the same short space of time, the Germans have taken 2 million prisoners of war and forced 10 million Belgians, Luxembourgers, Dutch and French to flee their homes. Furthermore, the Germans bombed Paris on 3 June resulting in 200 casualties – a foretaste of things to come.

As soon as they reach the city, the Germans requisition the La Pitié-Salpêtrière hospital on the Left Bank and that of Lariboisière next to the Gare du Nord. The facilities are henceforth reserved for wounded members of the Wehrmacht. Soon, they are staffed exclusively by German doctors. Jack's main concern is to keep the occupiers out of *his* hospital. Together with the American Hospital's governor-general, Aldebert de Chambrun, he devises an inventive strategy that he pursues throughout the war: his beds will only be occupied by American and French patients – before a bed is even vacated, he sends cyclists to alert the elderly, who are in on the conspiracy, and recruits them to come and occupy the beds. Aldebert de Chambrun also succeeds in concluding an agreement with the French railways (SNCF), who promise to transport injured *cheminots* to the American Hospital in the event of accidents and war. Thanks to his delicate position – de Chambrun is the father-in-law of Josée Laval, daughter of the Vichy prime minister Pierre Laval – he also ensures that the American Hospital is responsible for treating the British prisoners in the POW camps. With such interventions, the hospital avoids taking a single *boche* [German soldier] during the entire conflict. For German patients, the American Hospital is always full.

As the war progresses, the situation in Paris deteriorates. The American Hospital is also reaching the end of the road. Despite aid from the USA, the heating has already been adapted to run on inferior coal, food is being purchased on the black market at Les Halles, and meat – the scarcest of all

Doctor Jack and nurse Toquette

commodities – is smuggled inside. A 15-metre-deep groundwater well is dug to ensure sufficient water. In the absence of gas for the stoves, food is cooked on open fires in the garden. Medical instruments are also sterilised in the flames. In the garages, the staff raise six piglets. These are the activities that take place above ground. Beneath the hospital, deep in the basement, is a series of secret rooms and an operating theatre, both of which are functioning. There, Jack and his team tend hundreds of injured pilots, parachutists and resistance fighters in the utmost secrecy, thus enabling them to return to the conflict.

OPERATION SUSSEX

The wounded men are smuggled into the hospital under the cover of night. It is a perilous undertaking: anyone found guilty of helping or sheltering an Allied parachutist is put before the firing squad on Mont Valérien. One of the people brave enough to run the risk is Mme Andrée Goubillon, owner of the café at 8, Rue Tournefort. She is involved in the top-secret 'Sussex Plan', a large-scale military intelligence operation designed to gauge the situation in occupied France. Orchestrated by the Allies in London, Operation Sussex is intended to pave the way for the Normandy landings. From November 1943, the Bureau Central de Renseignements et d'Action (BCRA) [Central Bureau of Intelligence and Operations], established in 1940 by General de Gaulle in London, recruits more than 200 French volunteers. They are trained for this sensitive mission in British camps. Dropped back behind enemy lines, they are mainly operational in Northern France and Paris. From January 1944 until the liberation of Paris in August, Andrée Goubillon hides no fewer than forty-two Sussex parachutists in her small café, which – note well – is adjacent to a Gestapo office.[4]

AVENUE BOCHE

Meanwhile, the Gestapo and other agencies have made it a point of honour to establish their offices on the prestigious Avenue Foch – a fitting revenge on the Marshal of the same name who had humiliated them in the previous war.[5] To prevent their apartment at 11, Avenue Foch being seized by the Germans, Dr Jackson brings his wife and son, who had decamped to the countryside, back to Paris. They are not exactly on good terms with the neighbours. Across the street, at no. 72, is a Gestapo office, while the security services 'live' just a little further up the street. No. 31 houses the dreaded Office for Jewish Affairs run by Theodor Dannecker, Eichmann's protégé, who is not only responsible for cleansing Paris of the Jews but also sanctions the Vélodrome d'Hiver round-up.[6]

Determined to do all they can to stop the barbarism of the occupiers, Jack and Toquette also join the Goélette-Frégate network. This provides military intelligence to Maurice Duclos, a.k.a. Saint-Jacques, who was on the staff of Charles de Gaulle, the commander of the Free French army. They allow their apartment to be used as a contact point and conduit. Smuggling pilots out of the hospital in disguise is quite an art. But surreptitiously bringing wanted persons into your home is a life-or-death game, especially if you live in the 'Avenue Boche', as the road is now called thanks to the myriad German administrative divisions and Pétainists it houses.

CAUGHT

In the spring of 1944, the French black shirts from the Milices [the militia established by the Vichy regime to aid the Germans] capture a Goélette-Frégate cell in La Bourboule, Auvergne. Founded in 1943 by Pétain, the 45,000 Milices volunteers – common law criminals, riff-raff and hooligans – are under the command of Joseph Darnand. They 'lighten the Gestapo's load' and are authorised to arrest, torture and kill. In La Bourboule, the Milices discover letters addressed to Dr Jackson at 11, Avenue Foch, Paris. On 24 May, they arrive at the American Hospital, bundle the doctor into a car and drive him to the Avenue Foch. To his immense surprise, they do not stop at the Gestapo's headquarters, but at his home. He is reunited with Toquette and Phillip, who are being held at gunpoint... and so the road to calvary begins.

They are initially imprisoned in Le Petit Casino, the Milices 'headquarters' in Vichy.[7] But on 7 June, just twenty-four hours after the Normandy landings, the black shirts hand them over to the Gestapo, out of fear that the Americans, who might possibly win the war, will mete out a harsh punishment for the Jacksons' arrest. On 15 July, with the Allies rapidly advancing, Jack and Phillip, along with 2,000 other prisoners, are put on a train to Dachau. For reasons that remain unclear, the train stops 20km south of Hamburg, in Neuengamme. Here, father and son go from being people to numbers: 36,462 and 36,461. Poles, Russians, Danes, French citizens and people of countless other nationalities are literally worked to death in Neuengamme, either as slaves in the brickworks or in the Walther munitions factory. At the slightest sign of resistance, they are shot or hanged in the courtyard.

In the meantime, Toquette has been transferred to Germany. She walks through the gates of the Ravensbrück camp on 21 August. In theory, it is not an extermination camp. Nevertheless, the prisoners drop like flies due to starvation and exhaustion. Most are employed as slave labour in the SS-run Texled fabric and leather processing plant or the Siemens arms factory.[8]

Doctor Jack and nurse Toquette

TOO LATE...

Five days after Toquette's arrival in Ravensbrück, Paris is liberated. Just too late to save the Jacksons. Under heavy fire from the Germans, the Allies are bearing down on Berlin. The British will not reach Neuengamme until the beginning of May 1945. During the eight months in which Phillip and Jack cling to life in the camp, according to Phillip's calculations the Germans kill some 35,000 fellow prisoners. Only a few thousand people survive. Aware of their atrocities, the SS try to eliminate all witnesses. Survivors are transported to the coastal town of Lübeck where they are loaded onto three ships: the *Athen*, the *Cap Arcona* and the *Thielbek*.

The Jacksons board the latter ship. Although the vessels are launched under SS command, the British order them back to port. They believe the boats to be filled with fleeing SS soldiers. The *Athen* turns around. But the SS crews on the other two ships refuse to comply, whereupon the vessels are bombed. Of the 7,000 prisoners aboard the two boats, 200 manage to swim ashore. Of these, 150 are shot by the SS, who are waiting on the beach. Phillip survives, as if by a miracle. He is standing in a line with the other survivors, the SS machine gun already pointing at them, when British tanks roll into view. The Germans flee.

Phillip never sees his father again. He is reunited with his mother, however, although she is badly injured and unable to walk. On 18 July 1945, two months after the German surrender, they finally embrace one another in Paris. Dr Jack could not save himself, but he will always be remembered for saving hundreds of lives during the two world wars. The American Hospital has never forgotten his heroic actions. To this day, it presents the annual 'Dr Jackson Award' to an exceptional hospital employee. With the courageous deeds of Jack and Toquette as the benchmark, it seems quite a challenge. Nor has Mme Goubillon been forgotten. Her café in the Rue Tournefort was renamed 'Café des Sussex' after the Liberation.[9] A modest commemorative plaque adorns the façade: '*Ici en 1943 et 1944 furent cachés et hebergés by Mme Andrée Goubillon 42 parachutistes français des réseaux du Plan Sussex*' [Here, in 1943 and 1944, 42 French parachutists from the Sussex Plan networks were hidden and housed by Mme Andrée Goubillon].

Doctor Jack and nurse Toquette

The middle-aged terrorist, Carlos, with his wife and lawyer, Isabelle Coutant-Peyre.

4

THE PARTY IN THE RUE TOULLIER

"Let's go!" Police superintendent Jean Herranz of the Direction de la Surveillance du Territoire (DST) gestures impatiently to his colleagues. And to the informant who has just 'sung': "You will accompany us!" The man must identify the friend he has denounced. The destination is house number 9 in the Rue Toullier, an immaculate street between the Panthéon and the Sorbonne. The police officers leave their weapons in the office and step into an anonymous car without a radio. "It was supposed to be for a verification," says the only survivor of the nuit brûlante *of 27 June 1975, "not for an arrest."*[1]

The party in the Rue Toullier

'SUNDAY AT ORLY'

The DST has been keeping an eye on a certain Michel Moukharbal since his return to France in mid-June 1975. With his long face and black moustache, this Lebanese member of the Popular Front for the Liberation of Palestine (PFLP) is thought to be a liaison officer for a militant in Paris. One day, the police officers see Moukharbal handing something to a man in the Rue Toullier. They later photograph him with the same man in a café. One week prior to the fatal events, the DST arrests Moukharbal. The police officers discover weedkiller in his flat, used for making explosives. The suspect admits to being sympathetic to the Palestinian cause but denies any connection with the man in the picture. After five days of interrogation and threats of deportation, Moukharbal 'sings' and promises to lead the police agents to 'Nourredine', his contact in the Rue Toullier. The DST officers have never heard of Nourredine.

Or at least, that's what they think. Nevertheless, France has been the extended battlefield of the conflict between Israel and Palestine since the autumn of the previous year. On Sunday 15 September 1974, the setting sun turns the leaves of the plane trees on the boulevards a bright copper red. On the corner of the Boulevard Saint-Germain and the Rue de Rennes, a man aged "between twenty and thirty" hurls a grenade into the ground floor of the Drugstore Publicis at the people inside. The complex, which comprises a cinema, boutiques, a perfumery and cafés, is owned by Marcel Bleustein-Blanchet, a Jewish entrepreneur and founder of the communications group Publicis. In the Drugstore, Parisians are licking ice creams and enjoying an end-of-weekend chat. The explosion makes a crater. On the busy terrace of the Brasserie Lipp next door, the waiters feel the displacement of air and witness people running outside in panic. They rush to their aid. There are victims strewn everywhere, amid a wreckage of blood and shards of glass, shoes and twisted aluminium. They offer first aid with table linen. The tally: two dead, thirty-four wounded.

"There will be more!" threatens a mysterious correspondent with a Spanish accent, if the French government does not immediately comply with the demands from the Japanese Red Army (JRA). For two days prior to the attack, the radical Marxist-Leninist terror group, trained in Palestinian camps in Lebanon, had been holding eleven people hostage in the French Embassy in The Hague.[2] The terror group is infamous for its ruthless tactics. In the name of the Popular Front for the Liberation of Palestine, the JRA had, two years previously, murdered twenty-six people at Lod Airport[3] in Tel Aviv. From the Anna Paulownastraat in The Hague, it is now demanding the release of one of its fellow fighters who is imprisoned in Paris. President Valéry Giscard d'Estaing, prime minister Jacques Chirac, and minister of the interior Michel Poniatowski, have just entered office[4] and have no appetite for further tragedies. The terrorists get their way and fly unhindered to Damascus with their liberated comrade and a sum of money. The eleven hostages survive the adventure. In Paris, the DST feverishly tries to unearth the identity of the 'correspondent', but its efforts are in vain.

A few months later, on 13 January 1975, a man with a sports bag appears on the terraces of Orly Airport, then still accessible to the general public. There is nothing at all suspicious about him. The airport is a symbol of technological progress and many families with children visit at weekends to watch the take-offs and landings, especially of the supersonic Concorde. Orly appeals to the popular imagination and, at that time, has more visitors than the Eiffel Tower: "When I go to bed at night / I hear the Boeings sing up high / I love them, my birds in flight / And I will seek them out by and by / When on Sunday I go to Orly / At the airport you see them take off / The planes for every country / For a whole life... there's something to dream of", is Gilbert Bécaud's forever-carefree song about this delightful activity in *Dimanche à Orly*.[5]

The situation takes a dramatic turn when the aforementioned man conjures up the parts of a rocket launcher from his bag, cold-bloodedly assembles the device and fires a grenade at a Boeing from the Israeli airline El Al. He misses his target and punctures a Yugoslavian Douglas DC9. No problem. Six days later he is back with two accomplices. The terrorist under his command throws grenades and fires upon passengers. Twenty-one wounded victims later, the perpetrators fly to Baghdad with two hostages. They have disappeared without a trace, thinks police superintendent Jean Herranz. He sees no connection with the informant Moukharbal, otherwise he would probably have never left his office unarmed for the visit to the Rue Toullier. Or was there a certain recklessness to his actions? It is Friday evening and the DST officers Raymond Dous and Jean Donatini, two colleagues that the police superintendent has rounded up for the verification, are enjoying an apéritif. The autopsy shows that Jean Donatini had 1.45g of alcohol in his blood.[6]

TERRORIST SCHOOL

When the police officers arrive in the Rue Toullier, it seems as though they're in for a pleasant continuation of their evening. Latino beats are emanating from the studio that Moukharbal points out to them. The house is occupied by swinging South American students from the Sorbonne. One of them has departed for home, for Caracas, Venezuela, that evening. The leaving party is still in full swing. Another Venezuelan in attendance is a certain Ilich Ramírez Sánchez,

The party in the Rue Toullier

the son of a wealthy lawyer who is fanatical about communism and the South American liberation movements. He names his eldest son 'Vladimir' and his youngest 'Lenin' after his idol. He also gives his middle son Lenin's middle name:[7] Ilich. In the evenings, Fidel Castro's endless speeches lull the boys to sleep, and during the day they prick up their ears for the exciting adventures of Che Guevara.[8] At the age of ten, Ilich is already a member of the Communist Youth of Venezuela. When his parents divorce, he follows his mother who decides to continue her studies at the London School of Economics. In 1968, his father wants to enrol him at the Sorbonne in Paris, the dream of every revolutionary parent. But the KGB, which is closely following the strikes and revolutions in France, devises an even better idea: someone with Ilich's domestic and political background must continue his studies at Moscow's Patrice Lumumba University. It is there that the revolutionary world leaders of tomorrow are being educated in the era of the Cold War and American imperialism.

A series of dissipated excesses[9] involving an abundance of vodka and women puts a premature end to the theoretical education of the future world leader. The wild party animal is expelled from the university. Ilich is not in need of words but deeds. He concludes his education at a PFLP training camp in the desert near Amman in Jordan. On the curriculum are firearms, bombs and grenades, planes, hostage-taking, disguises and vanishing acts, terror and international contacts – for example with Ulrike Meinhof. This is all considerably more thrilling than statistics about the third world economy.

Once he has mastered all these skills, Ilich is given his mission from PFLP leader George Habash: to put the movement on the map in Europe. After his first, failed attack on a member of the Jewish family which owns the British retailer Marks & Spencer in London, Ilich Ramírez Sánchez continues to enjoy his 'working holiday' in France. There, he brings the French government to its knees in the affair of the bombing on the Boulevard Saint-Germain and fine-tunes his rocket-launching skills at Orly Airport.

THE END OF THE PARTY

A few moments before the DST officers arrive in the Rue Toullier, Ilich is already there, a bottle of Johnnie Walker in one hand, a black suitcase in the other.[10] Before he hides the luggage in the bathroom, he shows its contents to the student Leyma Palomares: "Be careful of that".[11] The desire to impress girls is still a weak spot. The party starts. The drink is flowing, the salsa trumpets are sounding, and Johnny Colón gets everyone dancing with his steamy '*Tierra va a temblar*', the earth is going to shake.

Police Superintendent Jean Herranz and Officer Jean Donatini head upstairs, while Officer Raymond Dous waits downstairs in the car, with Michel Moukharbal, the informant. The music is playing loudly as Herranz and Donatini, clutching a photo, make their way to the man it depicts. "That's definitely not me", is the suspect's riposte. What a scandal to disturb him at a party, he will involve his embassy, the police will be informed. The temperature rises, the volume of the music falls. Everyone gathers round. Herranz frisks the man: unarmed. *Voilà!* To calm the mood a little, Leyma asks to speak. Edgar Marino, another student, starts playing guitar and sings *"pour tout le monde"*. A symbol of brotherhood.

During this short *détente* the 'suspect', who admits to having reacted somewhat 'nervously', offers Herranz and Donatini a swig from a bottle of Johnnie Walker. As Herranz puts the glass to his lips, he discreetly orders Donatini to fetch Dous, with the informant. The latter immediately points to the man in the photo: "It's him!" There's no escaping it, the police superintendent wants 'Nourredine' to go with them to the DST for questioning. "Let me just go to the toilet first." OK. Then the earth really does shake. Flashes of light and loud bangs fill the room. Dous and Donatini slump to the floor, a bullet between their eyes; Moukharbal gets two in the head; Herranz lies seriously injured, twitching in a pool of blood. The room is full of smoke, the front door is ajar. "I saw an armed individual running through the passageway that joins the two properties, jumping into the courtyard, and vaulting the dividing wall of 11, Rue Toullier. This individual sped off into the darkness",[12] a witness states. "I never knew the surname and first name of the man who fired at us", Police Superintendent Herranz explains in hospital. The gunman disappeared into the night. Jean Baklouti, then head of the DST, admits in an interview: "The affair was handled badly."[13]

The shooting in the Rue Toullier was perpetrated with heavy artillery: a Tokarev T33, 7.62mm, a Russian-made pistol. Only an experienced gunman could operate a murder weapon of this kind. It dawns on the DST that they are not dealing with a 'militant from the PFLP' but with a ruthless professional. His name is printed on the front page of *Le Quotidien de Paris*: "*WE'RE SEARCHING FOR CARLOS*".[14] *Libération* leads with "Carlos – DST: 3 – 0". The link has been made between London, The Hague, the Drugstore and Orly.

In the Rue Toullier, the professional killer slips up: there are fingerprints on three bottles and a number of glasses. The Police Judiciaire compares them to the prints that are sent from Venezuela: they are unmistakeably those of Ilich Ramírez Sánchez, a.k.a. Carlos. In the meantime, more photos become available. The most famous shows the terrorist with his round face and sideburns, which were in fashion at the time, and with large, black-framed glasses, "which made him look like a housefly".[15]

The party in the Rue Toullier

Two days later, the police raid the house at 11, Rue Amélie, a narrow connecting street between the Rue de Grenelle and the Rue Saint-Dominique, in the 7th *arrondissement*. The address is on a cheque that was in the possession of the late informant Moukharbal. The Columbian occupant confirms that Ilich "passed by" on the night in question, 27 July. "He made a call to London and wrote several letters." In his apartment, the police make a shocking discovery: "Around a dozen pistols, dynamite, plastic and twenty-eight grenades. The police laboratory confirms that the grenades are identical to those detonated at Orly. An American M26 grenade matches those used in the Drugstore on the Boulevard Saint-Germain. Four grenades of the same type were left behind after the hostage-taking drama in the French Embassy in The Hague."[16] At the bottom of an intercepted letter that Ilich sends to a Spanish friend in London that night is his signature: "Dear Angela, as you must know, things are very serious.... I have sent Chiquitin (Michel Moukharbal's nickname) to a better world for his treason. Kisses. Carlos." At Angela's home, the British police find a bag with weapons and lists of Ilich Ramírez Sánchez's future targets. From now on, and for evermore, he is merely Carlos' shadow.

The DST has the name, not the terrorist. At the end of a bumper year of operations, Carlos surprises the world with a red-hot Christmas present. On 21 December, terrorists under his command take eleven OPEC (Organization of the Petroleum Exporting Countries) ministers hostage during a meeting at its headquarters in Vienna. Amongst them are Sheikh Yamani, the Saudi Arabian oil minister, world-famous due to the oil embargo two years previously with which he tipped the balance of power over the much-coveted energy source in favour of the Middle East.[17] The whole world is watching with bated breath: "Terrorists raid OPEC oil parley in Vienna, kill 3", *The New York Times* reports on its front page. Two days later, on the other side of the world, *The Indian Express* writes: "Guerrillas release all remaining hostages". On the television news, viewers see a man with a leather jacket and beret *à la* Che Guevara negotiating on the tarmac of the airport in Vienna. Once again, Carlos succeeds in getting himself flown to his desired destination: Tripoli and Algiers, where he is granted asylum and disappears into the meanders of the PFLP in North Africa and the Middle East.

A SUCCESSFUL OPERATION

Carlos will strike again in France in the early 1980s. He plants bombs on trains (Paris-Toulouse: 5 dead, 77 wounded; the TGV at Tain-l'Hermitage and Marseille station: 5 dead and 54 wounded) and in the Rue Marbeuf in Paris: 1 dead and 66 wounded. With the latter attacks, Carlos wants to put pressure on the French government to free his right-hand man, Bruno Bréguet, and also his girlfriend, Magdalena Kopp, following their arrest for possession of several kilos of explosives. In this too he is successful. Carlos and Magdalena are reunited in 1985 in Damascus, where they live with their young daughter in one of the city's better neighbourhoods. In the established family tradition, they have named their child after one of their idols: Rosa, after Rosa Luxemburg,[18] the German radical socialist.

After the fall of the Berlin Wall, Carlos is no longer safe in the Eastern Bloc, his favourite haven between the bombings. After years of lying low in the Middle East and North Africa, the party is over. In August 1994, the terrorist is supine on the operating table of a surgical centre in the Sudanese capital Khartoum. Anaesthetised. His face is to be permanently changed beyond recognition. At the age of forty-five, the anti-imperialist fighter wants to enjoy a well-earned retirement, to elude the police forces who are hunting for him across the globe. This masterstroke is designed to give him peace and quiet. It works a treat, but not in the way that Carlos has imagined. This time the roles are reversed. Before the surgeon makes the first incision, a team from the DST enters the operating theatre and puts the still-sedated murderer on a plane to Paris.

Carlos has been living in a French prison ever since, where the only thing he has to kill is time. He is lovingly defended by his lawyer, *Maître* Isabelle Coutant-Peyre, the assistant of his previous lawyer, iconoclast Jacques Vergès[19] and, like Carlos, a girl from a bourgeois family. They marry in an Islamic religious ceremony in 2001. According to *Maître* Coutant-Peyre, everything was set-up by Mossad, the Israeli secret service, to discredit Carlos and the Palestinian cause. The French media regularly report on developments in the endless proceedings against the man, who in France alone has 15 dead and 200 wounded on his conscience.

But anyone who sees Carlos smiling beneath his carefully trimmed moustache on TV in 2019, is looking at a seventy-year-old with true Parisian Left-Bank looks: in the summer, a dark blazer with a nonchalant pocket square, white shirt with cashmere foulard and stonewashed jeans; in the winter, a fur shapka. Anyone who doesn't know any better would spontaneously invite him for a coffee on the terrace of the Café de Flore, Les Deux Magots or the Brasserie Lipp opposite. Perhaps not on that of the Emporio Armani Caffè next door. There used to be a small, convivial shopping complex on the site. The Drugstore Publicis.

The party in the Rue Toullier

A young Ho Chi Minh at the 1920 Tours congress that split the French socialist party (SFIO).

LEFT BANK, EAST

5

MADE IN PARIS: THE PEOPLE'S REPUBLIC OF CHINA AND THE WAR IN VIETNAM

For many, the Parisian university of La Sorbonne will be forever associated with the student protests of May '68. That intellectual hotbed, however, was already fomenting revolution long before this, back in the early years of the twentieth century. Revolution even became an export product; activists for the People's Republic of China and for the decolonisation of Laos, Cambodia and Vietnam had their revolutionary zeal ignited in Paris and took it home with them. This can be attributed largely to one man: Li Shizeng. In 1912, this Chinese alumnus of the Sorbonne founded the Travail-Études movement which attracts thousands of Chinese students to Paris, including two characters named Deng and Zhou. Young people are also travelling to the city from neighbouring Indochina, then under French rule. Their aim is to work in the French capital while also studying. Among them is a certain figure called Ho. But students will be students, after all, and Li's well-intentioned plan for instructing these youngsters in science, technology and public administration soon goes awry. Instead of learning how to govern administrations, what they actually master in Paris is how to overthrow them.

Made in Paris: the People's Republic of China and the war in Vietnam

LESSONS ON REVOLUTION

Li Shizeng is a philanthropist and an admirer of French culture, educated at reputable French institutions such as the École Agricole in Montargis, the Sorbonne and the Institut Pasteur in Paris. He is convinced that Western knowledge and science can help an archaic China progress. In Li's opinion, China has been treading water for more than fifty years, while the burgeoning world powers of Great Britain and France have been the beneficiaries. The governments of Britain and France had initiated a joint military expedition to China as far back as 1860. The British did so for commercial reasons, the French in order to smooth the way for Catholic missionaries. After taking over Canton, they set fire to the Imperial Summer Palace in Peking, but not without first looting the art treasures within – or, rather, 'bringing them to safety', according to Queen Victoria and the Empress of France, Eugénie. The former adds them to the British Museum, the latter puts them in the Château de Fontainebleau. Although little known in the West, that theft of more than 500 precious cultural treasures remains a dagger in China's heart.

Forty years later, at the beginning of the twentieth century, Li's ancestral land is still in serious crisis. Famine and devastating wars between indigenous warlords keep the country in a stranglehold. Meanwhile, Japan, Great Britain and France are dividing up the region between themselves into spheres of influence. In the end, it all becomes too much for Li Shizeng. He decides to create a new intellectual elite in China to confront these problems and effect change.

It is with this goal in mind that he establishes the Travail-Études movement. In excess of 4,000 promising students arrive in France to further their education, flocking to Paris in particular. While abroad, they are expected not only to learn, but also to work in order to finance their studies. This soon proves an explosive cocktail. At universities and colleges, these young Chinese students are initiated into the ideas underpinning the Enlightenment and the French Revolution. Never before have terms such as 'liberty', 'equality' and 'fraternity' reached their ears, still less words such as 'independence', 'revolution' and 'republic'. Likewise, it is in the factories and workshops that they also encounter their first socialists and communists. They too are unknown to them because in the early twentieth century not a single translation into Chinese yet exists of the ideas of Karl Marx. By contrast, his tenets have firmly taken root in industrialised countries such as France, and particularly in Paris, the city of revolutions and barricades. Before Li realises, it is too late: the lid to that Pandora's box is already open.

THE COMMUNE OF SHANGHAI

In Paris, a great many of the Chinese Communist Party's subsequent leaders lap up the ideas of Jean-Jacques Rousseau, Montesquieu, Voltaire and Marx. Let's begin with Deng Xiaoping. After his arrival in Marseille, the sixteen-year-old Deng starts work at the Laminoirs du Creusot, the steel mill run by the Schneider family, where he is immediately brought face-to-face with the misery of the proletariat. His next employer, the tyre manufacturer Hutchinson, sacks him because of his rebellious behaviour. His work file makes it clear: "Doesn't want to work, don't rehire". So, Deng heads off to Paris, where the communist militants at the Renault factories in Billancourt hone his political education until razor sharp. Meanwhile, another student arrives in Paris by the name of Zhou Enlai, subsequently premier of the People's Republic of China. He also catches the same revolutionary bug. In 1921, from his digs at 17, Rue Godefroy, a street behind the Place d'Italie, he founds the Chinese Communist Party in Europe – the forerunner to the Chinese Communist Party – together with several supporters from Travail-Études.[1]

Zhou is completely in thrall to the history of the French Revolution. He knows every detail. Above all else, it is the utter lack of compromise in its 'heads off' approach that he finds so wonderful. From Paris, he sends his fiancée in China a postcard of his great idol, Robespierre. On the back he scribbles a romantic reverie: "One day I shall also have to face the guillotine, but I hope it shall be arm-in-arm with you."[2] Quite what the young lady thought about this prospect is unknown. Zhou's words are prophetic: it won't matter a jot to him whether he is in fact shortened by a head. In the Shanghai of the late 1920s, he organises several workers' uprisings with his comrade Zhao Shiyan. Two of them fail, but a section of the city falls into their hands during their third attempt. With Paris once again the source of their inspiration, they name this acquisition the 'Commune of Shanghai'. The victory is short-lived. Just as in 1871, when Adolphe Thiers bathed the Paris Commune in blood, so it is for the Commune of Shanghai, with Chiang Kai-shek, the commander-in-chief of China's nationalist forces, quelling the uprising through mass executions, beheadings and widespread disappearances. Comrade Zhao Shiyan is beheaded. Zhou Enlai manages to flee. Perhaps his fascination for the guillotine temporarily escapes him.

In 1949, the Communists seize power under the inspirational leadership of their great helmsman, Mao Zedong, and announce the birth of the People's Republic of China. After 1956, Deng becomes secretary general of the Chinese Communist Party and, consequently, the most powerful man after Chairman Mao. He falls into disfavour during the Cultural Revolution. In 1975, however,

Made in Paris: the People's Republic of China and the war in Vietnam

when China finds itself brought to a wretched state thanks to the implementation of Mao's policies, Zhou Enlai succeeds in returning his Parisian comrade Deng to the centre stage. In the early 1980s, it is Deng Xiaoping who introduces the first far-reaching economic reforms to China. As a result, the People's Republic makes a great leap forward in only a few decades. Deng's 'open door policy', a form of socialism with capitalist features, continues to be the guiding principle for economic policy in China to this day. Where else but in Paris could Deng have learnt this combination of revolutionary ideas and hedonism? For Deng, the legacy of his five-year sojourn in France was a lifelong passion for French delicacies: wine, cheese, croissants and coffee. Nostalgically, he will compare the tea houses in his native province of Sichuan with the cafés of France, frequently reminiscing about his favourite establishment on the Place d'Italie in Paris.[3]

UNASSUMING PATRIOT

By 1890, when Ho Chi Minh was born in Central Vietnam as Nguyen Sinh Cung, the French had divided the country into three states: Cochin China (South Vietnam), Annam (Central Vietnam) and Tonkin (North Vietnam). In 1887, along with Cambodia and Laos, these were consolidated as the Indochinese Union. France governs Indochina via a colonial administration, without the participation of the people. That is to put it rather mildly: according to the young Ho, the French rule under a reign of terror. He longs to escape, and in 1911 boards a French steamer as a ship's galley assistant, sailing halfway round the world. After spending time in Boston and London, he arrives in Paris in 1917. France is then in the thick of the First World War, and the October Revolution is in full swing in Russia. The 'red echo' of the latter reverberates throughout Europe, also reaching Ho in Paris. This unassuming young man's ability as a jack-of-all-trades enables him to keep his head above water: for example, as a master in Chinese calligraphy, a decorator of imitation Chinese antiques or retouching photographs. On one particular day, Parisians pick up their copy of the newspaper *La Vie Ouvrière* and read the following advertisement: "If you'd like to have a lifelong souvenir for your family and friends, have your photographs enlarged by Nguyen-Ai-Quoc. A splendid portrait in a splendid frame starting from 45 francs. 9, Impasse Compoint, Paris."[4] The fact that he signs this as Ai-Quoc, 'the patriot', points to his growing political consciousness. He pores over the same publication for news about his mother country and does not like what he reads. Slowly but surely, he starts to put pen to paper to jot down his political convictions and disseminate them.

In 1919, when the American president Woodrow Wilson comes to Paris to sign the Versailles Treaty to mark the end of the First World War, Ho decides to move up a gear in his approach. He feels he must be present in Versailles. Ho believes that President Wilson's new discourse on self-determination relates not only to the Western world but also to Asia. He dresses sprucely for the occasion. In his long coat, grey-striped trousers and top hat, he looks quite in keeping. However, what he is carrying under one arm is anything but acceptable to the assembled company in Versailles: *Les Cahiers de Revendications du Peuple Viet-Namien*. Nobody has any interest in hearing about this, and Ho is thrown out of the formal proceedings. 'Nobody' is perhaps misleading. Socialist leaders such as Léon Blum and Marcel Cachin feel that Ho's political courses of action are extremely courageous, and they approach him. The future Vietnamese freedom fighter becomes a socialist militant.

However, Ho feels that, with regard to the problems in his homeland, the socialist stance is far too tame. In 1920, at the famous Tours Congress for the socialist Second International, Ho and other dissatisfied socialists split away and set up their own party: the French Communist Party (PCF). They ally themselves with Moscow, becoming members of Comintern (the Communist or Third International). Before long the French and Americans will be hearing more from this skinny, goatee-bearded fellow whom they threw out at Versailles, leaving his demands to swirl about in the air and cross the cobblestones behind those palace gates.

Ho patiently perseveres with his political writing. From Paris, he focuses increasing attention on French oppression in Indochina, which includes his article '*Le sadisme colonial*'. It is this grisly tale of multiple rapes and child murders in a Vietnamese village that instils a deep hatred of Ho in the French government. Above all, it is his stinging comparison of French policy in Vietnam with the bloody suppression of the Paris Commune, the inspiration for which he took from the *Histoire de la Commune de 1871* by eye-witness Hippolyte Lissagaray. In 1923, Ho is ready for the next step: he relocates to Moscow for his 'further completion'. Then, thoroughly versed in the art of class struggle, he travels to Hong Kong, where he founds the Communist Party of Vietnam.

Ho – by then known as Ho Chi Minh [Bringer of Light] – has his first opportunity to further the Vietnamese cause in 1945. The French oppressor has become profoundly destabilised by the end of the Second World War. In France, the PCF and its trade union organisation, the Confédération Générale du Travail (CGT), are so strong that they are threatening the traditional political parties. This makes it precisely the right time for Ho to declare Vietnam's independence, casting himself as president. In so doing, he sets alight the powder keg of

Made in Paris: the People's Republic of China and the war in Vietnam

a long and gruelling war in Vietnam. First it is against the French, then still more intensely against the Americans on to whom, amid the Cold War climate, the shrewd French pass the buck of bringing the global advance of Communism to a halt.[5] Once the Americans are mired up to their necks in the swamp of Vietnam, the French get out, leaving their allies to clear up the mess alone. It is all for naught: Saigon, the South Vietnamese capital, falls on 30 April 1975. One year later, North and South Vietnam are united as the Socialist Republic of Vietnam. Saigon is renamed Ho Chi Minh City. Mission accomplished for Ho and his *Revendications du Peuple Viet-Namien.*

The Indochinese war for independence also had some unwelcome side-effects for France. In Vietnam, more than 5,000 Algerian soldiers have also been fighting in the French army against Ho Chi Minh. While so engaged, they learn two lessons: France is not invincible and a 'revolutionary war', such as that waged by the Viet Minh independence coalition, can result in liberation. In the late 1950s, when representatives from the Algerian National Liberation Front (FLN) pay a visit to Peking, Zhou Enlai receives the freedom fighters with full state honours. Algerian flags flutter at the airport and Mao Zedong thanks them for their 'contribution to the revolution'. Of greater significance for these FLN men is the pledge of 2 billion francs in war loans, mortars, submachine guns and 75mm ordnance.[7] Previously, they had also met in Hanoi with Ho Chi Minh, who assured them of the Democratic Republic of Viet Nam's moral support and who (in French) gave them a not unimportant piece of advice: *"Restez unis!"* [Stay united!].[8]

UNACCEPTABLE STUPIDITY

And then there is that other Parisian student who went on to enjoy a 'successful' career back in his homeland. Saloth Sar is an electrical engineering student in 1950s Paris. In 1951, he participates in the illustrious 80th anniversary commemoration of the Paris Commune, which by then has fired the imagination of the entire communist world. The story of the Commune also has a profound effect on the young Sar. With a touch of radicalism, he concludes that the Commune failed because the proletariat neglected to install dictatorial rule over the bourgeoisie from the outset.[9] Saloth Sar, better known as Pol Pot, swears that he will never commit an act of such "unacceptable stupidity" in the Cambodia liberated by his Khmer Rouge. Fortunately for the French, his infamous killing fields lie some 9,700 kilometres to the east of the Champs-Élysées. Between 1975 and 1979, the Khmer Rouge will send almost two million people to their deaths out of a population of seven million. This puts Pol Pot way out in front of Robespierre.[10]

Undeniably, the revolutionary spirit of Paris has brought its influence to bear on political developments in Asia. In turn, certain contemporary Parisian neighbourhoods still bear the mark of Ho Chi Minh City or Peking. The steady influx of Asian migrants accounts for these developments. Chinese and 'Indochinese' people can be seen migrating to France, chiefly for economic reasons, even during the Second Empire (1852-1870), when the French are on their 'journey of discovery' in Asia. A fully fledged wave of migration comes only during the First World War, when no fewer than 140,000 Chinese and Indochinese people arrive in the country. They are put to work in French factories and logistic networks, thereby ensuring the swift despatch of food and war materials to the Front, and also replacing their conscripted French colleagues in car factories such as Panhard & Levassor, Citroën and Renault.[11] Protracted armed conflicts in the Indochinese region – and French involvement in these battles – are later responsible for a permanent influx. After the fall of Saigon in 1975, a new flood of refugees appears from the wider region of Vietnam, Laos, Cambodia and southern China. Between 1975 and 1977, some 145,000 refugees from Indochina settle in France, 50 to 60 percent of whom are of Chinese descent.

Many congregate in Paris. This explains the Chinatowns overflowing with Asian restaurants, repair workshops, clothing establishments, supermarkets, dry cleaners, mobile phone stores, travel bureaux, jewellers, hairdressers, bank branches and stalls selling spices, rice and vegetables, all labelled in incomprehensible characters. Even the *dames faisant commerce de leur corps*[12] [ladies of the night] on the Boulevard de la Villette are Chinese. To visit the Rue de Belleville or the Tang Frères supermarkets in the Triangle de Choisy, south of the Place d'Italie, is to cross into another continent. Nowadays, many Parisians and tourists come to these little pieces of Asia-in-Paris in search of recipes for a culinary revolution. But once upon a time, it was the likes of Ho Chi Minh, Deng Xiaoping, Zhou Enlai and Pol Pot who came here seeking inspiration for their political revolutions.

Made in Paris: the People's Republic of China and the war in Vietnam

After the attack: François Mitterrand's bullet-riddled Peugeot 403.

6

MYTHERRAND

First a decorated civil servant in the Vichy collaborationist regime, then a resistance leader. First a far-right militant, then leader of the 'Union de la Gauche', a leftist coalition. First an anti-communist, then an ally of the French Communist Party. First a supporter of French Algeria, then a standard-bearer for independence. First an advocate of capital punishment in the colony, then an abolitionist. An enemy of the Fifth Republic who later became its champion. Married to Danielle Gouze but simultaneously the author of 1,217 love letters to Anne Pingeot.[1] In 1958, at the height of his ministerial career, the Algerian crisis unexpectedly conjures an old adversary back onto the political stage: General de Gaulle. Mitterrand takes a fall. He pulls out all the stops to clamber back up. Sometimes rather clumsily. It thus transpires that the man with a penchant for grandiose buildings such as La Grande Bibliothèque, La Grande Arche or Le Grand Louvre, also harbours one for Le Grand Guignol, money and women.

L'ALGÉRIE FRANÇAISE!

On Thursday 29 May 1958, six Dakotas take off from Le Bourget. It is early afternoon. With the utmost secrecy, they are due to collect the first contingent of paratroopers from Perpignan and fly them to Paris. The next day, on 30 May, the soldiers will occupy every strategic position in the capital. They will arrest the new prime minister, Pflimlin, the traitor of *l'Algérie française*, and the minister of the interior, Jules Moch. Other champions of Algerian independence, such as François Mitterrand, who recently nailed his colours to the mast on the issue, and Pierre Mendès France, leader of the Socialists, will also be arrested. If the Communist Party defies the coup – not unthinkable given it is the largest political party in the country – then its leaders, Jacques Duclos and Maurice Thorez, will also be jailed.[2]

The French military commanders in Algeria have long since washed their hands of the political dithering in Paris. None of the twenty-four prime ministers and twenty-two governments of the Fourth Republic,[3] now in its twelfth year, have been able to solve the question of French Algeria. But the troops have stood in the firing line the entire time, battling to protect French interests against an expanding and increasingly professional independence movement. French attitudes are the sticking point. Unlike other French overseas territories, such as Morocco and Tunisia, which gained independence in 1956, the people do not see Algeria as a colony but as an intrinsic part of France. The French inhabit an immense country, one that stretches all the way from Dunkirk on the Belgian border to Tamanrasset, the Tuareg capital in the Ahaggar massif on the border with Niger. Since 1830, a million French citizens have been building their lives on the opposite shores of the Mediterranean, cheek-by-jowl with 10 million Algerians.[4] In a land that can be reached by boat from Marseille in a single day, they run businesses, practise trades, build properties, raise families, and give their all. They tend the graves of their ancestors, who were born and bred in Algeria. Farmers, industrialists, people in the liberal professions, winegrowers, merchants, civil servants, soldiers: their futures are now at stake.

Senator Henri Borgeaud, owner of the vast La Trappe estate, is amongst them. He was born and raised in Algeria as a third-generation child. His two vineyards, Domaine de La Trappe and Chapeau-de-Gendarme produce, respectively, 40,000 and 45,000 hectolitres of wine. Borgeaud, who employs some 6,000 Algerians, is also the proprietor of orange farms and agricultural concerns, as well as the builder of schools and dispensaries. "*Il est à lui seul un état. Ses désirs sont des ordres*" [He is a state unto himself. His desires are orders].[5] Like many of his compatriots, both grand and humble, Borgeaud does not want to leave Algeria. By 1954, on the opposite shores of the Mediterranean, over 60,000 Algerians are living in Paris, their new home, and working in the factories around the capital.

The French may consider France and Algeria to be one and the same country, but in reality, their peoples couldn't be further apart. "The French had never bothered with education: only 15 per cent of Algerian men could read and write in 1954, and just 5 per cent of women."[7] Over 1,683,000 children were excluded from primary education, only 6,000 students entered secondary education and a mere 4,000 pupils received vocational training.[8] It is rich versus poor. The situation is untenable. Local and regional resistance groups have joined forces over the years to form the Front de Libération Nationale (FLN). It has been waging an open, unrelenting war of independence since 1954. In just four years, the casualties can be counted in the thousands and unspeakable atrocities have been committed. The French army feels completely abandoned by Paris in the fight for *l'Algérie française*.

The French are also still smarting over the loss of Indochina to Ho Chi Minh's communists four years earlier.[9] After years of heavy military losses, culminating in the ignoble fall of Diên Biên Phu on 7 May 1954, thousands of French citizens saw their possessions and livelihoods go up in smoke as their country retreated from the Asian region. The French and the *pieds noirs*[10] fear that history will repeat itself in Algeria. Therefore: no *indépendance* for *l'Algérie française*.

COOKING THE CARROTS (ALMOST)

Pflimlin's appointment as prime minister is the straw that breaks the camel's back.[11] His views on Algeria are overly liberal. It is a provocation, and yet another example of Parisian incompetence. Furious supporters of French Algeria storm the Government Palace in Algiers and proclaim a *Comité de salut public*, an alternative government. They have the backing of the army. Having seized power in Algiers, General Raoul Salan, commander-in-chief of the colonial troops in Algeria, and General Jacques Massu, the popular commander of the 10th Parachute Division, both want to turn the screws on Paris.

On 24 May, news reaches the French capital that a *Comité de salut public* has also seized political power in Corsica. The fever is spreading. The situation reaches boiling point with Pflimlin's appointment. With Algeria and Corsica in the hands of the military insurgents, General Salan sends a telegram to Paris: the army will not make peace with an *Algérie abandonnée*.[12]

Mytherrand

Only if there is a complete *volte face* – and it is a question of minutes not hours – and a new strong man takes charge of the country, a man who deserves the confidence of the generals, then, and only then, are the military prepared to abandon Operation Résurrection. Meanwhile, the 50,000 paratroopers stationed at the military bases in south-western France are poised and ready to dot the i's and cross the t's in Paris. All they are waiting for is the coded signal: "*Les carottes sont cuites*" [The carrots are cooked, meaning literally 'there is no turning back'].[13]

Thank God a *coup de théâtre* is underway – *in extremis* – in Paris. The Dakotas are flying over Limoges as René Coty, the last president of the turbulent Fourth Republic, delivers his speech to the Assemblée Nationale, stating that with the country on the brink of civil war, he was "turning towards the most illustrious of Frenchmen, towards the man who, in the darkest years of our history, was our chief for the reconquest of freedom and who refused dictatorship in order to re-establish the Republic."[14] With these words, Coty rolls out the red carpet for the man who, in 1944–45, brilliantly put France – defeated by Germany and financially ruined – back on the map of world powers as one of the victors of the war, alongside America, Britain and Russia. If *le Général* de Gaulle does not instantly heed Coty's call to form a new government and contain the Algerian crisis with immediate effect, not only will there be further bloodshed in Algeria, but also in the streets of Paris. In which case, France will founder like a rudderless ship. The situation is perilously close to the brink.

Meanwhile, in the apparent calm of La Boisserie, his country home in Colombey-les-Deux-Églises, the erstwhile saviour of France, General de Gaulle, has spent the last few months secretly preparing his return to power. His strategy is one of silence, patience, intelligence gathering and diplomacy. As the telephones are tapped at La Boisserie, his confidants slip in and out discreetly: former staff members, party leaders and diplomats who all want to sound out the General and learn what he might do for a country that has lost its way. Military personnel too, with whom he maintains direct communications, such as General Salan in Algeria, who doggedly begins his letters to de Gaulle with "*Mon Général*".[15]

But after bidding farewell to politics in 1946, the General does not want to create the impression that he is forcing himself on the situation at hand. A man of his stature – who must be thanked for ensuring that whenever the war is discussed, "it is not in terms of defeat, chaos, starvation, despondency and collaboration, but in those of glory and triumph"[16] – does not simply act of his own volition. No, a man of his calibre must be *invited*. Which is what President Coty does on bended knee. His entreaty is heard in Colombey. De Gaulle immediately condemns any act, from whichever quarter, that threatens the public order.[17]

General Salan rephrases his command: "*Les carottes ne sont pas cuites.*" [The carrots are not cooked]. The empty Dakotas double-back to Paris.[18]

THE GENERAL'S RETURN

General de Gaulle heads to the capital. He strides into the Elysée Palace in civilian clothes, past a bank of microphones and flashing cameras, at 7.30pm on 29 May. But the game has not yet been decisively won. The generals are waiting in the wings with their fingers on the trigger.[19] The draft telegram from General Salan to General Miquel, head of Operation Résurrection, pulls no punches: "30 May 10:30 – Operation Resurrection – will be launched on my order in the following situations: 1. If Gen. de Gaulle gives the command - 2. Gen. de Gaulle cannot form a govt., *Salut Public Republ.* - 3. communist insurrectional emergency – Salan."[20]

De Gaulle unveils his plans in the Assemblée the very next day. He wants to rule by proxy for six months. Parliament will be suspended and a new constitution written. For de Gaulle, the latter is vital. It will prevent the Assemblée from dropping its governments, as it often did during the Third and Fourth Republics. Furthermore, ministers must relinquish their parliamentary seats so as to eliminate conflicts of interest. But most importantly of all, de Gaulle is not returning to national politics to be immortalised in a portrait bust that will adorn the corridors of the Elysée Palace, as per previous presidents. No. He wants to be directly elected by the French people, to be invested with the power to lead the country by the citizens themselves, rather than being mandated by the electoral college.[21] Everyone in the orbit of the Palais Bourbon understands that it is a choice between de Gaulle or chaos. General de Gaulle is elected prime minister, on a six-month term, by 329 votes to 224. The country breathes a collective sigh of relief. The paratroopers remain in their barracks.

On 27 June, prime minister de Gaulle makes a televised address from the Hôtel Matignon, the French prime minister's residence on the Rue de Varenne: "... In referendums and elections, the ten million Algerians will have the same rights and duties as the French."[22] In his inimitable and paternalistic voice, he restores confidence and hope to the French: "It was dark yesterday. But this evening there is light." Then, as if personally to embrace the thousands of television viewers, he extends his arms to them: "Frenchwomen, Frenchmen, help me!"[23] The saviour is well and truly back. The French heed his call. Six months later, on 21 December 1958, 'prime minister' de Gaulle triumphs in the elections[24] to become 'President' de Gaulle.

Not every politician is thrilled with this result. In the eyes of many, the cunning old fox has played a clever hand. His privileged links to the military top brass; the explosive Algerian crisis and the related panic in Paris; the French people's hatred of the Fourth Republic, which inflicted governments upon them that sometimes collapsed in just a couple of days – all completely unworthy of a civilised country. Amongst the ranks of the disillusioned is François Mitterrand, holder of several ministerial positions in the shaky Fourth Republic. After becoming the minister of veterans and war victims at the age of thirty-one, he has climbed through the ranks. In 1954, in his capacity as minister of the interior, he condemns the creation of the Algerian FLN: "Algeria is France; the sole negotiation possible is war."[25]

Two years later, in 1956, in yet another government, Mitterrand becomes minister of justice.[26] His position on French Algeria is even more uncompromising. Meanwhile, the conflict has degenerated into a dirty war. No holds barred. The French army embarks on a campaign of air raids, bombings and torture, while the FLN retaliates with attacks and killings in both Algeria and France. The soldiers, many of whom have fought for France in Indochina, know that their leader is not infallible. Meanwhile, civilians, women and children are dying on both sides of the conflict.

But the odour of blood and gunpowder does not reach the Ministry of Justice on the sparkling Place Vendôme, next to the exclusive Ritz Hotel. Here, the air is scented with the smell of polished mahogany. "Negative opinion on the appeal", minister Mitterrand writes in blue ink on a stack of files, or "Appeal to be rejected".[27] These are his stock phrases for advising President Coty on which FLN fighters to pardon or execute. Mitterrand rejects thirty-eight out of forty-five such pleas.[28] The unlucky victims are beheaded in Algiers, Oran or Constantine, in north-eastern Algeria. It is like pouring oil onto a fire.

A year later, in January 1957, as a government minister, Mitterrand helps transfer the political power in Algeria to General Massu, in an attempt to eradicate the FLN. The result is a pattern of systematic torture and some 3,000 executions.[29] One of the victims is a young lawyer named Ali Boumendjel, a member of the militant Union Démocratique du Manifeste Algérien (UDMA). He became a member of the FLN after realising that non-violent resistance would never help the Algerians achieve independence. A month after the handover of power to General Massu, the French government gets cash on the nail: on 9 February, during the Battle of Algiers, Boumendjel falls into the hands of French paratroopers. Several weeks later, the resistance fighter jumps from the sixth-floor window of the barracks in which he is imprisoned.[30] Suicide. But in 2001, Paul Aussaresses, head of the French intelligence services in Algiers at the time, confessed to having personally commanded his subordinates "to kill him and make the crime look like suicide".[31] By the time the assassins throw the thirty-eight-year-old lawyer from the window, he has been interrogated and abused for forty-three days.[32] Boumendjel is just one case of many, but his 'suicide' is so egregious as to cause great consternation when debated in the Assemblée in Paris.[33]

The Assemblée is also concerned that the war is costing France millions,[3] while international condemnation is simultaneously mounting. Some ministers, such as Pierre Mendès France and Alain Savary, resign over the government's position on Algeria and slam the door shut on their way out. But not the minister of justice, François Mitterrand. Why not? His biographers Franz-Olivier Giesbert and Jean Lacouture both reach the same conclusion: "It is clear that, in his mind, La Place Vendôme was the antechamber of the Matignon.[35] First, minister of justice, then prime minister. Thus, Mitterrand hopes to be considered as someone who is tough enough: a person to whom the leadership of the country can be entrusted."[36]

CITOYEN FRANÇOIS

On 9 January 1959, the day after his appointment as president of the Republic, de Gaulle introduces his Cabinet. His prime minister is Michel Debré, a brilliant veteran and loyal confidant of the General[37] who, at his behest, will draft the Fifth Republic's new constitution. Debré's ministerial team includes many of Mitterrand's personal friends, but he, the man who has served the country with such distinction, has been overlooked. It is not wholly unexpected. There is no love lost between de Gaulle and Mitterrand. Their mutual disdain runs deep. All the way back to their first encounter in 1943, in Algiers. It was a debacle, and not without reason.

Having commenced his political career on the far right, Mitterrand was awarded the Ordre de la Francisque Gallique by Marshal Pétain, for services rendered to the collaborationist Vichy regime. An award that replaces the Republican values of *liberté, égalité* and *fraternité* with *travail, patrie* and *famille*. After subsequently defecting and joining the Resistance, Mitterrand backs General Giraud in the power struggle within the Comité Français de Libération Nationale (CFLN). Giraud loses, de Gaulle wins. Mitterrand establishes a resistance cell with a group of escaped prisoners of war. De Gaulle's nephew, Michel Cailliau, of all people, already controls a functioning unit. Cailliau warns the General that, given the above facts, the ex-Vichyist is not to be trusted.[38] All these setbacks torment Mitterrand like a boulder on his back. They push him down, closer to the ground. But that he will sink even lower is all his own doing.

The backdrop of François Mitterrand's life has changed dramatically since General de Gaulle became prime minister on 1 June 1958. Gone are

Mytherrand

official palaces, guards of honour, ministerial offices and receptions. Gone is the headed stationery. Gone is the chauffeur. Gone, too, are his party colleagues. Of his fourteen deputies from the Union Démocratique et Socialiste des Résistants (UDSR), ten immediately defect to de Gaulle, and come the *élections législatives* in November 1958, his party is decimated. Mitterrand is no longer *Monsieur le Ministre* but plain old *citoyen François*.

Putting bread on the table – *faire bouillir la marmite familiale* – is the concern he now shares with millions of other French people. As a lawyer, he must seek out court cases and clients. To this end, he associates himself with *Maître* Irène Dayan, wife of his close friend, Georges Dayan. The judges and magistrates enjoy the former minister of justice's tricks and are suitably impressed. He wins the case against film director Roger Vadim and Les Films Marceau, for example, who were sued for their racy television adaptation of *Les Liaisons dangereuses*.[39] Had he wanted it, Irène Dayan asserted, he could have carved out "an immense career as a barrister".[40] But it isn't for him. He can't wait to return to politics: to the guards of honour, the ministerial office, and the corridors of power. But to reach the top of the ladder once more, he must first start at the bottom. In March 1959, he wins the town hall of Château-Chinon, a small town in the Morvan. It is a start. A month later, he is co-opted into the Sénat. Things are starting to look up. Now, all that remains is a political agenda, some pros and cons. They are quickly found.

From the benches of the Palais du Luxembourg, he rails against "the privileged, the technocrats and the military who appropriated the levers of power in May 1958!"[41] Those who permit the war and atrocities in Algeria to continue unabated. Those who turn a blind eye to the paramilitary organisations that are threatening the politicians, writers and journalists who condemn *l'Algérie française*. What Mitterrand once deplored, he now champions: an independent Algeria. And the people he might once have supported (had he been given a nice ministerial post), he is now firmly against: de Gaulle and his government.

At a dinner party in the summer of 1958, just as the General and his allies are asserting their authority, the spirit of Fouquier-Tinville, the bloodthirsty prosecutor of the French Revolution, takes possession of Mitterrand: "There will never be enough lampposts on the Place de la Concorde to hang these usurpers",[42] the senator proclaims to his friends, Jacques Kosciusko-Morizet and Jean-Jacques Servan-Schreiber.[43] De Gaulle, dangling from a lamppost. For the time being, however, Mitterrand nurses his dream in solitude. The opposition is divided and Mitterrand, once used to playing first violin, is relegated to playing the triangle at the back of the orchestra. He desperately wants to conduct. The public needs to hear his voice again. To see what he represents. But how?

What touches the hearts of all French citizens? One thing: the war in Algeria! Sitting on the benches in the Palais du Luxembourg, the senator starts to sketch the outlines of a comeback plan.

THE OBSERVATORY AFFAIR

On the evening of 15 October 1959, after dining with close friends Georges and Irène Dayan, François Mitterrand departs for his residence on the Rue Guynemer. On the way home, he stops for a nightcap at the Brasserie Lipp on the Boulevard Saint-Germain. It is 11pm, which is still early for this establishment, located opposite Les Deux Magots and the Café de Flore. In full flow, black-waistcoated waiters hurry up and down the pavement, heads cocked, balancing trays laden with *choucroute royale* on their shoulders. Cutlery clatters, corks pop. Mitterrand surveys the scene. The person he is due to meet has stood him up. The ex-minister of justice climbs back into his dark blue Peugeot 403 and heads home.

"I was turning the corner, into the Rue de Seine, when I had the impression that I was being followed by individuals in a car. I could not distinguish the make or the colour. I followed their movements in my rear-view mirror. My suspicions were confirmed when I drove up the Rue de Tournon. It was then, when I arrived in front of the Palais du Luxembourg, that I tried to shake off my pursuers," he explained to the journalist from *Le Monde* later that night.[44]

Instead of turning right towards the Rue Guynemer, a long street that runs parallel to the Jardin du Luxembourg, Mitterrand turns left, onto the Rue de Médicis. The headlights are on his tail. At the fountain in the Place Edmond Rostand, his assailants draw close. They try to corner him. But Mitterrand accelerates and takes the wide Boulevard Saint-Michel. To no avail. He is almost overtaken at the École Nationale Supérieure des Mines. In desperation, he veers to the right, into the Rue Auguste Comte. Now's his chance. He is on the exposed Place André Honnorat, located between the Jardin du Luxembourg and the Jardin de l'Observatoire. The quarry pulls in by the pavement, flings the door open, and jumps from the car. Fearing the worst from his pursuers, the senator vaults the fence and disappears into the darkness.

Screeching brakes, machine-gun fire, bullets on metal, breaking glass. The assassins vanish into the night. Moments later, a staggering Mitterrand presses the bell of number 5, Avenue de l'Observatoire. The concierge immediately picks up the phone: Police! "It is likely that Mitterrand only survived thanks to his cool headedness",[45] report the newspapers. Seven bullet holes puncture the driver's side of the car: two in the rear wing and two each in the front and back doors.

Mytherrand

A bullet has perforated the driver's seat. Exactly where the former minister would have been sitting had he not kept his head. Everything points in one direction: to the far right, the Organisation de l'Armée Secrète (OAS), or another paramilitary opponent of Algerian independence. *Les ultras de l'Algérie française.*

The victim immediately appears on television. Danièle Breem, journalist for Radiodiffusion-Télévision Française (RTF): "*Monsieur le Ministre* [for this is how Mitterrand is still addressed], you have graciously welcomed us here, to your UDSR office, on the evening of the attack that, thanks to your presence of mind, you escaped. What can you tell us?" "Nothing," says a hesitant and sombre looking Mitterrand, "that I haven't already told your press colleagues. I'm not going to add anything that might increase the confusion in people's minds. But it is logical to think that this situation is the result of the passionate political climate created by extremist groups. I, like my political friends, am a patriot. I fight only for what is best for France, it is sad that this incitement has brought us to this point, that Frenchmen are fighting against Frenchmen. What more can I say? I think it is up to the competent services to conduct the appropriate investigation."[46] Photographs of the bullet-riddled Peugeot with shattered windows add weight to the story: Algerian conditions in central Paris.

LE GRAND GUIGNOL

The Left is outraged. The Parti Communiste Français (PCF), demands "the necessary measures to eliminate the conspirators and terrorists".[47] The communist trade union, the CGT, condemns this "unspeakable act" and rallies the workers to redouble their efforts "so that talks begin quickly and lead to a ceasefire in Algeria and the self-determination of the Algerian people."[48] *L'Humanité*, the PCF's newspaper, declares: "Demand the dissolution of the fascist gangs!"[49]

The hero who cheated death spends the weekend receiving journalists, politicians, friends and sympathisers from at home and abroad. On the Monday evening, 19 October, the Party office of the Union des Forces Démocratiques (UFD), sister party of the UDSR, led by Pierre Mendès France and others, meets to organise a rally against de Gaulle's Algerian policy. But the hero of the Observatory Affair still hasn't arrived, and it is now 6.30pm. He cannot attend, is the message conveyed by the secretariat. Nevertheless, Mendès France still decides to convene a press conference on Wednesday. He is gleefully anticipating the tragic demise of Debré's government. On Wednesday 21 October, Mitterrand is running late for the press conference at the Hôtel Moderne on the Place de la République, a favourite haunt of the champagne socialists. Mendès France is getting nervous when, all of a sudden, thunderous applause erupts from the back of the room. He's here! He's here! The new figurehead of the Algerian independence movement – the new leader in the fight against the extreme right – shakes hands, basks in the adulation and strides onto the stage through a guard of honour (how he has missed them!).

Eyebrows shoot up when Mitterrand bluntly declares that it might not be "*les ultras de l'Algérie française*" who wanted his skin, but that "the brain that put the gun in the hand is perhaps closer to the circles of power."[50] The inner circles of power! None other than President de Gaulle and prime minister Debré. They are responsible. They want to silence him. The halo of Che Guevara swirls above Mitterrand's balding skull as the end of Debré's government is spelt out in applause, embraces and endorsements.

The press and opposition have little time to hassle the government. The very next day, the mischievous delegate, Jean-Marie Le Pen,[51] jokes in the Assemblée corridors, "Ah friends! Tomorrow you'll see what you'll see. A real bombshell!"[52] It couldn't be worse. The blast stuns France. In the right-wing magazine *Rivarol*, a certain Robert Pesquet, a Poujadist[53] and former delegate, declared the assassination attempt had been faked, staged by Mitterrand with his help. *Pas vrai?* Well, lo and behold. Not only is Pesquet's court submission entirely accurate, but he also states that he posted two letters prior to the 'attack', in which he describes the events in detail and, obviously, in accordance with how they played out. He is accompanied to the post office on the Rue de Vaugirard by a court official, who opens the letter. His story is true from beginning to end. The other letter, with identical contents, was posted to an accomplice. Who also brandishes it at the media and police.

In his article, Pesquet describes how Mitterrand staged the attack on himself as a means of returning to politics. Algeria would be the motive. That they had concocted the plan over the course of three meetings: the last drink at the Brasserie Lipp, so that time wore on and the night drew in; the chase around the Jardin du Luxembourg; the so-called 'forcing the car off the road' by the fountain; the vault over the Jardin de l'Observatoire's fence, and the subsequent fusillade, carefully orchestrated to avoid wounding the former minister. To ensure seamless execution, Pesquet personally drove the attack car. His gardener, Abel Dahuron, fired the shots from a submachine gun supplied by a mechanic friend, André Pequignot. Mitterrand and Pesquet made three circuits around the park before they could enact the scheme. First, they encountered a couple kissing on the bench at the chosen spot. Next, a taxi drove into view. Third time lucky. After publication, Pesquet recapitulates his revelations at a well-attended press conference. On 23 October, *L'Aurore* quotes Pesquet: "I plotted with Mitterand!"[54] Blanket press coverage.

Mytherrand

BAZOOKA

The 'real bombshell' pitches the ambitious politician into a bottomless pit. Reactions range from outrage to hilarity. At the editorial office of *France Observateur*,[55] journalists stack chairs to the height of the Observatory's fence and try to leap over, in an attempt to prove whether or not the ex-minister is telling the truth.[56] Paris resounds with laughter.

Mitterrand confesses but spins a curious yarn in his defence. It was Pesquet who had approached him, he says, and confessed that he'd been ordered to 'liquidate Mitterrand', but out of a sense of sympathy, he couldn't go through with the plan. Instead, he would try and execute the plan, but it would unfortunately fail. He would then have to sell this story to his merciless commissioners. Pesquet would tell them it was beyond his control. That Mitterrand had stolen a march on him. In return for this 'lifesaving' information, Mitterrand had promised not to turn Pesquet over to the police. This story rattles all sides. Mitterrand is a wounded animal. Party colleagues are deserting him, political allies are turning their backs. "Friends witness him crying, they think he is close to suicide."[57]

Perhaps the full truth will never be known in the France of eternal and everlasting scandals, but the senator loses all credibility, as well as his parliamentary immunity. But it is Michel Debré, the prime minister, who twists the knife for the final time. A wound that he should never have inflicted. As former minister of justice, Mitterrand is fully apprised of Debré's suspected involvement in another malodorous case, *l'affaire du Bazooka*. One scandal hides another... On 16 January 1957, a plan was launched to topple General Salan and replace him with a military commander less synonymous with *l'Algérie française*. While Salan survived, his commandant, Rodier, was not so lucky. Debré, in sackcloth and ashes, is hauled before the minister of justice for questioning. But Mitterrand, under the guise of affection, hushed everything up because, as a minister, he too would have been implicated.[58] It seems to have slipped Debré's mind. Mitterrand now launches a full-scale attack on his *Bazooka* flank. The prime minister relaxes his grip. Too late. Debré has inadvertently served himself up as the enemy against which Mitterrand will now turn. Debré, the henchman of putschist de Gaulle, the oppressor of the Algerians. The stick with which Debré had wanted to push Mitterrand ever-deeper into the swamp, has now become the pariah's lifeline. He can use it to climb out of the mire – and he won't stop until he regains the centre stage.

THE ART OF EVASION

After establishing his own party, Convention des Institutions Républicaines, Mitterrand is named as the Left's candidate in the 1965 presidential elections. On Thursday, 9 September 1965, he writes to his mistress Anne Pingeot and declares: "*Anne, mon amour, Voilà c'est fait.* After long negotiations and doubts, now the certainty of a heavy burden: tonight at 6.00pm, following General de Gaulle's press conference, I announced that I am a candidate for the presidency of France. ... Deferre, Maurice Faure, Mollet and others from the Socialist Party have asked me *en bloc* to take up the gauntlet. *Bref, j'en suis là.*"[59]

Mitterrand loses to de Gaulle, the incumbent president, in the second round. In 1971, he becomes First Secretary of the Parti Socialiste and in 1974, as the Left's candidate, once again takes up the presidential gauntlet, this time against Valéry Giscard d'Estaing. Giscard triumphs in the second round. But Mitterrand is once more a player on the political stage.

It finally happens in 1981. François Mitterrand wins the presidential election, with 16 million votes to Giscard's 15 million. Meanwhile, the rocambolesque Observatory Affair is all but forgotten, although many new scandals follow in its wake, including: blasting the Greenpeace ship *Rainbow Warrior* out of the water; the illegal eavesdropping of critics in *Les Ecoutes de l'Elysée*;[60] the acceptance of bribes; insider trading in relation to Péchiney, a French aluminium concern, by friends and political associates; and the clandestine sale of arms to Iran.[61]

Mitterrand gets away with it all, miraculously. Even the suicide of his socialist prime minister, Pierre Bérégovoy, in 1993 – on 1 May no less – and that of his close associate, François de Grossouvre, who shoots himself in the head at the Elysée Palace a year later, fail to rattle him. Nor the lost millions earmarked for a Franco-African summit in Bujumbura; nor the taxpayer-funded accommodation, transport and protection for his second family;[62] nor the political launch of the entrepreneurial hustler, Bernard Tapie; nor the million-dollar theft from the coffers of the Elf-Aquitaine oil company. A French journalist once described Mitterrand's chicanery – his unique talent for navigating the fallout of such scandals – as *L'art de l'esquive*, the art of evasion.[63] The president is pleased to share the lessons he learnt from the Observatory Affair with his protégés: "Keep a low profile. Let the storm pass. You'll be fine."[64] And while François Mitterrand manages to deflect the flying debris with silence, indignation or denial, it still leads to cracks in the myth of the great man of the Left.

In 1994, after the publication of a controversial book[65] about the Left-wing leader's far-right past, party colleague Lionel Jospin said of Mitterrand,

Mytherrand

239

who was in the last year of his presidency: "One would like to dream of a simpler and clearer itinerary for the man who was the leader of the French Left in the 1970s and 1980s."[66] Guy Mollet, former leader of the French Socialists, a career minister and former prime minister, had already warned: "Mitterrand did not become a socialist, he learnt to speak socialist: nuance!"[67] The president is more Mitterrandist than socialist, switching political sides to secure his personal power.[68] But financial and political scandals, they are of all times and of all presidents. Love affairs too, with the exception of *Le Général*.

WOMEN

Yet why, in all of Paris, did Mitterrand choose that specific spot in the Jardin de l'Observatoire for his Le Grand Guignol performance? His intimate knowledge of the location is said to date all the way back to his assignations with a teenage girl named Marie-Louise Terrasse.[69] She first met the future president of the Republic on 28 January 1938, at one of the balls thrown by the École Normale Supérieure. It was here that François, twenty-one, stole the fourteen-year-old heart of the schoolgirl from the Lycée Fénélon. She accepted his marriage proposal but the lovers were separated by the war: François was captured in Germany during the early days of the conflict, and despite writing her multiple love letters, their relationship fizzled out by 1942. But it was not a wasted effort. It was an excellent training ground for the *graphomane amoureux,*[70] one that stood him in good stead with his subsequent conquests.

Next in line is Danielle Gouze. "She's pretty. I'll marry her!"[71] François exclaimed to his childhood friend, Roger-Patrice Pelat, whose insider trading later landed Mitterand in hot water. With his marriage in 1944, Mitterand does the right thing. François met Danielle at the end of the war, through her sister Christine, who was active in the Resistance. Christine and Danielle's parents were teachers, supporters of the Section Française de l'Internationale Ouvrière (SFIO) and amongst the Resistance fighters of the first rank. During the war, Danielle's father, Antoine Gouze, refused to list the Jewish children and teachers at his school. Sacked by the Vichy regime, he made ends meet by working as a private tutor. "One can well imagine that, after his [Mitterrand's] flirtation with the extreme right, his contribution to the Vichy regime, and receiving the Ordre de la Francisque Gallique from Pétain, marrying a girl from an authentic *résistance* family was a profitable investment."[72]

Although they will have three children, Pascal,[73] Jean-Christophe and Gilbert, their love does not run deep. When Madame Mitterrand questions him about his timetable for the day, her husband retorts coldly, "I did not marry you under the regime of the Inquisition."[74] Loneliness was the fate of the official wife of the president of the Republic, whose womanising created the image of "a compulsive collector of women, like those who collect Camembert labels".[75]

Through his *"Et alors?"* [So what?] response, everyone came to know Mazarine Pingeot, his illegitimate daughter by Anne Pingeot, born in 1974. When the forty-four-year-old married senator first declared his love for Pingeot – the daughter of one of his golfing acquaintances from Hossegor – she was just nineteen years old. His illegitimate son, Hravn Forsne, is more obscure. He was born to an utterly alone Christina Forsne, a Swedish citizen, at the Belvédère hospital in Boulogne-Billancourt on 12 November 1988. His father, Mitterrand, was just beginning his second term as president.[76] Christina, a journalist and Paris correspondent for the popular Swedish newspaper *Aftonbladet* (as well as for Swedish television), encountered the president of the Fédération de la Gauche Démocrate et Socialiste at a socialist congress in Stockholm in 1980. She was thirty-one, he was sixty-three. They remained together for years. Meanwhile, the letters continued to pour through Anne Pingeot's letterbox. Often on headed notepaper from the Sénat or Assemblée Nationale and, after 1981, on the stationery reserved for the exclusive use of *Le Président de la République*.[77] The letters invariably begin with *"Anne, mon amour"*, *"mon Anne chérie"* or *"mon amour d'Anne"*, interspersed with the occasional poetic reverie in which the Catholic socialist's disposition is never far away: "I love you with all my being, my love. You are Anne and these words alone will speak to you as much as the Bible of tenderness that I recite to myself."[78]

Big-hearted Mitterrand simultaneously divides his affections between Danielle, Anne and Christina. Unlike President François Hollande, a later Party colleague, Mitterrand has no need of a moped to see his mistresses. For a tête-à-tête with Anne, the president can leave his house on the Rue de Bièvre, cross the hectic Rue Saint-Jacques and Boulevard Saint-Michel, to reach the Rue Mazarine – did this inspire him when choosing a name for his daughter? – before entering the Rue Jacob. It is even easier to see Christina. Mitterrand just has to cross the Pont de l'Archevêché and the Pont Saint-Louis to reach the island of the same name, behind the Île de la Cité, where she lives. Nor must we forget Françoise Giroud, the editor-in-chief of the magazine *L'Express*, who confesses that Mitterrand had the ability to seduce even a stone.[79] The final love affair of the *graphomane amoureux* is with a law student, Claire,[80] who is fifty years his junior. When they kiss in 1988, she is twenty-two and Mitterrand seventy-two. The 'young colt' twists and turns between a European summit and a Cabinet meeting, and between phone calls to Helmut Kohl and to Margaret Thatcher. Claire provides a simple joy amidst the tumult of global politics, rapacious

Mytterrand

journalists, frustrated political schemers, and the looming spectre of death. She is the spring sunshine in the late autumn of his life.

Mitterrand even remained on good terms with his first love, Marie-Louise Terrasse, the girl he once met in the Jardin de l'Observatoire. After the war, she makes her debut as a television presenter under the pseudonym Catherine Langeais. She becomes one of France's most popular television personalities. The president does not give her a child, but she is the recipient of a badge of honour. In 1987, President Mitterrand elevates her to Chevalier de la Légion d'Honneur for services rendered. He penned over 300 letters to Marie-Louise, whom he called '*Mon Zou*'.[81] Which is 917 fewer than the 1,200-plus he composed to Anne Pingeot, which were published by Gallimard… and many more than Charles de Gaulle ever wrote to his beloved wife Yvonne. As if the *le Général* had time for such things.

Mytherrand

Picasso's irreverent birthday card to Stalin.

7

PICASSO'S 'RED PERIOD'

After the Second World War, the Parti Communiste Français (PCF) is as strong as iron. Not only is it the party of the Resistance, owing to its leading role in that underground organisation, but it is also the party of those executed by firing squad, owing to the heavy price paid by its members in that respect. At the same time, it has positioned itself as the party of reconstruction, the party of a French renaissance. In so doing, it has won the votes of hundreds of thousands of workers with dreams of earning a decent living once again. By engaging with themes such as anti-colonialism, anti-imperialism, world peace and, simply, the betterment of the masses, it has also had a magnetic effect on scientists, intellectuals and artists. One important convert to the cause is Pablo Picasso. The Party newspaper L'Humanité *salutes the painter of* Guernica *and* Les Demoiselles d'Avignon *as:* "Le plus grand des peintres aujourd'hui vivants dans le monde entier [The world's greatest living painter]."[1] *From within the Party's ranks, Picasso, who has already been through both a blue and a pink period, now finds himself caught up in a red one as well. It is not always a bed of red roses.*

Picasso's 'red period'

COMMUNISTS IN POWER

After the war, the party that Picasso joins is referred to by his friend Louis Aragon as *"la grande famille communiste"*.[2] Aragon is a renowned writer and poet, a member of the Académie Goncourt. Firstly, it is the party of the Resistance,[3] an image its leadership has diligently cultivated. In the immediate post-war period, the Communists also style themselves as the party of the 75,000 executed by firing squad.[4] The election posters proclaim: "75,000 communists were massacred by the *boches* or murdered by the Vichy traitors. Vote for the Communist candidates!"[5] Not *wholly* unjustified but a trifle overdone all the same. According to the respected researcher Serge Klarsfeld, it was at Fort Mont-Valérien – the gruesome execution site operated by the Nazis on the heights above the Seine overlooking the Bois de Boulogne – that some 1,007 members of the Resistance were executed by firing squad.[6] There is no doubt that, throughout the nation as a whole, communists paid a high and heavy price for their active role in the Resistance. However, one should not accept tallies arrived at by the same means as figures for grain and coal production in the Soviet Union. The *résistance* label confers on all the heroism of the few. Each party member feels *résistant*. It's a trump card.

The PCF is not only *le parti de la Résistance*, but also *le parti de la Renaissance française*[7] – the party of France reborn. It calls on all Frenchmen to roll up their sleeves for the reconstruction of the nation. This is how they win such enthusiasm and, not least, the votes of hundreds of thousands of workers who envisage jobs. By addressing forward-looking issues,[8] the Party is also able to persuade important writers, philosophers, scientists and artists to invest in a Party card. In the rapid-fire succession of administrations in power between 1944 and 1947, more than ten PCF ministers and secretaries of state take up office.[9] Moreover, by 1947, the Party has a membership of one million[10] – the largest in the country.

Even prior to the liberation of Paris on 25 August 1944, the communists have been getting ready to play a prominent role in post-war France. After all, was it not the Red Army that liberated Berlin? Likewise in Paris, was it not the communist resistance led by the Franc-Tireurs et Partisans (FTP)? Their leader, Colonel Rol-Tanguy, was a joint signatory along with General Leclerc, to the German capitulation by General von Choltitz. However, they have a competitor: General de Gaulle. He also wishes to lead the nation, but in his own way and with one particular nuance. First and foremost, de Gaulle is seeking unity once more among all the French. He realises only too well how the Germans trampled his country underfoot from the very outset of war, and France was thus defeated. De Gaulle knows that French unity is the only means by which to keep the real victors of the Second World War – the Americans, the British and the Russians – from meddling with the government of France.[11]

Consequently, he understands full well what he is saying into the microphone in his legendary speech of 25 August 1944 at the Hôtel de Ville. Gunfire is still ringing out here and there in the city, as the Germans have not yet been completely repelled. All the same, for thousands of thronging Parisians, it is this that they hear through the loudspeakers:

"Why should we hide the emotion which seizes us all, men and women, who are here, at home, in Paris that stood up to liberate itself and that succeeded in doing this with its own hands... Paris! Paris outraged! Paris broken! Paris martyred! But Paris liberated! Liberated by itself, liberated by its people with the help of the French armies, with the support and the help of all France: that's to say of the France that fights. That's to say of the only France, of the true France, of the eternal France."[12]

"... the only France, the true France and the eternal France": the trinity of powers that has sorted everything out, all by itself.

The Americans, the British, the Canadians and the other Allies who have fought side-by-side in the liberation of Europe can scarcely believe their ears. However, de Gaulle plays it brilliantly. Thanks to his Hôtel de Ville speech, he is able to solder a nation back together again, a nation in dire need of reconciliation and unity: "Royalists and republicans, left and right, Catholics and free-thinkers, white and coloured, rich and poor, literate and illiterate, men and women, townsfolk and country folk...."[13] In the final equation, this also includes Pétainists and Gaullists; let's leave Vichy behind us. Through his address, de Gaulle intends, above all, to turn a page on the past. The general even manages to style France as the victor!

Nevertheless, Moscow also deserves credit for triumphing over the Third Reich and is laying claim to a role in Europe. For that reason, the PCF, acting as the French radio antenna for Moscow, now has to put in place its own 'transmitters' in relation to politics, socio-economics and culture. One of those transmitter devices is Pablo Picasso. One month after the liberation of Paris, his friends, the literary tenors Louis Aragon and Paul Éluard, have carried out their mission, convincing the Spanish painter to join their party. The same front page of *L'Humanité* welcoming Picasso to the fold also tells its readers that the war is still not fully won: "*Goebbels appelle à une guérilla désespérée*" [Goebbels calls for a desperate guerrilla war], and near Montbéliard in the Vosges, another twenty-two Frenchmen have been killed by retreating Germans.[14]

Picasso's 'red period'

Picasso makes an auspicious start with the PCF. Beneath a drawing of one of his large bronzes, *L'homme à l'agneau*, a shepherd bearing a lamb in his arms, the poet Paul Éluard writes in *L'Humanité*: "All tenderness and the deepest integrity are embodied in the intent gaze of this man of the people. I bore witness to the intelligence and compassion with which Picasso thanked the French people by joining their Party: the party of those executed by firing squad."[15] Yes, that again. In propaganda, repetition pays.

ICE-COLD HEROISM

Picasso already enjoys international acclaim at the time of joining the Party. In 1900, at the age of nineteen, the Spanish government asks him, along with some other young artists, to take part in the Exposition Universelle in Paris. He then familiarises himself with the city and barely a year later has moved there to live, albeit in abject poverty. However, things soon start to look up. By 1936 he has already been appointed honorary director of the Prado in Madrid, and his works are being exhibited in Boston and San Francisco. In 1939 there is a prestigious retrospective exhibition – *Picasso: Forty Years of his Art* – displaying 344 of his works at the Museum of Modern Art in New York.[16]

In the meantime he has painted *Guernica*. On learning of the murderous bombardment of the Basque town by Franco's German and Italian allies on 26 April 1937, Picasso paints this monumental work in his new studio at the Hôtel de Savoie, 7, Rue des Grands-Augustins.[17] Picasso's attic space lacks sufficient height, and so he has to tilt the canvas at an angle in order to work. *Guernica* is to be exhibited in the Spanish pavilion at the 1937 Exposition Universelle in Paris. The result of Generalísimo Francisco Franco's coup d'état against the Republican government will be there for all the world to see: violence, blood and death. The Civil War is raging at the very moment of the exhibition. It will end only in 1939 with the victory of Franco, 'El Caudillo'. Franco turns Spain into a dictatorship, with help from Hitler and Mussolini.

The 1937 exhibition has a good deal more to it than *Guernica*. Although its theme is 'Arts et Techniques', this Exposition Universelle is, above all, an ideological confrontation between political parties that will be baying for each other's blood a few years later in the Second World War. The thirty million visitors[18] are impressed less by the art and technology and rather more by the two pavilions looming opposite each other like giants: the Third Reich and the Soviet Union. On the right bank, at the Place de Varsovie opposite the Eiffel Tower, each side bids to outdo the other through the medium of monumental architecture: national socialism versus communism. Atop a 25-metre-high plinth, their gaze cast skywards and suffused with fighting spirit, two gigantic labourers – one male, one female – brandish their respective hammer and sickle in *Worker and Kolkhoz Woman* by Vera Mukhina. The duo is fashioned from stainless steel and weighs 65 tons. Facing them, like a sentry, there is Hitler's bronze eagle. Perched atop a plinth 54 metres in height, the vast raptor clasps in its talons a laurel wreath encircling a swastika. The work is the creation of Albert Speer, architect to the Third Reich.

Adversaries though they may be, there is a marked similarity between the 'artistic' entries of the Third Reich and the Soviet Union: detachment, *froideur*, rectilinear sleekness, bare plinths and, above all, over-the-top bombast. Unlike these colossi of concrete and steel, the design for the Spanish republic's pavilion employs glass and timber. The gulf between the entries could not be greater. The same holds true within. Picasso's victims of Guernica, people and animals torn limb from limb, stand in stark contrast to the perfectly composed, athletic and heroic images from Nazi Germany and the Soviet Union. Anyone at the 1937 Exposition Universelle would have to be blind not to see that Europe is once again about to explode.

HAVING NOTHING ELSE TO DO

On 14 June 1940, German troops occupy Paris. During the war, Picasso keeps a low profile ensconced behind his double-gated entrance in the Rue des Grands-Augustins with its oblique view of the Seine. Although artists, collectors and dealers associated with 'degenerate' art are undergoing a time of hardship, including Picasso himself,[19] here and there in Paris the artist's works are still put on exhibition during the Occupation.[20] They even find buyers. Picasso suffers the same problem as everyone else in this period: money. Not that he is starving; he drives a sought-after Hispano-Suiza convertible and owns the Château de Boisgeloup in Gisors, a small town between Paris and Rouen. His studio in Boisgeloup contains his sculptures. In normal times, Picasso would sell his works via his art dealer, Daniel-Henry Kahnweiler. But Kahnweiler is Jewish and in hiding in the French countryside. In the nick of time, he has left his celebrated gallery in the care of his French – and Aryan – relative Louise Leiris. Louise continues his work with great dedication and prudence and, with Kahnweiler, she does everything she can to support Picasso during the war. The Jewish art dealer Paul Rosenberg, whose higher prices had succeeded in temporarily poaching the cash-astute Picasso from Kahnweiler, has also fled, in his case to New York where he opens a new gallery.

For Kahnweiler, Picasso's friend, confidant and dealer, the present circumstances are his second round of bad luck. In the First World War, the

Picasso's 'red period'

French government had confiscated the collection held by this heart-and-soul Francophile dealer because he was German. Now, in the Second World War, the Germans want to confiscate his collection because he is Jewish.[21] Picasso and Kahnweiler keep in touch and, after the war, Kahnweiler resumes his representation of Picasso until the death of 'his' painter in 1973.[22] Kahnweiler and Picasso will work together for more than sixty-five years. Now, however, with his dealer in hiding, Picasso is also selling work either directly to, or via, Nazi-tolerated galleries, such as the Galerie Charpentier in the Rue du Faubourg-Saint-Honoré, diagonally across from the Elysée Palace, and nowadays the headquarters of Sotheby's Paris. Picasso paints as much, if not more, under the Occupation as he did between the wars because, as he put it himself: "*Il n'y avait rien d'autre à faire.*" [There was nothing else to do][23]

On 26 September 1940, scarcely two months after the German occupation of Paris, art auctions resume at the renowned Hôtel Drouot, subject to adherence to the restrictions that have been imposed.[24] Despite the nation having just been overrun, it would appear that a great deal of money is still being paid for art. *L'Inondation* by Claude Monet goes for the record sum of 201,000 francs, followed by *Le Modèle, femme nue assise* by Auguste Renoir, earmarked for 101,000 francs. A much lower price – would it have been too great a political risk otherwise? – is offered for a few Picassos: *Nature morte au flacon* changes hands for 3,200 francs, a view of Dinard for 7,000, an *Athlète* for 41,000 and *La Guitare*, a bona fide Cubist work, for 26,000 francs. By the end of the war, however, prices for Picassos rise again in the manner of reinvigorating share prices after a crash. A collector pays 61,000 for a nude and 41,000 francs for a *Femme nue debout.*[25] Picasso is able to make a living from this, as well as pay the rent on the apartment for Marie-Thérèse Walter and their young daughter Maya. By now they have moved to the Boulevard Henri IV, between the Pont de Sully and the Bastille, where Picasso visits them from time to time. In terms of his love life during the war, there is no peace for Picasso on that front either. He has to divide his attention between three women simultaneously: Marie-Thérèse, Dora Maar and Françoise Gilot.

CLOSE CALLS

As the painter of *Guernica*, degenerate art and 'negroid' works, Picasso is definitely on the Nazis' radar. He could have fled to the United States, as did the surrealists Max Ernst and André Breton, or the painters Fernand Léger and André Masson.[26] However, Picasso chooses to remain living in occupied Paris, with Dora Maar: "I want to stay here because I *am* here. It's not really a badge of courage; it's more a sort of inertia."[27] Picasso is honest about matters. Outside, the war is raging; inside, he wants only two things – to paint and to sculpt.

He wants to cast bronze too, despite this being at a time in Paris when sculptures, such as those of François Arago, disappear within the smelting furnaces of the German war machine. As part of the 'Metal Plan' devised in collaboration with the Vichy government, the Nazis melt down 144 sculptures in Paris alone.[28] Every day or so, the great and the good of France vanish from their plinths: writers such as Victor Hugo and de La Fontaine; Republicans such as Gambetta, Raspail and Louis Blanc; Enlightenment thinkers such as Condorcet, Rousseau and Voltaire; despised adversaries from the First World War such as General Mangin and the British nurse Edith Cavell, killed by firing squad in Belgium. The Nazis know that while there is limited 'industrial benefit' to be had from this, the psychological impact will be devastating. Just how Picasso is able to keep casting bronze during the Occupation is anyone's guess. However, it is sometimes linked to his pre-war friendship with the German sculptor Arno Breker, now Hitler's professional art consultant. In 1942, Breker treats himself to a major exhibition of his own work at the Orangerie. During his residence in Paris, Breker enjoys the use of an apartment on the Île Saint-Louis recently expropriated from its Jewish occupant, Helena Rubinstein.[29] Picasso looks on with dismay. He also suspects that by some means or another Breker is protecting him from Nazi persecution.[30]

In May that same year, an advertisement for the sale of Picasso's works appears in *Je suis partout – Le grand hebdomadaire politique et littéraire*, an anti-Semitic collaborators' newspaper, occasionally carrying a quote from Adolf Hitler at the top of the page next to the title. The Drouot auction house has placed the advertisement.[31] Sales need to be made, regardless, because even the painter of *Guernica* has to live. As things turn out, it all goes very nicely for him, as it does in November 1943: in the restaurant Le Catalan, a little further down his street, and on a day without meat – meat is rationed – Picasso is collared by the inspectors of provisions while in the company of a *Chateaubriand* steak, *en flagrant délit*: caught in the act. The restaurant is forced to close for a month and Picasso is despatched with a fine.[32]

He has a close call with the Germans on two occasions. One fine day the Gestapo comes to call at the Rue des Grands-Augustins, asking him awkward questions. Was it not the case that Picasso, in 1935, sent a telegram to the Führer to protest against the death sentences passed on Albert Kayser and Rudolf Claus, German anti-fascists? Had he not, two years later, subjected the Third Reich to international ridicule with that communist dog's breakfast of a work *Guernica* at the Exposition Universelle of 1937? They threaten the painter,

Picasso's 'red period'

kick some of his works to pieces, and bark that they will be coming back. But they do not come back. That they refrain is thanks to Picasso's guardian angels among the Vichy police.[33] Even in that organisation, Picasso the survivor has his admirers and contacts. André-Louis Dubois of the Sûreté Nationale is on the spot straightaway and succeeds in seeing off the Gestapo. Maurice Toesca from the *préfecture de police* is also of assistance. He renews Picasso's residence permit such that the painter will not have to go in person to the *préfecture* each time, which would mean exposing himself to interrogations or complications.

The other occasion involves an anxious Picasso during a visit paid by Otto Abetz, Nazi Germany's ambassador in Paris. Abetz is a former fine arts teacher and a total vulture when it comes to the plundering of art.[34] At Picasso's studio, Abetz is reported to have picked up a photograph of *Guernica*: "*C'est vous qui avez fait ça?*" To this Picasso is said to have replied: "*Non, c'est vous.*"[35] A magnificent riposte, but probably a myth. According to his friend Matisse, Picasso would never dare give such an incautious answer. He is too diplomatic for that. In Picasso's dealings with people, his concern is first and foremost to ensure that he can paint. He is not engaged in either resistance or collaboration.

Be that as it may, he refuses to take part in the cultural tour involving French artists fraternising with their counterparts in Munich and Berlin. Derain, de Vlaminck and van Dongen do agree to go. The refusal is a source of regret for Gerhard Heller, chief of the Propaganda Team and organiser of the tour. Picasso is, after all, an internationally renowned artist, and the opportunity for a nice publicity stunt has been lost. Heller comes in person to the Rue des Grands-Augustins to urge Picasso to change his mind. On this occasion, while in Picasso's studio, Heller allows himself to be lectured about modern art by writer and literary critic Jean Paulhan. His hope is that this strategy might yet convince the painter. But Picasso does not take the bait. Perhaps he knows that at that same moment Paulhan is in the Resistance.[36] Picasso also receives visits from the German writer Ernst Jünger and other high-ranking, better 'cultured' Nazis. They always understand the value placed on a Picasso and accordingly pay the price as asked by the artist. But senior Nazis, such as Reichsmarschall Göring or Ambassador Otto Abetz, simply steal works from their rightful owners: Jewish collectors and art dealers.[37]

Despite his name, celebrity and contacts, Picasso cannot prevent his close friends Max Jacob and Robert Desnos from dying in German internment.[38] Max is the first to go. He had acted as witness at Picasso's marriage to Olga Khokhlova in 1918 but, long before that, in 1902, he had also shared a hotel room with Picasso at 5, Boulevard Raspail. There had been only the one bed and so Picasso painted at night and slept through the day. Vice versa, during the day

LEFT BANK, EAST

Max would peddle Picasso's paintings still dripping with paint. Max dies in the internment camp at Drancy in the northern suburbs of Paris. Robert is next. The resistance fighter is caught by the Gestapo. After a hellish tour through other camps, Robert ends up in Theresienstadt, where he dies on 8 June 1945. For his part, Picasso survives the war relatively unscathed. The tolerance of the occupiers towards Picasso is masterfully expressed by Pierre Assouline in his biography of Daniel-Henry Kahnweiler: "When you occupy France and would have the foreigners believe that the arts, literature and Parisian life have never flourished quite as well as they have under the jackboot, you don't then put a stop to Voltaire".[39]

FICKLENESS

Following the liberation of Paris at the end of August 1944, the PCF hails Picasso as *"le monument de la Résistance."*[40] It is an exceptional title for someone who, unlike his friends Paul Éluard and Louis Aragon, took not the slightest part in the Resistance. Picasso's resistance was like that of thousands of other Frenchmen: passive, symbolic, ambiguous.[41] One undeniable fact, however, is that the Nazis actually stole numerous works by Picasso from Jewish collectors and gallery owners. Even on 2 August 1944, twenty-three days before the liberation of Paris, sixty-four of his paintings are inside a train packed with looted art that the Nazis are still aiming to get out of Paris. It fails owing to an adventurous alliance between the Résistance Fer (the Resistance arm of the French railways) and the Allies.[42] In that self-same month, the PCF is promoting Picasso's work for Le Salon de l'Automne 1944. Even as German mortar fire continues to thunder a few hundred kilometres to the east, the event is already being rechristened in Paris as Le Salon de la Libération. At the Salon's opening, the painter of *Guernica* joins the Party. "This painting was not made to decorate the walls of an apartment; it is an offensive and defensive instrument of war against the enemy."[43] An exceptionally rare pronouncement about his own work. Yet the language is militant and well suited to that used by the Communists. Then again... they will come to rue the day that they ever pressed this fickle artist to their bosom.

"Picasso militant politique, communiste de surcroît! Quelle blague."[44] [Picasso a political militant and a communist to cap it all! What a joke.] Kahnweiler knows Picasso only too well: he who always runs counter to all dogma, he who always seeks the extremes whatever the discipline. But it is too late. By the time Kahnweiler arrives back in Paris, the PCF has already appointed Picasso as chairman of the Front National des Arts, whose mission is to examine a list of artist collaborators. Under his chairmanship, sanctions are imposed on

Picasso's 'red period'

'quisling' art critics and exhibition organisers, as well as artists such as Derain, de Ségonzac, Maillol, de Vlaminck and Oudot. Ten collaborationist professors are expelled from the École des Beaux-Arts.[45] Presiding over de-Nazification committees is not at all Picasso's style. To Kahnweiler's great relief, Picasso soon calls it a day in order to focus once more on his art.

Increasingly, the painter of *Les Demoiselles d'Avignon* is also swapping the fumes of Paris for the sunshine of the Mediterranean where, in 1946, he paints a beach scene peopled with animals and frolicking people playing music, a sailing boat bobbing amid the blue waves. The work is titled *Joie de vivre* and the sense is clear: the war is over. Life has returned.

After the Liberation, the Americans also come to Picasso for their slice of the pie. Millionaire Samuel Kootz immediately succeeds in buying some paintings from the master. One day Kahnweiler uncovers his technique. Kootz strolls out with a still life, leaving Picasso behind with the keys to a brand-new Oldsmobile.[46] Rapidly improving prosperity is not an unwelcome state of affairs for the artist; nonetheless, he also does something in return for the Party. On 8 January 1949, Picasso produces a lithograph of a white dove that is to become world famous: *La Colombe*. It becomes the poster for the World Congress of Partisans for Peace in Paris organised by the PCF. The most familiar version is the dove drawn by Picasso in one brushstroke, with an olive branch in its beak. By the beginning of the 1950s, however, a chill easterly wind is blowing that dove of peace off course.

Fresh artistic directives aim to help Moscow win the Cold War. The new cultural weapon is 'socialist realism'. Picasso needs to sit down when taking in its definition: "In essence socialist realism consists of faithfulness to the reality of life, however painful that might be, expressed through artistic images from a communist perspective. The ideological principles of and fundamental aesthetic guidelines for socialist realism are as follows: commitment to communist ideology; its use in the service of the people and the spirit of the Party; engagement in class struggle, humanism and internationalism; historical optimism; rejection of formalism and subjectivism, as well as naturalistic primitivism."[47] In short, the antithesis of his soul. Consequently, relations between Picasso and the Party do not really fare well from then on. However much he condemns war and violence in his work, the result never satisfies the directives from Moscow, which the PCF has made its own.

Evidence of this can be seen in the example of Picasso's *Massacre in Korea*. In this work from 1951, Picasso condemns American participation in the Korean War. Robotic servicemen aim their weapons at a small group of naked, weeping women: one pregnant, one with a child clutching at her arm, one with a baby at her breast, one with a child huddled against her in fear. They are to be shot at close range by the soldiers. This is Picasso's version of two well-known execution paintings: *The Third of May 1808*[48] by Goya and *The Execution of Emperor Maximilian*[49] by Manet. Except that Picasso's work is far more harrowing; here, it is not rebels or soldiers who are being executed, but women, children and babies. Once again it proves not good enough! *Les Lettres françaises* calls the content of the work "politically incorrect".[50] The Party would have preferred to see the Korean people depicted as fighters striving for a better – communist – world. Picasso's group of women displays only passive subjugation and they are not Asian in appearance. No, this is not socialist realism. All this criticism leaves Picasso at a total loss. For that matter, he has no wish to understand it and, increasingly, is tiring of the whole thing. Discussions on the subject are not his forte either. If someone asks him to explain a piece of work, he just raises the palm of his hand: "Don't speak to the pilot while the plane is in flight!"[51]

Conversely, one artist who certainly does have a good command of the 'socialist realism' discipline is André Fougeron, who has now been promoted as the official painter to the PCF. In his work *Atlantic Civilisation* (1953), a blue Cadillac (which might just as easily have been Picasso's Oldsmobile) sporting a huge chrome grille is thrusting forth aggressively; meanwhile a soldier is firing his rifle as he leans out from the car (materialism and aggression). A portly man with a tie is doffing his hat (a capitalist). To the right a ship is unloading coffins (meddling imperialist soldiers). People are living in tents (poverty). Children dance in a circle next to a gigantic electric chair (executions). This is unmistakably capitalist imperialism according to socialist realism. What a contrast with *Joie de vivre*.

'CHEERS, STALIN!'

What alienates Picasso from the Party still more is the similarity between its socialist realism and Nazi propaganda. A PCF poster from 1951 depicts a giant octopus with dollar signs in its eyes and an American flag on its menacing head. Its tentacles stretch all the way from Nord, the northernmost *département*, to the French Riviera: "*Les Américains en Amérique! Non, la France ne sera pas un pays colonisé!*" Another poster from 1952 shows an American plane dropping black spiders above Korea: "The Americans are spreading plague and cholera in Korea, in China. The whole world is under threat! Halt!" True or not, the fact is that Nazi posters depicting global Judaism also used the image of an all-devouring octopus. And on a poster for the prominent anti-Jewish exhibition *Le Juif et la France* held in Paris in 1941, black spiders can also be seen overwhelming

Picasso's 'red period'

the city: Jews, Bolsheviks and Freemasons.[52] Picasso has little time for art of that sort. None at all, in fact.

Lastly, there are the antics surrounding the famous 'Party portraits'. It all begins innocently enough. In 1945 – at which time he has been a Party member for a few months – Picasso is given the chance to produce a portrait of the great communist Paul Langevin. Langevin is a world-renowned scientist, a former student under Pierre Curie. The erudition of the physicist, who has been awarded numerous prizes and distinctions, radiates from his facial features. The portrait is approved and passed by the Party leadership. But then, in 1949, the PCF leadership gradually discovers just what sort of person they are dealing with when it comes to Picasso. This time he is commissioned to create a work to celebrate Stalin's seventieth birthday, "the greatest captain of all time and of all the peoples of the world".[53] *Ooh là là!* The Central Committee is expecting a work going beyond anything there has been before, on the grandest scale imaginable. Imagine their bewilderment when the artist, whom they themselves describe as "The world's greatest living painter", comes up with a card measuring 14 by 21 centimetres. On it he has scribbled, in Indian ink, a hand holding a glass of wine. In straggly, skewed lettering it bears the lofty ideological message "*Staline à ta santé*".[54] Fortunately, the ensuing tempestuous storm does blow over.

But then comes the king and queen of all dramas. When, on 5 March 1953, Joseph Stalin swaps Soviet paradise for eternity, half the world plunges into deep mourning. Likewise, half of France. Louis Aragon asks Picasso for his services: a dignified portrait of the universally loved secretary general of the Communist Party of the Soviet Union, the victor of the Second World War, the hero first to liberate a concentration camp on 22 July 1944[55] and who went on to conquer Berlin. He, the successor to Lenin, who saw to it after the war that America would not subdue the rest of the world, and so on and so forth. Picasso has already stopped listening.

Louis Aragon wants his eulogy to the great Stalin placed on the front page of *Les Lettres françaises* – a literary journal under the auspices of the PCF – accompanied by a portrait of the leader as illustrated by Picasso. It will be a unique artistic tribute. Both eulogy and portrait will be published on 12 March, involving an additional print run for *Les Lettres*. All well and good, except that what Picasso cobbles together this time would not resemble the great Communist leader if seen from a thousand paces. Instead of that powerful head with its impressive moustache, Picasso draws the first Frenchman to catch his eye in the Rue des Grands-Augustins. A mundane countenance with darkly outlined eyes and a moustache that 'droops' rather than 'projects', like a dustpan brush above the otherwise invisible mouth of Ioseb Jughashvili a.k.a.

Joseph Stalin. His head sports neither the grey hair of wisdom, nor the Soviet army cap with its red star, but instead something that looks like an unravelled, traditional Basque beret. Scandalous! The Central Committee is "deeply agitated and stricken". Readers cancel their subscriptions to *Les Lettres*. But the damage has been done. Picasso is dumbfounded. He knows Stalin only from posters on which he signals to factory workers the sun rising above their factories. But Picasso has no desire to copy that. Instead of glorifying Stalin, comrade Picasso draws his own version, and the emerging embarrassing caricature may well be unintentional and inadvertent. That is just how things go sometimes with this headstrong Spaniard.

On 18 March 1953, five days after publication of the offensive portrait, a message appears in *L'Humanité* (just above the typical crease where the paper was folded): "The party leadership of the French Communist Party wishes to express its wholesale rejection of the great Stalin's portrait in *Les Lettres françaises* of 12 March as produced by comrade Picasso, whose dedication to the working class is well-known to everyone. Moreover, it is regrettable that comrade Aragon, Central Committee member and director of *Les Lettres françaises*, which courageously fights for the development of realistic art, should have permitted this publication."[56] The Party leadership castigates and soothes at the same time. Picasso and Aragon are not the first by any means. Does Picasso care much any more about this public repudiation? Back in his native Spain, *El Mundo* writes: "In actuality, Picasso was never enthralled by Stalin. He joined the Party under the influence of friends such as Aragon, who brought him into the fold as a valuable trophy for the cause. Communist, millionaire, defiant to the last. And far more in thrall to the models on the Côte d'Azur than to an embalmed Lenin."[57]

HELLO FRANCO!

Once upon a time, on their arrival in Paris in the early 1900s, Picasso and his impoverished friends would sleep on old newspapers on the floor. None of them had a mattress. Their bedding of choice was *L'Intransigeant*, a newspaper title with spirit. It also had six more pages than the others[58] and so one slept more comfortably than on, say, *L'Aurore* or *Le Petit Parisien*. That is a time long past. Now, in addition to several properties in Paris, Picasso also owns a large estate north of Cannes. From his nineteenth-century villa, La Californie, he is able to look across from Golfe-Juan to the Cap d'Antibes peninsula. When it gets too busy there, he loves to go and paint at the old chateau of Vauvenargues, which he has also acquired. "*J'ai acheté la montagne Sainte-Victoire!*" he writes to his

Picasso's 'red period'

dealer, wild with enthusiasm.[59] "The mountain or the work by Cézanne?" asks Kahnweiler by return mail. Neither: "*un château!*" on the slopes of Mont Sainte-Victoire, the mountain so many times immortalised by Cézanne. That means something to Picasso.

Swimming with his children Claude and Paloma; watching bull fights; dining with friends; surviving troubles and quarrels with his current and former partners; seeing his wealth grow; making ceramics, and painting – these are all the things that keep Picasso busy. In 1956, when Soviet troops invade Hungary, *Le Monde* publishes yet another letter of protest to the PCF, with Picasso as a co-signatory.[60] However, the painter of *Les Demoiselles d'Avignon* shows greater enthusiasm posing in his signature striped top along with a weighty revolver and the cowboy hat received as a gift from American actor Gary Cooper.[61]

In 1968, Soviet tanks roll into Prague. But Picasso is not writing letters of protest anymore. Despite everything, he remains a faithful PCF member until his death, albeit in his own idiosyncratic style – for example, placed above his telephone at La Californie there is a list of direct phone numbers to VIPs he can always call. Alongside the number for Maurice Thorez, leader of the French communists, an indiscreet visitor might also notice the number for El Caudillo, Spain's dictator Generalísimo Franco.[62] That is Picasso's version of 'socialist realism'. Just don't go looking for it in his work!

Picasso's 'red period'

PART 5

MONCEAU
& BATIGNOLLES

1. The lady from the   p. 264
Rue de Chazelles
25 rue de Chazelles 75017

2. Dying 'for' France,   p. 276
dying 'at the hands of' France
63 rue de Monceau 75008

3. Victorine 'the shrimp'   p. 284
58 rue de Rome 75008

4. Righteous crimes I   p. 292
56 rue de Saussure 75017

5. Righteous crimes II   p. 304
47 rue Nollet 75017

6. Messieurs de Paris   p. 318
Cimetière de Montmartre 75018

1

THE LADY FROM THE RUE DE CHAZELLES

We find ourselves in the Rue de Chazelles, the time is the early 1880s. Contrary to what one might think, the residents are not bothered by all the deafening clanging and hammering. Quite the opposite in fact, it fills them with pride. Within their quarter of Paris, La Plaine Monceau, situated between Ternes and Batignolles, a vision is ascending skywards from Gaget, Gauthier & Cie, a workshop opposite the Parc Monceau. It inches higher and higher. Soon enough, across the rooftops of Paris, a gigantic woman can be seen peering through the scaffolding. Her head bears a diadem from which emanate seven spiked rays. Clasped to her breast, she holds a tablet on which is engraved "4 July 1776" – the Fourth of July – the date of the American Declaration of Independence. And held aloft, high above her head, she bears a torch to enlighten the world. Just as the Eiffel Tower becomes the symbol of France in 1889, so it is that six years earlier the Statue of Liberty – a gift from the French to the Americans – becomes the symbol for an entire nation. The United States of America.

‹ The Statue of Liberty rises above the rooftops around the Parc Monceau.

The lady from the Rue de Chazelles

FRENCH AMERICA

In 1745, French territory encompasses nearly half of present-day Canada and the United States. The Mississippi River divides the continent, flowing from its source in northern Minnesota to its delta in the Gulf of Mexico near New Orleans,[1] named after Philippe d'Orléans, the governor of France following the death of King Louis XIV. He remained regent until the late Bourbon monarch's great grandson, Louis XV, reached the age of majority. At that time, all the territory surrounding the river and to its east is French, aside from a narrow strip of eastern coastline plus the area around Hudson Bay. Nevertheless, British trading positions are better, and their colonist population is considerably greater than that of the French: almost two million against 55,000. In the wake of three wars that have seen the systematic expansion of British domains, a fourth conflict erupts that spells the end of French territory in North America. It lasts seven years, from 1756 to 1763. To resist the enemy, the French join forces with several American Indian tribes, including the Shawnee and the Algonquin. To no avail. France is defeated. French territory is ceded in its entirety to the British Empire. A triumph for George III, a scandal for Louis XV.

Yet it proves a pyrrhic victory. The war has drained Great Britain financially. Immediately afterwards, the British are obliged to despatch 10,000 officers and men to maintain order in the conquered territories. British expenditure increases tenfold in just one year: from 14.5 million pounds to 145 million.[2] To plug the hole in their coffers, the British Empire imposes a range of new taxes on its thirteen American colonies, as well as all manner of obligations and statutory prohibitions. An avalanche of rotten legislation.

It begins with the Sugar Act (1764), an even more stringent version of an earlier tax. The Currency Act (1764) forbids the thirteen[3] colonies from issuing paper currency as legal tender for public or private debts. The Quartering Act (1765) obliges the colonists to supply housing and provisions to British troops in America. The Stamp Act (1765) taxes the use of paper certificated with a seal or stamp and thus endowed with legal force. The Tea Act (1773) allows the British East India Company to sell its surpluses without paying duties. Effectively, this is a tea monopoly. There is great and growing opposition to the situation, culminating in the Boston Tea Party: colonists tip three entire shipments of British tea into the harbour. Given the scale of resistance against this raft of legislation, the British feel obliged to occupy Boston militarily, which leads in 1770 to the Boston Massacre.[4] Despite this, the penny has yet to drop for the British. The very territories that they have won at so much cost, they are now antagonising – as if blinkered to reality. The Coercive (Intolerable) Acts of 1774, and the Quartering

Act in particular, are the last straw: without either the owner's consent or any remuneration, British soldiers can now be lodged at anyone's property in any of the colonies. It is one Act of Parliament too far.

Punitive measures such as the closure of ports and the economic curtailment of their colonies only serve to accelerate the growth of local production and trade. American output of tea, cotton, wool and sugar skyrockets. New York, Philadelphia and Boston take it one step further. They jointly turn the tables and establish a non-importation front: nothing originating from the British Empire is welcome any more. The Daughters of Liberty, large numbers of women who spin and weave at home, furnish Americans with their own clothing. Homemade. By degrees, America's economy is becoming self-sustaining. The colonists' demand of "no taxation without representation", which was initially justified, now makes way for something else altogether: independence. It isn't mere 'representation' that Americans want, it's their independence.

All thirteen of the American colonies are in a state of rebellion by 1775. They want to be rid of the British once and for all. On 4 July 1776, they declare their independence, although this has yet to be fought for and won. London reels in shock. The British Empire fixes its bayonets and rolls out the cannon. Its naval fleet sets sail for the New World. Meanwhile, back in Versailles, Louis XVI, who has been on the throne for just two years, is rubbing his hands with glee. Officially neutral, he employs his admiral, Latouche-Tréville, to dispatch secret arms and troops to support the rebels. The young Marquis de Lafayette is also sympathetic to the American cause. At the age of twenty, he crosses the ocean and becomes *aide-de-camp* to General George Washington. Lafayette rises through the ranks and is soon helping to organise and command the troops. Very successfully. In 1777, a year after the declaration of independence, the British are trounced at Saratoga to the north-west of Boston. It is the signal to the French to join forces openly with the Americans. In 1781, Admiral de Grasse, along with 3,000 men, heads for Yorktown, Virginia, on Chesapeake Bay. There, he defeats the British fleet, while French troops under the Comte de Rochambeau, side-by-side with troops under George Washington, defeat the British on land.

A MISERABLE LITTLE ISLAND

This dramatic news is a blow for the British Empire. "We shall be reduced to a miserable little island, and from a mighty empire sink into as insignificant a country as Denmark or Sardinia!"[5] complains Lord Horace Walpole in Great Britain. On the other side of the Channel, Louis XVI is delighted. All the same, it is not at Versailles but in the Hôtel d'York at 28, Rue Jacob on the left bank of

The lady from the Rue de Chazelles

Paris that Benjamin Franklin, the Americans' representative in Paris, places his signature on the Treaty of Paris of 1783. In the settlement, the British formally acknowledge the newly independent United States of America. It is a milestone. The Americans are grateful to France for her support. The French see new commercial opportunities in the United States and are gratified that their country's standing has been restored in the Old World. It is a short-lived state of affairs, however. French support for American independence in turn bankrupted the French treasury, a fact partly responsible for the French Revolution.

Thirteen years before they cause such furore in the French Revolution, the ideas underpinning the Enlightenment are laid out in clear terms in the American Declaration of Independence: "We hold these truths to be self-evident that all men are created equal, that they are endowed by their Creator with certain unalienable Rights, that among these are Life, Liberty and the pursuit of Happiness."[6] After 1789, *liberté, fraternité* and *égalité* forge a deep bond between the two nations.

Those shared values even transcend the alternating political regimes in France. In 1803, when Napoleon needs money to finance his Grande Armée, he sells the French territories to the United States, then governed by Thomas Jefferson as president. History now refers to this as the Louisiana Purchase: 2,144,476 km^2 of land, equivalent to 22.3 per cent of the present United States, is transferred to the Americans for 15 million dollars.[7] There is a sting in the tail to the transaction; as a fledgling nation, the United States cannot possibly cover such a vast expense on its own, and thus borrows the sum from Barings Bank. So it is that a British bank is responsible for financing Napoleon's war machine, which the French emperor then proceeds to deploy against the British.

AN UNFORGETTABLE GIFT

In April 1865, some fifty years after the fall of Napoleon and almost a century after the American Declaration of Independence, the American Civil War (1861-1865) between the northern and southern states is settled in favour of the northern Union. Slavery is abolished and the Confederate states re-join the United States. In France, the Second Republic abolishes slavery in the French colonies somewhat earlier, in April 1848. Consequently, French republicans cheer on the decision adopted by the Americans. One particular member of this group is the French lawyer, politician and anti-slavery activist Édouard René de Laboulaye. He is relieved that "liberty, equality and fraternity have been victorious once more on the other side of the Atlantic". In France, Laboulaye is considered the world's greatest supporter of the United States. He feels that the Unionist victory, and thus republican values, must be immortalised. Laboulaye is also chairman of the

French Emancipation Committee against slavery that collects money to support freed slaves in the United States.[8] An idea hatches in his mind.

Early in the summer of that same year he invites a few friends to dinner. Above his home in the hamlet of Glatigny to the north of Versailles they see fluttering in the breeze, in fraternal solidarity, both the French tricolour and the stars and stripes[9] – the latter then bearing only thirty-five stars. Laboulaye's guests, all of them opposed to slavery, are intrigued. They have been invited to discuss an important idea relating to the 'profound friendship' between France and the United States. As guest of honour, the grandson of the Marquis de Lafayette is seated opposite the host. This evening, the heroic deeds of his grandfather, Rochambeau and de Grasse are recalled through a thick pall of cigar smoke. Costly cigars, as it turns out, because the dinner has an expensive objective: "In ten years' time, dear friends – in 1876 – we shall be celebrating the centenary of our American friends' independence. That deserves a gift! Something remarkable. Unforgettable!" To a man, the company agrees. At a sign from Laboulaye, the butler refills their glasses.

In addition to the grandson of the great Lafayette and assorted French politicians – some of whom are the same age as the calvados: *hors d'âge* ('beyond age') – a young man of twenty-three is also puffing away on his cigar in agreement. He is neither in the military nor in politics, he's an artist. A sculptor to be precise. Frédéric Auguste Bartholdi, born in Colmar and, later, a student at the Lycée Louis-le-Grand in Paris. While there, his well-to-do mother has him take classes at the studios of the sculptor Antoine Étex and the Dutch painter and sculptor Ary Scheffer.[10] It is the latter who opens Bartholdi's eyes to his artistic calling: sculpture. Bartholdi is awarded his *baccalauréat* in 1852, and a year later his mother sets him up in his own studio on the Rue Vavin, a street linking the Jardin du Luxembourg to the Boulevard Raspail. Bartholdi has been invited to Laboulaye's dinner on good grounds given that he has just immortalised his host by way of a hefty bronze bust. Laboulaye is terribly proud of the work. Bartholdi, *quel artiste*! The idea of presenting something unforgettable to the Americans strikes a chord with the young sculptor. In fact, he has just developed a unique idea for an entirely different purpose: a gigantic statue that could be ceremonially unveiled at the opening of the Suez Canal. The canal is a colossal project in which Emperor Napoleon III takes the greatest pride. The new maritime link between Port Said on the Mediterranean Sea and Suez on the Red Sea is a magnificent economic asset to the Second Empire and a political feather in the emperor's cap. At his studio on the Rue Vavin, Bartholdi sketches the form of an Egyptian woman.[11] From atop a pedestal at the entrance to the canal, she points ships in the right

The lady from the Rue de Chazelles

direction with her torch: *La Liberté éclairant l'orient* [Liberty enlightening the East]. However, at the actual site in question in the 'East', Ismail Pasha, the Khedive[12] of Egypt and the Sudan, has absolutely no truck with notions of *liberté* and the like. Consequently, in November 1869, Eugénie,[13] Empress of France, cuts the ceremonial Suez ribbon without Bartholdi and his *Liberté*. The disappointed artist is not given long to dwell on this rejection. Only a few months later, bullets start flying thick and fast.

A BLOODY SPECTACLE

In the summer of 1870, Emperor Napoleon III plunges France into a reckless war against Prussia. With hubristic cries of *"À Berlin! À Berlin!"* [To Berlin! To Berlin!] and banners flying, he departs the French capital. However, as early as 2 September he is compelled to surrender at the Battle of Sedan. Paris does not follow suit, meaning to fight on. Nonetheless, a few weeks after a French emperor, on bended knee, has handed over his sabre to Otto von Bismarck, the Prussians have encircled Paris and are starving its inhabitants into submission. After a bitter winter of freezing temperatures, famine and misery,[14] a broken France signs the armistice in January 1871. An inglorious end to the Second Empire. France receives a reparations order for 5 billion francs and must relinquish Alsace and Lorraine, the region in which Bartholdi was born.

The soldier-sculptor has barely cast off his uniform and laid down his arms when Laboulaye appears once again in the Rue Vavin. "The centenary, dear friend! 1876 approaches! A bare five years to go and still we have nothing!" Bartholdi has a lightbulb moment. From beneath dusty covers, he extracts *La Liberté éclairant l'orient*. "Why not something like this, a 'Liberty' for the Americans? Liberty is, after all, the greatest asset to possess, is it not, Laboulaye? *La Liberté éclairant l'orient* will become *La Liberté éclairant le monde*. You can't get a better fit than that, can you?" Laboulaye thinks it a capital idea. "That's it, our unforgettable gift!" Laboulaye sends Bartholdi off at once on a promotional trip to the United States.

He leaves behind a Paris in which all hell is breaking loose. While Bartholdi is seeking to export the notion of liberty to the United States, the conservative politician Adolphe Thiers is bloodily seeking to extinguish an uprising in his own city. Republicans, socialists, communists and anarchists, united in the Paris Commune, have no wish to comply with the surrender of France. Yet they are brought down, along with *liberté, égalité* and *fraternité*.

Liberty enlightening the world. In the minds of the republicans Bartholdi and Laboulaye it is, of course, crystal clear – except that, after the crackdown on the Paris Commune, the values of the French Revolution are a mere semblance of what they had once been in France. The victors over the Commune – the bourgeoisie and the aristocracy – are giving loud voice to their dreams of a new king and of the good old days under the *ancien régime*. But in the end the decision is for a president after all, and it is Field Marshal MacMahon who comes to power in the elections of 1873 – with the support of the monarchist majority in the Assemblée Nationale. Now that a conservative field marshal has become president of France, the German troops that have kept the nation under occupation for three years can return home in confidence. The reds have been muzzled and order reigns once again. However, whereas the bourgeoisie and aristocracy feel that MacMahon is heaven-sent, in terms of their shared dream he is Bartholdi and Laboulaye's worst nightmare. Just like the Khedive of Egypt and the Sudan, the new French government does not wish to be associated with *La Liberté*. So, it's a 'no' to the centenary of the American Revolution. Not a single cent of government money. Those cents will have to come from the pockets of the French. It will not be a gift from France to the United States at all. It is to be one from the French people to the American people.

THE FLAME OF AMBITION

In the interim, Laboulaye has risen from his position as a *député* for the Republicans to become a senator. With great aplomb, he sets up a committee of the Franco-American Union to garner support and raise funds. The statue is to cost 250,000 francs. A fortune at that time. The deal brokered in the United States is that France should pay for the statue, while the United States should pay for the site and pedestal. Bartholdi has already returned from his promotional trip to the United States before 1871 draws to a close. Letters of recommendation from Laboulaye have opened doors to American senators, industrialists, and even the president, Ulysses S. Grant. While abroad, Bartholdi has also found a suitable site for *La Liberté*: Bedloe Island, just off the coast of Manhattan. In her left hand *La Liberté* is to hold a tablet bearing the date of the American Declaration of Independence. The most important of symbols for the new nation.

In 1875, the year which sees the ceremonial opening of the Opéra Garnier in Paris, a new constitution also marks the start of the Third Republic.[15] On the political horizon, it is just possible to discern the outlines of liberty, equality and fraternity, as yet far off, fragile and frail. This is the moment seized upon by Laboulaye and Bartholdi in which they and their committee set the wheels of their money machine in motion. Newspaper articles, public speeches, banquets, shows, lotteries, donations, and even letter openers in the form of 'the lady with the torch' all combine to get the cash registers ringing. Charles Gounod composes the anthem

The lady from the Rue de Chazelles

La Liberté éclairant le monde for the new Opéra.[16] The full proceeds go towards the statue. Towns and villages, chambers of commerce, industrialists, trade associations and thousands of private individuals, even Le Grand Orient de France, the mother lodge of the Freemasons in France, to which Bartholdi belongs, all make their contribution. Money flows in and work on the project commences.

Bartholdi is not about to take any chances. Before shipping his statue across the Atlantic, he wants it fully assembled in Paris first. Every millimetre, every nut and every bolt must be right. He entrusts this extraordinary assignment to Gaget, Gauthier & Cie in the Rue de Chazelles. The firm is renowned for its grand-scale works and monuments. The contractors lease 3,000m² of space next to their premises for beating out three hundred copper plates to a thickness of 2.37mm. It is from these sections that *La Liberté* will rise.

Nevertheless, however expeditious the flow of donations and however diligent the labour of the metalworkers, the 1876 deadline is still missed. By the time of the American centenary of independence, only the arm bearing the torch is ready. Fortunately, Bartholdi is not just a successful sculptor, by now boasting commissions throughout France, but also a good salesman. A brilliant idea ensures that the flame of ambition is kept alight: at the Centennial Exposition of 1876 in Philadelphia, thousands of Americans will climb up into the giant arm towards the flame that will one day illuminate New York Harbor. The French display, which includes the torch of *La Liberté*, proves to be the event's most popular attraction. Photographs circle the globe. Miniatures, postcards and posters sell like hot cakes, helping to finance additional costs. The arm and torch are already on site and continue to attract visitors even after the exposition. In a letter of encouragement to the secretary of the Franco-American Union committee, Bartholdi writes: "I believe that the enthusiasts climbing up into the flame will undergo rather a strange sensation".[17]

FIENDISHLY HIGH

On the other side of the ocean, the Americans are now also showing their generosity. In that regard, the torch is being borne aloft by the New York lawyer and statesman William M. Evarts. The chairman of the Franco-American Union committee is a good choice. Evarts served the United States as a secretary of state, attorney general and senator. He is universally acknowledged and respected. In the United States, theatrical performances, art exhibitions, auctions and even boxing matches mobilise people to become believers in the *La Liberté* project. But it is above all *The New York World* which makes the difference. For months at a time, the publisher Joseph Pulitzer appeals to the conscience of American citizens. In his view, be they rich or poor, nobody can refrain and all should give what they can. "Let us not wait for the millionaires to give us this money. [*La Liberté*] is not a gift from the millionaires of France to the millionaires of America, but a gift of the whole people of France to the whole people of America."[18] Pulitzer sets an example: part of the proceeds from each new subscription to his newspaper will go towards funding the Statue of Liberty's pedestal. The campaign is a terrific success. Likewise for his newspaper: "Circulation of *The New York World* climbs to more than 600,000 copies and the newspaper tops the leader board for the most sales in the country."[19]

The Paris World's Fair (Exposition Universelle) opens its doors on 1 May 1878. It is the greatest one to date. Thirteen million people buy a ticket.[20] The government of the Third Republic wants to illustrate the fruits of its strategy by way of astonishing new inventions to promote the welfare of citizens. Such inventions can take their place alongside those of the most advanced nations in the world. On either side of the Seine, 53,000 exhibitors[21] pull out all the stops at pavilions designed to fire the imagination. Visitors marvel at all manner of miraculous machinery. Before their very eyes one machine can produce 84 tonnes of ice a day, another blows chilled dry air for the transport of food, yet another can produce one hundred horseshoes an hour, while a further machine provides visitors with a new taste sensation: carbonated drinks. A typewriter, an electric light bulb, an aluminium flying machine by Félix du Temple, a telephone by Alexander Graham Bell, and a phonograph by Thomas Edison...[22] the wonders never cease. But besides all of this, something else is attracting visitors like a magnet. Two years after the Centennial Exposition in Philadelphia, Bartholdi and Laboulaye are repeating their promotional stunt in Paris, this time with the head of *La Liberté*. Up to forty visitors can climb into it at one time and then look out over this extraordinary fair of the future, extending from the Trocadéro, across the Seine, up to the École Militaire on the Avenue de la Motte-Picquet. Hearts are gladdened, wallets are opened. Pierre-Eugène Sécretan, a French industrialist, donates 64 tonnes of copper to the cause. The project starts to grow wings.

Initial elation is tempered by the death of architect Eugène Viollet-le-Duc, designer of the interior work for the Statue of Liberty. Bartholdi has to go in search of a replacement. His choice is Gustave Eiffel – busily engaged in a certain other project for which he is to become world famous. The engineer-entrepreneur intends to suspend the copper form from a mobile steel truss – *La Liberté* must be able to withstand storms: bending is tolerable, but breakage is not. Engineers now also set to work at the Eiffel workshops in Levallois-Perret, only two kilometres to the east of the Rue de Chazelles. They work against the clock at both establishments, and in December 1882, four years before the

The lady from the Rue de Chazelles

110th anniversary of American independence, Bartholdi sends a fresh injection of adrenaline to the Americans: "We are advancing with speed and in the spring our colossus will be seen hovering above the Parc Monceau. It is already starting to become fiendishly high!"[23]

La Liberté is indeed fiendishly high. So high, in fact, that all 46 metres of her become the chief of all attractions in Paris. There is a deluge of families with children, photographers, engravers and painters. Part of the workshop roof has already been removed and, stage by stage, *La Liberté* gradually assumes her final form above Paris. But, even before she reaches completion, a shadow is cast over her crown. Had she been of flesh and blood, a certain event in May 1883 would have seen her face streaked with tears: the death of her animating force, Édouard de Laboulaye. Although the great admirer of all things American might have preferred to be transported to the 'happy hunting ground', in his case it turned out to be the 49th section of Père Lachaise cemetery. There, he lies in the company of – coincidentally enough – Eugène Delacroix, painter of *La Liberté guidant le peuple*.

In the autumn of 1885, apartments in the Rue de Chazelles become sunnier again, although in the process they lose their unique spectacle. *La Liberté* has been dismantled for shipment. On 17 June 1886, the French ship *L'Isère* reaches the shores of the United States. A sculptor is aboard, accompanied by 214 chests containing 350 component parts.

NO WOMEN, NEGROES OR JEWS

On 28 October 1886, one hundred and ten years after the American Declaration of Independence, Chauncey M. Depew, senator for New York, bids welcome to the highest authorities in the land: President Grover Cleveland, together with 600 invitees. Seated in the front row are Bartholdi and Ferdinand de Lesseps, the successful builder of the Suez Canal, who is also excavating a canal to cut across Panama. "We dedicate this statue to friendship among nations and to peace in the world. The spirit of liberty embraces all races in common brotherhood," says Depew. There follows a laudatory speech to the French comrades-in-arms Lafayette, Rochambeau and de Grasse, and to those who followed in their footsteps: Édouard de Laboulaye and Frédéric-Auguste Bartholdi, "the genius". In Depew's final words, distant history becomes all at once current: "The rays from this beacon ... will welcome the poor and persecuted with the hope and promise of homes and citizenship. It will teach them that there is room and brotherhood for all who will support our institutions and aid in our development, but that those who come to disturb our peace and dethrone our laws are aliens and enemies forever."[24]

With a tug on the cord, Bartholdi lets the gigantic flag fall. Joyous cannon fire thunders across the Hudson River, three hundred sea vessels sound their horns, and the bells ring out from all the churches in New York City. Gravely and calmly, *Liberty Enlightening the World* gazes out across the ocean and towards France, the country of her birth. The Americans are happy, the French proud. A statue from Paris now stands as a symbol for an entire nation, the United States of America. The Statue of Liberty – the lady from the Rue de Chazelles – subsequently graces all tourist brochures, postcards and posters.

It's all very well, of course, but something of a false note rings in the ear concerning that solemn inauguration. Although at that time there are already several African-Americans serving their country as elected representatives of the people, not a single one of them has been invited to the inauguration. Apart from Jeanne-Emilie Bartholdi and Tototte, the daughter of 'great Frenchman'[25] Ferdinand de Lesseps, not a single woman has been invited either. A group of suffragettes intends to disrupt the occasion from a boat hired for the purpose, but their protest disappears amid the smoke of the celebratory cannon fire. Joseph Pulitzer doesn't receive an invitation either, despite fulfilling the 'requirements' found in Depew's inauguration speech. As a youthful immigrant from Hungary, Pulitzer serves in the Lincoln Cavalry during the American Civil War. After the war he works in St Louis as a bellboy and waiter. At the municipal Mercantile Library he strives to hone his English as well as his knowledge of American law, which he respects as much as he does the institutions of the United States. He rises from the position of journalist to become a media magnate but, for the Americans applauding at the Statue of Liberty in 1886, he's still a Jew when all's said and done.

That said, by slow degrees Lady Liberty sets about her work, there on her pedestal opposite the Manhattan skyline, whatever the weather may throw her way. Six years after her official inauguration, the immigration centre on Ellis Island opens its doors. From then until its closure in 1954, more than 12 million[26] newcomers pass through, hailing from every part of the globe. Each new arrival, whoever it may be, is stopped in their tracks at the sight before them. In 1903, a sign of progress is also registered: a plaque comes to grace the Statue of Liberty with a sonnet by Emma Lazarus, a poet with Jewish roots:

"Give me your tired, your poor,
Your huddled masses yearning to breathe free,
The wretched refuse of your teeming shore.
Send these, the homeless, tempest-tost to me,
I lift my lamp beside the golden door!"

The lady from the Rue de Chazelles

Father and son, Moïse and Nissim de Camondo, in their garden on the Rue de Monceau.

2

DYING 'FOR' FRANCE, DYING 'AT THE HANDS OF' FRANCE

To get a better view of the movements below them, Lieutenant Nissim de Camondo pilots his plane higher. He is now flying at 2,800 metres. Equipped with a powerful Renault V8 engine, his pathfinder, a Dorand AR1 two-seater,[1] can climb to a height of 5,000 metres. Behind him, Lieutenant Louis Desessard takes photos of the enemy lines between Lunéville and the German border. After the French defeat by the Prussians in 1871, this runs diagonally through the département of Meurthe-et-Moselle. Cities such as Metz, Thionville, Mulhouse and Colmar now lie within the German Empire. Nissim checks his dashboard. He smiles. As the crow flies, he is just 300 kilometres from his family in Paris. At the Dorand's average speed, it would take him less than two hours to fold his father Moïse and his sister Béatrice in his arms. A glance in the mirror abruptly wipes the smile off his face. Behind him are three German fighter planes.

'DIED FOR FRANCE'

On Wednesday 5 September 1917, the third year of the First World War, Nissim and Louis take off from Villers-lès-Nancy for a new reconnaissance flight. It is just before midday. In this *département* filled with water and forests, the enemy positions are shrouded in mist. If they want sharp photos, they must wait for it to clear. Suddenly, the clicks of Louis' camera fall silent. "Shit", he swears, "Albatrosses! Behind us!" The new Albatross DIII fighter planes are single seaters and faster than their own model. One second later, their LMG machine guns tear up the sky between Remoncourt and Emberménil. Nissim's plane shudders under the rain of fire. "Louis! Louis!" Desessard does not reply. He dies instantly. The Albatrosses deliberately tail Nassim, out of reach of his heavy Vickers machine gun mounted on the front of the Dorand. Nissim executes a skilful swerve. In vain. He is hit by a fresh German salvo. He fires back cold-bloodedly with the lighter Lewis machine guns mounted on the rear of his plane. Bullseye! Screaming and with a plume of smoke pouring from its tail, one of the German fighter planes tumbles from the sky. For Nissim it is also too late, his Dorand is on fire. Nissim de Camondo and Louis Desessard crash behind enemy lines. They die for France – *morts pour la France*. These talented young men, 25 and 32 years old, had already been honoured several times for their courage and commended for the successful execution of dangerous missions. In 1920, Nissim would be posthumously included in the Ordre National de la Légion d'Honneur. Both entered the war as *poilus* in the trenches. Their commitment and tenacity saw them climb to the ranks of pilot and military photographer respectively. In civilian life, Louis was a watchmaker, the son of Jean Baptiste Desessard, a clogmaker from the Indre, and Nissim was an *administrateur*, the son of Moïse de Camondo, a banker from Paris, custodian of one of Europe's largest fortunes.

THE HOUSE OF THE WORLD

Born from the mists of the Mediterranean Sea, the Jewish banking family Camondo has been building up its wealth in this region since time immemorial. First as merchants, later as financiers. When Granada falls in 1492, the last bastion of the Moors in Spain, the family gradually retreats with its clients towards Constantinople. During their stay in the thriving city of Venice, their definitive name is shaped: a combination of Ca and Mondo. Just as in Venetian dialect the Ca d'Oro on the Grand Canal means 'the house of gold', so too does the Ca Mondo mean 'the house of the world', and rightly so because in the meantime the Camondo diaspora stretches far beyond the Mediterranean region. A few centuries after their exit from Spain, their activities stretch from modern-day Turkey to the Middle East, the Greek islands and the Balkans, Austria and Italy.

At the beginning of the nineteenth century, the patriarch Abraham Salomon Camondo is a financier not only of numerous industries, but also of the Ottoman state. He capitalises infrastructure works, urbanisation projects and covers the Turkish costs in the Crimean War (1853-1856). In 1867, he facilitates the unification of the country via his investments in the Italian railways. As a gesture of thanks, King Victor Emmanuel II elevates the family to the ranks of the nobility. A little *'de'* may now be added, *de* Camondo. Abraham is unmoved. His true preoccupation lies not with titles but with his business – and with the economic opportunities in the region. There are fewer and fewer possibilities in the empire of the sultans and pashas of the 'Sublime Porte' of the Near East.

Intrigued by the ideas of the Enlightenment, Abraham has long been scrutinising the developments in France. It fascinates him beyond measure. Napoleon III has commissioned the prefect of Seine, Georges-Eugène Haussmann to transform the capital city into a new metropolis. The first International Exhibition in France, held in 1855, is a resounding success: 23,954 exhibitors from thirty-six countries showcase their innovations, including numerous applications of the highly promising steam engine.[2] Even Queen Victoria pays a visit. Building projects such as the Hôtel du Louvre and the Palais de l'Industrie – larger than the Crystal Palace in London – are sprouting like mushrooms. Investors are establishing new companies left, right and centre, the majority with global import and export capabilities – not least in the French colonies in Asia and Africa. But the most important thing of all is that Jews in France have the same rights and obligations as French citizens. So isn't this where the new opportunities for growth lie?

'THE ROTHSCHILDS OF THE ORIENT'

When the innovative family faces headwinds in Constantinople in response to its ideas for reforming the Ottoman economy and education system, and the climate starts to become bleaker for Jews, the Camondos decide to reorient their business empire to the city of the future.

Arriving in Paris in 1869, they settle in the chic Rue de Monceau, at numbers 61 and 63. It is from here that they continue to expand their business empire. They are involved in the Chemins de fer portugais, the Compagnie internationale du gaz, the Crédit foncier franco-canadien, the Société nationale pour le commerce, l'industrie et l'agriculture dans l'Empire Ottoman, the Compagnie des eaux de Constantinople, the Banque impériale ottomane, the Société

Dying 'for' France, dying 'at the hands of' France

franco-belge de Tianjin, the Santa Fe Railway, the Sucrerie et raffinerie d'Egypte, the Compagnie internationale d'Orient, Anaconda Copper, the Société norvégienne de l'azote, the Société du naphte de Bakou, the Compagnie générale du gaz pour la France et l'étranger, the Compañía de los Ferrocarriles Andaluces, and others. In 1881 they set up the Ciments Portland du Boulonnais with a capital of 30 million francs.[3] In Paris, they are now 'The Rothschilds of the Middle East'.

From their age-old Jewish family tradition, Isaac and Moïse have had it drummed into them that they should always integrate into society, wherever they may be, and help care for it so that it develops for the good. They take this very seriously and become 'more French than the French'. As well as financiers, they also become prominent art collectors. They invest in the opera, in theatres and companies, and above all, in the big museums. The de Camondos have seats on the boards of numerous cultural institutions. Before his death in 1911, scion Isaac had already donated his entire art collection, with works by Manet, Monet, Degas, Cézanne, Sisley, Van Gogh, Corot and other leading artists, to the Louvre. Today, these can be enjoyed in the Musée d'Orsay. Isaac's business assets go to his cousin Moïse, the only beneficiary. But regardless of how hard they try to be good Frenchmen, ever-darker clouds are gathering above the de Camondos. Not because they are bankers, but because they are Jews.

JEWISH PLOT

In France, the tolerant tide of liberty, equality and fraternity is turning. The defeat by the Prussians in 1871 has left many feeling embittered. The relinquishing of Alsace and Lorraine and the shelling out of 5 billion francs in reparations to the now-unified Germany are bitter pills for the French to swallow. Deep anti-German sentiment is therefore rife, above all amongst army commanders, but also in the wider strata of French society. Culprits are therefore sought for the malaise – and found. An age-old scapegoat is dusted off. In 1886, journalist Edouard Drumont publishes his essay *La France Juive* [Jewish France], in which he lays the blame for the French defeat on a plot. A sinister conspiracy of Jewish capitalists is holding the French, their banks, their economy, their culture and their government in its grip with its all-pervasive tentacles. Was Achille Fould, minister of finance to Napoleon III (who declared war on the Prussians) not a Jew, for example? He may have been a Jew who converted to Protestantism, but he was a Jew nonetheless. In ensuring this poison is swallowed, Drumont is helped by a series of scandals in which Jews are involved, directly or indirectly, over this same period (1880-1900). The Deutz Affair,[4] the Bauer Affair,[5] the Dreyfus Affair,[6] the bankruptcy of the Union Générale,[7] the Panama scandal[8] etc.

These are widely reported in the press, in books and pamphlets. Added to the deep anti-German sentiment, there is now a gradually rising tide of anti-Jewish sentiment.

With the steady drip of information of this kind, a large section of French society turns against its Jewish fellow citizens. From Paris to Bordeaux and Lyon, windows of Jewish shops and businesses are smashed. In the midst of this socially threatening climate, it is not long before the de Camondos will also suffer a soul-crushing blow to the very heart of their family. In 1891, Moïse marries a Jewish banker's daughter Irène Cahen d'Anvers, who was immortalised as a child by Renoir in *La fille au ruban bleu*. A year later, their son Nissim, the future fighter pilot, is born. Two years later, he is followed by a daughter, Béatrice. In 1896, Moïse is shaken to the core when his wife Irène leaves him for Comte Charles Sampieri. Following the divorce of their parents, Nissim and Béatrice are raised by their father. To be able to marry Comte Sampieri, the Jewish Irène must be rebaptised as a Catholic. It is pure chance, but forty-five years later, this very same change of religion will save Irène Cahen d'Anvers from the Holocaust. Things will be very different for her daughter, son-in-law and grandchildren, however.

After the abrupt departure of Irène, Moïse throws himself into a new passion, collecting unique pieces of eighteenth-century furniture. To this end, he has the parental home in the Rue de Monceau demolished and a beautiful but outwardly discreet urban palace built in its stead. Behind the high walls of dressed stone, he will live with Nissim and Béatrice, happily surrounded by his collection. At least, that is his grand dream.

IN THE GARDEN BY THE PARC MONCEAU

Little of this transpires. The new Palais de Camondo is only just completed when the first shot is fired in the First World War. Nissim has been serving in the French army since 1911, an army which is preparing itself for a likely approaching war. As a *poilu* he only visits the Rue de Monceau during his infrequent military leave. There is a moving photograph of one such moment, in which Nissim and his father are chatting relaxedly in their rattan garden chairs beside the Parc Monceau. Moïse always carries this photo next to his heart after Nissim dies in 1917, 'for the honour of France'. Nevertheless, with his unlimited financial means, the banker could have taken his son to safety in the United States before the war. But no, family tradition forbids a de Camondo from doing such a thing.

A year after Nissim's death, Moïse's daughter Béatrice also disappears from the daily life in the Rue de Monceau. She marries Léon Reinach, a musician

Dying 'for' France, dying 'at the hands of' France

and member of a leading Jewish humanist family. The couple have two children, Fanny and Bertrand. They are adored by their grandfather Moïse, who is ageing and thinking about passing on his assets. With France in his head and his heart, he donates his city palace with its entire art collection to the French state so they can open it up as a museum in honour of his fallen son Nissim. This is now the small but beautiful Musée Nissim de Camondo.

His business assets are predestined for his daughter Béatrice and his grandchildren. When Moïse de Camondo dies on 14 November 1935 at 3.40pm, the lanterns are dimmed at the double gate in the Rue de Monceau. Inside on the *cour d'honneur*, Béatrice, her husband and their children close the shutters, overwhelmed with sorrow. But unaware that perhaps an even greater one awaits them.

'DIED AT THE HANDS OF FRANCE – MORTS PAR LA FRANCE'

This happens less than five years later. In June 1940, at the start of the German occupation of Paris, Moïse's grandchildren Fanny and Bertrand are already young foals of twenty and seventeen. But there is to be no more carefree frolicking in the fields for them. In 1941, the possessions of the Jewish families de Camondo and Reinach are confiscated. Léon Reinach protests. "Order from Berlin", is the Vichy government's reply. What more could the de Camondos have done for their fatherland than donate their art collections to the Louvre, and their city palace with its unique furniture collection to the French state? What more could they have done than support hundreds of good causes? What more than play an active role in French industry? What more than lose a son who died for God and his country, holder of the Légion d'Honneur? It is hard to be more French than this.

In the meantime, in the Château de Chambord, the Germans unscrupulously confiscate entire chests of art belonging to Jewish families who had entrusted their collections to the national museums. Amongst these were the Renoir with the portrait of Moïse's ex-wife and mother of Béatrice, *La fille au ruban bleu*. After the loss of their possessions, Béatrice, her husband and her children are coldly arrested in 1942 – Béatrice and her daughter Fanny on 5 December, Léon and his son Bertrand on 12 December. They are incarcerated in the transit camp at Drancy, the large marshalling yard to the north of Paris, from where the convoys to the concentration camps depart. In the meantime, Georges Duhamel, *secrétaire perpétuel* [permanent secretary] of the Académie française, nevertheless tries to intervene with Fernand de Brinon, French ambassador to Nazi Germany. The collaborator does not lose too much sleep over the matter. Other contacts are also approached, but no one is prepared to help. France looks the other way.

On the afternoon of Saturday 20 November 1943, a sinister train glides out of Bobigny station. On board are 1,200 Jews, including Léon Reinach and his children, Fanny and Bertrand. There are even younger children among the passengers: 83 of them are under twelve. Their convoy no. 62 arrives in Auschwitz five days later. In March 1944, his wife Béatrice follows in convoy no. 69. Upon her arrival, her husband and son turn out to have already been gassed and her daughter to have died of typhoid. The precise cause of death of Béatrice herself is unknown, but it is certain that she did not survive the camp.

Moïse de Camondo's timely death spared him from experiencing this tragedy. In his gem *Le dernier des Camondo,* author Pierre Assouline pricks the French war conscience. Of the war hero Nissim, his sister and her family, he writes: "If he died *for* France, then her husband and children died *at the hands of* France."

Dying 'for' France, dying 'at the hands of' France

Seen by all, known by none: Victorine Meurent.

3

VICTORINE 'THE SHRIMP'

No one has heard of her. Yet everyone has seen her. From Paris to New York, and from San Diego to Boston and Washington, naked or clothed, she stares her audience straight in the eye. In Le Déjeuner sur l'herbe *and* Olympia, *the most scandalous of works by Édouard Manet, the painter of modern life,[1] she attracts disgust and fury: this is no artistic nude of a Greek Galatea or a Roman Venus, but the vulgar nakedness of a brazen whore. The step from her role in Manet's paintings to her private life is quickly taken. Being a female artist's model is not an easy profession in the time of Victorine Meurent.*

BRAZEN NUDE

Between 1862 and 1873, Victorine Meurent poses for some eight works by Édouard Manet. She is naked in just two of them, *Le Déjeuner sur l'herbe* and *Olympia*,[2] both painted in 1863, the year after they meet.[3] The outcry that both works cause is legendary. On the one hand, this is due to a reluctance to accept Impressionism, the new art movement of which Manet is the pioneer and, on the other, to the way in which the artist depicts Victorine: naked, without embellishment, staring at her audience unabashed. This 'looking the viewer straight in the eye' is something she does in all these eight works by Manet. In *La Chanteuse de rue*,[4] from 1862, she is leaving a bar with a guitar in one hand, challengingly and suggestively pressing two cherries to her lips with the other. In *La Femme au perroquet* (1866) she poses in a long dress beside an African parrot, the talking, innocent companion of the prostitute who is killing time between two customers. The banal nudity, the cold gaze, the symbolism, all of this combined is enough to establish her reputation in the art world and, by extension, in the court of public opinion: Victorine, the tart.

The press is awash with disparaging comments. The majority are aimed at the painter, but certain barbs strike his model directly. Because of her unobtrusive stature, her unexceptional body and her pallor, the newspapers dub Victorine 'the shrimp'. Manet's Dutch wife, the piano teacher Suzanne Leenhoff, does not have a good word to say about Victorine either. First as his mistress and then as his wife, Suzanne occasionally posed nude for her husband – for example in the classically inspired *La Nymphe surprise*[6] from 1861. But now Manet has asked Suzanne to marry him, he doubts whether it is a good idea for her to continue posing for his new work, *Le Déjeuner sur l'herbe*, with which he once again wishes to battle with the jury of the Paris Salon[7]. His wife in the eye of the storm? No. He paints over Suzanne with Victorine.[8] In *Madame Manet*, an original book in which she talks about her life,[9] Manet's spouse is more relieved about the change than jealous of it: "In this way I am spared the scorn and mockery of the Parisian public."[10]

She also gives a dramatic twist to the truth about how her husband meets his new model: "One evening Édouard plucked a Parisian worker from the street. She was leaving an obscure café in the Rue Guyot.[11] She was holding a guitar in her hand. Édouard walked up to her and asked her if she wanted to pose."[12] Suzanne does not answer the letter that Victorine directs to her after Manet's death in which she asks for a financial contribution that she claims the painter once promised her.[13] Half a century later, Adolphe Tabarant, French journalist, writer and art critic,[14] paints an uncharitable picture of Victorine:

"Even before disappearing at the age of forty, Victorine is a wreck, fallen into drunkenness and depravity."[15] Manet's biographers keep silent about her, writers present her as an orphan or as a *lorette*,[16] named after the prostitutes who earnt their bread around the L'Église Notre-Dame-de-Lorette, whilst others speak of a premature death.[17]

This is particularly striking for someone who – at that time – would live to be over eighty. The real Victorine Meurent was born in 1844, the daughter of an engraver and laundry proprietor, in the parish of Sainte-Elisabeth in the Rue du Temple in the east of Paris. It is also where she was christened. From an early age, Victorine cherishes a secret ambition: to become an artist. She kills two birds with one stone. As a model, she gains a foothold within the 'sector' and earns her first independent wage. From the age of seventeen, she poses for Edgar Degas and Alfred Stevens, a Belgian painter working in Paris. In reality, Victorine meets Édouard Manet in a painter's studio and not on the street. Although this would have been perfectly plausible, given how disparaged the profession is.

PAINTING OR BEING PAINTED

The status of male artist's models had already declined sharply halfway through the nineteenth century. Long gone is the time when they lived in the Louvre (dressed in royal livery and carrying swords), were revered by the Académie Royale de Peinture et de Sculpture, and received a generous pension upon retirement. For female models, the situation is even worse. A female model is paid less than a man. The tutor to Manet and Stevens, the French classical painter Thomas Couture, pays his male models a salary of 19 francs per week, whilst Victorine receives 25 francs for posing for his pupils for an entire month.[18] What's more, models who pose for artists are not permitted also to offer their services at the famous Académie des Beaux-Arts. However extravagant the praise may be for their divine and elevated beauty, made incarnate on numerous prize-winning canvases, the female models do not grow rich from their attributes. That is not Victorine's primary goal. In between modelling stints, she hones both her pastels and her talent.

She hangs on. But the years as Manet's model are a trial. When she leaves her modest room in the Rue Maître-Albert, a narrow street that runs between the Quai de la Tournelle and the Quai de Montebello on the Seine, she glances first left and then right. Not that anyone recognises her. But since the violent reactions to *Le Déjeuner sur l'herbe* and *Olympia* she is not always confident that she will not be spotted. On the Batignollaise, the horse-drawn omnibus

Victorine 'the shrimp'

to Manet's studio in the Rue Guyot, she prefers to sit entirely alone. It is a long journey from the Left Bank to the northwest of the city, and she always takes a few newspapers along. But she can never relax, indeed the opposite is true. How many times has 'the shrimp', with a stab to her heart, immediately folded up her newspaper: "What is that odalisque with her yellow stomach supposed to be, that repulsive model, who has been fished out from who knows where, and yet depicts Olympia? Olympia? What Olympia? A courtesan of course", the influential *Le Figaro* writes.[19] *Le Constitutionnel* throws oil on the fire: "An unimaginably vulgar representation."[20] Nevertheless, *Olympia* is accepted by the Salon jury of 1865. A victory for Manet who, unlike his younger Impressionist friends, has chosen the official Paris Salon as his battleground.[21] But Victorine? It is not known whether tears welled up in her eyes, but the reviews will certainly not have given her pleasure. A year later, after the portrait with the parrot, she swaps France for the United States. Does she want to build on her career as a painter there, or is she following a lover? We are in the dark about this period.[22] Ironically, *La Femme au perroquet* follows Victorine to America, where the work *is* valued. It is the first canvas by Manet to enter a museum.[23] It is exhibited at the Metropolitan Museum of Art in New York as early as 1889.

After a stay of six or seven years, Victorine Meurent returns to Paris, determined to exhibit her own work. She takes additional portrait classes and enrols at the Académie Julian, a successful private school founded by Rodolphe Julian, which at its height has six ateliers spread across Paris. In women-only studios, ladies can become proficient in painting male models [posing in their underwear!].

BUT IT NEVER WORKS OUT

When Manet finds out that Victorine is back in the city, he convinces her to pose for a new work. This time, she will be fully clothed. Better still, it is to be a kind of 'mother with child'. But clothed or not, child or no child, the relationship between the public and Victorine never works out, even though more than ten years have passed since the unveiling of *Le Déjeuner sur l'herbe* and *Olympia*. This is apparent from the tomatoes that are thrown at model and painter alike at the prestigious Paris Salon of 1874. This is where the new work, *Le Chemin de fer*, also known as *Gare Saint-Lazare*,[24] is first shown to the public. But the title is irrelevant: there is no trace of either a railway or a station in the painting.

MONCEAU AND BATIGNOLLES

Yet they are emphatically present. As is Victorine Meurent who, as a demure childminder or the loving mother of the girl beside her, sits on a low wall beneath the railway fence. Manet paints her in the garden of his friend, Alphonse Hirsch,[25] at 58, Rue de Rome,[26] right next to Saint-Lazare station. The artist demonstrates that he is in touch with modernity and the grand building works that Haussmann is executing all over the city: in the background to the right he shows a piece of the new Pont de l'Europe,[27] and to the left a glimpse of the façade of his studio at 4, Rue de Saint-Pétersbourg, a street on the other side of the railway tracks.

In the work, a blonde girl in a white dress with a large blue bow watches the steam rising from an invisible locomotive. She is safe and is separated from the railway by a black iron fence. Beside the child, a woman looks up enquiringly from her open book, a finger between the pages as if she would like to continue reading. She is dressed head to toe in the latest Parisian fashions of autumn 1873:[28] a full-length, dark-blue dress with white stitching and large buttons, a wide, open collar, and long sleeves with white lace that reveals nothing. Around her neck she wears a black ribbon. [The same as Olympia wears around her neck – did Manet do this intentionally?]. On her head is a dark hat with a few flowers, on her lap a sleeping lapdog and a folded fan. Regardless of the bourgeois, homely way that Manet paints Victorine this time around, the work provokes furious reactions: "Two incurably mad women [*folles*] watch the train from behind the bars of their cell" is the arch description in *Le Journal*. Beneath a cartoon of the painting in *Le Tintamarre, hebdomadaire satirique et financier* is a rhyme:

> *Ce tableau d'un homme en délire*
> *A pour étiquette, dit-on*
> *'Le Chemin de fer'. Il faut lire*
> *'Chemin de fer pour Charenton'*

[Etiquette dictates that this tableau of a human being in a state of delirium be called 'The Railway'. It should read 'Railway to Charenton']29

Charenton-le-Pont, southeast of Paris, is home to the famous institute for the mentally ill. This is the last canvas for which Victorine poses for Manet. The French may be laughing at the painting, but the Americans welcome it with open arms. After purchasing the work from Paul Durand-Ruel, the 'Impressionist

Victorine 'the shrimp'

merchant' with a gallery in New York and the first to pay Manet for a work, sugar magnate Henry Osborne Havemeyer and his wife Louisine leave *Le Chemin de fer* to their son Horace. In 1956, the latter donates it to the National Gallery of Art in Washington.

In 1876, the year in which the Salon jury rejects two works by Manet,[30] Victorine Meurent proudly exhibits her own work at the Paris Salon. *Le Jour des rameaux* [Palm Sunday],[31] shows a young girl with long brown hair, flushed cheeks and a palm branch in her hand. In another, *Autoportrait*, she looks severe. A courtesan? Here she seems the absolute opposite, like a determined woman intent on holding her own. She creates the same impression as in her portrait by Alfred Stevens, entitled *Le Sphinx de Paris* (1870).[33] Victorine takes part in the Paris Salon,[34] and in 1903 is admitted to the Société des Artistes Français, which has been organising the annual Salon since 1880. She has finally made her secret dream a reality.

In around 1905, Victorine, now past sixty, exchanges the hectic Paris for the peaceful Colombes. In the village set in the bend of the Seine where it curves majestically between Argenteuil and Nanterre, she lives for the last twenty years of her life with her friend Marie Dufour, a piano teacher. Whether or not she was Manet's lover is a commonly asked question. There is frequent allusion to "their long artistic and amorous relationship".[35] But this is another myth and this is the reason why – Manet died of syphilis. To prevent the disease from further ravaging his body, the renowned Parisian surgeon Paul Tillaux[36] amputates Manet's lower left leg on 20 April 1883. After the operation there are complications. Ten days later, the painter of *Olympia* and the driving force behind the Impressionists is dead. He is just 51. Victorine lives to at least the age of 83. She has never complained of syphilis. Encircled by her friend Marie's care, she peacefully lays down her brushes and palette beside her bed in Colombes. For "a wreck, fallen into drunkenness and depravity" that's pretty good going.

Victorine 'the shrimp'

4

RIGHTEOUS CRIMES I

The house of Madame Herbelin and her niece, the artist Madeleine Lemaire, at 31 Rue de Monceau is certainly not the most prestigious of premises to be found in the vicinity of the chic Parc Monceau. However, it has its charm. Lilacs thrive in the modest front garden... but they've just been trampled. Clément Duval and his companion haven't come here for such delights. "Hold that lantern higher!" Walls are crammed with paintings. "Roses and still more roses, good grief!" The proprietor, Madeleine Lemaire, exhibits her work at the Salon de Paris, illustrates books by Marcel Proust,[1] and is not without merit in terms of her still lifes and floral subjects. "Useless petty bourgeois rubbish!" She holds a salon every Tuesday from April to June. Scions of the nobility and other rogues of the first order trip over themselves to attend. It only heightens the sense of repugnance felt by these intruders. In their wake, they leave flames to lick at Madame Lemaire's property, while 'bringing to safety' all of her jewellery and silverware. Duval stands before the judge with his head held high. He is no thief, on the contrary. He is the bringer of justice. "Why did you set fire to the house as well?" queries the judge. "To be honest, it was pointless," admits the anarchist, "the parasites weren't at home."[2]

‹ Ravachol, the popular bomber.

Righteous crimes I

'WE'LL NEVER BE ABLE TO KILL ENOUGH OF THEM'

Parasites, fripons, rapaces. Parasites, rogues and vultures. This says it all about the *Versaillais*: the collective name for the senior officer class and bourgeoisie who, in May 1871, allow their political lackey, the conservative politician Adolphe Thiers,[3] to steep the Paris Commune in blood. He installs the Assemblée Nationale not in republican Paris but in regal Versailles.

Stationed in Paris itself, there are more than 100,000 national guardsmen who, with the army, have defended the city against the Prussians. Overnight, the new government halts their wages. The suspension of rental payments, which allowed Parisian families more or less to manage during the war, is also repealed. The populace is plunged into poverty and rebellion. The Garde Nationale sides with them. As the flames of Paris spread to other cities, civil war threatens to engulf the nation. To restore things to order, Thiers dispatches men from Versailles to Paris; it is a small army made up of remnants cobbled together from the defeated French troops. The callous ruthlessness employed by the *Versaillais* to accomplish their mission inflicts deep wounds.

The annihilation of a whole swathe of the Parisian population is well documented;[4] in the *Semaine sanglante* [Bloody Week] alone – the final week of the Paris Commune running from 21 to 28 May – 3,000 *communards* die in the battle with the *Versaillais*, and 20,000 men and women are executed by firing squad in the streets of the capital without any form of trial. 35,000 others are arrested, including 651 children between the ages of seven and fifteen. Afterwards, another 960 die while imprisoned in camps, and 514 in the prison fortresses off the French coast, while 4,170 others are deported to New Caledonia. The toll among the *Versaillais* does not begin to compare: 877 dead and 76 hostages shot by firing squad, including Monseigneur Darboy, the archbishop of Paris. After his victory, Adolphe Thiers addresses the Assemblée Nationale, then in session at the palace in the gilded Opéra Royal, telling them that justice and order, humanity and civilisation have triumphed. Concerning the tens of thousands who have died among the supporters of the Commune, a *Versaillais* general is succinct: "*On en tuera jamais assez!*"[5] [We'll never be able to kill enough of them!]

The physical scars left behind from the Commune remain visible long afterwards in the form of townhouses in ruins and government buildings reduced to ashes[6] by cannon fire from either the *communards* or the *Versaillais*. At the Place Vendôme, Napoleon's triumphal column has been blasted to smithereens. But there are also invisible scars, beneath the surface. Many Parisians are incensed and harbour a deep hatred on account of those who have died, been executed, exiled or imprisoned. For some, this hatred is because they themselves have been beaten, mutilated or had their livelihoods ruined.

Whereas the ruling classes resume their lucrative places in the ministries, bank branches or management offices in the immediate post-Commune years, the working classes must return to the drudgery of the workshops, coal mines or iron foundries. Life reverts to its normal pattern in Paris. But tensions between the ruling and working classes are palpable. It doesn't take much to disrupt this apparent peace or unsettle the establishment again; no, it won't take much to set the fuse properly alight once more and ensure that justice is done.

BLACK FLAGS AND DYNAMITE

The latter becomes the anarchists' mission. Disgruntled or deprived, injured or indignant, they meet together in the wake of the emerging labour movement, which is trying to channel the growing torrent of men, women and children along a course that serves their best interests. Through its organisations, making advances under the red flag, they wish to bring about change via participation in the parliamentary process. The anarchists do not. They don't wave a red flag but a black one, their colour of choice. Neither do they have the patience for hoping to improve their lot by gradual degrees. They want it now. If that doesn't come to pass via the masses, then the alternative is to take individual action. Their dreams of the future involve a paradise without government or property, and in which everyone is equal. That is the essential idea outlined by their spiritual leader Pierre-Joseph Proudhon. He is the first to introduce the term 'anarchy'[7] and to translate anarchist ideas into a 'fitting language'.[8] As an example for your consideration: "Property is theft! Your enemy: the state!"[9]

This philosopher is admired by writers such as Octave Mirbeau and Emile Verhaeren,[10] publicists such as Elisée Reclus, Jean Grave, Félix Fénéon and Laurent Tailhade, and artists such as Camille Pissarro and Paul Signac. Russian nationals Mikhail Bakunin and Peter Kropotkin follow in Proudhon's footsteps. They have both traded the dictatorship of the tsar for the tolerance of France, where they busy themselves with class struggle. But however radical their writing and lectures may be – at an anarchist congress in the Swiss Jura, Kropotkin presses for propaganda "by means of words, daggers, pistols and dynamite"[11] – in reality these theoreticians couldn't hurt a fly. That said, their publications do inspire others who, with less enlightened minds and not as much eloquence, are filled with wrath. They will devote themselves to the practical side of the struggle.

In Paris, the anarchists congregate in clandestine clubs such as *Les Amis de Robespierre*, *Les Partisans de la Dynamite* and *La Panthère des Batignolles*,

Righteous crimes I

named after the district in the 17th *arrondissement* in the northwest of the city. *La Panthère* might sound more evocative of a frivolous local bordello rather than a group engaged in social struggle, but this couldn't be further from the truth. Their leader is a much-wounded, battle-hardy veteran of the Franco-Prussian War, demoted for his rebellious conduct: Clément Duval, locksmith. He has a score to settle.

Bomb making is the sole topic at the inaugural meeting of his new club. In its edition of 15 October 1882, *L'Etendard révolutionnaire* announces the initiative with pride: "Up until now the anarchists from Batignolles were content to be affiliated with various other clubs in Paris. Now, however, they are sufficiently numerous to establish their own group, one that will go by the name of *La Panthère des Batignolles*. On the agenda: the manufacture of hand grenades. We invite other anarchist groups to place this topic on their agendas as well, and to share with one another such observations as may be gleaned from this topic. New members are welcomed by Eugène Caron, leather worker, 39, Rue de Monceau."[12] That is three houses away from Madame Lemaire. Has Caron been keeping an eye on the parasites' comings and goings, and tipping off Duval about the address of his wealthy female neighbour? Clément Duval's break-in at the Rue de Monceau introduces a new term to the anarchist vocabulary: *la reprise individuelle* [individual reclamation].[13] He does not 'rob' Madame Lemaire; rather, he 'unburdens' her of her silverware and jewellery (valued at 15,000 francs[14]) and her property. It is completely revolutionary and a *cambriolage justicier* [an avenging act of burglary],[15] the proceeds of which will serve to finance anarchist propaganda. It never gets that far. Two weeks after the break-in, the revolutionary thief is apprehended in Batignolles on the premises of his fence at 56, Rue de Saussure. "I arrest you in the name of the law!" cries Sergeant Rossignol. Duval turns around and plants his pocketknife[16] in the officer's chest: "And I'll have you in the name of liberty!"[17]

'I'LL BLOW UP THE LOT OF YOU!'

The Assizes. The opening of the court session takes place at the Cour d'Assises de la Seine on 11 January 1887. Uproar. Under no circumstances will Duval have himself addressed as the accused. He is the *accuser*. He has written out his complaint against the crow-like judges in their black robes, also sending this to sympathetic journals such as *Le Révolté*.[18] In front of a packed courtroom, Duval hauls the judges over the coals: "If you want the head of yet another anarchist, take mine. On the day of justice, it is you who will have to be held accountable. I hope that on that day the anarchists will know what they must do. And that they will show no pity. Even then they will never victimise as many people as you do every day. ... It is not theft that I have committed, but a just restitution in the name of humanity. The money was to fund revolutionary propaganda, both in written and active forms. ... In your white lead factories you play unashamedly with human lives. Workers are first crippled, only to meet with death afterwards. In your mercury gilding factories the workers first lose their hair and then die in terrible agony. ... Children are kept an entire week, five or six hundred feet underground, in the darkness of the mines. When at last, they see the light of day, it's straight into the army and off to some war or other! ... For the women it is still worse than for the men. How many girls arrive from the country in good health only for you to turn them into anaemic creatures or flesh for your pleasure? ... No, I am no thief, but rather a victim of robbery. A bringer of justice. I am the enemy of individual ownership and say along with Proudhon: property is theft! That anarchistic, logical resolution will have you shaking to the core. Well then, rulers, magistrates, exploiters of every hue, on this day you will be lost![19] Thereafter, you will be done for. *Vive l'anarchie!*"

The presiding judge has had enough. Six policemen haul the unruly Duval out of the chamber. "*Je vous ferai tous sauter!*" [I'll blow up the lot of you!] His repeated cry is heard from the corridors: "*Je vous ferai sauter! Tous!*"[20] The following day, the court sentences Clément Duval to death. The fact that the sergeant has survived is immaterial. Public opinion does not side with the death sentence. The people of Paris understand his actions and his defence plea.

The gulf between the obscenely rich and the poverty-stricken is too great. Meetings are organised throughout the city urging support for Duval. Two weeks after the verdict, five hundred sympathisers and curious onlookers flock together for a day of solidarity at La Boule Noire, nowadays a concert hall, at 120, Boulevard de Rochechouart: "*Les lois on doit s'en foutre. On s'est foutu déjà du bon Dieu et tout a bien marché!*" [Let's take no heed of laws at all. We've already been heedless of God and that's gone fine!][21]

A resolute voice resounds from the small stage at La Boule Noire. The shouting subsides, silence descends. It is Louise Michel who speaks, the Commune's 'Red Virgin',[22] newly returned from years of exile in New Caledonia: "Duval's action is one of social war that will be repeated by thousands."[23] Applause! In his *Almanach anarchiste*, Sébastien Faure writes: "Accused of theft, of looting the *hôtel* Lemaire and of the attempted murder of that copper Rossignol, Duval, an impecunious worker, convinced that there is no legitimate basis for individual property, did indeed steal. Not for himself, but in support of propaganda. For the court of assizes, his stance was '*admirable de résolution et de sincérité*'."[24] An example of resolve and sincerity. Yielding under the pressure of public opinion,

Righteous crimes I

and to redress the spate of bombings, the president of the French republic, Jules Grévy, commutes Duval's death sentence to one of hard labour for life. But on Devil's Island, off the coast of French Guiana, it all amounts to the same thing.

One of Duval's followers, Alexandre Marius Jacob, declares before the court and to the press that he steals only from the rich – and among them only from entrepreneurs, investors, clergy, judges and the military. Never from doctors or architects "because they do useful things".[25] Notaries, on the other hand, do not. If property is theft, then Bakunin and Kropotkin see the radical extermination of notaries as a necessary precondition for a successful revolution. *Boom!* All property titles gone in a flash![26] So far, each conviction has launched a new campaign of action, and each such action a new conviction. Meanwhile, "*Vive l'anarchie!*" has been resonating in law courts and on scaffolds from Lyon to Paris. But it is an event in a town in the north of France that fires the starting gun for a new *spirale infernale* in the capital.

LILIES-OF-THE-VALLEY AND BULLETS

On 1 May 1891, some twenty years after the Paris Commune, the dam of apparent social calm finally breaks. It happens in Fourmies, a textile town eight kilometres from the Belgian border. There, in a total of thirty-seven wool and cotton spinning mills, men, women and children work for up to fifteen hours a day.[27] Their lives are dictated more by the rhythm of the flying shuttle and the factory whistle than by that of the church bells.

That year a dozen or so young women are at the head of the May Day procession. Not arrayed in communist red but in the innocent white of Maytime lily-of-the-valley. Félicie Tonnelier (Pennelier) is handing out sprays of these blooms to bystanders; they are the only splash of colour amid the drab surroundings. But wait... there is also a flag, the *Tricolore*. It goes without saying that the flag is allowed, but... the bosses of the two largest factories, Les Fourneaux and its competitor La Sans-Pareille, are for once of like mind: May Day should be an ordinary working day in Fourmies. Mayor Augustin Bernier, fed up with the strikes for an eight-hour day and a factory owner himself, has drummed up the gendarmes and the army. However, red flags are indeed being flown at the factories. There have been skirmishes and arrests since morning. With the working day almost at an end, the weavers have yet to weave and the textile spinners have yet to spin. It calls for punishment. Commandant Chapus does the deed:[28] *Fire!*

Abbot Margerin and his two assistant priests come running over, arms flailing in the air: "Stop! In the name of God, stop!" The sources differ, but between nine and twelve people are killed. Whatever the tally, eight of the victims are aged between eleven and twenty. Félicie Tonnelier was seventeen. The first body to be lifted up is that of another young woman. On the ground next to her lies the sprig of lily-of-the-valley that she was carrying. It's the eighteen-year-old Maria Blondeau, "the top of whose skull was completely blown off".[29]

A faithful illustration[30] of the *fusillade de Fourmies* occupies the whole front page of *Le Petit Parisien*, the newspaper that enjoys the nation's highest circulation. Public opinion is one of shock, the anarchists are *enragés*. On that same day of 1 May 1891, leaving aside the events in Fourmies, the anarchists hijack the socialists' march at the Place de Clichy in Paris. After the parade, the battle! This time it's the anarchists themselves who open fire. A few slightly injured gendarmes later, the three gunmen are treated to sabres in the gendarmerie. Perhaps it is to purge all centres of industry from the rot within that the public prosecutor *Maître* Bulot and *Juge* Benoît sentence the three to hard labour.

THE UNJUST JUDGES

Ravachol, the new anarchist talent, feels it is all too hard and unjust. In early March 1892, it all kicks off. *Boom!* On the Boulevard Saint-Germain, a majestic townhouse is blown to pieces. *Juge* Benoît has barely recovered from the blow when a fresh explosion occurs, this time in the Rue de Clichy, blasting away the roof of his colleague, *Maître* Bulot. Meanwhile, a bomb explodes in the hated Lobau Barracks behind the Hôtel de Ville. During the suppression of the Paris Commune, this is where the *Versaillais* executed between two and three thousand *communards* by firing squad. In the same month of March, the windows of the Princess de Sagan's mansion in the Rue Saint-Dominique are blown off their hinges; when half of Paris is living in poverty, you don't host decadent balls.

Ravachol becomes a folk hero. The popular song '*La Carmagnole*' – *Dansons la Carmagnole/ Vive le son / Vive le son du canon* – is renamed '*La Ravachole*': *Dansons la Ravachole ... Vive le son de l'explosion*. Other crimes are conveniently attributed to him as well: the looting of a rich countess's tomb, the murder of a 92-year-old hermit who had amassed a fortune from begging, and a double murder. Ravachol denies these charges, and his guilt is never proven. Conversely, Ravachol takes pride in the bombings. He preaches his passion for dynamite and anarchy up to the very last moment. The executioner Anatole Deibler precisely records his observations of each beheading in his logbook *Carnets d'exécutions*.[31] From his perspective, Deibler refers invariably to the falling of the blade as *le moment suprême*. He has seen 395 of these over the course of half a century. In Ravachol's case he writes: "He kept shouting furiously that he felt

Righteous crimes I

no regret for his deeds. He denounced the bourgeoisie, the magistrates and the chaplain. From the door to his cell all the way up to the scaffold, he sang and cried out obscenities [*des mots orduriers*] and at the *moment suprême*: '*Vive l'anarchie!*'" Ravachol inspires a new set of followers. The engraver Charles Maurin portrays him as a saint. His powerful head is not framed by stained glass but by the guillotine. Behind him emerge the rays of a new dawn.

Dynamite continues to be 'on trend'. One month after Ravachol's arrest, Théodule Meunier throws a bomb into the Café Véry on the Boulevard de Magenta where a waiter had betrayed his idol to *les vaches*, the police. Another of Ravachol's admirers, Émile Henry, sends dynamite to the prestigious headquarters of the Société des Mines de Carmaux in the Avenue de l'Opéra. The Société is exploiting its miners. With all of these explosions going on in the city, the wary concierge places the suspicious package on the pavement. A policeman carries it cautiously to the nearest police station in the Rue des Bons-Enfants. *Boom!* Five policemen dead, one gravely injured. The anarchists' posters exclaim: "*A notre tour nous disons: on en tuera jamais assez!*"[32] [We, in turn, say: we'll never be able to kill enough of them!]

Another act of revenge for Ravachol's death springs from the mind of Auguste Vaillant. He proceeds to launch a homemade explosive device into the Chambre des Députés. *La dynamite au Palais-Bourbon!*[33] shrieks *Le Petit Parisien* across the whole of its front page for 10 December 1893. Although only a few *députés* are slightly wounded, with no-one killed, Vaillant still receives the death penalty. Sadi Carnot, president of the French Republic, refuses to grant him mercy. It is a decision that will cost the statesman dearly only a few months later. The attack on the Assemblée Nationale – dubbed the *palais de l'injustice* by the anarchists – is applauded in sympathetic sections of the press. Laurent Tailhade, journalist, poet and libertarian speaker: "*Qu'importent les victimes si le geste est beau?*"[34] [What do the victims matter as long as the gesture is noble?]

Barely three months later, early in 1894, there is a series of new bomb explosions in retaliation for Vaillant. One of these detonates in the popular Café Terminus at the Gare Saint-Lazare. This time, the sympathetic press condemns the incident. After all, the casualties include ordinary people waiting for a train, the people's children. Some weeks later, a bomb kills a passer-by in the Rue Saint-Jacques, while another damages a townhouse in the prestigious Faubourg Saint-Germain district. A third explodes too soon; on 15 March the Belgian anarchist Désiré Joseph Pauwels plans to blow up the church of La Madeleine. He fails to factor in divine providence, and the bomb explodes on the church steps in the anarchist's pocket.[35]

To start, the *saumon Chambord*, followed by the *perdreaux à la vigneron*, with a delicious *corbeille glacée* for dessert. Laurent Tailhade, who has just defended the Assemblée Nationale bomber, is yielding to the temptations afforded by the menu at Chez Foyot, an exclusive restaurant on the Rue de Condé, adjacent to the Théâtre de l'Odéon. Busily sparring with assorted politicians, bankers and their *maîtresses* – he is a notorious *provocateur* with more than thirty duels under his belt – Tailhade is deeply engaged in discussion. Moreover, he is enjoying the company of these delightful mistresses every bit as much as he is the exquisite burgundy. *Boom!* Blood, shards of glass and flames. The lecturer loses an eye. Oh well... as long as the gesture is noble.

THE 'VILLAINOUS LAWS'

Had President Carnot been able to see into the future, he might well have shown mercy to Auguste Vaillant, the Assemblée Nationale bomber. On 24 June, the president finds himself the guest of honour in Lyon, where his role is to lend further panache to the Exposition Internationale et Coloniale. Just fifteen minutes after his arrival, he is lying on the ground in convulsions. It takes no more than a moment for him to hear the words *"Vive l'anarchie!"* before the Italian anarchist Sante Geronimo Caserio has plunged his knife into Carnot's heart. In a salon at the official residence of the prefect for Lyon, the most eminent doctors and surgeons from the city's medical faculty attempt to save the life of their president. Dr Antonin Poncet, a professor of surgery, operates on him and is assisted by four of his peers.[36] They are unable to staunch the bleeding. At precisely twenty minutes to one, in the early hours of Monday 25 June 1894, the president of the French republic succumbs to his wounds. The country is in shock. Enough is enough.

The Assemblée Nationale, by now expert in the field, votes for a package of laws aimed at the root-and-branch eradication of anarchism. It is not only 'gang leaders' who are to be punished, but also those who assist and sympathise with them. A police report from the same year lists no fewer than five hundred anarchists in Paris.[37] Five hundred too many. Many are picked up in mass arrests, others flee the country. In a grand trial, *Le procès des Trente*, which opens two months after the president's assassination, the anarchists' intellectual leaders – often publishers and journalists from the affiliated press, such as Jean Grave, Félix Fénéon, Emile Pouget and Sébastien Faure – are convicted and given long prison sentences. Their anarchist publications, *Le Père Peinard* and *Le Révolté*, cease printing. *Les lois scélérates* – the 'villainous laws', as they are termed by the anarchists – have done their job.

Righteous crimes I

Although the flames of *la terreur noire* die down in France, the embers of anarchism smoulder on elsewhere in the world and with angry resurgences. Three years after the assassination of President Carnot, prime minister Antonio Cánovas del Castillo of Spain is shot dead. A year later, in 1898, the Empress Elisabeth of Austria, better known as Sisi, is stabbed to death with a sharpened file. In 1900, King Umberto of Italy is on the receiving end of a bullet. And in 1901, President William McKinley of the United States shares the same fate. This catalogue of assassinations directed at heads of state comes to a provisional close in 1912 with the shooting of Spain's prime minister, José Canalejas y Méndez. All the perpetrators plead anarchism as their excuse and, in their turn, pay for their actions with death. Martyrdom.

Although by the end of the nineteenth century the anarchists in France have all been killed, imprisoned or exiled, they are not forgotten. New 'confessors of the faith' may yet arise from their black ashes with "*ni dieu, ni maître*" on their lips.

Righteous crimes I

Excelsior on the trail of the tragic bandits.

5

RIGHTEOUS CRIMES II

Cracking pistols and carbines, whining engines and screeching tyres, orders from gunmen, the groans of the wounded and the rattles of the dying. In Paris, an orgy of violence heralds the resurgence of a phenomenon that everyone believed had fizzled out: righteous criminals. They are back. In the last few days before Christmas 1911, the anarchist bandits tragiques [tragic bandits] raise hell. For four months, they hold the city in their grip with extreme violence, and with an innovative weapon: the car. At the steering wheel: Jules Bonnot. At the trigger: his gang, the Bonnot Gang.

A BODY IN THE WOODS

"Yesterday morning, Mr Blondeau, watchman, heard two shots during his tour of inspection. He initially thought he was dealing with poachers, but on approaching was astonished to see a grey automobile by the side of the road. Alongside the vehicle he observed an individual undressing a motionless man. As the watchman drew near, the motorist jumped into the car and sped off. The automobile bore the numberplate 701-S-2. The victim was still breathing but died after mumbling a few unintelligible words. The unidentified man had two wounds, caused by bullets from a revolver,"[1] the newspaper *Excelsior* reports to its readers on Wednesday 29 November 1911.

Le Petit Parisien – its modest title does not lead one to suspect that this is France's biggest newspaper with a circulation of 1.3 million[2] – has a bad feeling about the news: "This affair at Le Châtelet-en-Brie seems incredibly mysterious and hugely troubling."[3] *Le Petit Parisien* is usually right. Its recipe for success is simple: it combines reliable reporting with unvarnished common sense. The editorial staff know everything there is to know about the disturbing events in the city and all its mysteries. Including those surrounding the anarchist violence that had engulfed France fifteen years previously. Its subscribers could not get enough of it. It boosted its circulation to unprecedented heights. But the readers remember the bombing spree of the *anarchistes illégalistes* in Paris only too well. An explosion of violence that only died away after the murder of the French president. Is it starting again?

In fact, it is already underway. Sitting at the wheel of the car from Le Châtelet-en-Brie is Jules Bonnot, anarchist on the run. In Lyon, things became too hot for him to handle. In Paris, on the other hand, he knows where to go. In Romainville, a place beyond Belleville, to the northeast of the city, stands an innocent-looking country villa in the midst of a garden. An ideal retirement property for any successful Parisian merchant. But nothing is what it seems. Shrouded in a semblance of rural tranquillity, it is actually used by the editorial team of *L'Anarchie*.

RATHER BLOOD THAN INK

The founder of the weekly magazine is the iconic anarchist, Albert Libertad. He has long admired Ravachol and the other bombers.[4] All of whom were devotees of the 'individual reclamation' theory, which allows people to reclaim what has been taken from them through the organised exploitation of the state and employers. Libertad cannot proclaim his sympathies from the rooftops because of the strict laws prohibiting anarchism[5] which hang over his head like a sword of Damocles. Libertad, who walks with crutches due to a disability affecting his lower legs, also organises well-attended *causeries populaires* [popular conversations]. He loves to provoke, and to this end enjoys interrupting church services. During mass on Sunday 5 September 1897, in the Sacré-Coeur Basilica, the pompous temple that was built by the *Versaillais* in celebration of their victory over the *communards*, he curses God and his worshippers. It is the talk of Paris. *L'Anarchie* is thriving at this point: with 22,000 subscribers, the magazine is head and shoulders above its competitors. These are *Le Libertaire* (circulation 7,000) from Sébastien Faure, who commits theft as a revolutionary act, and *Les Temps Nouveaux* (circulation 8,000) from Jean Grave, who adopts a more moderate tone.[6] Of the three, *L'Anarchie* is far and away the most combative. What more could you expect of a publisher who attacks God and the police alike with his crutches. 'Neither God nor master'.

The figures who frequent the editorial office of *L'Anarchie* include those who do not just do battle with their pens – some prefer to spill blood rather than ink! Although they do not actually write, their names will soon be in all the papers: Octave Garnier, baker's boy; Eugène Dieudonné, apprentice furniture-maker; André Soudy, grocer's assistant; René Valet, locksmith; Edouard Carouy, metalworker; Étienne Monier, gardener and florist; Marius Metge, chef; and Raymond Callemin, typesetter. The others call him Raymond *la Science*, due to his pedantic boasting about his erudition: "I know a thing or two. According to my friends, my head contains just as much science as the books."[7] The oldest among them is Jules Bonnot, mechanic. Had they stuck to their own professions, they would probably have died peacefully in their beds.

Wanted for multiple crimes, the *illégalistes* hide out in Romainville. At the same time, the editorial office of *L'Anarchie* is a safe house for affiliated activists. In this hideout, Jules Bonnot tells his version of the story from Le Châtelet-en-Brie: when he and his accomplice are inspecting their pistols at the side of the road, a shot is accidentally fired. His accomplice is still conscious but bleeding heavily from a head wound. A watchman approaches from afar. Bonnot has no choice.[8] With a second shot, he finishes off his comrade and roars off in his La Buire *double phaeton*, a brand-new car, stolen from the garage of a wealthy Lyonnaise textile manufacturer.

The Le Châtelet-en-Brie watchman's detailed description of the car, the distinctive La Buire *double phaeton*, puts the detectives on the trail of Bonnot & Demange, 'repairs to automobiles, motorcycles and cycles' in Lyon. For a long time, the suspicious pair have stolen more cars than they have repaired. Petit-Demange has already been arrested, but his partner has disappeared.

Righteous crimes II

The car too. At *commissariats* and *préfectures* from Lyon to Paris, telegrams are ticking and telephones are ringing. Wanted: Jules Bonnot!

Bonnot lost his mother at a young age. When he was just thirteen his father found him work as an apprentice mechanic in the Peugeot factories, but it was not long before the troublemaker was out on his ear. Before he reaches the age of twenty, he already has a long criminal record. But there is a bright spot. The army, at which the anarchists rail, attracts Bonnot. He serves three years in the infantry, where he hones his mechanical skills – and his shooting ability. Following his army service, he works in a succession of garages. But because he spends more time preaching about anarchy than tightening bolts or screws, he acquires a bad reputation. One that rapidly spreads. His marriage to the seamstress Sophie Burdet produces a son, Louis Justin; but because of Bonnet's life as an *illégaliste*, his wife takes the child and leaves her husband. She follows her new man to Switzerland. The child takes his name and Bonnot never sees them again. To find employment, he travels from city to city. He is finally able to start work at the newly established Berliet car factory in Lyon. He also learns to drive, something new for that era – in 1907, by no means everyone can do such a thing. It opens new horizons. Ink will flow about this achievement, from Paris to New York.

CHRISTMAS BULLETS

Bang! Bang! On 21 December 1911, four days before people wish one another a *Joyeux Noël*, two shots turn the blue uniform of Ernest Caby red. The bank courier slumps down before the door of the Société Générale in the Rue Ordener. He didn't see the car approaching, it happened in a flash. Caby conscientiously clasps the bag containing the cash and securities. Then a second individual appears. While his companion tries to prise the bag loose, he raises his revolver.[9] *Bang!* Caby lets go. Shooting at the inquisitive market traders who stick their heads above their stalls, the car disappears with screeching tyres behind the bend of the Rue des Cloys. Bystanders come running from houses and doorways to bend over the victim, not yet realising that in their street, in the shadow of the Butte Montmartre, history is being written: the first motorised hold-up.[10]

Quelle aventure! Unprecedented! The newspapers are filled with reports and eye-witness accounts. Not to mention conjecture. When the car – this time a Delaunay-Belleville – is found in Dieppe, the police suspect the culprits have fled to England. In London, the Société Générale offers a reward of 12,500 francs for anyone with information that leads to the perpetrators of the reckless attack on their courier. But Caby – miraculously – has survived his gunshot wounds.

On the photos that Mr Jouin, the astute second-in-command of the Sûreté de Paris shows him on his sickbed, he points to someone. That's the man!

It is Octave Garnier.[11] Another figure makes him hesitate. It is Edouard Carouy, a good friend of Garnier and known to Mr Jouin for counterfeiting. Both are on the list of visitors to the house in Romainville that the Sûreté are watching. *Bang! Bang!* On Christmas Eve 1911, it is not the bells of Saint-Vincent-de-Paul that ring out. What people hear, instead, are gunshots in the Rue Lafayette. They are coming from the Manufactures réunies d'armes et de sports, which is diagonally opposite the church. When the pious Parisians emerge from Saint-Vincent, the shop windows lie in smithereens on the pavement. Taken aback, they cross themselves for a second and a third time. *Mon Dieu!* Revolvers, carbines and precision rifles have also been stolen from under the Christmas tree at a firearms retailer on the Boulevard Haussmann. Gleaming Smith & Wessons and Winchesters. Well-oiled Brownings as well… and bullets, thousands of bullets. An alarming development.

The season's greetings have not yet finished when, on the second day of the new year, the residents of Thiais awake to the news of an atrocity. In the hamlet to the south of Paris, a terrible crime has been committed. An elderly man and his housekeeper have been murdered in their sleep, writes *Le Petit Parisien* on 4 January 1912. The 93-year-old Mr Moreau, a rich private investor (*rentier*), and his 72-year-old housekeeper, Madame Arfeux, have been killed with a hammer. This is about more than money, Mr Jouin suspects. Is anger or hate mixed up in this somewhere?

The pieces of the puzzle begin to fall into place. Car thefts, the roadside murder in Le Châtelet-en-Brie, the hold-up of the bank courier in the Rue Ordener, and at the arms shop in the city centre, the break-in at the Romainville post office, the violent murder and robbery of the *rentier* and the housekeeper. Bonnot, Carouy and Garnier, anarchists. It begins to dawn on the second-in-command of the Sûreté. New 'righteous criminals' are at work. Ravachol, Vaillant, Henry and Caserio are resurrected! In new guises and with a new style. The dynamite has been replaced by guns, the lone bombings by the actions of an orchestrated gang: the Bonnot Gang.

Monsieur Jouin orders a raid at *L'Anarchie*. The police not only find the stolen stamps from a recent break-in at the Romainville post office, but also pistols from the armoury in the Rue Lafayette. The two ringleaders who took up the torch after the death of Albert Libertad are imprisoned. These are Rirette Maîtrejean, a seasoned anarchist, and Victor Kibalchich, who will later become known as Victor Serge, a supporter of Leon Trotsky, founder and first leader of the Russian Red Army. Others continue their mission. The culpability for the

Righteous crimes II

violence lies with capitalism, which spares no one. "Yes", writes *L'Anarchie* on 22 February, "Garnier and Carouy are members of our community. Anarchists. Well, you wicked people [*gens infects*], we swear to you that as long as your kind proliferates there will always be burglars, thieves and murderers."[12]

A GOLDEN AGE FOR NEWSPAPERS

The Sûreté may know their names, but they don't know their location. The nefarious automobile is still on the move. Five days after the proclamation in *L'Anarchie*, it races at full throttle through the Rue d'Amsterdam. At the Gare Saint-Lazare, coachmen curse and pedestrians shake their fists as they leap to safety. When the driver attempts to cross the junction to the Rue du Havre, he finds police officer François Garnier in his way. Stop! The servant of the law is given some help. An omnibus is unintentionally blocking Bonnot's path. "Madmen!" the officer shouts, notebook in hand. He jumps onto the running board of the car.

Bang! Bang! Bang! Three shots ring out from the back seat, *L'Humanité* writes. Officer Garnier falls backwards like a dislodged hand puppet, *Le Petit Parisien* discloses. "A crazy car in Paris!" is the *Excelsior's* headline. "A police officer killed!" The newspapers vie to report on the Bonnot affair. Just as in the era of Ravachol and the first bombers,[13] the press lap it up. The journalists scurry to obtain the latest news about the case. *Le Petit Parisien* and *Excelsior* lead the pack. Unlike the *Le Petit Parisien* and other big newspapers – such as *Le Journal* (circulation 995,000), *Le Petit Journal* (circulation 850,000) and *Le Matin* (circulation 647,000)[14] – *Excelsior* informs its readers through a new medium: photography. "For those unable to read,"[15] explains the newspaper in its first edition of 16 November 1910, *Excelsior* is the perfect means of betterment. Armed with their Vest Pocket Kodaks – the American firm is advertising its new, compact device in the French newspapers – the reporters from *Excelsior* are all over the place. Their unique 'I was there!' style drives up the newspaper's circulation to 110,000 in a single year.[16] Journalists from almost every title conduct their personal investigations, search for possible perpetrators, and offer tips to the police. In turn, the police leaks information and pictures to the editors.

The new generation of righteous criminals also uses the newspapers as a mouthpiece. "Mr Editor of *Le Petit Parisien*, I would be most grateful to you if you would publish the correction below as a response to the rumours that the police are spreading about me." It is soon apparent that the letter is poking fun at police inactivity: "Every morning, when I read my newspaper in the Jardin du Luxembourg, which is in such a sad state because there is not a single policeman to be seen in the vicinity, I smile like the Mona Lisa and think to myself: what tall stories. Yours sincerely, Edouard Carouy."[17] The Sûreté is furious, the *préfecture de police* incandescent with rage. Octave Garnier also picks up his pen: "Do not think that I am fleeing from your agents. Rather, I think that they are running away from me. All this will end in a battle between the formidable arsenal that society has at its disposal and myself. I know that I will lose, I am the weakest. *Mais j'espère bien faire payer cher votre victoire.*"[18] [But I hope to make you pay dearly for your victory.] In the press and the court of public opinion, the police are the fall guys. The first thing to do to remedy the situation is to replace Mr Lépine, *L'Humanité* writes. The newspaper publicly demands the dismissal of the prefect of the Paris police.

FAST CARS, MERCILESS GUNMEN

On 25 March 1912, Jules Bonnot is up and about early. It's going to be a busy working day. At 8.20am he has already passed Orly, deep in the Forêt de Sénart. In the same forest where the stagecoaches to Lyon were ambushed, the roar of a powerful engine grows louder. This is music to Bonnot's ears. In the distance, a gleaming De Dion-Bouton appears in the dawn light. Bodywork and wheels in the same dark blue, decorated with a yellow stripe, two headlights, two copper lanterns and two spare tyres. *Une merveille.* But also fast and reliable – Bonnot knew what he was doing when he chose the car. This gem needs to be delivered to its owner who is on holiday in Cap Ferrat, near Nice – driver Mathillé and mechanic Cérisol are tasked with this not-unpleasant task. Halfway through the forest, they slow down for the man waving a white handkerchief. Breakdown. The hand with the handkerchief drops, but his other appears with a pistol. *Bang! Bang!* Straight into the head and heart of Mathillé. Five accomplices emerge from the bushes. *Bang! Bang!* Mortally wounded, Cérisol crumples to the ground.

At 10.30am, barely two hours after the ambush in the Forêt de Sénart, the De Dion-Bouton appears in the tranquil Chantilly, outside the northern city limits of Paris. *Bang!* Behind their counter, which has been shot to pieces, two employees of the Société Générale lie lifeless in a pool of blood. A third is seriously injured. The gunmen steal 50,000 francs. A lookout with a long coat and bowler hat waits beside the thrumming getaway car. He fires at curious passers-by on the street with his automatic rifle. He loves this weapon. Indeed, it's his pride and joy. Sporting his trademark hat and overcoat, he lets himself be photographed with the weapon as he stares into the camera. This photo betrays him: it is the anarchist André Soudy. Known from now on as *"l'homme à la carabine"* [the man with the carbine].

Righteous crimes II

The next day's newspapers spew out their disgust. On the cover of *Excelsior*, two hands hold a choke chain to the throats of Carouy, Garnier and Bonnot: "100,000 to the person who apprehends them!" promises the Société Générale. The government also takes an interest. Under the chairmanship of Raymond Poincaré, a year later the president of France, the Council of Ministers approves new loans for the Sûreté générale and for the Sûreté de Paris: 540,000 francs, 96,000 francs of which are for the urgent purchase of eight cars. In 1907, Georges Clemenceau, prime minister and minister of the interior, and Célestin Hennion, chief of the Sûreté générale, had already created the Brigades Régionales de Police Mobile. But they were not effective. The twelve brigades, spread over the whole country, only had four De Dion-Boutons between them, which were "always broken down".[19] It was not until 1912, due to the Bonnot affair, that every brigade gained a car. The remainder of the new funding is spent on more officers, extra telephone equipment and modern weaponry.

SECRET WEAPON

But the Sûreté de Paris' most effective weapon is not made of metal but of flesh and blood. It is Mr Jouin. With the accuracy of a dedicated seamstress, he unravels all the threads from his network of informants. His patience and precision are rewarded. Along with his deputy, Colmar, he apprehends the first accomplices. The small fry led to bigger fish. A breakthrough! He catches the first core members of the gang: Marius Metge, the chef, and Eugène Dieudonné, the furniture-maker. When he leaves his home at 47, Rue Nollet, the latter is not carrying a wood planer, but two loaded Brownings, a cosh, and an escape route to Switzerland. The house, in the heart of Batignolles, serves as a hideout[20] for the gang, as Mr Jouin well knows.

New leads bring the deputy to André Soudy, the man with the carbine. Soudy suffers from tuberculosis and, as it turns out, has decided to take the air at the coast. Disguised as tourists, Mr Jouin and Colmar approach the bandit. Their picnic basket is not filled with croissants and cider, but pistols and handcuffs. They arrest the tuberculosis patient at Berck-Plage station. On 3 April, they again triumph with the arrest of Carouy. Four days later, they capture Raymond *la Science*. A few days after this, the successful duo also catches Etienne Monier, the gardener and florist. This is a triumph for the Sûreté.

If Jules Bonnot is the revolutionary who makes the French capital and its pallbearers quake in their boots, then Mr Jouin is the hero of all those yearning for order and justice. Even the bandit Monier compliments him: "I would rather be arrested by you than by any other police officer, you know. You are a courageous and skilled [*habile*] man, and you are appreciated in our milieu."[21] These are words that give Mr Jouin greater pleasure than a medal.

Why on earth does the successful inspector head to Ivry, just outside Paris, accompanied only by Colmar and a small escort? In the hamlet where the Marne and the Seine converge, suspects have been flagged in a warehouse. It could be something big. So why not deploy more men? Have the successes gone to his head? Does he hope to shoot the target on his own? In any case, after the smooth apprehension of two suspects, Mr Jouin asks them to show him around the building. 'There's no one here', they reply. Nevertheless, Mr Jouin climbs up the ladder to the upper floor. In the first room: nothing. In the second: even less. 'They don't know what a broom is around here', Colmar jokes light-heartedly. Suddenly, the trained eyes of Mr Jouin discern a human form. The shadow veers to the right but the deputy at the Sûreté still manages to grab him. A glimpse of his face makes the blood curdle in Mr Jouin's veins. Watch out! He shouts to Colmar behind him. Watch out! It's not at his assistant that the rain of bullets from Bonnot is directed, however, but at himself. Jouin is dead. Colmar fires back. But Bonnot is a better shot. And is gone.

"Alas", eulogises Théodore Steeg, minister of the interior, his voice trembling: "Today a new name is being inscribed on the marble plaque of heroes." In a full-blown state funeral, prime minister Poincaré leads the funeral procession, followed by his ministers, the vice-chair of the Assemblée Nationale, and numerous other dignitaries. Black horses in long caparisons pull several canopied mourning carriages. In the first of these lies the late Mr Jouin, whilst the others are filled to the brim with flowers and wreaths. Along the route to Notre-Dame thousands of subdued spectators doff their hats. "A brilliant career lay ahead of him", orates Mr Lépine, still in post as prefect of the Paris police, in his eulogy. "It has been shattered."[22]

THE END OF THE SPECTACLE

The murder of the much-loved police officer makes an impression. On 28 April, four days after the fatal shooting in Ivry, Bonnot is spotted. The concerted efforts of every police force, all of which want to avenge Jouin's death, lead to an isolated two-floor shed in Choisy-le-Roi, to the south of Paris. In front of the building is a billboard: Garage Dubois. Xavier Guichard, head of the Sûreté and the late Mr Jouin's boss, leads the siege of the run-down building with his brother Paul Guichard. Lépine is en route with back-up: a company of the Garde Républicaine, the elite troops. Police officers and firemen are streaming in from nearby villages. When two battalions of the Infanterie Coloniale turn up, it is as

Righteous crimes II

though Choisy-le-Roi is at war. From behind every tree and every wall, and out of every window in the surrounding area, hundreds of gun barrels are trained on the building. The members of the local shooting clubs are in their element. They too are permitted to join in the gunning down of the bandit.[23]

When Guichard gives the sign, a volley of gunfire erupts. From an opening in the wall of his hideout, Bonnot fires back. New salvos ring out. Bonnot does not give way; on the contrary, he wounds several of the besiegers. Lépine grows nervous. At 9.30am, he convenes a council of war. Then the elite troops step in. They shoot with new Lebel rifles, their bullets effortlessly piercing the walls of the building. But Bonnot still does not give an inch. The machine gun, bring the machine gun! This needs to be fetched from Versailles or Vincennes. It would take too long.

The young Lieutenant Fontan comes up with a more ingenious idea: dynamite! The favourite weapon of the anarchists themselves.[24] The photos taken by journalists at the scene show Fontan leading a high-sided cart up to the building, pulled by a white horse. It is filled to the brim with straw and several sticks of dynamite. Everyone waits with bated breath. Nothing. The wick has gone out. At the second attempt, the dynamite – to loud applause from the now more than 4,000 spectators – blows a number of stones out. "Oooohhhhh!", the public reacts in disappointment, as if a player has missed a goal and hit the post in a football match. At the third attempt, this time with a triple charge, the dynamite reduces an entire wall to rubble. The roof catches fire: "Bravo!" The Garde Républicaine and the other units fire continuously into the dark opening. Only a spiralling wisp of smoke emanates from the interior. No response.

According to legend, Jules Bonnot made a final sortie crying "*vive l'anarchie!*" [long live anarchy] as the building was stormed. But this is not correct. With a mattress tied around him as a shield, he lies mortally wounded on the floor. "His mouth like the jaws of a predator, his eyes wild, raging. Hideous!"[25] The body of an accomplice is lying downstairs, Dubois. Jules Bonnot, thirty-five years old, dies on the journey to the Hôtel-Dieu hospital. Of the nine bullets in his body, six have struck his head.[26] Amongst the smouldering rubble and shards of glass lies a piece of paper. Bonnot's last words. Not a diatribe against capital, church or state, but an attempt to set the record straight about suspects and about the gang member Dieudonné.[27] With this, he saves several lives.

When Bonnot is taken away, it is as if the fields and roads around the smouldering ruin are themselves in motion. Everyone rises. Families pack the remains of their picnics into their baskets. Folding chairs are collapsed. Reporters hurry back to their editors. The fire brigade dismantles its floodlights, and the film crew from Pathé,[28] who have recorded the firework display, packs up its camera. The spectacle is over.

Two weeks later, on the evening of 14 May 1912, the newspaper sellers are again yelling. "The bandits have been identified. Third edition. Read all about it!"[29] This time, it is the final gang members, Garnier and Valet, who have been cornered. They are hiding in a house beneath a viaduct in Nogent-sur-Marne. Promising stuff! The Parisian taxis make a killing out of the news and offer to ferry spectators from the boulevards: "For Nogent, two francs per seat!"[30]

The siege is a superlative sequel to Choisy-le-Roi: even more dynamite and even more troops. By the afternoon of the following day, the crowds of disaster tourists are starving. An innkeeper telephones "to have some barrels of beer transported by a motorised lorry."[31] It is 2.30am when the battered bodies of Garnier and Valet are carried out. The superhuman effort of the army and the police, just to catch two bandits, elicits a cynical remark from the publisher of *Le Crapouillot*: "The first victory of the French army since Sedan."[32]

FREEDOM FIGHTERS OR CRIMINALS?

In the *préfecture de police* on the Quai d'Orsay, medals are handed out, while beneath the walls of the La Santé prison on the Boulevard Arago, heads are rolling. Anatole Deibler, the executioner who fifteen years earlier beheaded Ravachol, Henry, Vaillant and Caserio, "approaches with a lantern and minutely inspects the installation. Then he nods with the air of a guild master who is satisfied with the workmanship."[33] He lets the blade fall on André Soudy, Raymond *la Science* and Etienne Monier. In his *Carnets d'exécutions*, which he has been carefully keeping since he first stepped onto the scaffold, he notes under Soudy, "an enemy of work".[34] Dieudonné escapes the guillotine. Thanks to the notes of the dying Bonnot, his death penalty is commuted to a life sentence of forced labour. Metge and Carouy receive the same punishment. Before the end of the court case, the latter swallows a poison capsule and dies in his cell. Victor Kibalchich and Rirette Maîtrejean, the militant publishers of *L'Anarchie* are, respectively, sentenced to five years in prison and acquitted.

At the Dubois garage in Choisy-le-Roi, at the place where Jules Bonnot was 'killed in action', the official receiver, Girard, and clerk of the court, Bourlès, hold a large public auction of the bandit's paraphernalia. Posters for the 'major auction' inform the public that numerous objects are damaged by fire, bullets or dynamite. A charred motorcycle is sold for 400 francs, an iron bed rail for 3.50 francs, and the bedsheets in which the bandit last slept for 8 francs. The 'major auction' yields the paltry sum of 1,423 francs.[36]

Righteous crimes II

The explanation is clear. Unlike the scions of the first generation, their descendants do not target aristocrats or deputies, and certainly not a president of the republic. Apart from a few rich car owners and an elderly *rentier*, all the victims of the Bonnot Gang are ordinary workers, 'children of the people': a chauffeur and a mechanic, a bank courier, a housekeeper, several bank clerks and policemen. This results in a rapid cooling of popular sympathy. It also explains why the members of the local shooting clubs in the Choisy-le-Roi area participate in the shooting of Bonnot. It was as if he were a rabid dog they were hunting. Are the members of the second generation of *anarchistes illégalistes* righteous criminals? Or are they disguising ordinary crimes amid the folds of the black flag? Where is the boundary "between heinous crimes and anarchist ideology?"[37] In any case, with the second generation there is less ideology and more violence involved. It is as though Bonnot and his associates are disinclined to convince the general public of the ideas of Proudhon or Bakunin, but simply want to cause them pain. To give them a first-hand taste of how outcasts live. In court too – in contrast to the political arguments of Duval, Ravachol, Henry or Vaillant – there is little grandiose discourse to be heard. No debate or discussion, simply: *Bang!*

Within his own ranks, Bonnot receives a moving eulogy the week after his death, printed in *L'Anarchie*: "Bonnot, who pistol in hand went to steal the gold of the bourgeois from the briefcase of the Société Générale, was an anarchist. Bonnot, who for months fooled all the Guichards[38] of the Sûreté, was an anarchist. Bonnot, who defended his freedom with a Browning, was an anarchist. Bonnot, who defended social equality, alone against the cops [*la flicaille*], the army, the magistrature and the mass of respectable citizens, was an anarchist. When that life and this death go hand in hand with efforts before which even a Spartan bows, when Bonnot, shot at by a whole regiment, in the sights of 500 Lebel rifles, his skull burst open with dynamite, when Bonnot, wounded, probably dying, takes up a pencil and writes: Mme Thollon is not guilty, neither is Gauzy, nor is Dieudonné, nor Petit-Demange, nor Mr Thollon. When a man does such deeds, well, at that moment he reaches the peaks of moral beauty."[39] A saint for some, a devil for others.

Jules Bonnot also enters the history books. With his criminal driving skills, he makes the news on the other side of the world. On 12 April 1912, two weeks before his death, *The New York Times* immortalises him in its columns as "the demon chauffeur". This devilish driver appeals to many people's imaginations for a long time. Bonnot and his gang are resurrected in books, television series, comics and films.

In one of these, *La Bande à Bonnot* from 1968, filmmaker Philippe Fourastié casts a Belgian in the role of Raymond *la Science* – for *la Science* was actually born in Brussels. The actor who played the gang member so spiritedly was truly able to inhabit his character's skin. Could this be because he lived for a time at the gang's safe house in the infamous Rue Nollet in Batignolles? On 11 August 1958, ten years prior to the film, upon arrival at a charming little hotel in the cité Lemercier[40] he writes his initials in the guestbook: J.B. Not Jules Bonnot, of course. But Jacques Brel, the famous Belgian songwriter and singer.

Righteous crimes II

6

MESSIEURS DE PARIS

"The executioners grab her from behind, throw her quickly onto the board and push her neck under the blade; the rope is pulled, the blade flashes as it falls, there is a dull thud, and already Sanson is grabbing a bloody head by the hair and brandishing it above the square. The crowd suddenly bursts forth with a wild 'Vive la République!'" This is how Stefan Zweig described the beheading of Marie Antoinette on 16 October 1793 in his biography of the French queen.[1] She falls beneath the blade of the novice Henri, son of Charles-Henri Sanson (1739-1806), the most famous executioner in Paris. He launches his son, the next member of the dynasty, quite literally on the shoulders of the unfortunate queen. Beheadings will continue in the country of human rights until 1977. It's a good living for two executioner dynasties.

‹ Monsieur de Paris, Anatole Deibler
(far right), with his assistants.

Messieurs de Paris

ROYAL BEHEADER

Nine months previously, Henri's father – Charles-Henri Sanson – had beheaded his own employer, King Louis XVI, the husband of Marie Antoinette, for Chevalier Charles-Henri Sanson de Longval, to give him his full title, is the royal executioner. The Sanson family, now in business for seven generations, has seen major technical evolutions in their field: from quartering, to breaking on the wheel and hanging; and from beheadings with swords to, most recently of all, the arrival of the guillotine. According to its inventor, Doctor Joseph-Ignace Guillotin, the machine has the unique advantage of being 'pleasant' for its victims. "My machine [the guillotine] will take off a head in a twinkling and the victim will feel nothing but a refreshing coolness on the neck", is how Dr Guillotin defends his invention before the Assemblée Nationale Constituante. Another advantage of the guillotine is its equity. For centuries, noblemen have been beheaded with the sword while the common working man could expect all manner of ends, from the wheel to burning at the stake. The guillotine puts a definitive end to this discrimination. Henceforth, workers and noblemen will all be equal in the face of death.

What's more, the new instrument will prove extremely useful, given the huge volumes of executions that are to come. Nicolas Jacques Pelletier, an ordinary murderer, is the first human guinea pig to test the guillotine, which up to that point has been tried on animals and cadavers. He mounts the scaffold, erected in front of the town hall, on 25 April 1792. It is a success. Clean and quick, incomparable to a manual beheading. Sanson is soon familiar with the new technique. Once he had warmed up, "it took him just thirty-six minutes to chop off twenty-two heads, and he was remarkably satisfied with this additional proof of the national razor's effectiveness".[3] The revolutionary Reign of Terror that governs France in 1793-1794[4] sees thousands of heads roll, both male and female: nobles, the bourgeoisie, merchants, clerics and other anti-revolutionaries. Between 14 June and 28 July 1794, Sanson chops off 1,306 heads. To encourage him to maintain his tempo, the executioner is paid a premium[5] for every one that rolls. Sanson must keep pace with Antoine Fouquier-Tinville, the revolutionary public prosecutor, who has a boundless enthusiasm for prescribing the death penalty. From its inception in late 1792 to the Reign of Terror's end, 40,000 heads submit to the blade.[6]

In the spring and summer of 1794, when the Reign of Terror is on its last legs, Sanson's business enjoys an unprecedented peak. To the mass of revolutionary traitors are added the *sans-culottes* who have fallen into disgrace. First, the leaders of the nonetheless radical Cordeliers, such as Jacques-René

Hébert, who himself fervently argued for the beheading of Louis XVI and Marie Antoinette. Sanson executes him on 24 March. Barely two weeks later, on 5 April, a new series of revolutionaries who have fallen into disfavour climb the scaffold, including the famous Georges Danton. "He is a shadow of his former self. The giant of the tribune now looks like an emaciated lawyer."[7] Camille Desmoulins, the man who five years ago called for the storming of the Bastille from beneath the arcades of the Palais Royal, now loses his head. All norms have been abandoned.

But Sanson is particularly irked when the hard-line Maximilien Robespierre himself, along with his remaining supporters, appears on his scaffold on 28 July. Robespierre and the other condemned prisoners are in a terrible state by this point. The manner of their arrest the evening before in the Maison-Commune, as the town hall is known during the Revolution, however dramatic, is quite incredible: "Augustin Robespierre, Maximilien's brother, jumps out of a window and breaks his thigh. Georges Couthon throws himself down the grand staircase in his wheelchair. Le Bas puts a bullet through his own head. Maximilien Robespierre does the same, but only succeeds in shattering his lower jaw."[8] The driving force behind the Reign of Terror is still alive. To avoid obstructing the falling guillotine blade, with a single tug Sanson removes the cloth that is holding Robespierre's loose cheek in place. Amid violent cries of pain, the head of the revolutionary leader rolls into the basket. His body is thrown, along with all the others, into a mass grave behind the Parc Monceau and sprinkled with quicklime.

Still Sanson cannot rest. The next day, and the day thereafter, the Tribunal Révolutionnaire sends a further eighty-seven revolutionaries to the guillotine. "Another Terror is beginning", is how writer Eric Hazan[9] describes the end of the French Revolution and the commencement of a period of revenge. During the White Terror, named after the colour of the monarchy's flag, royalists hunt down the last supporters of the Red Terror across the country. The Sanson family is unperturbed; this puts fresh bread on the table.

BY THE HEADS OF HIS CLIENTS...

Just like their forefathers, the Sansons looked on as today's clients abruptly became tomorrow's victims. It is the fate of a dynasty. For the executioner's family, it was ever thus and ever will be so. For almost a century and a half, from 1688 to 1836, the Sansons have retained control of their empire in this way. They are familiar with the art of a sustainable enterprise. That this family business survives the *ancien régime*, the French Revolution, the *directoire*, the Consulate,

Messieurs de Paris

the First Empire, two Restorations, the July Monarchy, not to mention all the intervening political turbulence, is quite remarkable.

Feared and respected, the executioner of Paris has traditionally been above the law. He must be addressed as "Monsieur de Paris" [Gentleman of Paris], he pays no rent and has "*le droit de havage*" [the right to take]: at markets he can take whatever he likes – and can carry. During the *ancien régime*, the executioner is also an 'Officier du Roi' [officer of the king], a title which is handed down from father to son. The torture that precedes an execution is also part of his job description. His financial security increases in line with a decrease in urban security because he is literally paid... with the heads of his clients.[10] In Paris, the Sansons are permitted to supplement their earnings by selling 'their' bodies on to 'doctors and surgeons'. To that end, Charles-Henri Sanson dissects the corpses in his spare time. However, they are deprived of the right to sell the clothing of the victims during the French Revolution as they now have to donate it to the poor. They may, however, sell on the hair of their 'clients' to wigmakers.

The Sansons, along with other French executioners, also enjoy the 'privilege' of consanguinity. Whilst the Church forbids marriages between family members, it turns a blind eye in the case of this profession. After all, no one wants to marry an executioner's child. The young Sansons are therefore obliged to seek their brides and bridegrooms amongst the daughters and sons of the executioners of Lyon, Toulouse or Bordeaux. The juvenile Charles-Henri Sanson is compelled to leave his convent school at Rouen after he is unmasked as an executioner's son. It is a lucrative but hard and lonely trade.

Nevertheless, the executioner is only human and he too has feelings. He might be artistic, for example: to make a change from cutting off heads, the sensitive Charles-Henri Sanson enjoys playing his violin or cello.[11] Or he might be grieving. Gabriel, one of Charles-Henri's sons, has a fatal accident at a young age. While assisting his father, he holds up a severed head to exhibit it to the crowd, slips in the blood, falls from the scaffold and breaks his neck.[12] Or he might face a moral quandary: "The executioner Sanson who, in hindsight, is horrified by his acts, repents, and every 21 January pays for a mass in memory of the king."[13] An annual mass in atonement for that exceptional day in 1793 when Sanson sent Louis XVI to join his ancestors. Just in case it hasn't gone down well up there!

THE HEAD BENEATH THE SKIRTS

As democracy flourishes, trade for the Sansons declines: fewer and fewer people receive the death penalty. What's more, the family line ends ignominiously due to the last descendant's gambling addiction. Henri-Clément "was homosexual, had many adventures and racked up huge debts."[14] These are so enormous that he ends up pawning the guillotine, which is entrusted to the care of the executioner, to settle his dues. The City of Paris is obliged to buy it back. The family business shuts up shop forever. Henri-Clément himself ends up behind bars in 1836. Later, in his *Sept générations d'exécuteurs, 1688-1847: mémoires des Sanson* [Seven Generations of Executioners, 1688-1847: Memoirs of the Sansons], he reflects upon a rich family history, punctuated by many last words in the face of death.

When Marie Antoinette accidentally steps on Sanson's foot when climbing the scaffold, she excuses herself: "I beg your pardon, I didn't do that on purpose." Madame du Barry, the powerful mistress of Louis XV, who wound the whole of Versailles around her little finger, tries to do the same with Sanson: "Just one moment, Mr Executioner", whereupon the executioner thrusts her beneath the blade. The Marquis de Charost bids him an exceedingly polite farewell: "Goodbye Sir and keep up the good work." Jean Sylvain Bailly, scientist, writer, politician and member of the Académie Française, had the courage to defend Marie Antoinette at her trial. He is also sentenced to death, as are Tronchet and Malesherbes, her husband's lawyers. When he is addressed by the crowd while on the scaffold: "Are you trembling, Bailly?", he replies: "Yes, but only from the cold." This may be true as he lost his head in the month of November. In his book, Henri-Clément Sanson also demolishes a few myths, such as the story of the 'talking head'. The head of a nobleman – by definition a pervert – flies into the crowd like a football during an execution, straight under the skirts of a young woman. Bystanders clearly hear it shouting: "*Ooh là là!*" That story, Henri-Clément writes, is nothing but fiction.

EXECUTED IN PARIS, WEATHER OVERCAST, 4.58 AM

The descendent of another dynasty of executioners, Anatole Deibler, carefully notes the weather conditions and the exact hour that Paul Gorguloff is decapitated. The Russian *agent provocateur* and anarchist murdered none other than the president of the republic, Paul Doumer, on 6 May 1932. The Deibler dynasty is not as old as that of the Sansons but it is certainly noteworthy, chiefly because the last Deibler, Anatole, has bequeathed us his detailed *Carnets d'exécutions* [Execution Diaries].[15] After every beheading, the 'Monsieur de Paris', in the privacy of his study in the Rue de Billancourt, not only notes down the name, date, place, time and weather conditions – very clear weather, shimmering heat, or hot weather, for example – but also his own verdict on the crime in question.

Messieurs de Paris

His notebooks containing his observations, his view of the offenders and their motives, his compassion for the victims, as well as the description of their livelihoods and their living conditions, the reactions of the public and the commentaries in the press, are a unique social document.

The Deiblers started out as executioners in Württemberg, Germany. But they emigrated to Dijon in France at the beginning of the nineteenth century. It is here that Joseph Deibler becomes an assistant executioner. His diligence sees him promoted to executioner-in-chief successively of the *départements* of Cantal and Île-et-Vilaine. He apprentices his son Louis to Antoine Rasseneux, the executioner of Algiers. The latter has plenty of work – and a daughter. The young Louis Deibler marries Zoé-Victorine. Two years later, on 29 November – the month of remembrance – in the year 1863, baby Anatole is born. A new dynasty is in the making.

While Anatole is learning the trade, his father Louis is promoted to assistant executioner (second class) in Paris. The capital is full of opportunities: executions in France are restructured after the Franco-Prussian War of 1870/1. Local executioners are abolished. Henceforth, a single executioner will place his talent at the disposal of the whole country. Louis Deibler is appointed to the role. With his team he works out of Paris and travels to the cities where his services are called for, from Lille to Corsica, and from Strasbourg to Rennes. The 'Monsieur de Paris' travels by train; '*les bois de justice*', as the dismantled guillotine is known, travel with him, as do his assistants, who maintain the precious equipment.

Who can imagine Louis' delight in 1885, when his son Anatole, who has just turned twenty-two, can officially start work with his grandfather Rasseneux in Algiers. Anatole's maternal grandfather, in the meantime, has been appointed executioner for North Africa. It is here that Anatole begins his first *Carnet*. In his early annotations, he limits himself to the essentials: "Executed in Algiers on 9 September 1885, man by the name of Arcano, Francisco (Italian national)... convicted of murder and theft in broad daylight of a Jewish travelling salesman, on the road to Guyotville, near Algiers."[16]

After a few years' practice in French North Africa, Anatole is back in Paris. Just as the city is once again being shaken to its core. In the final decade of the nineteenth century, anarchists[17] are throwing bombs at judges, restaurants, police stations, businesses and a certain person in the Assemblée Nationale. Their campaign ends in 1894 with the murder of the president of the republic, Sadi Carnot. The perpetrators are beheaded one by one, by father Louis, with Anatole assisting him. This is a tumultuous time. Sympathisers of the beheaded try to kidnap the executioner and steal the tools of his trade.[18] Deibler moves to a different *quartier* near the Porte de Saint-Cloud, where his house and his family are under permanent guard. All of this has a detrimental effect on the executioner's mental health. Louis Deibler has been feeling hesitant and unwell for some time. His hands tremble so violently that this is visible to the public. To crown it all, an even worse fate befalls him: he is diagnosed with haemopho-bia, a fear of blood. Louis Deibler has presided over the decapitation of some 360 heads. His son will do even better.

BLOOD-CURDLING

Anatole is now almost thirty and – what other choice does he have? – is married to another executioner's daughter, Rosalie Rogis. On 27 December 1898, he accepts the post of Exécuteur en chef des hautes oeuvres de la République [Chief Executer of the Republic]. With this comes a further change. The guillotine, which up to that point has been housed beneath the prison walls in the Rue de la Roquette, beside the Bastille, is moved to the La Santé prison on the Left Bank. It is not erected in the obscure Rue de la Santé but placed in plain view, adjacent to the busy Boulevard Arago, which can accommodate a crowd. The people are curious to see Louis Deibler's successor. In the same way that all Paris anticipates a new actor's debut at the Comédie Française, the Parisians eagerly look forward to Anatole's first appearance.

The twenty-nine-year-old Joseph Vacher, 'the shepherdess killer', is said to be guilty of fifty murders. He confesses to murdering "six young girls, four young boys, an old woman and also of killing a young child." On the final day of the year 1898, the press is jostling around the monster and the executioner. The debutant executioner does an excellent job. Paris has its celebrities and this week the spotlight is on Anatole Deibler, dubbed the "best executioner in France" by journalists.[19]

His fame transcends France's borders. In 1911, Deibler receives a Chinese delegation who come to investigate the wonderfully effective blade that is being used in the country of human rights. Convinced by Deibler's expert explanation, Peking orders several guillotines.[20]

As Deibler ages, one senses a growing desire in his *Cahiers* to justify having severed all those heads. Is he thinking about his own appearance before the Almighty, as his colleague Charles-Henri Sanson might have done at the same age? He therefore greatly emphasises the wrongdoers' aberrations. A mother-and child-killer slays Mme Bertrand with a hammer and cuts her throat with a razor "then he beats the head of little Octave to a pulp with the same instrument".[21] When Mme Boutard's children start to cry upon hearing their mother's

Messieurs de Paris

screams emanating from the barn, her murderer comes to reassure them: "It's the pigs that are screeching."[22] These are just a few of the many horrors. Certain convicts show absolutely no remorse for their deeds. When the chaplain says a prayer for the salvation of the eighteen-year-old thief and murderer Casimir Veignal, he mocks the clergyman: "Tears? I forgot to bring my onions to make me cry!"[23] Although the stories of the offenders and their victims are spectacular, to put it mildly, Deibler is not writing for an audience but for himself. He does not exaggerate anything, does not invoke an atmosphere, does not seek sensation. On the contrary, he notes the details with the accuracy of a coroner. In the case of the day labourer Henri Nicolas, who slits his employer's throat with a razor, Deibler notes: "The spinal column was exposed, the larynx, the pharynx and the arteries had been severed."[24]

Many of those sentenced to death are infamous: the eleven-time, widow-killer Henri Landru; the *'Chauffeurs de la Drôme'*, thieves and murderers from the region around Valence; the second generation anarchists with Liabeuf and the Bonnot Gang;[25] the bloodthirsty train robber Jacques Charrier, who turns the carefree dreams of well-to-do Parisians on Le Train Bleu (which transports them from the Gare de Lyon to the Riviera in luxurious sleeping compartments) into a nightmare; Olivier Henri, a.k.a. 'The Tiger', the ringleader of a gang of murderers in the region between Roubaix and Mouscron in Belgium. All are dissected in the *Cahiers*. Deibler also explores their gains in minute detail. Landru, for example, earned some 35,642 francs from his eager-to-marry widows, as well as "furniture, jewellery, linen and clothes".[26]

Deibler's career is progressing smoothly. Yet there is a certain darkness to Anatole's. Rosalie bears a son, but the baby dies after five months. Later the couple have a daughter, Marcelle – unsuitable for the profession. Yet the business still remains in the family. Anatole Deibler asks his brother-in-law Jules-Henri Desfourneaux to assist him. They continue together until the end of January 1939, when the last of the Deibler heads rolls into the basket. A week later, after leaving his house on 2 February – the winter is harsh and the executioner is tired – Deibler collapses and dies on the platform of the Porte de Saint-Cloud metro station. He was on his way to the Gare de Montparnasse to travel with his assistants to Rennes where a condemned prisoner awaited him. Said prisoner is given an unexpected 24-hour reprieve. Number 396, Maurice Pilorge, is decapitated by Jules-Henri Desfourneaux – he had murdered his friend, a male prostitute. Pilorge escapes Anatole Deibler's *Cahiers*. Between 1885, the year of his first beheading, and 1939, that of his last, the final great 'Monsieur de Paris' has personally 'despatched' 395 criminals.

MONCEAU & BATIGNOLLES

ICE CREAM AND CHAMPAGNE

Although the Sansons and the Deiblers ensured the uninterrupted fulfilment of the sentences issued by the changing regimes, they sometimes encountered political headwinds. During the French Revolution, the trailblazing administration throws Sanson, formerly a servant of the king, into prison. He is occasionally released to conduct an execution. But "once the guillotine was going full tilt, he was permanently freed".[27]

Later, Anatole Deibler also encounters setbacks. The new French president, Armand Fallières, a republican from the Parti Radical, stops all executions in 1906. Deibler makes ends meet by selling champagne.[28] A year later, the French take to the streets to demand the death of the child-killer Soleilland. "Long live Deibler! Down with Fallières!" The president holds out for a further two years. The brutal murders and robberies of Théophile Deroo, Canut Vromant and the Pollet brothers, Auguste and Abel, eventually oblige him to cave in to public pressure. The Hazebrouck bandits predominately strike just across the border, in Belgium. Dadizele, Pollinkhove, Krombeke, Rumbeke, Dottenijs and Roesbrugge have the dubious honour of being mentioned in Deibler's *Cahiers* as crime scenes. In January 1909, Anatole beheads the four gang members in Béthune in northern France. Twenty minutes before dawn, as prescribed.

The First World War also puts a spanner in the works for Deibler. With the Germans overrunning the north and east of the country, there is suddenly less work for him. There are three times fewer executions than normal. But Anatole and Rosalie manage to survive. They open a convalescent home for war victims in their summer residence in La Baule, on the Atlantic coast. It is relatively successful.

One day, Deibler makes a journey from the safe Atlantic coast to the dangerous Veurne. The Belgian government, which has stopped executions, wants to set an example. A certain Émile Ferfaille, Quartermaster Sergeant with the 2nd Heavy Artillery Regiment, had become engaged to two women. One of them, the twenty-year-old Rachel Ryckewaert, is four months pregnant when he murders and robs her on 27 October 1917 in the garden of Florimond Seru, a vegetable grower. King Albert I refuses to show the murderer any clemency. He wants to avoid signalling that, by committing a crime, soldiers can end up safely in a cell and thus escape the dangers of the Front. But because the crime was committed against a private citizen in this instance, the murderer cannot appear before a firing squad. An alternative solution is sought – and found. France is delighted to assist. Deibler arrives under German artillery fire in the front-line town, where buildings are blazing. He immediately carries out the sentence, in between two air-raid alerts.[29]

Messieurs de Paris

After Desfourneaux's term of office, André Obrecht, a nephew of Anatole Deibler, is appointed executioner of France. But unlike the Sansons and the Deiblers, Obrecht cuts off just sixty-five heads over a twenty-five-year period, from 1950 to 1975. It is impossible to make a living from the profession. He also runs an ice cream factory. Incidentally, Obrecht looks more like a well-off small businessman in archive photos: "You would never have thought that Mr Obrecht was an executioner. With his hat and fashionable jacket, he looked totally normal, like someone who was going to buy a baguette or submit his betting slip."[30]

Marcel Chevalier, who succeeds Obrecht in 1976, sees things going firmly downhill. He will only be required to perform two executions because on 10 September 1977, under the leadership of President Valéry Giscard d'Estaing, the last head rolls. Not in Paris but in Marseille: that of Hamida Djandoubi, sentenced to death for the violent murder and rape of a twenty-one-year-old woman. It would not be until 1981 that the death penalty was finally legally abolished in France under President François Mitterrand.

Fortunately, the Sansons and the Deiblers did not have to contend with this drop in their income. The latter repose beneath the pink granite of their family tomb in the cemetery at Boulogne-Billancourt. The descendants of the Sansons, the most illustrious dynasty of executioners in Paris, are considerably more discreet. They lie beneath a layer of moss in a forgotten row in the cemetery in Montmartre. It is November when we finally find the grave. It is adorned with yellow chrysanthemums. Could it be that someone still loves them?

Messieurs de Paris

ENDNOTES

DEEL 1

RIGHT BANK
WEST

1. ROSE VALLAND'S WAR

1 Rose Valland, *Le front de l'art – Défense des collections françaises 1939-1945*, revised edition of the 1961 work by the Réunion des musées nationaux, 2016: 82.
2 Valland: 84.
3 Pierre Assouline, *L'homme de l'art, D.-H. Kahnweiler 1884-1979*, Éditions Baland, 1988, published in Gallimard's 'Folio' series, 2013: 532.
4 Catalogue to the exhibition *21, rue de la Boétie*, La Boverie Expo Liège & Tempora, based on the book *21, rue de la Boétie* by Anne Sinclair, Éditions Grasset & Fasquelle, 2012: 66.
5 Isabelle Le Masne de Chermont & Didier Schulmann in Valland: 9.
6 Idem 4: 66.
7 Idem 4: 67.
8 Other German Expressionists such as Barlach, Beckmann, Heckel, Hofer, Kirchner, Lehmbruck, Levy, Macke, Marc, Marckx, Modersohn-Becker, Müller, Nolde, Pechstein, Rohlfs and Schmidt-Rottluff.
9 Jean-Patrick Duchesne, idem 4: 131.
10 Valland: 342 & 393.
11 Rose Valland mentions "Mmes Andre Chamson, Maxime Kahn and Guynet": 48.
12 Valland: 51.
13 Valland: 52.
14 Jean-Marc Dreyfus, *Le catalogue Goering*, Flammarion, 2015.
15 Pierre Assouline, *Le Portrait*, Gallimard, 2007: 217. An original history of the French branch of the Rothschild family, as seen through the eyes of Betty de Rothschild, wife of James, founder of the French dynasty. He was immortalised on canvas by Jean-Auguste- Dominique Ingres in 1848. Other Jewish collections that were looted include those belonging to Schloss, Kann, David-Weill and Lévy de Benzion.
16 Assouline: 532.
17 Hal Vaughan, *Sleeping with the Enemy*, Vintage Books; Random House, 2011: 152.
18 Emmanuelle Polack, Philippe Dagen, *Les Carnets de Rose Valland – Le pillage des collections privées d'œuvres d'art en France pendant la Seconde Guerre mondiale*, Fage Éditions, 2019. The citation is taken from the handwritten notebook, *Archives du Louvre*, with page reference 24.
19 Assouline: 221. Here, the author makes an apt comparison between the Drancy marshalling yard and the Jeu de Paume triage centre. One transports people, the other works of art, but the destination is the same: the Third Reich.

20 Valland: 348.
21 Assouline: 237–246.
22 Pierre Assouline, *Le dernier des Camondo*, Gallimard, 1999: 294: "*En leguant à l'Etat mon hôtel et les collections qu'il renferme, j'ai en vue de conserver dans son intégralité l'oeuvre à laquelle je me suis attaché [...] qui a été une des gloires de la France, durant la période que j'ai aimée entre toutes.*" This is now the Musée Nissim de Camondo, named after Moïse's son, and located at 63, Rue de Monceau.
23 Anne Sinclair, *21, rue La Boétie*, Éditions Grasset & Fasquelle, 2012: 156.
24 The Résistance-Fer was the resistance movement within the SNCF, the French railway company.
25 Rose Valland became a captain in the French army and travelled with the Monuments, Fine Arts and Archives programme, better known as the 'Monuments Men', which was led by Captain Rorimer. They headed east on a mission to trace stolen works and return them to their rightful owners. In 1947, she headed the central art recovery centre in Berlin, and in 1952 she was appointed curator of the Musées nationaux de France. Rose devoted the rest of her life, which she spent alongside her British friend Joyce Heer, to art. She died on 18 September 1980 in Ris-Orangis, a commune between Paris and Fontainebleau. She lived to the age of 81 and received numerous awards: Chevalier de la Légion d'honneur, Médaille de la Résistance française, Medal of Freedom (US), Ordre du Mérite, Officier des Arts et Lettres. She was honoured with a plaque on the façade of the Musée du Jeu de Paume in 2005.
26 Sinclair: 169 and Valland: 349.

2. CHANEL VERSUS WERTHEIMER

1 Bruno Abescat & Yves Stavridès, 'Derrière l'empire Chanel. La fabuleuse histoire des Wertheimer', *L'Express*, 4 July 2005 and www.arretsurimages.net/media/pdf/histoire_chanel.pdf.
2 Alexis Gregory, *Place Vendôme*, Assouline Publishing, 2004: 98.
3 Gregory: 85.
4 Tilar J. Mazzeo, *The Secret of Chanel N°5*, Harper Perennial, 2010: 60.
5 Abescat & Stavridès 2005. Epinard, the Wertheimers' most successful racehorse, was the centre of attention. For the Grand Prix de Deauville in 1922, Pierre Wertheimer flew his jockey to France on his private plane, an Amiot 22.
6 Mazzeo: 95.
7 Mazzeo: 126.
8 Vincent Bouvet & Gérard Durozoi, *Paris Between the Wars*, Thames & Hudson, 2012: 365.
9 Bouvet & Durozoi: 169.
10 Abescat & Stavridès, 2005.
11 Hal Vaughan, *Sleeping with the Enemy*, Vintage Books; Random House, 2011: 18.

Endnotes

12　Jean-Paul Cointet, *Paris 40-45*, Perrin, 2001: 95.

13　Annie Lacroix-Riz, *Industriels et banquiers français sous l'Occupation*, Armand Colin, 2013: 515.

14　Lacroix-Riz: 533.

15　Lacroix-Riz: 535.

16　Lacroix-Riz: 547.

17　Abescat & Stavridès, 2005.

18　Alex Kershaw, *Avenue of Spies*, Crown Publishers, 2015: 17.

19　Vaughan: 169.

20　Abescat & Stavridès 2005.

21　Vaughan: 50–51.

22　Mazzeo: 177.

23　Mazzeo: 183.

24　The Wertheimers do not discuss the extent of their fortune. The company made its first official financial statement in 2018, and only to quell rumours of a possible IPO [initial public offering]. In 2017, it generated revenues of $10 billion, profits of $2 billion and experienced growth of 18.5% over the previous year. In 2019, Chanel Inc. generated over $12 billion in sales with an operating profit of $3.5 billion. The company took a hit in 2020, due to the pandemic, but still realised $10.1 billion in sales, with an operating profit of more than $2 billion: www.chanel.com/gb/financial-results/.

3. NAPOLEON III, THE FORGOTTEN EMPEROR

1　Éric Anceau, *Ils ont fait et défait le Second Empire*, Tallendier, 2019, 29. In this book, Anceau, professor of history at the Sorbonne and a specialist on the Second Empire, discusses twenty-five figures who, as either supporters or opponents, helped shape Napoleon III's policies.

2　Anceau: 31.

3　Eric Hazan, *L'Invention de Paris*, Seuil, 2002: 336.

4　Anceau: 18.

5　Anceau: 42.

6　Pierre Milza, *Napoléon III*, Perrin, 2004.

7　Gérard Unger, author of *Histoire du Second Empire*, Perrin, 2018, cited in *Géo Histoire 36* (thematic edition 'Napoléon III et le Second Empire'), 2017/2018: 69.

8　Eric Meyer (ed.), 'Edito: Le neveu réhabilité', in: *Géo Histoire 36* (thematic edition 'Napoléon III et le Second Empire'), 2017/2018: 3.

9　Eric Hazan, *Le tumulte de Paris*, Éditions la fabrique, 2021: 54.

10　Béatrice de Rochebouët, 'Champ de bataille Napléonien aux Invalides, L'installation d'une œuvre d'art contemporain au-dessus du tombeau de l'Empereur suscite la colère des historiens. Hommage ou profanation?' *Le Figaro*, 30 April 2021: 34–35.

4. ARLETTY'S HEART

1　Françoise Pélisson-Karro, 'Régie théatrale et mise en scène, 1911-1939', *Septentrion*, 2014: 121.

2　Tilar J. Mazzeo, *The Hotel on the Place Vendôme*, Harper Perennial, 2014: 79.

3　Marc Laudelot & Patrick Fremeaux, *Arletty*: interview with Marc Laudelout (testimonies about Louis-Ferdinand Céline, Albert Paraz, Roger Nimier, Robert Le Vigan, Sacha Guitry, Paul Chambrillon, Marcel Aymé, Georges Simenon, Trotsky and Jean Cocteau), Frémeaux & Associés, 2007, 1 CD.

4　Claude Singer, 'Les contradictions de l'épuration du cinéma français 1944-1948', in: *Raison présenté* 137, (2001): 3–37.

5　Laurent Jullier & Martin Barnier, *Une brève histoire de cinéma 1895-2015*, Pluriel, 2017.

6　Pierre Fournié, *Présumées coupables – Les grands procès faits aux femmes*, L'Iconoclaste; Archives nationales, 2016.

7　In this regard, see: https://www.nouvelobs.com/rue89/rue89-chroniques-parisiennes/20140810. RUE0535/arletty-mon-c-ur-est-francais-mais-mon-cul-est-international.html

5. LENIN'S YELLOW JERSEY

1　On 23-24 February 1903, Lenin presented four lectures on '*Les conceptions marxistes dans la question agraire en Europe et en Russie*' at the École des Hautes Études Sociales in Paris.

2　They initially lived at 24, Rue Beaunier and later at 4, Rue Marie-Rose. The latter property was subsequently acquired by the PCF (Parti Communiste Français) and converted into a (small) museum. It is now home to the editorial offices of the magazine *l'Europe*. Khrushchev visited in 1963 and Georges Marchais gave Gorbachev a tour.

3　Jean Fréville, *Lénine à Paris*, Paris: Éditions Sociales, 1968: 62.

4　The Tour de France was launched in 1903.

5　Jean-Christophe Collin, 'Lénine, cycliste parisien avant l'heure', *L'Equipe*, 20 October 2017.

6　Irancy wine is a northern Pinot Noir, a type of grape grown in Burgundy, with vineyards located in the communes of Irancy, Cravant and Vincelottes, along the Yonne. Barrels of wine were smoothly transported to Paris along the river.

7　Bill McGann & Carol McGann, *The Story of the Tour De France: 1903-1964*, Dog Ear Publishing, 2006: 30–35.

8　Ben B. Fischer, 'The Paris Operations of the Russian Imperial Police', 1997: https://www.cia.gov/static/87bb92c0a274fdf9beb87b5163efd4ef/Okhrana-The-Paris-Operations.pdf.

9　André Salmon, *La Terreur noire*, Paris: Union Générale d'Éditions, 1959: 61.

10　Fréville: 160.

11　David Charpentier, 'Histoire: sur les traces de Lénine à Paris', *Le Parisien*, 29 October 2017.

12 Laura Marx and Paul Lafargue are buried together in Père Lachaise cemetery opposite the Mur des Fédérés, which honours the victims of the Paris Commune.

13 Nadezhda Krupskaya, cited in Collin 5.

14 Collin 5.

15 Fréville: 151–152.

16 Lenin, cited in Collin 5.

17 Geert Van Goethem, 'De internationale arbeiderssportbeweging tijdens het interbellum': "The new Union Internationale d'Education Physique et Sportive du Travail, subsequently better known as the Internationale Sportive de Lucerne, wanted to unite all workers' supporters, whatever political affiliation they professed. However, this obvious attempt to keep communist-oriented organisations within the movement was almost immediately countered by the establishment of the Internationale Rouge Sportive in Moscow in 1921. This organisation's attitude towards the Lucerne International was determined by the Communist International (Comintern) strategy; as a result, the two internationals clashed fiercely between 1921 and 1934."

18 Geert Mak, *In Europe – Travels through the Twentieth Century*, Harvill Secker, 2007.

19 Fréville: 161.

20 Fréville: 157.

21 Fréville: 162.

22 Fréville: 75.

23 French architect Henri Labrouste was born in Paris on 11 May 1801 and died in Fontainebleau on 24 June 1875. After attending the École des Beaux Arts in Paris, he studied classical architecture in Rome for six years. After returning to Paris, he opened a training centre for architects. Labrouste was one of the first architects to work with new materials, such as iron, glass and brick. He designed the Bibliothèque Sainte-Geneviève opposite the Panthéon and renovated the Bibliothèque Nationale de France in the Rue de Richelieu in its entirety. The library's Salle Labrouste reopened to students and researchers in 2016 after an extensive restoration programme.

24 Jean-François Lasnier, 'Un nouvel écrin: la Salle Labrouste, Connaissance des Arts', special edition no. 726, INHA: 23.

25 Paul Chemetov & Bernard Marrey, *Architectures, Paris 1848-1914*, catalogue to the 1976 exhibition of the same name, organised in Bon Marché, Rue de Sèvres, Paris: 34.

26 The Café de la Rotonde opened in 1911.

27 leftinparis.org/people/trotsky/

28 Fréville: 226.

29 Collin 5.

6. JOHN LAW'S 'SHITTY SHARES'

1 Niall Ferguson, *The Ascent of Money – A Financial History of the World*, Penguin Books, 2009: 127.

2 Claude Cueni, *Het Grote Spel*, Querido; Knack, 2009: 117.

3 Ferguson: 138.

4 John Law, *Money and Trade Considered, with a Proposal for Supplying the Nation with Money*, 1705; cited in Nicolas Buat, *John Law: La dette ou comment s'en débarrasser*, Les Belles Lettres, 2015: 51.

5 Louis XIV issued the Edict of Fontainebleau on 18 October 1685. It revoked the Edict of Nantes (1598) and suspended freedom of religion to the Huguenots (French Protestants). Deprived of their rights once more, thousands of Protestants fled the country.

6 Alex Gregory, *Place Vendôme*, Assouline, 2004: 44.

7 Ferguson: 139.

8 Gregory: 44.

9 Place Vendôme 18 (formerly the Place Louis-le-Grand) is now home to the Haute Joaillerie Chanel.

10 James Buchan, *John Law – A Scottish Adventurer of the Eighteenth Century*, MacLehose, 2018, in which the banknote 'Dix livres Tournois' no. 3606746 is reproduced. See also: *Billets de la Banque royale de John Law. 10 livres tournois*, 1720. Approximately 14cm long. Musée de la Monnaie, 11, Quai de Conti, Paris.

11 Gregory: 45.

12 Ferguson: 141.

13 The League of Augsburg (Grand Alliance) was brokered by William III of Orange, later King of England, Ireland and Scotland, between the Holy Roman Emperor Leopold I, the Kings of Spain and Sweden and the Elector of Brandenburg, amongst others. It was a defence mechanism against the constant threat from Louis XIV's France. France and the League of Augsburg clashed in the Nine Years' War (1688-1697).

14 Buat: 204–205.

15 Ferguson: 148–149.

16 Buat: 193.

17 Graph showing the share prices of the Compagnie des Indes in Paris: www.winton.com/longer-view/the-mississippi-bubble

18 *Agioteurs* are stock market speculators. See Buat: 195.

19 Gregory: 46.

20 Gregory: 46.

21 Ferguson: 145–146.

22 Cueni: 394.

23 Ferguson: 150.

24 Idem 23: 154.

Endnotes

DEEL 2

RIGHT BANK
EAST

1. LES GRANDES HORIZONTALES

1   Arthur Japin, *Mrs Degas*, Amsterdam; Antwerp: Uitgeverij De Arbeiderspers, 2020: 296. *Mrs Degas* is a wonderful novel about the relationship – which in this case is something more than a relationship – between Edgar Degas and Estelle, the wife of his younger brother René. Edgar was initially in love with Estelle. The passage about the ballerinas is based on the information given in the novel's epilogue.

2   The expression *'s'offrir une danseuse'* [literally 'treating oneself to a dancer'] is still used in France to describe spending a lot of money on a pleasure or passion. It refers to business acquisitions driven by the private interests of the entrepreneur or investor, as opposed to the expectation of growth or profit. Certain entrepreneurs, especially those involved in media and football, enjoy having a side interest in addition to their primary business. In France, Bernard Arnault, of the luxury goods group LVMH which has a turnover of €53.7 billion (2019), is also the long-time owner of French business newspaper *Les Echos*, which he acquired after selling his previous indulgence, *La Tribune*. Furthermore, the Dassault family, original name Bloch, with interests in defence and aviation, and with a turnover of €7.3 billion (2019), also owns the newspaper *Le Figaro*. In the Netherlands, Martijn van der Vorm also owns *Het Financieele Dagblad* through the holding company Hal Invest, with a market capitalisation of €10 billion (2019). Whether these activities contribute to consolidation is unimportant. Little can spoil an owner's pleasure in his *danseuse*, not even years of losses, as with *Les Echos*.

3   Certain *grandes horizontales* had children at the start of their career: Valtesse de la Bigne was a mother of two; la Païva, Liane de Pougy and Sarah Bernhardt all had a child.

4   Dominique Kalifa, *Paris – Une histoire érotique, d'Offenbach aux Sixties*, Payot, 2018: 120.

5   Gabrielle Houbre, *Le livre des courtisanes – Archives secrètes de la police des mœurs*, Tallandier, 2007. The book exposes the extent to which the police and authorities of the Third Republic recorded the names, addresses, contacts, habits, investments and profits of the known prostitutes: *Courtisanes, Demi-Mondaines* and *Grandes Horizontales*.

6   Mimi Pinson, the *grisette* from the poem of the same name by Alfred de Musset, is an enduring symbol of the lowest category of worker in the 'paid love' profession.

7   Claire Castillon, 'Coucher pour arriver', *Paris Match*, 5 August 2014.

8   Marie-Aude Bonniel, 'Les Folies Bergère: "La plus belle salle de ce genre à Paris" selon Le Figaro de 1869', *LeFigaro.fr*, 3 May 2016.

9   'Ego' is also the pen name with which she signed her autobiography *Isola*, Dentu, 1876.

10   Valtesse de la Bigne's *lit de parade* can now be admired in the Musée des Arts Décoratifs, 107, Rue de Rivoli, Paris.

11   The French gallerist Paul Durand-Ruel participated in the American Art Association of New York's prestigious annual exhibition in 1886, showing 300 works from the Havemeyer collection. At the time, no one in France wanted to buy Impressionist paintings, especially as certain canvases had been stamped 'refused' (*refusé*) by the Salon de Paris. American industrialists formed a new and interested audience for the works. Henry and Louisine Havemeyer were amongst Paul Durand-Ruel's first and most prominent American clients. Shortly after his successful visit to the United States, the dealer opened a gallery in New York.

12   The Casino de Paris, 16, Rue de Clichy, in the 9th *arrondissement*, is one of the most famous music halls in Paris. Although its name suggests a gambling den, the venue is dedicated to concerts and performances. The Casino de Paris still sells posters of *Emilienne d'Alençon et ses ânes savants*.

13   Florence Montreynaud, *L'aventure des femmes: XXe et XXIe siècle*, Nathan, 2006.

14   Hal Vaughan, *Sleeping with the Enemy – Coco Chanel's Secret War*, Vintage Books, 2001: 6.

15   Montreynaud, 2006.

16   The enchanting Cirque d'Hiver at 110, Rue Amelot, designed by the architect of the Gare du Nord, Jacques Hittorff, is still open.

17   Gabriella Asaro on histoire-image.org/fr/etudes/liane-pougy-charme-ambiguite-belle-epoque.

18   Idem 17.

19   Idem 17.

20   Bernard Briais, *Au temps des frou-frous – Les femmes célèbres de la Belle Epoque*, France-Empire, 1985: 41.

21   Yannick Ripa, 'Cléo de Mérode ou la mauvaise réputation', *Mensuel* 455, January 2019.

22   Ripa 2019.

23   Kalifa: 115.

24   Cléo de Mérode, *Le Ballet de ma vie*, Pierre Horay, 1955. Reissued in 1995 and 2015.

2. 'WHY DID THEY KILL JAURÈS?'

1 Koen Koch, *Een kleine geschiedenis van de Grote Oorlog 1914-1918*, Ambo; Manteau, 2010: 81.
2 'Déclaration du Bureau Socialiste International', *l'Humanité*, 31 July 1914: "... *Les prolétaires allemands et français feront sur leur gouvernement une pression plus énergique que jamais afin que l'Allemagne exerce sur l'Autriche une action modératrice et que la France obtienne de la Russie qu'elle ne s'engage pas dans le conflit...*"
3 Sophie De Schaepdrijver, *De Groote Oorlog*, Olympus, ed. 2002: 52.
4 Geert Mak, *In Europe – Travels through the Twentieth Century*, Harvill Secker, 2007.
5 Barbara Tuchman, *De kanonnen van augustus*, Uitgeverij De Arbeiderspers, ed. 2000: 56–60 and Koch: 136–137.
6 Tuchman: 65.
7 Catrine Clay, *Three Royal Cousins Who Led the World to War*, Walker Books, 2007.
8 Tuchman: 7.
9 Clay: 256-257.
10 Hans Andriessen, in *Het proces tegen Wilhelm II*, Lannoo, 2016 cites Dobrorolski: "*Der Krieg war bereits beschlossene Sache und die ganze Flut von Telegrammen zwischen der Regierungen Russlands und Deutschlands stellte nur eine mis en scene eines historischen Dramas vor.*" (Dobrorolski. S., *Die Mobilmachung der Russischen Armee 1914*: 20, 21).
11 Clay: 384–385.
12 Marcel Cachin, 'Jaurès assassiné', reprint of the article published in *L'Humanité* on 1 August 1914.
13 Andrew Hussey, *Paris, The Secret History*, Viking, 2006.
14 Idem 12.
15 *Jean Jaurès et la Défense Nationale, Discours sur la loi de 3 ans prononcé à la Chambre des Députés par Jean Jaurès les 17 et 18 juin 1913*. His speech was later published by *l'Humanité* and sold for 1 franc. Sales exceeded 100,000 copies in 1917.
16 https://www.assemblee-nationale.fr/histoire/ guerre_14-18/loi_3_ans/index.asp.
17 gouv.fr: "*La Cour prend un arrêt accordant un franc de dommages et intérêts à la partie civile, et condamne la partie civile aux dépens du procès envers l'État. Madame Jaurès est donc condamnée à payer les frais de justice.*" Raoul Villain, after many trials and tribulations, arrived in Ibiza in 1932. Anarchists captured the island in 1936, two months after the outbreak of the Spanish Civil War. The Italians sent planes to Franco's aid and bombed Ibiza. Villain perished in the chaos.
18 Translation of the song by Jacques Brel:
"If by misfortune they survived
It was to go to war
It was to end at war
Under the orders of some swordsmen
Who were demanding half-heartedly
That they go open in the field of horror

Their twenties which didn't have the chance to be born
And they died in full fear
All miserable, yes our kind Master
Covered with field horsetails, yes our Sir.

Ask yourself pretty youth,
The time of the shadow of a memory,
The time of the blow of a sigh,
Why did they kill Jaurès?
Why did they kill Jaurès?"

3. SELLING THE EIFFEL TOWER

1 Volker Saux, '1925 – Retour sur une escroquerie géante', *GEO Histoire* 27, June-July 2016: 78–79.
2 Jan Veliger, 'Victor Lustig – The man who (could have) sold the world', Broadcast Archive, Czech Radio, www.radio.cz, 15 October 2003. Other sources describe different amounts. It was a substantial sum, that much is certain.
3 Jeff Maysh, 'The Man Who Sold the Eiffel Tower. Twice', *The Smithsonian Magazine*, 22 August 2012, www.smithsonianmag.com/history. Jeff Maysh also wrote the audiobook *Handsome Devil* on Victor Lustig (Kindle Single, 2017).
4 Idem 3.
5 James Johnson & Floyd Miller, *The Man Who Sold the Eiffel Tower*, Doubleday & Company Inc., 1961: 126.

4. ATTILA

1 Nicolas Chaudun, *Haussmann au crible*, Éditions des Syrtes, 2000: 76.
2 Henri Bayard, *Mémoire sur la topographie médicale du IVe arrondissement de Paris, recherches historiques et statistiques sur les conditions hygiéniques des quartiers qui composent cet arrondissement* – Extract from *Annales d'hygiène publique et de médecine légale*, vol. XXVIII, Part 1, Paris: J.-B. Baillière, 1842.
3 https://data.bnf.fr/10741990/ alexandre_francois_baudet-dulary/.
4 Chaudun: 78.
5 Also in this book, see the chapter: *Napoleon III, The Forgotten Emperor*.
6 Éric Anceau, *Ils ont fait et défait le Second Empire*, Tallandier, 2019: 182.
7 H.L. Wesseling, *Scheffer, Renan, Psichari – Een Franse cultuur- en familiegeschiedenis*, Prometheus, 2017: 203.
8 Chaudun: 91.
9 Chaudun: 125–127.
10 Alexandre Lacroix, *Voyage au centre de Paris*, Flammarion, 2013: 17.
11 Chaudun: 151.
12 Graham Robb, *Parisians*, Picador, 2011.
13 Anceau: 184.

Endnotes

14 Chaudun: 25.
15 Walter Benjamin, 'Parijs, hoofdstad van de XIXe eeuw', published in *Kleine filosofie van het flaneren*, Uitgeverij SUA Amsterdam, 1992: 23.
16 Anceau: 182.
17 Idem 1.
18 Anceau: 181.
19 Chaudun: 111–112.
20 Anceau: 187.
21 Jules Simon, cited in Chaudun: 112.

DEEL 3

LEFT BANK WEST

---

1. ODÉONIA

1 Charles Glass, *Americans in Paris – Life and Death Under Nazi Occupation 1940-1944*, Harper Press, 2009: 26.
2 *Les Annales politiques et littéraires* was a weekly magazine published on Sundays, compiled and written by illustrious names from the established literary and political milieu. It regularly published archival texts by Leconte de Lisle or Alphonse Daudet. *Les Annales politiques et littéraires* was extremely successful, especially amongst the bourgeoisie and those in the provinces. The magazine boasted a circulation of 200,000 in 1917.
3 Vincent Bouvet & Gérard Durozoi, *Paris between the Wars*, Thames & Hudson, 2012: 343.
4 Christine Martinez, 'Adrienne Monnier', https://www.francebleu.fr/emissions/les-gens-d-ici/pays-de-savoie/adrienne-monnier-rencontre-sylvia-beach-episode-4.
5 Gérard Bonal, *Des Américaines à Paris*, 1850-1920, Tallandier, 2019: 339.
6 Glass, idem 1, cited the American composer Virgil Thompson who, like Aaron Copland and George Antheil, came to Paris to study music with Nadia Boulanger: 26.
7 Glass, idem 1, cited Janet Flanner, *The New Yorker*'s Parisian correspondent and Sylvia and Adrienne's friend: 26.
8 Bonal: 337.
9 Glass: 29.
10 The Croix de Guerre is a French decoration for bravery that was first awarded on 8 April 1915, in the second year of the First World War. It was also given to army divisions, fleet and air forces, and to individual soldiers. Not to be confused with the Croix de Guerre de Vichy that was issued during the Second World War.
11 Equal Justice Initiative: https://johnedwinmason.typepad.com/john_edwin_mason_photogra/2017/11/charlottesville-african-american-veterans-world-war-one.html.
12 An overview of the events of the Red Summer of 1919 can also be found on the Equal Justice Initiative website.
13 https://www.bbc.com/news/av/world-us-canada-46596066.
14 Bonal: 341.
15 Letter from Gertrude Stein to Frances Streloff from 1939. Streloff founded the Gotham Bookmart bookstore in 1920, in New York. The letter is mentioned in Bonal, endnotes: 370.
16 Bonal cited the French writer André Chamson: 341.

17 Bouvet & Durozoi: 343.

18 Glass: 30.

19 Stephen Cleary, *Discovering 20th-century Literature – Writers in Paris*, British Library, 25 May 2016.

20 Bouvet & Durozoi: 343.

21 'In Praise of Sylvia Beach', www.thehemingwayproject.com/2018/08/22/in-praise-of-sylvia-beach/, 22 August 2018: author not recorded.

22 The Buci market is a stone's throw from the Rue de l'Odéon, just across the Boulevard Saint-Germain.

23 Walter Benjamin did not keep his freedom for long. He was arrested by Spanish forces in the Pyrenees and extradited to France where Marshal Pétain's collaborationist government was in power. Walter Benjamin committed suicide on the eve of his extradition.

24 Gisèle Freund emigrated to Argentina after fleeing Paris but later returned to the French capital. She is buried in the Montparnasse cemetery.

25 Bonal: 337.

26 Glass: 1.

27 In addition to Drieu la Rochelle, other collaborators include Lucien Rebatet, Abel Bonnard, Ramon Fernandez, Henri Bidou, Marcel Jouhandeau, Robert Brasillach and Bernard Fay, who was made director of the Bibliothèque Nationale de France. One of his first acts was to 'lend' – i.e. give away – an exceptional collection of hunting books to Reichsmarschall Göring.

28 *Finnegans Wake* was published in 1939.

29 The American Embassy was closed in May.

30 Including that of *Ulysses*.

31 Benoist-Méchin translated sections of *Ulysses* into French for the edition published by Adrienne Monnier in 1929.

32 Sylvia Beach dived into the Foyer des Étudiantes, 93, Boulevard Saint-Michel.

33 Anne Thoraval, *Paris, les lieux de la Résistance*, 6 Parigramme, 2007: 57. *Éditions de Minuit* was founded by Jean Bruller, Pierre de Lescure, Yvonne Paraf and Yvonne Desvignes. Printing was done at 35, Rue Tournefort, 15 minutes' walk from the Rue de l'Odéon.

34 Glass: 388.

35 Sylvia Beach, cited in Glass: 387.

36 Adrienne Monnier, cited in Glass: 408.

2. BONNY AND LAFONT

1 Marie-Cécile de Taillac, *La Comtesse de Palmyre*, Belfond, 1999: 231.

2 Jean-François Muracciole, *La Libération de Paris*, Tallendier, 2013: 134.

3 Anne Thoraval, *Paris – Les Lieux de Résistance*, Parigramme, 2007: 76–77.

4 Julian Jackson, *A Certain Idea of France – The Life of Charles de Gaulle*, Allen Lane, 2018: 37. Charles de Gaulle was close to his niece Geneviève. He admired her religious devotion, her political conviction,

her work in the Resistance and her unifying role in the family. After the war, Geneviève de Gaulle campaigned within the Fourth World movement against poverty and exclusion in France. She was the first woman to be awarded the Grand Cross of the Legion of Honour in 1998. That same year, she published a book about her time in the Ravensbrück camp, *La Traversée de la Nuit* (Seuil, 1998).

5 *La Terreur* (c. 5 September 1793-28 July 1794), or 'Reign of Terror', is a term historians use to designate the two periods during the French Revolution when France was ruled by a special executive that relied on force, illegality and repression.

6 Jean-Paul Cointet, *Paris 40-44*, Perrin, 2001: 220.

3. THE HYENA OF THE GESTAPO?

1 Marceline Loridan (née Rozenberg) lived at this address from 1964 until her death in 2018, along with her second husband, the Dutch filmmaker Joris Ivens, who died in 1989. Marceline was deported to Auschwitz-Birkenau at the age of 16, in the same convoy as Simone Veil. She survived and was liberated by the Red Army from the Theresienstadt camp at the end of the war. Loridan and Ivens, who was thirty years her senior, met in 1963.

2 Marceline Loridan-Ivens [in collaboration with Elizabeth D. Inandiak], *Ma vie Balagan*, Robert Laffont, 2008.

3 In Raymond Ruffin's two biographies of Violette Morris, things go from bad to worse in the space of fifteen years. From collaborator and national traitor in the 1989 biography, to bloodthirsty hyena hunting down Jews and resistance fighters and single-handedly torturing them to death in the 2004 edition. See, Raymond Ruffin, *La diablesse – La véritable histoire de Violette Morris*, Paris: Pygmalion, 1989 and *Violette Morris – La hyène de la Gestap*, Le Cherche Midi, 2004.

4 Marie-Josèphe Bonnet, *Violette Morris – Histoire d'une scandaleuse*, Perrin, 2011: 36.

5 This is a work by the French painter Pierre-Victor Galland, commissioned by industrialist Jean-François Cail, original builder of the property, which also extends along the Boulevard Malesherbes.

6 Bonnet: 41.

7 Bonnet: 44.

8 Gilbert Charles, 'Jeux Olympiques féminins', *Le Figaro*, 21 August 1922: 1.

9 France Culture, March 2019: www.radiofrance.fr/franceculture/podcasts/serie-le-cas-violette-morris.

10 Bonnet: 73.

11 Brassaï, *The Secret Paris of the '30s*, Thames & Hudson, 1976. The book is not paginated but the picture is reproduced in the chapter entitled 'Sodom and Gomorrah'.

12 Paris was occupied on 14 June 1940.

13 The BCRA was led from London by the legendary 'Colonel Passy', real name: André Dewavrin.

14 The Maginot Line was a French defence line built between 1930 and 1938. It ran from the border with Belgium, Luxembourg and Germany in the north, and the border with Italy in the south.

15 Also in this book, see the chapter: *Bonny and Lafont*.

16 Bonnet: 212.

17 Bonnet: 155.

18 https://www.youtube.com/watch?v=OFn-sQCcaVY.

19 As described by Raymond Ruffin on Wikipedia. Anyone searching for Violette Morris across numerous sites will still find Ruffin's fiction repeated as fact. Today, only one sentence refers to Marie-Josèphe Bonnet's 'rehabilitation'. During my own quest for Violette Morris, I discovered that she is always branded 'the hyena of the Gestapo'.

20 Raymond Ruffin, *La Diablesse – La véritable vie de Violette Morris*, Pygmalion Watelet, 1989.

21 Raymond Ruffin, *Violette Morris – La hyène de la Gestap*, Le Cherche Midi, 2004.

22 Annie Lacroix-Riz, *Industriels et banquiers Français sous l'Occupation*, Paris: Armand Colin; HER Paris, 2013. The book is an adapted and augmented reissue of the 1999 edition. Her unparalleled precision makes it a confrontational read. As part of her research, Lacroix-Riz lists countless individuals, holdings, banks and companies, and chronicles their evolution both before and during the Second World War. She proves, in no uncertain terms, that French *haute finance* and *grande industrie* were not simply 'forced' to collaborate with the enemy, but consciously chose to do so out of preference for the Nazi political and social model. Not only this, but they evaded punishment after the war.

23 Bonnet: 226.

24 Lacroix-Riz: 644.

25 Lacroix-Riz: 38.

26 Lacroix-Riz: 644.

27 Lacroix-Riz: 39–40.

28 Lacroix-Riz: 52.

29 Lacroix-Riz: 52.

30 Lacroix-Riz: 652.

31 Lacroix-Riz: 654.

32 Also in this book, see the chapter: *Chanel versus Wertheimer*.

33 Roger Grenier – *Brassaï – Correspondance 1950-1983*, Gallimard, 2017: 10.

34 France Culture: idem 18.

4. BOILLOT, THE TORPEDO

1 Also in this book, see the chapter: *Why Did They Kill Jaurès?*

2 The Vélodrome d'Hiver was used as a temporary prison for the thousands of Jewish women and children who were rounded-up on 16 and 17 July 1942. This operation is now referred to as the Vélodrome d'Hiver round-up. The building was demolished in the 1970s.

3 www.britannica.com/topic/automobile-club.

4 Between 1914 and 1918, the German army had twenty-six Uhlan regiments (3 guard divisions, 16 Prussian, 3 Saxon, 2 Württemberg and 2 Bavarian). These were separate combat forces but most operated as part of an infantry division. Their mission was to gather intelligence and conduct 'blitzkrieg' attacks.

5 Koen Koch, *Een kleine geschiedenis van de Grote Oorlog 1914-1918*, Ambo; Manteau, 2010: 141.

6 Barbara Tuchman, *De kanonnen van augustus, de eerste oorlogsmaand van 1914*, De Arbeiderspers, 1962: 537.

7 Also in this book, see the chapter: *Castor and Pollux*.

8 Tuchman: 536.

9 At that time, Joseph Joffre was still a general; he was appointed commander-in-chief of the French armies on 7 August 1914. He only became marshal in 1916.

10 Tuchman: 239.

11 *La Vie au grand air* was an illustrated sports magazine largely comprising illustrations and voluntary contributions about cycling and, later, motor sports and aviation. It was published from 1898 to 1922, with a break from 1914 (when many of its contributors were called to arms) until June 1916.

12 Idem 11: *La Vie au grand air*.

13 Thierry Lentz, https://www.napoleon.org/histoire-des-2-empires/articles/des-napoleoniens-dans-la-grande-guerre/

14 Tuchman: 157.

15 Tuchman: 524.

16 Tuchman: 523.

17 Tuchman: 541.

18 histoire-image.org/fr/etudes/taxis-marne?i=1034.

19 Sophie De Schaepdrijver, *De Groote Oorlog*, Olympus, 2002: 94.

20 Cordelia Bonal, 'Non. Les taxis de la Marne n'ont pas sauvé Paris', https://www.liberation.fr/societe/2014/08/03/non-les-taxis-de-la-marne-n-ont-pas-sauve-paris_1074013/.

21 Lentz on www.napoleon.org.

22 René Chambe, *Le commandant de Rose – Créateur de l'aviation de chasse*, Forces aériennes françaises, October 1966: 389.

23 www2.culture.gouv.fr/LH/LH021/PG/FRDAFAN83_OL0268091v001.htm.

24 *L'Eclair Comtois*, 19 May 1916.

25 *La Guerre Aérienne Illustrée*, 14 December 1916: 79.

26 www.memoiredeshommes.sga.defense.gouv.fr.

27 The Targa Florio was a motor race for sports cars organised by the Sicilian entrepreneur Vincenzo Florio which, from 1906, was held annually on a street circuit in Sicily. The speed race was held until 1977, after which it was replaced by the Targa Florio Rally.

28 *Omnia*, 1 September 1921, via gallica.bnf.fr/ark:/12148/bpt6k9805259m/f2.

DEEL 4

LEFT BANK EAST

1. CASTOR AND POLLUX

1 Menu of 25 December 1870, Voisin restaurant, Paris.
2 Bismarck was Ambassador to France for several months in 1862.
3 *Les Séries*: Also in this book, see the chapter: *Napoleon III, The Forgotten Emperor*.
4 See isgeschiedenis.nl/nieuws/otto-von-bismarck-en-de-eenwording-van-duitsland.
5 This is Von Moltke 'the Elder': Helmuth Karl Bernhard von Moltke (1800-1891). The German general and field marshal, chief of staff of the Prussian army for 30 years, is widely considered to be one of the greatest military strategists of the second half of the nineteenth century. He is also called Moltke the Elder to distinguish him from his cousin Helmuth von Moltke, 'the Younger', who commanded German troops at the outbreak of the First World War.
6 Éric Anceau, *Ils ont fait et défait le Second Empire*, Tallandier, 2019: 318.
7 Anceau: 319
8 Alain Frerejean & Claire L'Hoër, *Le Siège et la Commune de Paris – Acteurs et témoins racontent*, l'Archipel, 2020: 13.
9 https://www.herodote.net/Le_premier_serviteur_de_l_Etat_-synthese-430.php.
10 In 1856, the French, along with Great Britain, the Ottoman Empire and the Kingdom of Sardinia, defeated Russia in the Crimean War. In 1859, France and Sardinia, led by Victor Emmanuel II, defeated the Austrians at Solferino.
11 Napoleon III, *Proclamation de l'Empereur*, Imprimerie de C. Desrosiers, 1870 via gallica.bnf.fr/ark:/12148/btv1b530286661?rk=42918;4.
12 Frerejean & L'Hoër: 14
13 Frerejean & L'Hoër: 14
14 Frerejean & L'Hoër: 15
15 The Rue du 4 Septembre runs from the Opéra Garnier to the Palais Brongniart, Paris' former stock exchange building, where it turns into the Rue Réaumur.
16 The Third Republic was the republican regime which governed France from 1870 to 1940, although its constitution was not created until 1875. It was the first regime since the start of the French Revolution to have a degree of longevity. Revolutions, coups and wars were the cause of numerous regime changes between 1789 and 1870. France's capitulation at the start of the Second World War led directly to Marshal Philippe Pétain's Vichy regime and the abrupt end to the Third Republic.
17 Frerejean & L'Hoër: 27.
18 Frerejean & L'Hoër: 27.
19 Frerejean & L'Hoër: 54.
20 Frerejean & L'Hoër: 184.
21 Frerejean & L'Hoër: 75.
22 Maurice d'Irrisson d'Hérisson, *Journal d'un officier d'ordonnance*, 1885, reissued by Collection XIX in 2016.
23 Prior to the French Revolution, the animals enjoyed a peaceful existence in the well-maintained Ménagerie Royale, the royal zoo at Versailles. After forcing the royal family back to Paris on 6 October 1789, the *sans-culottes* wanted the Ménagerie to follow suit. Ordinary people could henceforth enjoy this former royal amusement. The zoo was moved to the Jardin des Plantes, a popular park on the Left Bank.
24 *Le Figaro* of 24 January 1871.
25 Pierre Milza, *L'Année terrible – La guerre franco-prussienne, septembre 1870 – mars 1871*, Perrin, 2009: 391.
26 Frerejean & L'Hoër: 91.
27 The *Semaine sanglante* [Bloody Week] alone claimed 21,000 lives: 800 *Versaillais*, 4,000 people killed on the barricades and another 16,000 executed, half of whom had not taken up arms.
28 The Hôtel de Ville, Palais des Tuileries, Palais-Royal, Palais de Justice, Palais d'Orsay, Ministère des Finances, Gare de Lyon, several theatres and urban palaces, the Gobelins (a building housing valuable tapestries and carpets) and the La Villette food warehouses, amongst other buildings, all went up in flames during the *Semaine sanglante*, which was the last week of the Commune.

2. THE SECRET OF THE GRAND MOSQUE

1 Alex Kershaw, *Avenue of Spies*, New York: Crown Publishers, 2015: 41–42. As the war progressed, the Gestapo also requisitioned the buildings at house numbers 82, 84 and 86 in the Avenue Foch. Parisians nicknamed the street '*l'avenue boche*'.
2 Michel Renard, 'Résistance à la Mosquée de Paris: histoire ou fiction?', www.nouvelobs.com/Rue 89, 16 November 2016.
3 Perry Pierik, *Neu Turkestan aan het front – Islamitische soldaten in dienst van de Waffen-SS*, Aspekt, 2019.
4 Designed by French architects and built between 1920 and 1926, the mosque includes a library, a prayer hall, a school/madrassa, a restaurant with teahouse, a hammam and a garden. The complex covers an area of 7,500 square metres, including 3,500 square metres of gardens.
5 Renard, 2016.
6 Jean Corcos, *La Grande Mosquée de Paris sous l'occupation – Entre vérités et légendes*, Tribune CRIF, Conseil représentatif des Institutions Juives de France pour les relations avec les Musulmans, 3 June 2013.
7 The Vélodrome d'Hiver round-up took place on 16 and 17 July 1942. The French police helped round-up thousands of women and children

Endnotes

in Paris. Their husbands and fathers had already been deported in 1941, and the story spread by the French police was that they would be reunited in Germany. The 1941 deportees were, in fact, already dead. They had been gassed immediately upon arrival in Auschwitz. The victims of the Vel d'Hiv round-up, as it is known in abbreviated form, were first taken to the immense Vélodrome, where they were imprisoned for a week without food, drink or attention. They were then despatched to camps in the Loiret (Pithiviers and Beaune-la-Rolande), where the children were separated from their mothers. The victims were sent onwards to Drancy, the large marshalling yard north of Paris, and then to Auschwitz, where everyone, without exception, was gassed upon arrival.

8 Renard, 2016.

9 On the arrest of Si Kaddour Benghabrit, see Mohammed Aïssaoui, *L'étoile jaune et le croissant*, Gallimard, 2012: 27. The SS note of 24 September 1940 to General Weygand is reproduced in full.

10 M. Faivre, 'L'Armée d'Afrique et l'armée coloniale des origines à 1962', *Revue L'Algérianiste* 131, September 2010.

11 Berthe (Beïa) Halali was still able to 'postpone' her arrest until 1943 by marrying a certain André Valaix at the age of seventeen. She is listed in two sources: Archives Nationales [Arch. AN-F/9/5735 et 5748, *fiches d'internement, extraites du fichier du camp de Drancy (adultes) et de celui des enfants internés à Drancy. Suivant l'arrêté du 29 mars 2001 portant apposition de la mention 'Mort en déportation' sur les actes et jugements déclaratifs de décès paru dans le Journal officiel n° 144 du 23 juin 2001*, p. 10016, *Valaix, née Halali (Berthe, Beïa) le 16 décembre 1926 à Bône (Algérie), est décédée le 7 septembre 1943 à Auschwitz; son fils, Claude André Valaix, né le 21 février 1943 à Paris (15e), est décédé, près de trois semaines plus tard, le 30 septembre 1943, dans le même camp d'extermination*] and Jean Laloum, 'Persécution et déportation des Juifs du Constantinois', *Le Journal des Tournelles* 26, November 2017: 16–22: 20. Tournelles is the Rue des Tournelles, behind the Place des Vosges, where a large synagogue is located.

12 See Corcos: 105, in which Albert Assouline's article from *L'Almanach du combattant* of 1983 is printed.

13 Corcos: 25–26 and 104.

14 Cited in Renard, 2016.

15 See, amongst others: Michel Renard, Daniel Lefeuvre & Benjamin Stora in the dossier 'La Mosquée de Paris sous l'occupation, 1940-1944' on etudescoloniales.canalblog.com/archives/2011/10/09/22292189.html of 9 October 2011; Ethan Katz, 'Did the Paris Mosque Save Jews? A Mystery and Its Memory', *The Jewish Quarterly Review* 102, Spring 2012: 256–287; Jean Laloum, 'La Mosquée de Paris sous l'Occupation', *Cinéma et Histoire* 1, 2012.

16 On this, see amongst others: Corcos: 42–49, plus the interview with Mohammed Aïssaoui by Youssef Aït Akdim: 'Dire que Juifs et Arabes

ont marché ensemble reste tabou', *Jeune Afrique*, 3 December 2012.

17 Katia Kukawka, 'Avant Avicenne, l'hôpital franco-musulman de Bobigny', *La Revue du Praticien* (56) 10, 31 May 2006.

18 Yad Vashem is Israel's official memorial to the victims of the Holocaust. It is dedicated to: preserving the memory of the Jews who were murdered; echoing the stories of the survivors; honouring Jews who fought against their Nazi oppressors and gentiles who selflessly aided Jews in need; and researching the phenomenon of the Holocaust.

19 Renard, 2016.

20 Corcos: 35–36.

21 Aïssaoui, 2012.

22 Aïssaoui, 2012: 169.

3. DOCTOR JACK AND NURSE TOQUETTE

1 Charles Glass, *Americans in Paris*, Harper Press, 2010: 1–2.

2 Glass: 66

3 André Guérin, *Chronique de la Résistance*, Place des éditeurs, 2010: 260.

4 Anne Thoraval, *Paris – Les lieux de la Résistance*, Parigramme, 2007: 57.

5 Marshal Foch led the great Allied offensive that caused the Germans to retreat. It commenced on 28 September and ended with the Armistice of 11 November 1918. Foch personally delivered the armistice terms to the German delegation in his railway carriage at Compiègne. He refused to make any concessions. The fact that Foch also remained Allied commander-in-chief during the armistice period, when the Allied armies occupied the entire left bank of the Rhine and some of its riverside cities, created bad blood in Germany. He also chaired the discussions on extensions to the armistice. Furthermore, Foch urged the French government to make tough demands at the peace negotiations, which began in Paris in early 1919. He wanted the Rhineland to be politically detached from Germany and to act as a buffer state under French military control. Only this way, he warned, could future German aggression be avoided. The Germans could not stomach this level of humiliation. The 'occupation' of 'his' avenue can therefore be seen as the first act of revenge.

6 During the Vélodrome d'Hiver (Paris, 16 and 17 July 1942) round-up, over 3,000 Jewish women and children were rounded up with the cooperation of the French police, detained and eventually sent to the gas chambers of Auschwitz. Fewer than 100 detainees survived the mass arrest. Also in this book, see the chapter: *The Secret of the Grand Mosque*.

7 Alex Kershaw, *Avenue of Spies*, New York: Crown Publishers, 2015: 127.

8 Glass 2010: 395.

9   The eatery is now called 'Le Resto'. The plaque remains in place.

4. THE PARTY IN THE RUE TOULLIER

1   Karl Laske, 'Carlos refait la fusillade de la rue Toullier', *Libération*, 19 December 1997.
2   The hostage situation at the French embassy in The Hague lasted from 13 to 17 September 1974.
3   Now Ben Gurion International Airport.
4   The new president and government assumed office in May 1974.
5   Gilbert Bécaud wrote 'Dimanche à Orly' in 1963.
6   Karl Laske, '27 juin 1975, trois morts rue Toullier à Paris. Un carnage signé Carlos', *Libération*, 12 December 1997.
7   Vladimir Ilyich Ulyanov: Lenin.
8   Thierry Oberlé, 'Carlos, tueur sans frontières', Lefigaro.fr, 7 August 2008. Che Guevara was killed in Bolivia in 1967.
9   Alexandre Lacroix, *Voyage au centre de Paris*, J'ai Lu; Flammarion, 2013: 82.
10 Lacroix: 83.
11 Samuel Bartholin, 'La décennie de Carlos, ou la dérive sanglante d'un militant', Slate.fr, 8 December 2016: statement by Leyma Palomares, eyewitness.
12 Idem 6.
13 m.ina.fr/video/CAB97143790/carlos-rappel-rue-toullier-video.html
14 Idem 13, this report also shows the contemporaneous newspaper headlines.
15 Lacroix: 82.
16 Idem 6.
17 *The Financial Times*, 'Opec Linchpin Who Humbled the West', 27-28 February 2021: 6.
18 Rosa Luxemburg was a German Marxist politician, philosopher and revolutionary. Born in 1871 to a Polish-Jewish middle-class family, she and Karl Liebknecht played a leading role in pre-First World War Germany as members of the Spartacus movement. On the night of 15-16 January 1919, Luxemburg and Liebknecht were captured, interrogated in Berlin's Eden Hotel and murdered by a member of a Freikorps (Marine Brigade Ehrardt). Rosa Luxemburg's corpse was hurled into the Landwehr Canal, into which hundreds more murdered (alleged) Spartacists were also thrown. It was not until 31 May that Luxemburg's body was fished out of a lock. She was buried with Karl Liebknecht at the Zentralfriedhof in Berlin-Friedrichsfelde on 13 June 1919. Also in this book, see the chapter: *'Why Did They Kill Jaurès?'*
19 Jacques Vergès defended 'personalities' such as war criminal Klaus Barbie, a string of African dictators and Khieu Samphan, Brother number 4 of the Khmer Rouge with a PhD in Economics from the Sorbonne. Saloth Sar, Brother number 1, is better known as Pol Pot.

5. MADE IN PARIS: THE PEOPLE'S REPUBLIC OF CHINA AND THE WAR IN VIETNAM

1   Michel Pinçon & Monique Pinçon-Charlot, *Paris, quinze promenades sociologiques*, Éditions Payot et Rivages, 2009: 196.
2   Dennis Bos, *Bloed en Barrikaden*, Wereldbibliotheek, 2014: 566.
3   Jung Chang & Jon Halliday, *Mao – The Unknown Story*, Anchor, 2006.
4   Stanley Karnow, *Paris in the Fifties*, Times Books; Random House, 1997: 215.
5   Barbara W. Tuchman, *The March of Folly*, Abacus, 1984: 290-448, see chapter 5, 'America Betrays Herself in Vietnam'.
6   Pierre Miquel, *La guerre d'Algérie*, Fayard, 1993: 78.
7   Miquel: 403.
8   Miquel: 403.
9   Bos: 529.
10 During the Reign of Terror, a period during the French Revolution from 1793 to 1794, between 40,000 and 55,000 people were executed, typically by guillotine.
11 Eric Hazan, *A Walk Through Paris – A Radical Exploration*, London; New York: Verso, 2018: 7–8.
12 Eric Hazan, *Le tumulte de Paris*, Éditions La Fabrique, 2021: 32.

6. MYTHERRAND

1   François Mitterrand, *Lettres à Anne*, 1962-1995, nrf Gallimard, 2016.
2   Clément Steuer, *Susini et l'OAS – Collection Histoire et perspectives méditerranéennes*, Éditions L'Harmattan, 2004: 33.
3   The Fourth Republic was the period between the promulgation of the new constitution and the resignation of Charles de Gaulle in October 1946 and his return to power in 1958. The Fourth Republic ended on 4 October 1958. On 28 September 1958 a referendum had been held which supported the new constitution and the creation of the Fifth Republic. De Gaulle was elected president in January 1959. The Fifth Republic commenced with his appointment.
4   Pierre Daum, 'Combien sont-ils?' *Le Monde diplomatique*, May 2008: www.monde-diplomatique.fr.
5   Pierre Miquel, *La guerre d'Algérie*, Fayard, 1993: 91.
6   Miquel: 127.
7   Geert Mak, *In Europe – Travels through the Twentieth Century*, Harvill Secker, 2007.
8   Milquet: 160.
9   Also in this book, see the chapter: *Made in Paris. The People's Republic of China and the War in Vietnam*.
10 *Pieds noirs* was a term used to refer to settlers (colonists) in Algeria until the end of the Algerian War in 1962. In a broader sense, the term is also used for French people who left Morocco or Tunisia when those countries gained independence.

Endnotes

11 Pierre Pflimlin was leader of the Christian democratic Mouvement Républicain Populaire (MRP).
12 Julian Jackson, *A Certain Idea of France – The Life of Charles de Gaulle*, Allen Lane, 2018: 459.
13 Jackson: 469.
14 Jackson: 470.
15 Letter dated 24 May 1958 from Salan to de Gaulle.
16 Idem 7.
17 Miquel: 343.
18 Jackson: 470.
19 Pierre Miquel, *La guerre d'Algérie*, Fayard, 1993: 342–343.
20 Draft telegram from General Salan to General Miquel dated 30 May 1958.
21 De Gaulle will only obtain it via a referendum in 1962.
22 Serge Berstein, *Allocution radio-télévisée du 27 juin 1958, prononcée à l'Hôtel Matignon*, fresques.ina.fr/de-gaulle/fiche-media/Gaulle00014/allocutionradio-televisee-du-27-juin-1958-prononcee-a-lhotel-matignon.html.
23 Miquel: 91.
24 A college of 80,000 cast their votes for the French president but he was not directly elected at that time.
25 Jackson: 447
26 The government of prime minister Guy Mollet, leader of the French Socialists.
27 François Malye (with Philippe Houdart), *Les guillotinés de Mitterrand*, www.lepoint.fr/politique/les-guillotines-de-mitterrand-31-08-2001-56908_20.php.
28 Miquel: 342–343.
29 www.lepoint.fr/politique/les-guillotines-de-mitterrand-31-08-2001-56908_20.php
30 Miquel: 284.
31 *Le Monde*, 3 March 2021: www.lemonde.fr/afrique/article/2021/03/03/guerre-d-algerie-emmanuel-macron-reconnait-qu-ali-boumendjel-a-ete-torture-et-assassine-par-l-armee-francaise_6071747_3212.html.
32 On 2 March 2021, during the reception for Boumendjel's grandchildren at the Élysée Palace, President Emmanuel Macron acknowledged 'in the name of France' that Boumendjel had been tortured and killed by the French army.
33 Milquet: 284–285.
34 www.lemonde.fr/idees/article/2009/10/31/le-cout-de-la-guerre-d-algerie_1261060_3232.html
35 The Place Vendôme is the synonym for the Ministry of Justice, Matignon is the synonym for the official residence of French prime ministers.
36 www.lepoint.fr/politique/les-guillotines-de-mitterrand-31-08-2001-56908_20.php#11: "*Il est clair que dans son esprit la Place Vendôme était l'antichambre de Matignon. Il espérait, après ce passage à la Justice, avoir été assez dur pour qu'on lui confie la direction du pays*."
37 Michel Debré was a scion of a liberal-conservative Jewish family, who converted and became a Protestant. During the Second World War, he made his mark in the Comité Français de Libération Nationale (CFLN) led by de Gaulle. Here, Debré was responsible for recruiting and selecting the confidants who would hold key posts after the liberation of France. A brilliant intellectual himself, Michel Debré founded the Ecole Nationale d'Administration (ENA), from which the country's future leaders were recruited as of 1945. After de Gaulle's return in June 1958, he wrote the new constitution for the Fifth Republic with Couve de Murville and others.
38 Jackson: 660.
39 *Les Liaisons dangereuses* is an eighteenth-century French epistolary novel by Pierre Choderlos de Laclos. It has been filmed several times: *Les Liaisons dangereuses* (1959) with Jeanne Moreau and Gérard Philipe; *Les Liaisons dangereuses* (1979), directed by Charles Brabant; *Dangerous Liaisons* (1988), directed by Stephen Frears, with Glenn Close, John Malkovich, Michelle Pfeiffer and Keanu Reeves; *Valmont* (1989), directed by Miloš Forman, with Annette Bening, Colin Firth and Meg Tilly; *Les Liaisons dangereuses* (2003), directed by Josée Dayan, with Catherine Deneuve.
40 Catherine Nay, *Le Noir et le Rouge, ou l'histoire d'une ambition*, Grasset, 1984: 343.
41 Nay: 346.
42 Nay: 349.
43 Jacques Kosciusko-Morizet was a former resistance fighter, intellectual and diplomat. Jean-Jacques Servan-Schreiber was the founder and editor-in-chief of the [then] left-wing intellectual magazine *L'Express* in which Sartre and Camus also argued against *l'Algérie française*.
44 *Le Monde*, 'Les circonstances de l'attentat contre M. Mitterrand', 17 October 1959.
45 Miquel: 342–343.
46 Danielle Breem, *L'Affaire de l'Observatoire*, fresques.ina.fr/mitterrand/fiche-media/Mitter00131/laffaire-de-l-observatoire.html.
47 Nay: 351.
48 Nay: 351.
49 Nay: 351.
50 Nay: 352.
51 Jean-Marie Le Pen, later leader of the Front National, was at the time *député* for *Les Indépendants de Paris*, the autonomous Parisian federation of the *Centre national des indépendants et paysans* (CNIP).
52 Jackson: 447.
53 A supporter of Pierre Poujade, a French populist politician after whom the movement *Poujadism* was named. The *Union de défense des commerçants et artisans*, founded by Poujade, was an important political movement in France between 1953 and 1958. It rapidly lost supporters and influence during the Fifth Republic.
54 *L'Aurore* of 23 October 1959: 1.
55 *France Observateur* later became *Le Nouvel Observateur* and later still, was simply called *L'Obs*.

56 Nay: 355.

57 Claude Askolovitch, *François Mitterrand et l'attentat de l'Observatoire*, www.franceinter.fr/emissions/histoire-et-politique/histoire-et-politique-12-mars-2017.

58 Michel Onfray, *Vies parallèles, de Gaulle – Mitterrand*, Robert Laffont, 2020: 276–278.

59 Mitterrand: 409.

60 The scandal whereby journalist Edwy Plenel, editor-in-chief of *Le Monde*, actress Carole Bouquet and 148 other public figures were illegally bugged from the Élysée Palace at the behest of Mitterrand.

61 Philippe Broussard & Jean-Marie Pontaut, *Les grandes affaires de la Ve République, scandales, écoutes, malversations*, L'Express Poche, 2012: 227–378.

62 Mia Doornaert, *Ontreddderde Republiek – Zoektocht naar de ziel van Frankrijk*, Uitgeverij Polis, 2017: 183.

63 Gilles Gaetner, *Mitterrand – L'art de l'esquive*, in Broussard & Pontaut: 376–377.

64 Gaetner: 376.

65 Pierre Péan, *Une jeunesse française, François Mitterrand 1934-1947*, Pluriel, 1994. A detailed book by an investigative journalist. I consulted the reissued edition by Fayard/Pluriel 2010.

66 Jean Garrigues with Christine Clerc, Hervé Gattegno, Catherine Nay, Christophe Barbier, Renaud Dély, Sylvain Courage and Michèle Cotta, *La république des traîtres de 1958 à nos jours*, Tallandier, 2018: 144.

67 Onfray: 102. Here, the author cites the following work: Jacques Attali, *C'était François Mitterrand*, Fayard, 2005.

68 Doornaert: 10.

69 Nay: 349.

70 Onfray: 168.

71 Philip Short, *Mitterrand – A Study in Ambiguity*, Bodley Head, 2013.

72 Onfray: 169.

73 Pascal was François Mitterrand and Danielle Gouze's first child. He was born in 1945 but died two months later. Jean-Christophe was born in 1946 and Gilbert in 1949.

74 Onfray: 170.

75 Onfray: 170.

76 Onfray: 169.

77 Mitterrand: letter 1180: 1174.528.

78 Mitterrand: letter 464: 646.

79 Doornaert: 163.

80 Solenn de Royer, chief reporter for *Le Monde*, used the pseudonym 'Claire' for the student whose existence she revealed in her book *Le dernier secret*, published by Grasset in 2021.

81 Jérémie Maire, www.vanityfair.fr/actualites/diaporama/francois-mitterrand-et-les-femmes-de-sa-vie/5619.

7. PICASSO'S 'RED PERIOD'

1 *l'Humanité*, 5 October 1944: 1.

2 Marcel Cachin, 'Picasso a apporté son adhésion au Parti de la Renaissance française', *l'Humanité*, 5 Octobre 1944, reproduced in *Picasso et la Guerre*, Paris: Gallimard, 2019: 222.

3 There was also the Gaullist resistance of the Forces françaises de l'intérieur (FFI), but it was Colonel Rol-Tanguy, leader of the communist Francs-tireurs et partisans (FTP), who began the liberation of Paris even before Leclerc's second armoured division entered the city. It is also often forgotten that the PCF endorsed National Socialism after the non-aggression pact between Germany and the Soviet Union was concluded in August 1939. PCF leader Maurice Thorez, incidentally, stayed in Moscow during the war. Although the pact tore the party apart internally, there was no resistance. The common enemies of the PCF and Nazi Germany were London, the US, the banks, international capitalism, world Jewry and the Gaullists – especially the latter after the Appeal of 18 June 1940, in which General de Gaulle called for resistance to the Vichy government and the German occupiers. Meanwhile, the French and German working classes were united against international capitalism. It was only after 22 June 1941, when Hitler attacked the Soviet Union via Operation Barbarossa, that the PCF switched tactics and went underground.

4 Michel Lefebvre, 'Le parti et la Résistance', *Le Monde*, 9 December 2006: "*Le PCF s'est présenté, après la guerre, comme 'le parti des 75 000 fusillés'.* Jean-Pierre Besse & Thomas Pouty, in *Les Fusillés, répression et exécutions pendant l'Occupation 1940-1944* (édition l'Atelier), estimate that "4,520 people were shot in France during the war, 80% to 90% of them communists." www.lemonde.fr/societe/article/2006/12/09/le-parti-et-la-resistance_843770_3224.html.

5 Text of an election poster from *Les Archives du PCF*: archives.seinesaintdenis.fr/ark:/naan/a011550068576OlcB44. Full text of the poster: "*75.000 communistes ont été massacrés par les boches ou assassinés par les traitres de Vichy. Ils sont l'honneur et la fierté du parti des fusillés. Du parti de la Renaissance française. Du parti de l'unité ouvrière et de l'union de tous les républicains. Français ! Françaises ! pour être fidèles à la mémoire de ces héros qui sont morts pour que vive la France VOTEZ pour les listes communistes d'Union Républicaine et Résistante.*"

6 Anette Levy-Willard, 'Mont Valérien, Klarsfeld corrige le nombre de fusillés', *Libération*, 30 March 1995: "*Selon Serge Klarsfeld, ce ne sont pas 'plus de 4.500 résistants', mais 1.007 hommes qui ont été fusillés au mont Valérien, dont 174 juifs. Chiffre qui correspond d'ailleurs à celui de la Libération: dans un rapport préparé pour la commémoration par le général de Gaulle, le 1er novembre 1944, on parle 'd'environ un millier de personnes' fusillées au mont*

Endnotes

Valérien. Depuis huit ans, Serge Klarsfeld demande que le chiffre de 4.500 soit changé en 'plus de 1.000 résistants' sur la stèle en granit du 'mémorial de la France combattante'. Il espère que la vérité pourra être désormais inscrite avant le 8 mai prochain, cinquantième anniversaire de la capitulation de l'Allemagne. Déjà, il avait fait apposer, pour le bicentenaire de la Révolution française, une plaque à proximité du Mémorial du mont Valérien en souvenir des 161 résistants juifs fusillés (chiffre qu'il avait à l'époque) 'qui ont combattu pour leur dignité et leur liberté".

7   Cachin: 222.
8   PCF causes included the reduction of unemployment, gender equality, anti-colonialism, anti-imperialism, freedom, world peace and the edification of the working classes.
9   Eight ministers (Tillon, Billoux, Thorez, Croizat, Paul, Casanova, Arthaud, Marrane) and three Secretaries of State (Patinaud, Lecoeur and Gosnat).
10 Koen Hoondert, *El pintor politico – Een onderzoek naar het politieke leven van Pablo Picasso,* Master's degree thesis, Politics & Culture, Utrecht University, 2011.
11 De Gaulle feared an AMGOT administration for France: Allied Military Government of Occupied Territories.
12 www.gouvernement.fr/ partage/9406-Llib%C3%A9ration-de-Paris
13 Michel Onfray, *Vies parallèles, de Gaulle – Mitterrand,* Robert Laffont, 2020: 90–91.
14 Cachin: 222.
15 Cachin: 222.
16 Carsten-Peter Warncke & Ingo F. Walther, *Picasso,* Taschen, 1997: 705.
17 *Guernica* is a 1937 painting by Picasso. It depicts the bombing of Guernica during the Spanish Civil War and measures 3.49 x 7.76 metres. *Guernica* can be seen at the Museo Reina Sofía in Madrid.
18 Sylvain Ageorges, *Sur les traces des Expositions universelles Paris 1855-1937,* Parigramme, 2006: 166–167.
19 Also in this book, see the chapter: *Rose Valland's War.*
20 Pierre Assouline, *L'homme de l'art D.-H. Kahnweiler 1884-1979,* Gallimard, 1988: 527.
21 Assouline: 528.
22 Anne Sinclair, *21, rue la Boétie,* De Bezige Bij Antwerp, 2012: 119.
23 Assouline: 540.
24 Also in this book, see the chapter: *Rose Valland's War.*
25 The works and prices are taken from *Picasso et la Guerre,* Paris: Gallimard, 2019: 159.
26 Assouline: 521.
27 *Picasso et la Guerre,* Paris: Gallimard, 2019: 161.
28 Christel Sniter, 'La fonte des Grands Hommes – Destruction et recyclage des statues parisiennes sous l'occupation' in *Terrains et Travaux* 2007 no. 2, www.cairn.info/

revue-terrains-et-travaux-2007-2-page-99.htm.
29 Anne Sebba, *Les Parisiennes – How the Women of Paris Lived, Loved and Died in the 1940s,* Weidenfeld & Nicholson, 2016: 120.
30 Cachin: 150 & 161.
31 Assouline: 540.
32 Jean-Paul Cointet, *Paris 40-44,* Perrin, 2001: 126.
33 Ageorges: 161.
34 Also in this book, see the chapter: *Rose Valland's War.*
35 Sinclair: 164. Anne Sinclair recounts this anecdote as if it came from 'a German officer'. This perhaps increases the chances of it being a myth; in other literature it is Otto Abetz (*Picasso et la Guerre,* Paris: Gallimard, 2019, p. 161). Elsewhere, it is Arno Breker. Of course, this does not detract from the brilliance of this short exchange.
36 Cointet: 176.
37 Also in this book, see the chapter: *Rose Valland's War.*
38 Max Jacob in 1944 and Robert Desnos in 1945.
39 Assouline: 540.
40 *Picasso et la Guerre,* Paris: Gallimard, 2019: 162.
41 *Picasso et la Guerre,* Paris: Gallimard, 2019: 162.
42 Also in this book, see the chapter: *Rose Valland's War.*
43 Various authors, *Regards sur la peinture 2 – Picasso,* Paris: Éditions Fabri, 1988: 26.
44 Assouline: 560.
45 *Picasso et la Guerre,* Paris: Gallimard, 2019: 239
46 Assouline: 624.
47 Corina Mila, *Picasso-Staline et l'esthétique communiste,* thesis defended on 4 September 2017, New Sorbonne University Paris 3: 12.
48 *Tres de Mayo* [The Third of May] by Goya is dated 1814.
49 *L'Exécution de Maximilien* [The Execution of Emperor Maximilian] by Manet is dated 1868-1869.
50 Hoondert: 71.
51 Assouline: 639.
52 Lucie Fougeron, 'Propagande et création picturale: l'exemple du PCF dans la Guerre Froide', *Magazine Sociétés et Représentations,* October 2001: 269–84.
53 Cachin: 222.
54 Picasso, *Staline à ta santé* [Stalin, to your health], 1949, pen and ink drawing, 215 x 14 cm, Musée National Picasso-Paris.
55 Onfray: 86. Majdanek camp was liberated by the Russians on 24 July 1945.
56 Front page of *l'Humanité* of 18 March 1953.
57 Mila: 35. Here Mila quotes an article from *El Mundo* of 20 May 2010 by Eduardo Suarez: 'Picasso, el mal communista'.
58 Assouline: 101.
59 Assouline: 614.
60 Warncke & Walther: 715.
61 Warncke & Walther: 721.
62 Assouline: 680.

DEEL 5

MONCEAU & BATIGNOLLES

1. THE LADY FROM THE RUE DE CHAZELLES

1 Also in this book, see the chapter: *John Law's 'Shitty Shares'.*
2 Barbara Tuchman, *The March of Folly*, Abacus, 2001: 157.
3 Delaware, Pennsylvania, New Jersey, Georgia, Connecticut, Massachusetts, Maryland, South Carolina, New Hampshire, Virginia, New York, North Carolina and Rhode Island. They are symbolised by the 13 stripes in the American flag.
4 The Boston Massacre happened on 5 March 1770. British soldiers fired on American civilians before the Old State House, the seat of the British governor, in Boston, Massachusetts. It is widely considered to mark the start of the American quest for independence.
5 Tuchman: 276.
6 www.britannica.com/topic/Declaration-of-Independence/The-nature-and-influence-of-the-Declaration-of-Independence.
7 Johan Op de Beeck, *Napoleon*, part. 2: 'van keizer tot mythe', Manteau, 2014: 37.
8 Chelsea Bengier, 'The Shocking Secret You Didn't Know about America's Most Iconic Monument', June 2020, bestlifeonline.com/statue-of-liberty-slavery.
9 The American flag had 35 stars in 1865. West Virginia had just been added and the next star would be for Nevada.
10 H.L. Wesselink, *Scheffer, Renan, Psichari, een Franse cultuur- en familiegeschiedenis 1815-1914*, Prometheus, 2017: 134.
11 Pierre Vidal, *Frédéric-Auguste Bartholdi 1834-1904: par l'esprit et par la main*, Créations du Pélican, 1994: 31.
12 *Khedive* was the title of the governor of Egypt from 1867 to 1914. It was first applied to Governor Ismael, a descendant of Muhammad Ali Pasha, in 1867. Although the *khedives* notionally ruled under the sultan of the Ottoman Empire, they were in fact semi-autonomous leaders.
13 Also in this book, see the chapter: *Napoleon III, The Forgotten Emperor.*
14 Also in this book, see the chapter: *Castor and Pollux.*
15 The Third Republic was the republican regime that governed France from 1870 to 1940, although its constitution was not created until 1875. It was the first regime since the start of the French Revolution to have a degree of longevity. Revolutions, coups and wars were the cause of numerous regime changes between 1789 and 1870. France's capitulation at the start of the Second World War led directly to Marshal Philippe Pétain's Vichy regime and the abrupt end of the Third Republic.
16 Gounod composed the hymn in 1876, the year the Statue of Liberty was to be donated. The final stanza is unequivocal about the sculpture's mission: '*Je porte au loin dans la nuit sombre / Quand tous mes feux sont allumés / Mes rayons au vaisseau qui sombre / Et ma lumière aux opprimés!*'
17 www.autographes-des-siecles.com/produit/frederic-bartholdi-et-la-construction-de-la-statue-de-la-liberte/.
18 www.nps.gov/stli/learn/historyculture/joseph-pulitzer.htm.
19 Seymour Topping, *Biography of Joseph Pulitzer*, www.pulitzer.org/page/biography-joseph-pulitzer.
20 Orlando Figes, *The Europeans – Three Lives and the Making of a Cosmopolitan Culture*, Metropolitan Books, 2019.
21 Sylvain Ageorges, *Sur les traces des Expositions Universelles – Paris 1855-1937*, Parigramme, 2006: 46–75.
22 Idem 20.
23 Idem 17.
24 www.columbia.edu/cu/lweb/digital/collections/cul/texts/ldpd_5655298_000/pages/ldpd_5655298_000_00000009.html?toggle=image&menu=maximize&top=&left=.
25 Donald Barr Chidsey, *The Panama Canal*, Wildside Press, 2016: 73.
26 Lesley Kennedy: www.history.com/news/immigrants-ellis-island-short-processing-time#:~:text=More%20than%2012%20million%20immigrants,United%20States%20in%201907%20alone.

2. DYING 'FOR' FRANCE, DYING 'AT THE HANDS OF' FRANCE

1 Denis Albin, 'Ltt Nissim de Camondo, Observateur-Pilote', albindenis.free.fr /Site_escadrille/escadrille033.htm.
2 Sylvain Ageorges, *Expositions universelles Paris 1855-1937*, Parigramme, 2006: 18.
3 Pierre Assouline, *Le dernier des Camondo*, Gallimard, 1999: 128.
4 The Deutz Affair. After the fall of Napoleon, the house of Bourbon reclaimed the throne in 1815. France reverted to Catholicism. To enhance his career prospects, Simon Deutz, son of France's Chief Rabbi, converted to the faith in Rome, with much fanfare. He achieved this through the intercessions of Marie-Caroline of Bourbon-Two Sicilies, better known as the Duchesse de Berry, niece-in-law of the last Bourbon kings, Louis XVIII and Charles X. Under his new 'Catholic' name, Hyacinthe de Gonzague, Deutz became the duchess' trusted advisor. A description that would later leave a bitter aftertaste. After the 'Citizen King' Louis-Philippe d'Orléans expelled Charles X from the country in 1830, other

Endnotes

members of the Bourbon family also fled, including the Duchesse de Berry. Two years later, she secretly entered France and tried to incite a rebellion against Louis-Philippe. Deutz knew her hiding place and denounced her to Adolphe Thiers, Louis-Philippe's interior minister, for the sum of 500,000 francs. The betrayal caused an uproar in France and the Chief Rabbi was asked to denounce his son. He refused. Then the opposite happens. De Gonzague, the Catholic, converts back to Judaism and reclaims his previous name, Simon Deutz. The affair fuels French suspicions that Jews have a 'Judas quality' to them.

5 The Bernard Bauer Affair. This Hungarian Jew, also the son of a rabbi, converted to Catholicism in 1852, at the age of twenty-five. Louis-Napoleon, nephew of Napoleon Bonaparte, had seized power as emperor and created the Second Empire in Paris. Bauer was a fluent orator and was appointed the personal confessor to Empress Eugénie, wife of Louis-Napoleon. She secured him multiple promotions, including in Rome. Thanks to Empress Eugénie, Bauer became *Monsignor*. In this capacity, he became an ardent supporter of the imperial couple. But when the Emperor and Empress, together with the Second Empire, were toppled by the Franco-Prussian War in 1870, 'Monsignor Bauer' suddenly fell prey to a crisis of faith. With his paymasters exiled, the Monsignor renounced his Catholic vows and reclaimed his Jewish identity. Moreover, the newly reconverted Bernard Bauer married the young actress Elisabeth Lévy. Yet more oil poured onto the anti-Semitic fire.

6 The Dreyfus Affair. The Dreyfus Affair was a judicial scandal that erupted in 1894. It had major repercussions for French politics until 1906. Jewish-French officer Alfred Dreyfus was falsely accused of being a spy for Germany and, as such, was sentenced to life imprisonment on Devil's Island off the coast of French Guiana. In 1898, Emile Zola published *J'accuse* in the newspaper *L'Aurore*, a plea in support of Dreyfus. He was not reinstated until 1906. Like no other scandal before it, the Dreyfus Affair tore France apart.

7 The bank l'Union générale was founded in 1875 by monarchist Catholics. Taken over by the Catholic industrialist Paul Eugène Bontoux in 1878, it collapsed due to his mismanagement. A huge number of French Catholics lost their savings. The blame was quickly shifted to Jewish bankers, with the Rothschilds being a prime target.

8 The Panama Scandal: after his success with the Suez Canal, diplomat Ferdinand de Lesseps applied for a public loan to finance a new canal connecting the Atlantic to the Pacific. The money, raised from over 800,000 underwriters, was not used for the works themselves, but to produce further fundraising propaganda. Baron Jacques de Reinach (no relation to Léon Reinach, husband of Béatrice de Camondo), a Jew, was involved in the scheme. In 1893, father and son de Lesseps were convicted of fraud. Cornelius Herz and Jacques de Reinach, two Jewish administrators, 'had a lucky escape': Herz fled to England and Reinach committed suicide. Again, this soured French public opinion.

3. VICTORINE 'THE SHRIMP'

1 Charles Baudelaire cited in Ton van Kempen & Nicoline van de Beek: *Madame Manet – Muziek en Kunst in het Parijs van de impressionisten*, Uitgeverij Het Archief Collectief, 2014: 81. For Baudelaire, Manet was not an Impressionist but a Realist, a painter of modern life. No epic scenes from mythology or heroic wars, nor Greek or Roman goddesses, but a waitress with glasses of beer (*La Serveuse de bocks*), a drunkard (*Le Buveur d'absinthe*), a mother and child by a railway (*Le Chemin de fer*), a rag picker (*Le Chiffonnier*), a man with guitar and a girl with a musical score (*La Leçon de musique*), a beach (*La Plage de Boulogne*), an elderly man with book (*Le Liseur*) and above all: he paints 'his' women 'as they are'.

2 Both works can be admired today in the Musée d'Orsay in Paris.

3 Édouard Manet and Victorine Meurent met in 1862 through the Belgian painter Alfred Stevens, who was then working in Paris. Manet and Stevens knew each other as pupils of the French painter Thomas Couture, who specialised in works depicting classical antiquity.

4 *La Chanteuse des rues* now hangs in the Museum of Fine Arts in Boston.

5 *La Femme au perroquet* can today be seen in the Metropolitan Museum of Art in New York.

6 *La Nymphe surprise* belongs to the Museo Nacional de Bellas Artes in Buenos Aires.

7 Le Salon de Peinture et de Sculpture de l'Académie des Beaux-Arts, or the Salon de Paris for short, was founded in the late seventeenth century and operated until 1880. In that year, the French statesman Jules Ferry decided that the Académie should no longer have a monopoly on the organisation of the annual exhibition. The Société des Artistes Français took over the running of the Salon de Paris in 1881.

8 Van Kempen & Van de Beek: 89.

9 Van Kempen & Van de Beek. Their remarkable book *Madame Manet* is partly based on the research conducted by the British art historian and curator Juliet Wilson-Bareau, an authority on Francisco Goya and Édouard Manet. She was the Slade Professor of Fine Art at the University of Oxford from 1993 to 1994.

10 Van Kempen & Van de Beek: 90.

11 The Rue Guyot is now the Rue Médéric in Batignolles. Manet had his studio at no. 8 from 1860 to 1872.

12 Van Kempen & Van de Beek: 89.

13 Van Kempen & Van de Beek: 299–300.

14 Van Kempen & Van de Beek: 348. Tabarant authored several books on the Impressionists, especially on Manet: *Manet et ses oeuvres* was published in 1947.

15 V.R. Main, 'The Naked Truth', *The Guardian*, 2008: www.theguardian.com/lifeandstyle/2008/oct/03/women.manet

16 Debra Finerman, *Mademoiselle Victorine*, New York: Three Rivers Press, 2007: 6. This book is a novel but is presented as 'the life of'. Consequently, the protagonist is not Victorine Meurent but Victorine Laurent, supposedly the most desirable courtesan in Paris.

17 Idem 15.

18 Ross King, *The Judgment of Paris: The Revolutionary Decade That Gave the World Impressionism*, Bloomsbury, 2006.

19 Jules Claretie on *Olympia* in *Le Figaro* in 1865.

20 Ernest Chesneau in *Le Constitutionnel* in 1865.

21 Whereas the Impressionists, whose works were rejected by the Salon de Paris and stamped on the reverse with an 'R' for *Refusé*, participated in the Salon des Refusés or organised their own exhibitions (the first Impressionist exhibition took place from 15 April to 15 May 1874 at photographer Nadar's studio on the Boulevard des Capucines), Manet sought recognition for his work through the official Salon.

22 Even Margaret Seibert, who wrote her doctoral thesis on Victorine Meurent, states in *A biography of Victorine-Louise Meurent and her role in the art of Edouard Manet*, Ohio State University 1986: 238–239: "The precise dates of this journey, her destination, and in whose company she travelled are not known. Nevertheless, it has never been doubted that she made the journey, for she herself once mentioned it in a letter." The letter that Margaret Seibert references is reproduced in Van Kempen & Van de Beek: 299–300.

23 Paul Durand-Ruel, *Memoirs of the First Impressionist Art Dealer (1831-1922)*, Flammarion, 2014: 260. *La Femme au perroquet* and *L'Enfant à l'épée* were both shown at the Metropolitan Museum of Art in 1889.

24 *Le Chemin de fer* or *La Gare Saint-Lazare* was painted in 1873 and can now be seen in the Museum of Fine Arts, Boston. The painting owes its alternative title, *La Gare Saint-Lazare*, to Paul Durand-Ruel, art dealer to the Impressionists, who gave it a more 'Parisian-sounding' name to help it sell in the United States.

25 Eric Hazan, *L'invention de Paris*, Seuil, 2002: 440.

26 King: 406.

27 The Pont de l'Europe was part of Georges-Eugène Haussmann's redevelopment of the area around the Gare Saint-Lazare. It was constructed between 1865 and 1868.

28 Julie Malaure, 'Le Chemin de Fer, une réflexion sur la peinture signée Manet', *Le Point*, 25 January 2013.

29 Pierre Assouline, *Grâces lui soient rendues – Paul Durand-Ruel, le marchand des impressionnistes*, Gallimard, 2002: 182.

30 Manet dossier, Musée d'Orsay: www.musee-orsay.fr/fr/collections/dossier-manet/chronologie.html.

31 *Palm Sunday* was only 'discovered' in 2004 and can be seen today in the Musée municipal de l'art et d'histoire in Colombes.

32 Self-portrait by Victorine Meurent from the catalogue of the Galerie Edouard Ambroselli catalogue, Rue Drouot, Paris.

33 *Le Sphinx de Paris* can be seen today in the San Diego Museum of Art.

34 Main, see 15. After her participation in 1876, Victorine Meurent exhibited at the Salon de Paris in 1879, 1885 and 1904.

35 *Le Chemin de fer*, wikipedia.org: "*Il s'agit du dernier portrait du modèle fétiche [sic] de l'artiste, Victorine Meurent, sans doute réalisé en hommage à leur longue relation artistique et amoureuse.*"

36 Van Kempen & Van de Beek: 280. "*Paul Jules Tillaux: Franse arts en chirurg in Parijs. In 1879 werd hij lid van de Académie de médecine. Van 1868 tot 1890 was hij directeur van het Amphithéatre d'Anatomie des Hôpitaux de Paris.*" [Paul Jules Tillaux: French physician and surgeon in Paris. He became a member of the Académie de médecine in 1879. From 1868 to 1890, he directed the Amphithéatre d'Anatomie des Hôpitaux de Paris].

4. RIGHTEOUS CRIMES I

1 *Les Plaisirs et les Jours* by Marcel Proust is a collection of prose poems and novellas. Published in 1896 by Calmann-Lévy, it was Proust's debut book.

2 mirror.anarhija.net/tabularasa.anarhija.net/mirror/l/lp/le-probleme-du-vol-clement-duval-fr.html.

3 After the French defeat in the Franco-Prussian War [1870-1871], Thiers was appointed head of the new conservative government.

4 Jean Baronnet, Johan Pas & Xavier Canonne, *Le Temps des cerises*, Pandora Publishers; Éditions de l'Amateur; Musée de la Photographie de Charleroi, 2011: 21.

5 André Salmon, *La Terreur noire*, vol. 1, Paris: Union Générale d'Éditions, 1959: 292.

6 The Hôtel de Ville, the Palais des Tuileries, the Palais d'Orsay (containing the Court of Audit and the Council of State or Ministry of Finance), the Château de Meudon, the home of Adolphe Thiers, captain of the *Versaillais*, residences on the Rue Royale and the Rue de Rivoli, and others.

7 Barbara Tuchman, *De trotse toren – Europa en de Verenigde Staten aan de vooravond van de Eerste Wereldoorlog*, Agon, 1987: 89.

8 Salmon 1: 10.

9 Salmon 1: 11.

10 Emile Verhaeren regularly wrote poems for the Parisian anarchist magazines *Les Temps Nouveaux* and *L'Almanach du Père Peinard*.

11 Tuchman: 97–98.

12 *L'Etendard révolutionnaire* of 15 October 1882, Gallica.bnf.fr: 4.

13 Luc Sante, *Parijs, stad van het volk*, Uitgeverij Polis, 2016: 293.

Endnotes

14 Clément Duval, *Je suis l'ennemi de la propriété individuelle. Déclaration de Clément Duval aux assises, le 11 janvier 1887*: infokiosques.net.

15 Salmon 1: 108.

16 *Eustache* – Parisian argot for dagger, knife.

17 Duval: 14.

18 maitron.fr/spip.php?article153910.

19 Duval: 14.

20 lareto.free.fr/PDF/alphabet/Duval.pdf.

21 Anarchiv.wordpress.com/2017/10/24/les-anarchistes-et-la-condamnation-de-clement-duval/.

22 Louise Michel, born on 29 May 1830 in Vroncourt-la-Côte, in Haute-Marne, died on 9 January 1905 in Marseille. Michel was a teacher, militant anarchist, freemason and feminist. She led one of the 'vigilance committees' in the Franco-Prussian War and joined the barricades during the Paris Commune that followed the conflict. Although known as 'the Red Virgin', Louise Michel was a staunch anarchist who waved the black flag and, even after her return from exile, remained committed to the cause.

23 Idem 21.

24 Salmon 1: 122.

25 Sante: 296.

26 Salmon 1: 51.

27 Michel Labori & Jean-Marc Tetier, *Le féodalisme industriel – Patronat textile et révolte ouvrière du 1er mai 1891 à Fourmies*, SIDES, 1995: 28.

28 André Pierrard & Jean-Louis Chappat, *La fusillade de Fourmies: premier mai 1891*, Miroirs, 1991: 114.

29 Salmon 1: 153.

30 The illustration was made from photographs by M. de Perron, as *Le Petit Parisien* mentions at the bottom of the page.

31 Anatole Deibler, *Carnets d'exécutions 1885–1939*, consulted via: collections-aristophil.com. The notebooks were sold through this antiquarian bookshop for 20,800 euros. They are detailed in the book by Gérard A. Jaeger, *Anatole Deibler – L'Homme qui trancha 400 têtes*, Paris: Éditions du Félin, 2001.

32 Salmon 1: 292.

33 *Le Petit Parisien*, 10 December 1893. The Assemblée Nationale is housed in the Palais Bourbon.

34 Tuchman: 122 & Sante: 300.

35 Tuchman: 124 & Sante: 300–301.

36 www.interieur.gouv.fr/Actualites/Dossiers/Grandes-et-petites-histoires-du-patrimoineprefectoral/24-juin-1894-L-assassinat-du-president-Sadi-Carnot-a-Lyon.

37 Sante: 295.

5. RIGHTEOUS CRIMES II

1 Frédéric Lavignette, *La Bande à Bonnot à travers la presse de l'époque*, Éditions Fage, 2008: 18. *Excelsior* of 29 November 1911.

2 Lavignette: table of newspaper titles and their print runs taken from Claude Bellanger, *Histoire générale de la presse française* and Christophe Charle, *Le siècle de la presse*: 12.

3 Lavignette: 18. *Le Petit Parisien* of 29 November 1911.

4 Also in this book, see the chapter: *Righteous Crimes I*.

5 After the assassination of the French president, Sadi Carnot, in Lyon in 1894, strict laws were passed that banned membership or sympathy for anarchist organisations or publications. The anarchists themselves referred to them as '*les lois scélérates*', or the 'villainous laws'.

6 Lavignette: table of newspaper titles and their print runs taken from Claude Bellanger, *Histoire générale de la presse française* and Christophe Charle, *Le siècle de la presse*: 12.

7 Lavignette: *Excelsior* of 8 April 1912: 257.

8 Three versions exist on this point: the press version is that Bonnot shot his comrade Platano dead in an argument over the division of the spoils from a prior job. Bonnot's own version was that he and Platano were inspecting the gun, which went off unexpectedly. Platano was shot in the head and Bonnot fired the second shot, finishing Platano off as a watchman was approaching. Rirette Maîtrejean's version, as she later testified in *Le Matin* of 24 August 1913, may be the correct account: Platano was simply murdered by Bonnot. The Italian had just inherited 27,000 francs from his parents, a small fortune. Twenty-seven 1,000-franc notes were later recovered from one of Bonnot's mistresses in Lyon.

9 Lavignette: *Le Petit Parisien* of 22 December 1911: 67.

10 André Salmon, *La Terreur noire*, vol. 2, Paris: Union Général d'Éditions, 1959: 213.

11 Salmon: 216.

12 Lavignette: *L'Anarchie* of 22 February 1912: 124.

13 Also in this book, see the chapter: *Righteous Crimes I*.

14 Lavignette: table of newspaper titles and their print runs taken from Claude Bellanger, *Histoire générale de la presse française* and Christophe Charle, *Le siècle de la presse*: 12.

15 Lavignette: *Excelsior* of 16 November 1910: 15.

16 Idem 6.

17 Lavignette: *Le Petit Parisien* of 10 January 1912: 106.

18 Salmon: 230.

19 Guillaume Bernard, 'La Bande à Bonnot: entre crimes crapuleux et idéologie anarchiste', *Revue française de criminologie et de droit pénal*, vol 5, October 2015, www.rfcdp.fr/numeros/numero-5-octobre-2015#ancre1.

20 A *planque* is a hiding place, a hideout.

21 Lavignette: *Le Matin* of 25 April 1912: 280.

22 Lavignette: 372.

23 Salmon: 243.

24 Also in this book, see the chapter: *Righteous Crimes I.*

25 Lavignette: *Le Petit Parisien* of 29 April 1912: 339.

26 Lavignette: 350–351.

27 The handwritten message literally says: "*Madame Thollon est innocente. Gauzy aussi. Dieudonné aussi, Petit Demange aussi. Mr Thollon aussi*", signed: Jules Bonnot.

28 Luc Sante, *Parijs, stad van het volk*, Uitgeverij Polis, 2016: 306.

29 Lavignette: *Le Journal* of 16 May 1912.

30 Lavignette: *Le Temps* of 16 May 1912.

31 Lavignette: *Le Journal* of 16 May 1912.

32 Salmon: 242.

33 Lavignette: *L'Action Française*, 22 April 1913.

34 Gérard A. Jaeger, *Carnets d'Exécutions d'Anatole Deibler 1885–1939*, l'Archipel, 2004: 104.

35 Lavignette: 412.

36 Lavignette: *Excelsior* of 13 May 1913.

37 Idem 19.

38 Brothers Xavier and Paul Guichard both worked for the police. Xavier as *chef de la Sûreté de Paris* and Paul as *chef de la police municipale*. They were in charge during Bonnot's siege in Choisy-le-Roi.

39 Jean Maitron & Anne Steiner cite *L'Anarchie*, 9 May 1913: maitron.fr/spip.php?article153821.

40 The hotel was then called the Hôtel du Châlet and was located at number 11 in the Cité Lemercier. Jacques Brel rented a room from 11 August 1958 until his departure for the Marquesas but did not live at the hotel permanently. Today, the Cité Lemercier is an oasis of peace and greenery, paved with time-honoured *pavés*. It has been closed to the public for many years.

8 Hazan: 385.

9 Hazan: 386.

10 Nicolas d'Estienne d'Orves, *Dictionnaire Amoureux de Paris*, Plon, 2015: 240.

11 Joris Verbeurgt, *Weldra zal ik onder de guillotine liggen – Grace Elliott: ooggetuige van de Franse Revolutie*, Uitgeverij Vrijdag, 2019: 243.

12 Jonathan Moore, *Hung, Drawn, and Quartered: the story of execution through the ages*, Quid & New Burlington, 2019.

13 Sylvie Yvert, *Mousseline la Sérieuse – J'étais la fille de Marie-Antoinette*, Éditions Héloïse d'Ormesson, 2016: 200.

14 Philip Freriks, *De Meridiaan van Parijs*, Uitgeverij Conserve, 2003: 49.

15 Idem 6.

16 Jaeger: 65.

17 Also in this book, see the chapter: *Righteous Crimes I.*

18 Jaeger: 25.

19 Jaeger: 27.

20 Jaeger: 268.

21 Jaeger: 85.

22 Jaeger: 223.

23 Jaeger: 110.

24 Jaeger: 223.

25 Also in this book, see the chapter: *Righteous Crimes II.*

26 Jaeger: 113.

27 De Saint-Agnès: 73.

28 Estienne d'Orves: 241.

29 Jaeger: 286.

30 François Foucart, *Dernier mots – Les condamnés face au guillotine et au peloton*, Via Romana, 2018, in 'Zoom avec Elise Blaise', TVL, 29 October 2018.

6. GENTLEMEN OF PARIS

1 Stefan Zweig, *Marie Antoinette*, Uitgeverij IJzer Utrecht, 2019: 422.

2 Yves de Saint-Agnès, *Guide du Paris Révolutionnaire*, Perrin, 1989: 41.

3 Simon Schama, *Citizens: A Chronicle of the French Revolution*, Random House, 1989.

4 *La Terreur* (1793-1794), or the Reign of Terror, is the period of the French Revolution when Robespierre led the *Comité de salut public*. During the Reign of Terror, an estimated 35,000-40,000 people were executed, civic liberties curtailed, and freedom of speech abolished. The Reign of Terror ultimately drowned in its own blood with the beheading of Robespierre on 28 July 1794 at today's Place de la Concorde.

5 De Saint-Agnès: 100.

6 Gérard A. Jaeger, *Carnets d'Exécutions d'Anatole Deibler 1885–1939*, l'Archipel, 2004: 16.

7 Eric Hazan, *Une histoire de la Révolution française*, La Fabrique éditions, 2012: 338.

Endnotes

BIBLIOGRAPHY

Ageorges S., *Sur les traces des Expositions universelles, Paris 1855-1937*, Parigramme, 2006

Aïssaouï M., *L'étoile jaune et le croissant*, Gallimard, 2012

Almasy P., *Paris*, Prestel, 2001

Anceau E., *Ils ont fait et défait le Second Empire*, Tallandier, 2019

Anderson P., *Lineages of the Absolutist State*, Verso, 1974

Assouline P., *Grâces lui soient rendues – Paul Durand-Ruel, le marchand des impressionnistes*, Gallimard Collection Folio, 2002

Assouline P., *L'homme de l'art – D.-H. Kahnweiler 1884-1979*, Gallimard, 1988

Assouline P., *Le dernier des Camondo*, Gallimard, 1999

Assouline P., *Le portrait*, Gallimard, 2007

Attali J., *C'était François Mitterrand*, Fayard, 2005

Attali J., *De joden, de wereld en het geld*,

Averbode/Ten Have, 2003

Baird J., *Victoria, koningin*, Nieuw Amsterdam, 2017

Barnes J., *The Man in the Red Coat*, Jonathan Cape, 2019

Barr Chidsey D., *The Panama Canal*, Wildside Press, 2016

Bayard H., *Mémoire sur la topographie médicale du IVe arrondissement de Paris, recherches historiques et statistiques sur les conditions hygiéniques des quartiers qui composent cet arrondissement – Extrait des 'Annales d'hygiène publique et de médecine légale'*, vol. XXVIII, Part 1, Paris, J.-B. Baillière, 1842

Beaurepaire P. Y., *La France des Lumières 1715-1789*, Berlin, 2001

Becquet H., *Marie Thérèse de France – L'orpheline du Temple*, Perrin, 2012

Benjamin W., *Kleine filosofie van het flaneren*, Uitgeverij SUA Amsterdam, 1992

Berten C., *Femmes sous l'occupation*, Stock, 1993

Boespflug B. & Billon B., *Paris fait son cinéma*, Éditions du Chêne, 2014

Bonal G., *Des Américaines à Paris, 1850-1920*, Tallandier, 2019

Bonnet M. J., *Violette Morris – Histoire d'une scandaleuse*, Perrin, 2011

Borrus K., *One Thousand Buildings of Paris*, Black Dog & Leventhal Publishers, 2003

Bos D., *Bloed en Barrikaden*, Wereldbibliotheek, 2014

Bousquel F., *Paris 17e arrondissement 1900-1940*, Parigramme, 2015

Bouvet V. & Durozoi G., *Paris Between the Wars*, Thames & Hudson, 2012

Brassaï, *Le Paris secret des années 1930*, Gallimard, 1976.

Brassaï, *The Secret Paris of the '30s*, Thames & Hudson, 2001

Brassaï, *Marcel Proust sous l'emprise de la photographie*, Gallimard, 1997

Braude M., *De onzichtbare keizer, Napoleon op Elba*, Uitgeverij Balans, 2019

Breker A., *Paris, Hitler et moi*, Presses de la Cité, 1970

Briais B., *Au temps des frou-frou: les femmes célèbres de la Belle-Epoque*, France-Empire, 1985

Broussard P. & Pontaut J. M., *Les grandes affaires de la Ve République – Scandales, écoutes, malversations*, L'Express Poche, 2012

Brown D., *The Da Vinci Code*, Doubleday, 2003

Buat N., *John Law – La dette ou comment s'en débarrasser*, Les Belles Lettres, 2015

Buchan J., *John Law – A Scottish Adventurer of the Eighteenth Century*, MacLehose, 2018

Buisson S. & Fresia M., *La Ruche – Cité des artistes*, Éditions Alternatives, 2009

Burke P., *Popular Culture in Early Modern Europe*, Temple Smith London, 1978

Chambon J., *Geschiedenis van een martelaarskerk – Het protestantisme in Frankrijk tot aan de revolutie*, Oosterbaan en Le Cointre, 1951 / Stichting de Gihonbron, 2004

Chang J. & Halliday J., *Mao – Het onbekende verhaal*, Forum-Amsterdam, 2005

Chantin J.P., *Le Jansénisme*, Éditions du Cerf, 1996

Chaudun N., *Haussmann au crible*, Éditions des Syrtes, 2000

Bibliography

Chemetov P. & Marrey B., *Architectures, Paris 1848-1914*, exhib. cat., Secretaire d'État à La Culture/La Caisse Nationale Des Monuments Historiques, Paris, 1976

Clay C., *Three Royal Cousins Who Led the World to War*, Walker Books, 2007

Cointet J.P., *Paris 40-44*, Perrin, 2001

Cooper D., *Henri de Toulouse-Lautrec*, Nouvelles Éditions Françaises, 1957

Coquart E., *Marthe Richard – De la petite à la grande vertu*, Payot, 2006

Cueni C., *Het Grote Spel*, Querido/Knack, 2009

d'Estienne d'Orves N., *Dictionnaire Amoureux de Paris*, Plon, 2015

d'Estienne d'Orves N., *Marthe Richard ou les beaux mensonges*, Calman Levy, 2018

d'Irisson Hérisson M., *Journal d'un officier d'ordonnance*, 1885, republished by Collection XIX, 2016

de Gouvion Saint-Cyr A., *Brassaï – Pour l'amour de Paris*, Flammarion, 2013

de Mérode C., *Le Ballet de ma vie*, Pierre Horay, 1955

de Rosnay T., *Elle s'appelait Sarah*, Éditions Héloïse d'Ormesson, 2006

De Royer, S., *Le dernier secret*, Grasset, 2011

de Saint-Agnès Y., *Guide du Paris révolutionnaire, 1789-1795*, Paris Musées / Perrin, 1989

De Schaepdrijver S., *De Groote Oorlog*, Olympus, ed. 2002

de Taillac M.C., *La Comtesse de Palmyre*, Belfond, 1999
Decaux A., *C'était le XX siècle, III: La guerre absolue (1940-1945)*, Perrin, 1998

Delorme J.C. & Dubois A.M., *Passages couverts Parisiens*, Parigramme, 1996

Demurger A., *The Persecution of the Templars*, Profile Books, 2020

Deutsch L., *Métronome, l'Histoire de la France au ritme du métro parisien*, Essai (Poche), 2014

Deutsch L., *Métronome 2, Paris intime au fil des rues*, Michel Lafon, 2016

Doornaert M., *Ontredderde Republiek – Zoektocht naar de ziel van Frankrijk*, Polis, 2017

Dreyfus J.M., *Le catalogue Goering*, Flammarion, 2015

Durand-Ruel P.L. & Durand-Ruel F., *Paul Durand-Ruel – Memoirs of the First Impressionist Art Dealer* (1831-1922), Flammarion, 2014

Elder M., *A Giverny chez Claude Monet*, Paris Bernheim-Jeune, 1924

Faux E., Legrand T. & Perez G., *La Main droite de Dieu – Enquête sur François Mitterrand et l'extrême droite*, Seuil, 1994

Ferguson N., *The Ascent of Money, a Financial History of the World*, Penguin Books, 2009

Figes O., *The Europeans – Three Lives and the Making of a Cosmopolitan Culture*, Metropolitan Books, 2019

Finger B. & Karel W., *Opération 'Vent printanier' – 16-17 juillet 1942, La rafle du Vel'd'Hiv*, Éditions La Découverte, 1992

Finnerman D., *Mademoiselle Victorine*, Three Rivers Press, 2007

Foucart F., *Derniers mots – Les condamnés face au guillotine et au peloton*, Via Romana, 2018

Frerejean A. & L'Hoër C., *Le Siège et la Commune de Paris – Acteurs et témoins racontent*, l'Archipel, 2020

Freriks P., *De meridiaan van Parijs*, Conserve, 2003

Fréville J., *Lénine à Paris*, Éditions Sociales, 1968

Gallo M., *Henri IV – Un roi français*, XO-Éditions Paris, 2016

Garrigues J. (ed.), *La république des traitres de 1958 à nos jour*s, Tallandier, 2018

Gautrand J.C., *Eugène Atget, Paris*, Taschen - Bibliotheca Universalis, 2016

Gauvard C. (ed.), *Présumées coupables – Les grands procès faits aux femmes*, L'Iconoclaste et les Archives Nationales, 2016

Giesbert F.O., *François Mitterrand, une vie*, Éditions du Seuil, 1977

Giesbert F.O., *Histoire intime de la Ve République, Le Sursaut*, Gallimard, 2021

Giesbert F.O., *Histoire intime de la Ve République, La Belle Epoque*, Gallimard, 2022

Glass C., *Americans in Paris – Life and Death under Nazi Occupation 1940-1944*, Harper Press, 2009

Gregory A., *Place Vendôme*, Assouline, 2004

Grenier R., *Brassaï – Correspondance 1950-1983*, Gallimard, 2017

Guérin A., *Chronique de la Résistance*, Place des éditeurs, 2010

Haag M. & Haag V., *The Rough Guide to The Da Vinci Code*, Penguin Books, 2004

Hackett F., *François Ier*, Payot, 1984

Hazan E., *A History of the Barricade*, Verso, 2015

Hazan E., *A Walk Through Paris – A Radical Exploration*, Verso, 2018

Hazan E., *L'invention de Paris*, Seuil, 2002

Hazan E., *Le tumulte de Paris*, La fabrique éditions, 2021

Hazan E., *Une histoire de la Révolution française*, La fabrique éditions, 2012

Hennig J.L., *Espadons, Mignons et autres monstres – Vocabulaire de l'homosexualité masculine sous l'Ancien Régime*, Éditions Cherche Midi, 2015

Higgs D., *Queer Sites – Gay Urban Histories Since 1600*, Routledge, 1999

Hillairet J., *Connaissance du Vieux Paris*, Payot & Rivages, 1993

Hoondert K., *El pintor politico – Een onderzoek naar het politieke leven van Pablo Picasso*, master's degree thesis in political and cultural history, Utrecht University, 2011

Houbre G., *Le livre des courtisanes – Archives secrètes de la police des mœurs*, Tallandier, 2007

Hussey A., *Paris, The Secret History*, Viking, 2006

Jackson J., *A Certain Idea of France – The Life of Charles de Gaulle*, Allen Lane, 2018

Jaeger G.A., *Anatole Deibler – L'Homme qui trancha 400 têtes*, Éditions du Félin, 2001

Jaeger G.A., *Carnets d'Exécutions d'Anatole Deibler 1885-1939*, l'Archipel, 2004

Jamet F., *One Two Two: 122 rue de Provence, Paris*, Olivier Orban, 1975

Japin A., *Mrs Degas*, De Arbeiderspers, 2020

Jeanneney J.N., *Le duel: une passion française 1789-1914*, Seuil, 2004

Johnson J. & Miller F., *The Man Who Sold the Eiffel Tower*, Doubleday & Company Inc, 1961

Jones D., *De Tempeliers – De opkomst en ondergang van de tempelridders*, Omniboek, 2019

Kahnweiler D.H., *Les sculptures de Picasso – Photographies de Brassaï*, Éditions du Chêne, 1949

Kalifa D., *Paris – Une histoire érotique, d'Offenbach aux Sixties*, Payot, 2018

Kamen H., *Alva – Een biografie*, Houtekiet, 2005

Karnow S., *Paris in the Fifties*, Times Books/Random House, 1997

Kershaw A., *Avenue of Spies*, Crown Publishers New York, 2015

King R., *The Judgment of Paris: The Revolutionary Decade That Gave the World Impressionism*, Bloomsbury, 2006

King R., *Waanzin en betovering – Claude Monet en de waterlelies*, De Bezige Bij, 2017

Koch K., *Een kleine geschiedenis van de Grote Oorlog 1914-1918*, Ambo/Manteau, 2010

Labori M. & Tetier J.M., *Le féodalisme industriel – Patronat textile et révolte ouvrière du 1er mai 1891 à Fourmies*, SIDES, 1995

Lacout D. & Lançon C., *La mise à mort de Jean-Edern Hallier*, Presses de la Renaissance, 2006

Lacouture J., *Mitterrand, une histoire de Français – Les risques de l'escalade*, Seuil, 2006

Lacouture J., *Mitterrand, une histoire de Français – Les vertiges du sommet*, Seuil, 2012

Lacroix A., *Voyage au centre de Paris*, J'ai Lu – Flammarion, 2013

Lacroix-Riz A., *Industriels et Banquiers Français sous l'occupation*, Armand Colin, 2013

Lanzmann C., *De Patagonische haas, Mémoires – Het bewogen leven van de maker van Shoah*, De Arbeiderspers, 2011

Laurence-Maire C., *Les convulsionnaires de St-Médard: miracles, convulsions et prophéties à Paris aux XVIIIe siècle*, Gallimard 1985

Lavignette F., *La Bande à Bonnot à travers la presse de l'époque*, Éditions Fage, 2008

Law J., *Money and Trade Considered: With a Proposal for Supplying the Nation with Money*, A. Foulis, 1705

Bibliography

Lemestre M., *Madame Sphinx vous parle*, Eurédif, 1974

Lemonier M. & Dupouy A., *Histoire(s) du Paris libertin*, la Musardine, 2003

Lévy C. & Tillard P., *La grande rafle du Vél d'Hiv*, Robert Laffont, 1967

Mak G., *In Europe – Travels through the Twentieth Century*, Harvill Secker, 2007

Mazzeo T.J., *The Secret of Chanel N° 5*, Harper Perrennial, 2010

McCullough D., *The Greater Journey – Americans in Paris*, Simon & Schuster, 2011

McGann B. & McGann C., *The Story of the Tour De France: 1903-1964*, Dog Ear Publishing, 2006

Merki C., *L'Amiral de Coligny – La maison de Chatillon et la révolte protestante 1529-1572*, Plon, 1909

Michel L., *La Commune*, Stock+Plus, 1978 (originally published in 1898)

Mila C., *Picasso-Staline et l'esthétique communiste*, thèse soutenue le 4 septembre 2017 Université Paris III

Miller A., *Puur*, Xander Uitgevers, 2012
Milza P., *L'Année terrible – La guerre franco-prussienne, septembre 1870 – mars 1871*, Perrin, 2009

Milza P., *Napoléon III*, Perrin, 2004

Miquel P., *La guerre d'Algérie*, Fayard, 1993

Mitterrand F., *Lettres à Anne*, 1962-1995, nrf Gallimard, 2016

Montreynaud F., *L'aventure des femmes: XX et XXI siècle*, Nathan, 2006

Moore J., *Hung, Drawn, and Quartered: The Story of Execution Through the Ages*, Quid & New Burlington, 2019

Muracciole J.F., *La Libération de Paris*, Tallendier, 2013

Nay C., *Le Noir et le Rouge, ou l'histoire d'une ambition*, Grasset, 1984

Noguères H., *La Saint-Barthélemy, 24 août 1572*, Robert Laffont, 1959

Onfray M., *Vies parallèles – De Gaulle-Mitterrand*, Robert Laffont, 2020

Op de Beeck J., *De Zonnekoning – Glorie & schaduw van Lodewijk XIV*, Horizon, 2018

Op de Beeck J., *Het hart van Napoleon*, Horizon, 2016

Op de Beeck J., *Napoleon, deel 1 – Van strateeg tot keizer*, Manteau, 2014

Op de Beeck J., *Napoleon, deel 2 – Van keizer tot mythe*, Manteau, 2014

Op de Beeck J., *Napoleons nachtmerrie – 1812: hoe de keizer en zijn soldaten ten onder gingen in Rusland*, Epo, 2012

Op de Beeck J., *Waterloo – De laatste 100 dagen van Napoleon*, Manteau, 2013

Ouvrard L., *La prostitution – Analyse juridique et choix de politique criminelle*, Harmattan, 2000

Pascal C., *L'Eté des quatre rois*, Plon, 2018

Pascal C., *La chambre des dupes*, Plon, 2020
Pauwels J., *Het Parijs van de sansculotten – Een reis door de Franse Revolutie*, Epo, 2007

Paxton R.O., *La France de Vichy 1940-1944*, Seuil, 1973

Péan P., *Une jeunesse française – François Mitterrand 1934-1947*, Pluriel, 1994

Pierik P., *Neu Turkestan aan het front, islamistische soldaten in dienst van de waffen SS*, Aspekt, 2019

Pierrard A. & Chappat J.L., *La fusillade de Fourmies: premier mai 1891*, Miroirs, 1991

Pinçon M. & Pinçon-Charlot M., *Paris, quinze promenades sociologiques*, Payot & Rivages, 2013

Polack E. & Dagen P., *Les Carnets de Rose Valland – Le pillage des collections privées d'œuvres d'art en France pendant la Seconde Guerre mondiale*, Fage Éditions, 2019

Queneau R., *Connaissez-vous Paris?*, Gallimard, 2011

Richard M., *Ma vie d'espionne – Au service de la France*, 1935

Robb G., *De ontdekking van Frankrijk*, Atlas, 2008

Robb G., *Parisians*, Picador, 2011

Roberts A., *Napoleon De Grote*, Prometheus Bert Bakker, 2015

Rosbottom R.C., *Toen het licht uitging in Parijs – De lichtstad tijdens de Duitse bezetting 1940-1944*, Spectrum, 2015

Ruffin R., *La diablesse – La véritable histoire de Violette Morris*, Pygmalion Watelet, 1989

Ruffin R., *Violette Morris – La hyène de la Gestap*, Le Cherche Midi, 2004

Salmon A., *La terreur noire*, Union Générale d'Éditions, Paris, 1959

Sante L., *Stad van het volk – Het andere Parijs*, Polis, 2016

Schama S., *Citizens: A Chronicle of the French Revolution*, Random House, 1989.

Sebba A., *Les Parisiennes – How the Women of Paris Lived, Loved and Died in the 1940s*, Weidenfeld & Nicholson, 2016

Seibert M., *A Biography of Victorine-Louise Meurent and Her Role in the Art of Edouard Manet*, Ohio State, 1986

Short P., *Mitterrand – A Study in Ambiguity*, Bodley Head, 2013

Shovlin J., *Trading with the Enemy: Britain, France, and the 18th Century Quest for a Peaceful World Order*, Yale University Press, 2021

Sinclair A., *Rue La Boétie 21*, De Bezige Bij, 2012

Soboul A., *Histoire de la révolution française, deel 1, de la bastille à la gironde*, Gallimard, 1962

Soboul A., *Histoire de la révolution française, deel 2, de la montagne à Brumaire*, Gallimard, 1964

Steuer C., *Susini et l'OAS – Collection Histoire et perspectives méditerranéennes*, Éditions L'Harmattan, 2004

Taieb K., *Ik schrijf u vanuit het Vel d'Hiv – De teruggevonden briefjes van geïnterneerde joden in het Vélodrome d'Hiver van Parijs* – Karakter Uitgevers BV, 2011

Thoraval A., *Paris, les lieux de la Résistance*, Parigramme, 2007

Thoraval J., *Les grandes étapes de la civilisation française*, Bordas, 1972

Tichauer E., *Grâce à mes yeux bleus j'ai survécu*, Editeur Les impliqués, 2017

Tuchman B., *De kanonnen van augustus*, De Arbeiderspers, 2000

Tuchman B., *De trotse toren – Europa en de Verenigde Staten aan de vooravond van de Eerste Wereldoorlog*, Agon, 1987

Tuchman B., *The March of Folly*, Abacus, 2001

Valland R., *Le front de l'art – Défense des collections françaises 1939-1945*, revised edition of the 1961 work by the Réunion des musées nationaux, 2016

van Kempen T. & van de Beek N., *Madame Manet – Muziek en kunst in het Parijs van de Impressionisten,* Het ArchiefCollectief, 2014

Vaughan H., *Sleeping With the Enemy – Coco Chanel's Secret War,* Vintage Books – Random House, 2001

Verbeurgt J., *Weldra zal ik onder de guillotine liggen – Grace Elliott: ooggetuige van de Franse Revolutie*, Uitgeverij Vrijdag, 2019

Vidal P., *Frédéric-Auguste Bartholdi 1834-1904: par l'esprit et par la main*, Créations du Pélican, 1994

Warncke C.P. & Walther I.F., *Picasso*, Taschen, 1997

Weiss C. & Manfrin R.P., *Regards sur la peinture 2 – Picasso*, Éditions Fabbri, Paris, 1988

Wesseling H.L., *Scheffer, Renan, Psichari, een Franse cultuur- en familiegeschiedenis 1815-1914*, Prometheus, 2017

White E., *De flaneur, een wandeling door de paradoxen van Parijs*, Atlas, 2002

Wildenstein D., *Claude Monet – Biographie et catalogue raisonné*, La Bibliothèque des Arts, Lausanne and Paris, 1974-1991

Willemin V., *La Mondaine – Histoire et archives de la Police des Mœurs*, Hoëbeke, 2009

Woodham-Smith C., *Queen Victoria – Her Life and Times*, Cardinal Books, 1975

Yvert S., *Mousseline la Sérieuse – J'étais la fille de Marie-Antoinette*, Éditions Héloïse d'Ormesson, 2016

Zamoyski A., *Napoleon – De man achter de mythe*, Uitgeverij Balans, 2018

Zweig S., *Marie Antoinette*, Uitgeverij IJzer, 2019

exhib. cat., 21, *rue de la Boétie*, La Boverie Expo Liège & Tempora, based on the book 21 *rue de la Boétie* van Anne Sinclair, Éditions Grasset & Fasquelle, 2012

exhib. cat., *Manet 1832-1883*, Metropolitan Museum of Arts, 1983

exhib.cat., *Picasso et la Guerre*, Gallimard – Musée de L'Armée – Musée National Picasso-Paris, Gallimard, 2019

Bibliography

INDEX OF PEOPLE

Abbott, Berenice 138
Abetz, Otto 24, 25, 58, 60, 252
Abetz, Suzanne 58
Achard, Marcel 57
Adler, Friedrich 100
Aïssaoui, Mohammed 200
Albert I of Belgium 327
Alexander II of Russia 66
Alfonso XIII of Spain 32
Alphand, Adolphe 121
Amiot, Félix 35, 36, 37
Anderson, Margaret 139
Anderson, Sybil 96
André, Emilienne (d'Alençon) 88, 91
Antigny, Marie-Ernestine (Blanche d'Antigny) 66, 88, 89, 92
Apollinaire, Guillaume 134
Arago, François 251
Aragon, Louis 143, 246, 247, 253, 256, 257
Araùjo de Païva, Albino Francisco de 94
Arcano, Francisco 324
Arletty (Léonie Bathiat) 12, 54, 55–61
Armand, Alexander 68
Armand, Inessa 68
Assouline, Albert 198–200
Assouline, Pierre 253, 283
Astorg, Georgette 200
Attila 13, 117, 123, 125
Aussaresses, Paul 232
Babou, Hippolyte 47
Bader, Théophile 32, 33, 34, 37
Bailleul, Claude 155, 162, 165
Bailleul, Henri 155, 162, 165
Bailly, Jean Sylvain 323
Baker, Joséphine 138
Baklouti, Jean 215
Bakunin, Mikhail 295, 298, 316
Balsan, Etienne 91
Baltard, Victor 121
Barillet-Deschamps, Jean-Pierre 121
Barnacle, Nora 139
Barnaud, Jacques 164, 165
Barnes, Djuna 138
Barney, Natalie Clifford 138
Barrelet de Ricout, Charlotte Sylvie (Toquette) 204
Barry, Madame du 323
Bartholdi, Frédéric-Auguste 269–275
Bartholdi, Jeanne-Emilie 275
Bathiat, Léonie (see Arletty)
Baudelaire, Charles 47
Baudet-Dulary, Alexandre 118
Bayard, Henri 118
Beach Whitman, Sylvia 144

Beach, Sylvester 135
Beach, Sylvia 132, 133, 135, 136, 138, 139, 141, 142, 144
Beauharnais, Hortense de 42
Beauharnais, Joséphine de 42
Beauvoir, Simone de 95, 96
Beaux, Ernest 32
Bécaud, Gilbert 213
Behr, Kurt von 20, 28
Belgrand, Eugène 121, 122
Bell, Alexander Graham 273
Belmondo, Jean-Paul 91
Benjamin, Walter 124, 141
Benoist-Méchin, Jacques 143
Bérégovoy, Pierre 239
Berg, Else 22
Berger, Jean-Jacques 120
Berkani, Derri 198
Bernhardt, Sarah (Rosine) 88, 89, 96
Bernheim, Françoise 141, 143
Bernier, Augustin 298
Bichelonne, Jean 165
Bischoffsheim, Raphaël 92
Bismarck, Otto von 51, 52, 95, 183, 184–187, 190, 191, 270
Blanc, Louis 44, 47, 251
Blanke, Kurt 36
Blériot, Louis 68
Bleustein-Blanchet, Marcel 212
Blier, Bernard 61
Blondeau, Maria 299
Blücher, Gebhard Leberecht von 192
Blum, Léon 223
Boillot, André 176
Boillot, Georges 168–172, 175, 176
Boillot, Louis 176
Bonaparte, Napoleon 13, 119, 184, 185, 192
Bonaparte, Napoleon III (Louis-Napoleon) 41, 42, 43, 45, 46, 47, 119
Bonnard, Pierre 27
Bonnet, Marie-Josèphe 161–163, 166, 308
Bonnière, Suzanne 134
Bonnot, Jules 66, 305–317
Bonny, Pierre 146–152, 160
Borgeaud, Henri 228
Boumendjel, Ali 232, 233
Bouts, Dirk 27
Braque, Georges 22, 25, 27, 61
Brassaï 159, 166
Brasseur, Pierre 57
Breem, Danièle 236
Bréguet, Bruno 217
Breker, Arno 251
Brel, Jacques 108, 317

Index of people

357

Breton, André 135, 250

Briand, Aristide 94

Brinon, Fernand de 282

Brooks, Romaine 138

Bruller, Jean 211

Bugeaud, Thomas-Robert 118

Buguet, Henri 90

Bullard, Eugene 137

Bullitt, William 204

Bülow, Karl von 171, 173

Burdet, Sophie 308

Caby, Ernest 308

Cachin, Marcel 99, 223

Cahen d'Anvers, Irène 281

Cailliau, Michel 233

Caldwell, Erskine 139

Callemin, Raymond 307

Camondo, Abraham Salomon 279

Camondo, Béatrice de 281

Camondo, Isaac de 280

Camondo, Moïse de 27, 276, 278, 282, 283

Camondo, Nissim de 276–278, 281, 282

Canalejas y Méndez, José 302

Cánovas del Castillo, Antonio 302

Capel, Boy 32

Carné, Marcel 57, 58, 61

Carnot, Sadi 300–302, 324

Caron, Eugène 296

Carouy, Edouard 307, 309–312, 315

Caserio, Sante Geronimo 301, 309, 315

Cassou, Jean 143

Castelnau, Édouard de 172

Castiglione, Virginia Oldoini di 89

Castro, Fidel 214

Cavaignac, Eugène 45–47

Cavelier de La Salle, Robert 76

Cavell, Edith 251

Cézanne, Paul 21, 27, 258, 280

Chagall, Marc 22

Chambrun, Aldebert de 205

Chambrun, René de 34, 35, 60

Chamillart, Michel 78

Chanel, Gabrielle (Coco) 12, 32–37, 56, 58, 91, 165

Chassaigne, Anne-Marie (Liane de Pougy) 93

Chaudun, Nicolas 125

Chevalier, Marcel 328

Chiang Kai-shek 221

Chirac, Jacques 126, 213

Choltitz, Dietrich von 28, 246

Choron, Alexandre-Etienne 190

Christiaens, Josef 170

Citroën, André 32

Clemenceau, Georges 312

Cléo de Mérode 89, 95–97

Cleveland, Grover 274

Cocteau, Jean 33, 159

Cointet, Jean-Paul 150

Colbert, Jean-Baptiste 78

Colón, Johnny 214

Condorcet, Nicolas de 251

Considerant, Victor 118

Convert, Pascal 53

Cooper, Gary 258

Corneille, Pierre 77

Corot, Jean-Baptiste 280

Cottens, Victor de 120

Coty, René 230, 232

Coubertin, Pierre de 157

Courbet, Gustave 92, 93

Coutant-Peyre, Isabelle 210, 217

Couthon, Georges 321

Couture, Thomas 287

Cranach, Lucas 24

Curie, Pierre 256

Dannecker, Theodor 206

Danton, Georges 321

Darboy, Georges 294

Darnand, Joseph 207

Daudet, Alphonse 188

Davioud, Gabriel 121, 122

Dayan, Georges 234, 235

Dayan, Irène 234, 235

Deboos (Monsieur) 190

Debré, Michel 233, 236–238

Deferre, Gaston 239

Degas, Edgar 25, 27, 88, 280, 287

Deibler, Anatole 299, 315, 323, 32–328

Deibler, Joseph 324

Deibler, Louis 324, 325

Deibler, Marcelle 326

Delabigne, Émilie-Louise (Valtesse de la Bigne) 89, 90

Delacroix, Eugène 125, 274

Demange (Petit-Demange), Albert Joseph 307, 316

Deng Xiaoping 221, 222, 225

Depew, Chauncey M. 274, 275

Derain, André 22, 252, 254

Deschamps, Eugène 121, 122

Desessard, Jean Baptiste 278

Desessard, Louis 277, 278

Desfourneaux, Jules-Henri 326, 328

Desmoulins, Camille 321

Desnos, Robert 252

Detaille, Édouard 90

Diaghilev, Serge 33, 69

Dietrich, Marlene 33

Dieudonné, Eugène 307, 312, 314–316

Dincklage, Hans von 34, 37, 56
Djandoubi, Hamida 328
Dobrorolski, Sergei 103
Dolié, René 104
Donatini, Jean 213, 215
Dos Passos, John 136, 138
Doumer, Paul 323
Doumergue, Gaston 112
Dous, Raymond 213, 215
Drieu (*Maître*) 152
Drieu la Rochelle, Pierre 141
Drumont, Édouard 280
du Temple, Félix 273
Dubail, Auguste 172
Duboc, Paul 65
Dubois, André-Louis 252
Duc d'Uzès 91
Duclos, Jacques 228
Duclos, Maurice 207
Dufour, Marie 290
Dufy, Raoul 27
Duhamel, Georges 140, 282
Dunoyer de Segonzac, André 27
Durand-Ruel, Paul 289
Dürer, Albrecht 24
Duval, Clément 293, 296–298, 316
Edison, Thomas 273
Edward VII of the United Kingdom 91, 94, 103
Eichmann, Adolf 206
Eiffel, Gustave 48, 273
Eliot, T.S. 136
Elisabeth of Austria 302
Éluard, Paul 247, 248, 253
Engels, Friedrich 41
Ensor, James 22
Ernst, Max 26, 250
Étex, Antoine 269
Evarts, William M. 272
Falguière, Alexandre 96, 97
Fallières, Armand 327
Faulkner, William 138
Faure, Maurice 239
Faure, Sébastien 297, 301, 307
Favre, Jules 123, 191
Fénéon, Félix 295, 301
Ferroukhi, Ismaël 199
Ferry, Abel 101
Ferry, Jules 123
Flanner, Janet 138
Foch, Ferdinand 103
Fonvielle, Wilfrid de 188
Forsne, Christina 241
Forsne, Hravn 241

Forster, E.M. 139
Fougeron, André 255
Fould, Achille 47, 280
Fouquier-Tinville, Antoine Quentin 234, 320
Fourastié, Philippe 316
Francis I of France 23
Franco, Francisco 140, 248
Franklin, Benjamin 415
Franz Ferdinand of Austria-Hungary 100
French, John 174
Freund, Gisèle 140, 141
Gallieni, Joseph 171–174
Gambetta, Léon 90, 95, 187, 188, 251
Garbo, Greta 33
Garnier, Charles 50
Garnier, François 310
Garnier, Octave 307, 309, 310, 311, 312, 315
Garrigou, Gustave 65
Garros, Roland 68
Gauguin, Paul 22, 27
Gaulle, Charles de 149, 160, 165, 206, 207, 227, 230, 231, 233, 234, 236–239, 242, 246, 247
Gaulle, Geneviève de 148, 149
Gaulle, Yvonne de 242
Gautier, Théophile 95
George III of Great Britain and Ireland 266
George V of the United Kingdom 103
Ghika, Georges 93
Gide, André 135, 140, 141
Giesbert, Franz-Olivier 233
Gilot, Françoise 250
Giraud, Henri 233
Giroud, Françoise 241
Giscard d'Estaing, Valéry 212, 239, 328
Godivier, Marcel 65
Goebbels, Joseph 24, 247
Goldwyn, Sam 33
Goncourt, Edmond & Jules 95
Gorguloff, Paul 323
Göring, Hermann 20–22, 24, 25, 34, 56, 252
Goubillon, Andrée 206, 208
Gounod, Charles 271
Goux, Jules 170, 171
Gouze, Antoine 240
Gouze, Christine 240
Gouze, Danielle 227, 240
Grant, Ulysses S. 271
Grasse, François Joseph Paul de 267, 269, 274
Grave, Jean 295, 301, 307
Grenier, Roger 166
Grévy, Jules 298
Grison, Georges 90
Grossouvre, François de 239

Index of people

359

Grosvenor, Hugh 37
Guevara, Ernesto (Che) 214, 216, 237
Guichard, Paul 313
Guichard, Xavier 313, 314
Guillotin, Joseph-Ignace 320
Guimard, Hector 56
Guitry, Sacha 57, 58
Habash, Georges 214
Hadot, Jules-Hadrien 124
Halali, Berthe (Beïa) 198
Halali, Brahim 199
Halali, Simon (Salim) 198–200
Hammett, Dashiell 136
Hardouin-Mansart, Jules 52
Harting, Arkady Mikhailovich 66, 68
Hausen, Max von 171
Haussmann, Eugénie 124
Haussmann, Georges-Eugène 13, 48, 49, 116, 117–126, 279, 289
Haussmann, Henriette 118
Haussmann, Valentine 118
Havemeyer, Henry Osborne 290
Havemeyer, Horace 290
Havemeyer, Louisine 290
Hazan, Eric 321
Heap, Jane 139
Hébert, Jacques-René 321
Heller, Gerhard 252
Hémery, Henri 162
Hemingway, Ernest 136, 144
Henckel von Donnersmarck, Guido 94
Hennion, Célestin 312
Henry, Emile 300, 309, 315, 316
Henry, Ernest 170
Herbelin, Mathilde 293
Herranz, Jean 211, 213, 215
Herz, Henri 94
Himmler, Heinrich 149, 160–162, 196, 197
Hirsch, Alphonse 289
Hitler, Adolf 13, 21, 22, 24, 160, 163, 164, 166, 248, 249, 251
Ho Chi Minh (Nguyen Sinh Cung) 12, 218, 222–225, 229
Hohenzollern-Sigmaringen, Leopold von 185
Hollande, François 241
Hopner, Serafima 68
Howard, Harriet 44
Huebsch, Ben 139
Hugo, Victor 45, 46, 51, 118, 188, 251
Ingres, Jean-Auguste-Dominique 27
Isabella II of Spain 185
Ivens, Joris 156
Jackson, Sumner 202–204, 206, 207
Jacob, Alexandre Marius 298

Jacob, Max 252, 253
Jaujard, Jacques 20, 23, 28
Jaurès, Jean 99–102, 104–108
Jeanson, Henri 61
Jefferson, Thomas 268
Joffre, Joseph 102, 172–175
Jospin, Lionel 239
Jouin, Louis-François 309, 312, 313
Joyce, James 132, 139, 141
Julian, Rodolphe 288
Jünger, Ernst 252
Justin, Louis 308
Kahnweiler, Daniel-Henry 25, 249, 250, 253, 254, 258
Kamenev, Lev 70
Karsavina, Tamara 69
Kayser, Albert 251
Khokhlova, Olga 251
Klarsfeld, Beate 199
Klarsfeld, Serge 246
Klee, Paul 22, 26
Kluck, Alexander von 171, 173
Knochen, Helmut 150, 151, 160, 162, 195, 196
Koestler, Arthur 141
Kokoschka, Oskar 22
Kootz, Samuel 254
Kopp, Magdalena 217
Kosciusko-Morizet, Jacques 234
Kosciusko-Morizet, Nathalie 71
Kropotkin, Peter 295, 298
Krupskaya, Nadezhda 64, 67, 68, 70, 71
Kümmel, Otto 24
La Fontaine, Jean de 251
Laboulaye, Édouard René 268–271
Labrouste, Henri 70
Lachmann, Esther (La Païva) 94
Lacouture, Jean 233
Lacroix-Riz, Annie 163, 164
Lafargue, Paul 67
Lafayette, Gilbert du Motier de 34, 136, 267, 269, 274, 309
Lafont, Henri 146–152, 160
Lafourcade, François 65
Lagerfeld, Karl 37
Laharpe, Octavie de 124
Lamarque, Jean Maximilien 118
Lamartine, Alphonse de 44, 45, 46, 389
Landrieu, Philippe 104
Landru, Henri Désiré 326
Lang, Georges 164
Langevin, Paul 256
Langle de Cary, Fernand de 172
Lanrezac, Charles 172
Larbaud, Valéry 140

Latouche-Tréville, Louis-René-Madeleine de 267

Laurencin, Marie 27

Lautenschlager, Christian 169, 171

Laval, Josée 35, 56, 60, 205

Laval, Pierre 35, 56, 160, 205

Law of Lauriston, Jane 74

Law of Lauriston, John 73–80

Law of Lauriston, William 74

Lawrence, D.H. 138

Lazarus, Emma 275

Le Bas, Philippe 321

Le Fort, Léon 122

Le Pen, Jean-Marie 237

Lear, Fanny 89

Leblanc, Robert 161, 163

Lebreton, Marco 67

Leclerc, Philippe 28, 36, 144, 246

Ledru-Rollin, Alexandre 46, 47

Leenhoff, Suzanne 286

Léger, Fernand 25, 26, 250

Lehideux, François 164, 165

Leiris, Louise 25, 249

Lemaire, Madeleine 293, 296

Lenglen, Suzanne 157

Lenin, Vladimir 12, 62–71, 214, 256, 257

Leopold II of Belgium 91, 94, 96, 97

Lépine, Louis 311, 313, 314

Lesseps, Ferdinand de 51, 274, 275

Lesseps, Tototte de 275

Li Shizeng 219, 220

Libertad, Albert 306, 307, 309

Lifar, Serge 34

Lissagaray, Hyppolyte 223

Longworth de Chambrun, Clara 144

Lonsdale, Michael 199

Loridan, Marceline 156

Losada, Alberto 71

Louis Philippe of Orléans 42–44

Louis XIII of France 77, 148

Louis XIV of France 75–77, 148, 266

Louis XV of France 75, 266, 323

Louis XVI of France 267, 320–322

Louis XVIII of France 42

Lubomirski, Aleksander Ignacy 90

Lustig, Victor 110, 112–115

Luxemburg, Rosa 100, 217

Maar, Dora 250

MacMahon, Patrice de 271

Macron, Emmanuel 53

Maillol, Aristide 254

Maîtrejean, Rirette 309, 315

Malesherbes, Chrétien-Guillaume de Lamoignon de 323

Mamy, Jean 59

Man Ray 141

Mandel, Georges 58

Manet, Édouard 91, 255, 280, 285, 286, 287, 288, 289, 290

Mangin, Charles 14, 251

Mansfield, Katherine 138

Mao Zedong 221, 224

Marais, Jean 159

Margerin (Abbot) 298

Marie Antoinette (Archduchess Maria Antonia of Austria) 319–321, 323

Marie Louise of Austria 42

Marino, Edgar 215

Martel, Thierry de 204

Marville, Charles 121, 122

Marx, Karl 41, 220, 221

Marx, Laura 67

Marx, Pierre 148

Masson, André 250

Massu, Jacques 229, 232

Matisse, Henri 22, 138, 252

Maupas, Emile de 47

Mauriac, François 143

Maurin, Charles 300

Maurois, André (Herzog, Émile Salomon Wilhelm) 140

Mazarin (Cardinal) 107, 308, 309, 313

McKinley, William 302

Meinhof, Ulrike 214

Mendès France, Pierre 228, 233, 236

Metge, Marius 307, 312, 315

Meunier, Théodule 300

Meurent, Victorine 284–290

Michel, Louise 297

Michelangelo 23, 27

Milhaud, Darius 33

Miller, Henry 141

Miller, Robert V. 114

Millerand, Alexandre 171, 172

Miquel, Roger 231

Mirabeau 186

Mirbeau, Octave 295

Miró, Joan 26

Mitchell, Louis 137

Mitterrand, Danielle (see Gouze, Danielle)

Mitterrand, François 71, 226–228, 232–242, 328

Mitterrand, Gilbert 240

Mitterrand, Jean-Christophe 240

Mitterrand, Pascal 240

Moch, Jules 228

Modigliani, Amedeo 22, 27

Mollet, Guy 239, 240

Moltke, Helmuth (Johannes Ludwig) von 102, 172–174

Moltke, Helmuth (Karl Bernhard) von 184

Monet, Claude 27, 250, 280

Index of people

361

Monier, Etienne 307, 312, 315
Monnier, Adrienne 132–134, 144
Monnier, Philiberte 134
Montesquieu 221
Moreno, Daniël 71
Morgan, Claude 143
Morizet, André 71
Morny, Charles de 47, 49, 51, 88, 89
Morris, Jacques 156, 157
Morris, Louise Marie 156
Morris, Paul 156
Morris, Violette 154–163, 165, 166
Moukharbal, Michel 212, 213, 215, 216
Murat, Joachim Joseph Napoléon 89
Mussolini, Benito 248
Nadar 96
Navarre, Jean 176
Nicholas II of Russia 94, 96, 101, 102
Nijinska, Bronislava 33
Nijinsky, Vaslav 69
Noailles, Adrien Maurice de 75
Oberg, Karl 160, 162
Obrecht, André 328
Offenbach, Jacques 90, 123, 184
Ollivier, Emile 124
Orbison, Eleanor 135
Orsini, Felice 50
Otero, Agustina Caroline (La Belle Otero) 88, 89, 93, 94, 96
Oudinot, Nicolas Charles 89
Oudot, Roland 254
Owen, Robert 44
Palomares, Leyma 214
Pasteur, Louis 51
Paulhan, Jean 140, 143, 252
Pauwels, Désiré Joseph 300
Pelat, Roger-Patrice 240
Pelletier, Nicolas Jacques 320
Pequignot, André 237
Pereire, Emile 51, 123
Pereire, Isaac 51, 123
Perier, Casimir-Pierre 118
Persigny, Victor de 43, 45, 47–49, 89, 120
Pesquet, Robert 237, 238
Pétain, Philippe 160, 175, 207, 233, 240
Pflimlin, Pierre 228, 229
Philippe I, Duke of Orléans 75, 77, 78, 266
Pianori, Giovanni 50
Picard, Ernest 123
Picasso, Claude 258
Picasso, Pablo 12, 22, 25–28, 33, 138, 140, 245–258
Picasso, Paloma 258
Pingeot, Anne 227, 239, 241, 242

Pingeot, Mazarine 241
Pissarro, Camille 21, 295
Poincaré, Raymond 101, 103, 171, 312, 313
Poisson, André 113, 114
Pol Pot (Saloth Sar) 224, 225
Pompidou, Georges 121
Poncet, Antonin 301
Poniatowski, Józef Michał 89
Poniatowski, Michel 213
Pontchartrain, Louis Phélypeaux de 78, 95
Pouget, Emile 301
Pound, Ezra 136
Prévert, Jacques 57, 61, 135
Proudhon, Pierre-Joseph 46, 295, 297, 316
Proust, Marcel 293
Pulitzer, Joseph 272, 273, 275
Queneau, Raymond 13, 273
Rambuteau, Claude-Philibert Barthelot de 119
Ramírez Sánchez, Ilich (Carlos) 213–216
Raspail, François-Vincent 46, 251
Rasseneux, Antoine 324
Rasseneux, Zoé-Victorine 324
Ratibor und Corvey, Ernst von 196
Ravachol 293, 299, 300, 306, 309, 310, 315, 316
Reclus, Elisée 295
Reinach, Bertrand 282, 283
Reinach, Fanny 282, 283
Reinach, Léon 281–283
Renan, Ernest 95
Renault, Louis 164, 165
Renoir, Pierre-Auguste 21, 27, 250, 281
Reutlinger, Léopold-Émile 96
Ribbentrop, Joachim von 24, 25
Richelieu (Cardinal) 76, 77
Rivière, Jean-Marquès 60
Robespierre, Augustin de 321
Robespierre, Maximilien de 14, 221, 224, 321
Roblin, Louis-Henri 69
Rochambeau, Jean-Baptiste Donatien de Vimeur 136, 267, 269, 274
Rodier, Robert 238
Rodriguez, Joaquim 71
Rogis, Rosalie 325
Rognat (Baron) 175
Rol-Tanguy, Henri 246
Rolier, Paul 188
Romains, Jules 135, 140
Rosenberg, Alexandre 28
Rosenberg, Alfred 20, 25
Rosenberg, Paul 25, 27, 249
Rossi, Tino 59
Rothschild, Betty de 27
Rothschild, James de 187

Rousseau, Jean-Jacques 221, 251
Rubens, Peter Paul 24
Rubinstein, Helena 251
Ruffey, Pierre 172
Ruffin, Raymond 161, 162
Saillet, Maurice 144
Saint-Arnaud, Armand Jacques Leroy de 47
Sakakini, Élisabeth 156, 162
Salan, Raoul 229–231, 238
Sampieri, Charles 281
Sanson (de Longval), Charles-Henri 319–323, 325, 327, 328
Sanson, Gabriel 322
Sanson, Henri 319
Sanson, Henri-Clément 323
Sari, Léon 90
Sarkozy, Nicolas 71
Sarton du Jonchay, Christian 159
Savary, Alain 233
Scheffer, Ary 269
Schlumberger, Jean 140
Schueller, Eugène 164, 165
Scott Fitzgerald, Francis 136
Scotto, Vincent 138
Sécretan, Pierre-Eugène 273
Servan-Schreiber, Jean-Jacques 234
Shalaby, Mahmoud 199
Si Kaddour Benghabrit 194–200
Signac, Paul 295
Simon, Jules 126
Sinclair, Anne 27
Sisley, Alfred 280
Soehring, Hans-Jürgen 56, 60
Solano, Solita 138
Somia, Ahmed 199, 200
Sorel, Cécile 96
Soudy, André 307, 311, 312, 315
Speer, Albert 249
Spuller, Eugène 188
Stal, Ludmila 68
Stalin, Joseph 244, 256, 257
Steeg, Théodore 313
Stein, Gertrude 138
Stevens, Alfred 287, 290
Stora, Benjamin 199
Straumann, Marcelle Eugénie 137
Swanson, Gloria 33
Tabarant, Adolphe 286
Tailhade, Laurent 443, 448, 449
Taittinger, Pierre 164, 165
Tapie, Bernard 239
Tardieu-Boganim, Oro 200
Tencin, Claudine de 78

Tencin, Pierre-Paul Guérin de 78
Terrasse, Marie-Louise (Catherine Langeais) 240, 242
Texier, Richard 52
Thiers, Adolphe 43, 46, 47, 119, 124, 191, 221, 270, 294
Thomas, Gregory 36
Thomas, René 169
Thorez, Maurice 228, 258
Tillaux, Paul 290
Toesca, Maurice 252
Toklas, Alice Babette 138
Tonnelier (Pennelier), Félicie 298
Toulouse-Lautrec, Henri de 27
Tourbillon, Robert 112
Trichet, Alexandre Jacques 188
Trochu, Louis Jules 191
Tronchet, François Denis 323
Trotsky, Leon 64, 309
Tuchman, Barbara 172
Turbiaux, Edmond 188
Umberto I of Italy 302
Utrillo, Maurice 27
Vacher, Joseph 325
Vadim, Roger 234
Vaillant, Auguste 300, 301, 309, 315, 316
Valadon, Suzanne 26
Valéry, Paul 134
Valet, René 307, 315
Valland, Rose 19, 20, 23–25, 27
Van Dongen, Kees 252
Van Dyck, Anthony 24
Van Eyck, Jan & Hubert 22, 24
Van Gogh, Vincent 22, 280
Vandervelde, Emile 100
Vardaman, James K. 137
Vaufreland, Louis de 36
Veil, Simone 199
Vergeot, Eléonore 44
Vergès, Jacques 217
Verhaeren, Emile 295
Vermeer, Johannes 27
Viannay, Philippe 148
Vibert 188
Victoria, Queen of the United Kingdom 49, 50, 120, 220, 279
Villain, Raoul 106, 107
Viollet-le-Duc, Eugène 273
Viviani, René 101, 103, 171
Vlaminck, Maurice de 22, 27, 252, 254
Voltaire 221, 251, 253
Vuitton, Louis 49
Wagner, Jeanne 148, 149
Walewski, André 175
Walpole, Horace 267

Index of people

Walter, Marie-Thérèse 250
Washington, George 267
Wellesley, Arthur (Duke of Wellington) 192
Werner, Anton von 191
Wertheimer, Alain 38
Wertheimer, Gérard 38
Wertheimer, Paul 32, 34, 37
Wertheimer, Pierre 30, 32, 34, 36–38
Weygand, Maxime 197
Whitman, George 144
Widmaier-Picasso, Maya 250
Wilde, Oscar 97
Wildenstein, Georges 25
Wilhelm I of Prussia 51, 184, 185, 187, 190, 191
Wilhelm II of Germany 91, 102, 103, 173
Wilson, Woodrow 223
Wood, Thelma 138
Woolf, Virginia 138
Woolsey, John 139
Yamani, Ahmed Zaki 216
Zhao Shiyan 363
Zhou Enlai 221, 222, 224, 225
Zinoviev, Grigori 70
Zuccarelli, Paolo 170
Zweig, Stefan 319

ACKNOWLEDGEMENTS

I was helped by a number of specialists during the search for my Parisian souls, and I owe them a debt of gratitude: Johan Op de Beeck for his suggestions on the stories in which *his* characters, the Sun King and Napoleon, make indirect appearances; Nicoline van de Beek and the late Ton van Kempen, authors of the sublime *Madame Manet*, connoisseurs of Impressionism in general and of Edouard Manet in particular, for their advice on *Victorine, the shrimp*; Michel Vermote of the AMSAB Institute of Social History and specialist on Nazi art theft, for his remarks on the chapter about the Jeu de Paume's courageous assistant curator, Rose Valland.

Raf Vandenbussche searched high and low for the original documents, photographs and illustrations that bring my characters to life. Being able to quote directly from the notes on a *Compagnie du Mississippi* share or from the *Tarif des filles du Palais-Royal* all adds – I hope – to the reader's pleasure.

Paris is one of the crossroads in the history of Europe. I would therefore like to thank political intellectual – or intellectual politician – Herman Van Rompuy, former EU President, who knows European history like no other, for reading several stories.

That the 'narrator' always had the upper hand over the 'historian' in this book was the heavy task that my good friend, cultivated reader and classicist, Stefaan Couvreur, took upon his shoulders. *'Truth, well told'* was the touchstone of his strict but invariably fair judgement. And delete, Dirk!

Frieke Rogiers is a native French speaker, unlike myself. She provided invaluable tips on how to put a curse or joyful cry in the mouths of the numerous Parisians who populate this book.

I would like to thank translator Helen Simpson and editor Derek Scoins for their expert advice, which now makes my characters feel at home in the language of Shakespeare.

Without the dedicated organisational talent of Hadewych Van den Bossche, the creative design work of Tim Bisschop and the diligent picture research of Séverine Lacante, this book would not be in your hands today.

Nor would it be as beautiful or immaculate. They were all encouraged by the unwavering enthusiasm of Gautier Platteau, publishing director of Hannibal Books, whom I thank for his initial confidence in this project, expressed at the kitchen table in Ghent.

Un grand merci and *amitiés* to my Parisian friends Gérard and Jeanne Fournier and Xandrine Charpentier, who opened several doors for me in the city, and to all the friends and lovers of Paris who encouraged me during the writing process. In particular, I would like to thank Johan Thijs, Bart and Michou Van Hooland, Marc and Nadine Saverys, Bernard Tuypens, Peter Quaghebeur and Piet Vroman.

And finally, after years of marital bliss, who wouldn't be delighted to keep discovering new qualities to their greatest love? The happiness was all mine. If one person made me believe in this book, uplifted me in dark times and tempered my reckless euphoria, guided me in choices and decisions regarding characters, always patient and never turning her head away from 'that book again', it is Birgit, mother and stepmother of our children and devoted grandmother, to whom this book is lovingly dedicated.

Dirk Velghe

COLOPHON

TEXT
Dirk Velghe

TRANSLATION
Helen Simpson

COPY-EDITING
Derek Scoins

IMAGE RESEARCH
Raf Vandenbussche
Séverine Lacante

IMAGE EDITING
Séverine Lacante

PROJECT MANAGEMENT
Hadewych Van den Bossche

DESIGN
Tim Bisschop

TYPESETTING
Jef Cuypers
Chloé D'hauwe

INDEX
James De Coninck

PRINTING AND BINDING
Wilco, Amersfoort,
The Netherlands

PUBLISHER
Gautier Platteau

ISBN 978 94 6466 640 3
D/2023/11922/27
NUR 680/693

HANNIBAL
BOOKS

© 2023 Hannibal Books
www.hannibalbooks.be

All rights reserved. No part of this publication may be reproduced or transmitted in any form or by any means, electronic or mechanical, including photocopy, recording or any other information storage and retrieval system, without prior permission in writing from the publisher.

Every effort has been made to trace copyright holders for all texts, photographs and reproductions. If, however, you feel that you have inadvertently been overlooked, please contact the publisher.

PHOTO CREDITS

Cover image: Brassaï, *Les Amoureux de la place d'Italie*, c. 1932, Centre Pompidou, MNAM-CCI, Dist. RMN-Grand Palais / Jacques Faujour

BnF (p. 30)

Bridgeman (p. 54)

Centre Pompidou, MNAM-CCI, Dist. RMN-Grand Palais / Georges Meguerditchian (p. 154)

Collections des Archives diplomatiques du Ministère des Affaires étrangères (p. 18)

Getty Images (pp. 132, 226, 264, 292, 318)

Mémorial de la Shoah / Collection Gérard Silvain (p. 194)

Imageselect (pp. 40, 86, 110, 146, 168, 218)

Isopix (p. 210)

Musée Carnavalet – Histoire de Paris (p. 116)

Paris, Les Arts Décoratifs, Musée des Arts Décoratifs (p. 276)

Public domain (pp. 62, 98, 182, 202, 284, 304)

Rijksmuseum (p. 72)

RMN-Grand Palais (Musée national Picasso-Paris) / Adrien Didierjean (p. 244)

This book was published with the support of Flanders Literature (www.flandersliterature.be).